Shojo Beat

ping
on Roses

Vol. 7

Story & Art by
Rinko Ueda

Stepping on Roses

Volume 7
CONTENTS

Story Thus Far

During the Meiji Era, Sumi Kitamura was living a life of poverty and taking care of young orphans that her elder brother Eisuke brought home from the streets. Then, in order to pay off Eisuke's debts, she marries Soichiro Ashida, the heir to a wealthy conglomerate. This is a marriage of convenience, and people don't know her true background, but Soichiro and Sumi begin to have feelings for each other.

Soichiro's friend Nozomu is in love with Sumi, and he publicly announces that he will divorce his wife Miu. Miu attacks Sumi with a knife, and Soichiro is injured while protecting Sumi. Later, Sumi unwittingly agrees to be the guarantor for a loan Eisuke is making. When it's revealed that Eisuke has been embezzling money from Soichiro's company, Sumi and Soichiro find themselves in trouble as Eisuke tells everyone that Sumi is his sister!

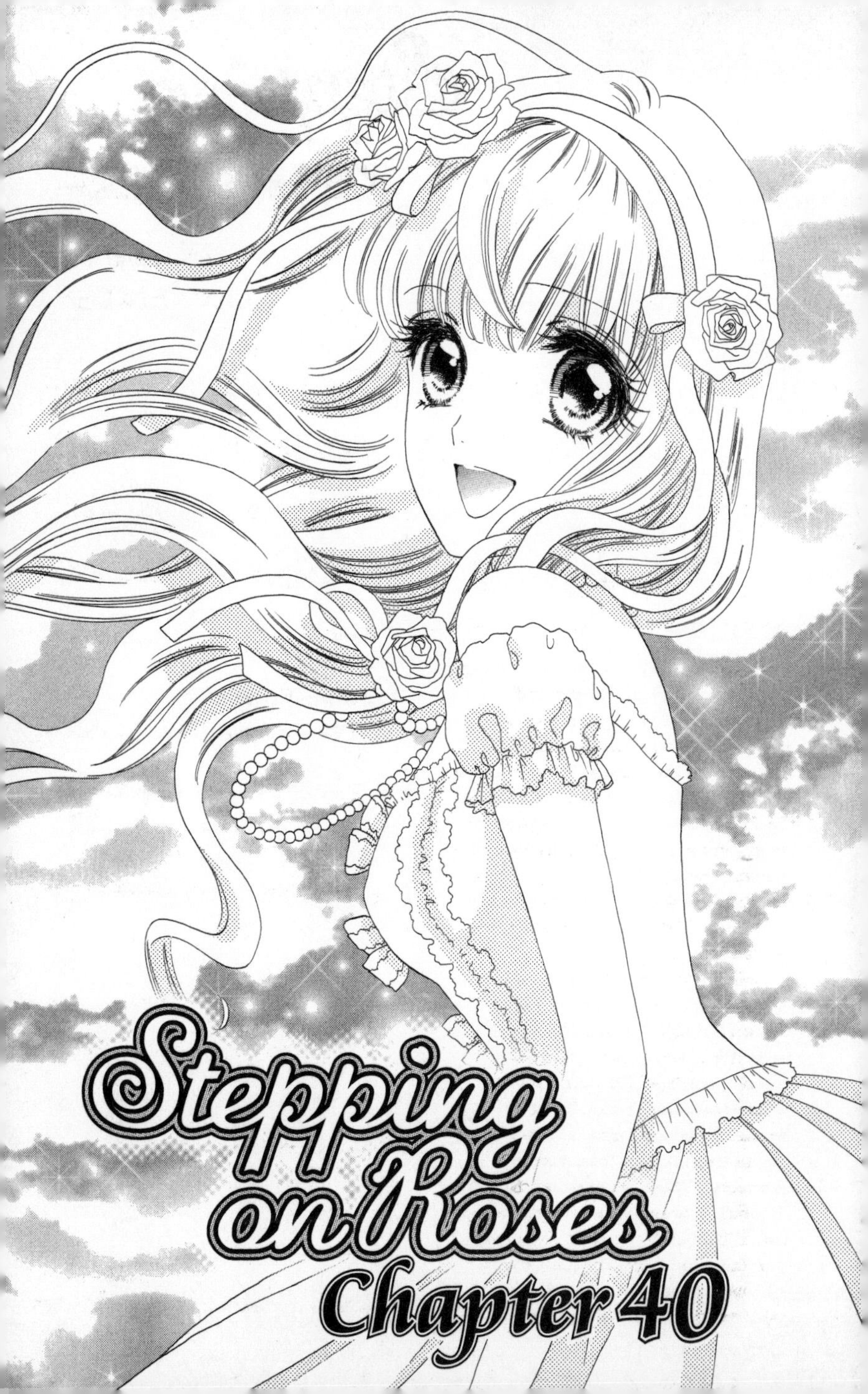
Stepping on Roses
Chapter 40

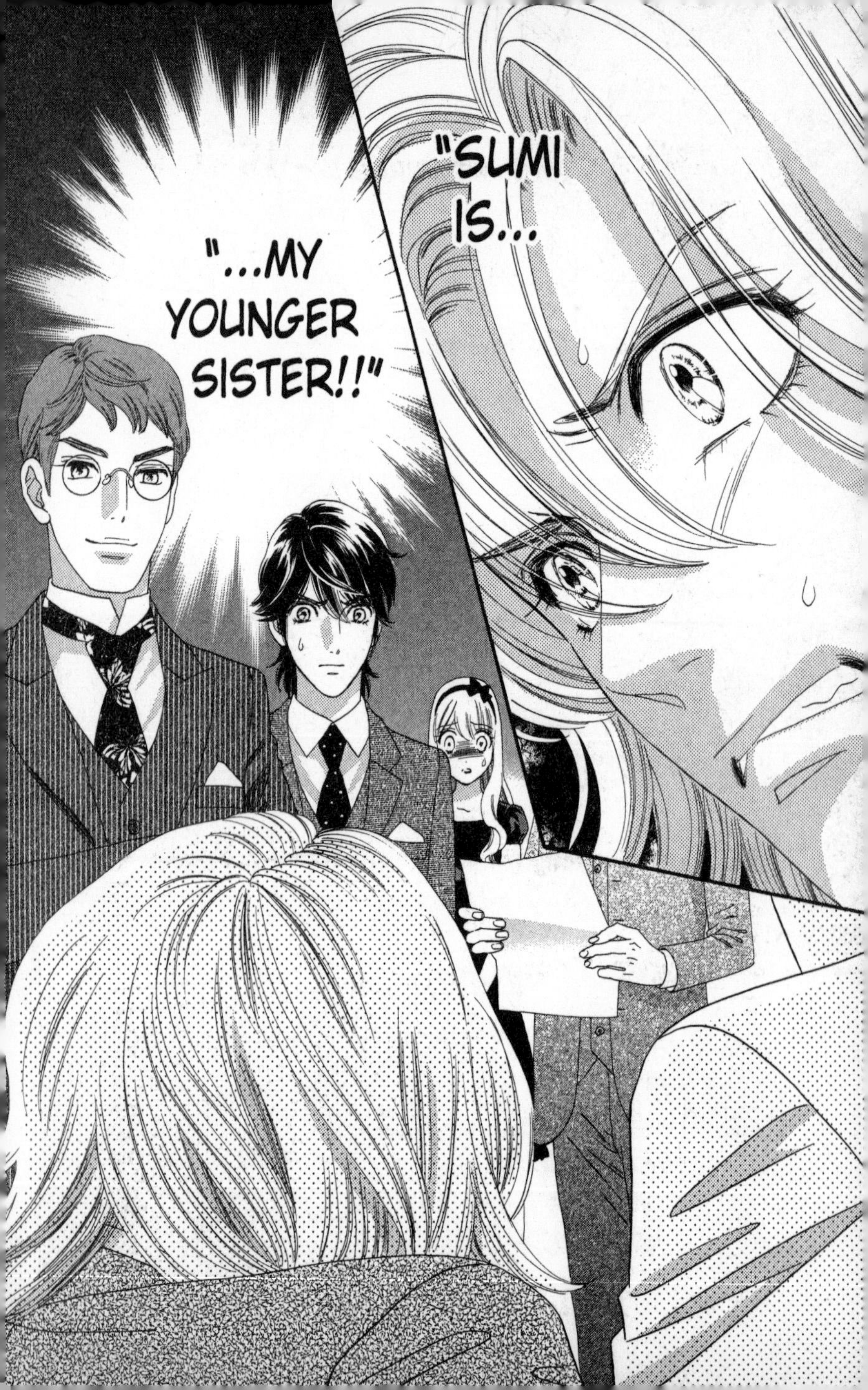
"SUMI IS...
"...MY YOUNGER SISTER!!"

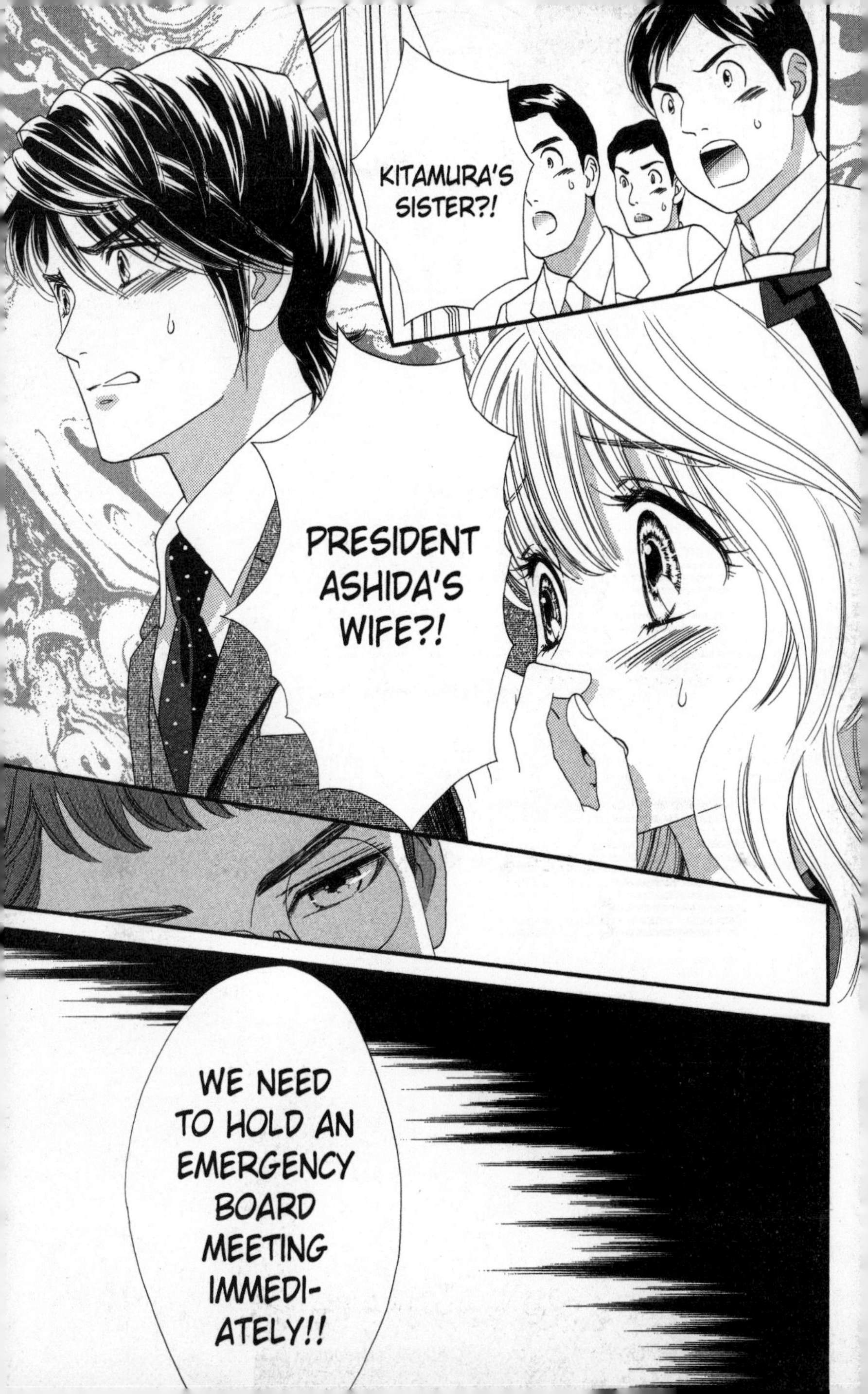
KITAMURA'S SISTER?!
PRESIDENT ASHIDA'S WIFE?!
WE NEED TO HOLD AN EMERGENCY BOARD MEETING IMMEDI-ATELY!!

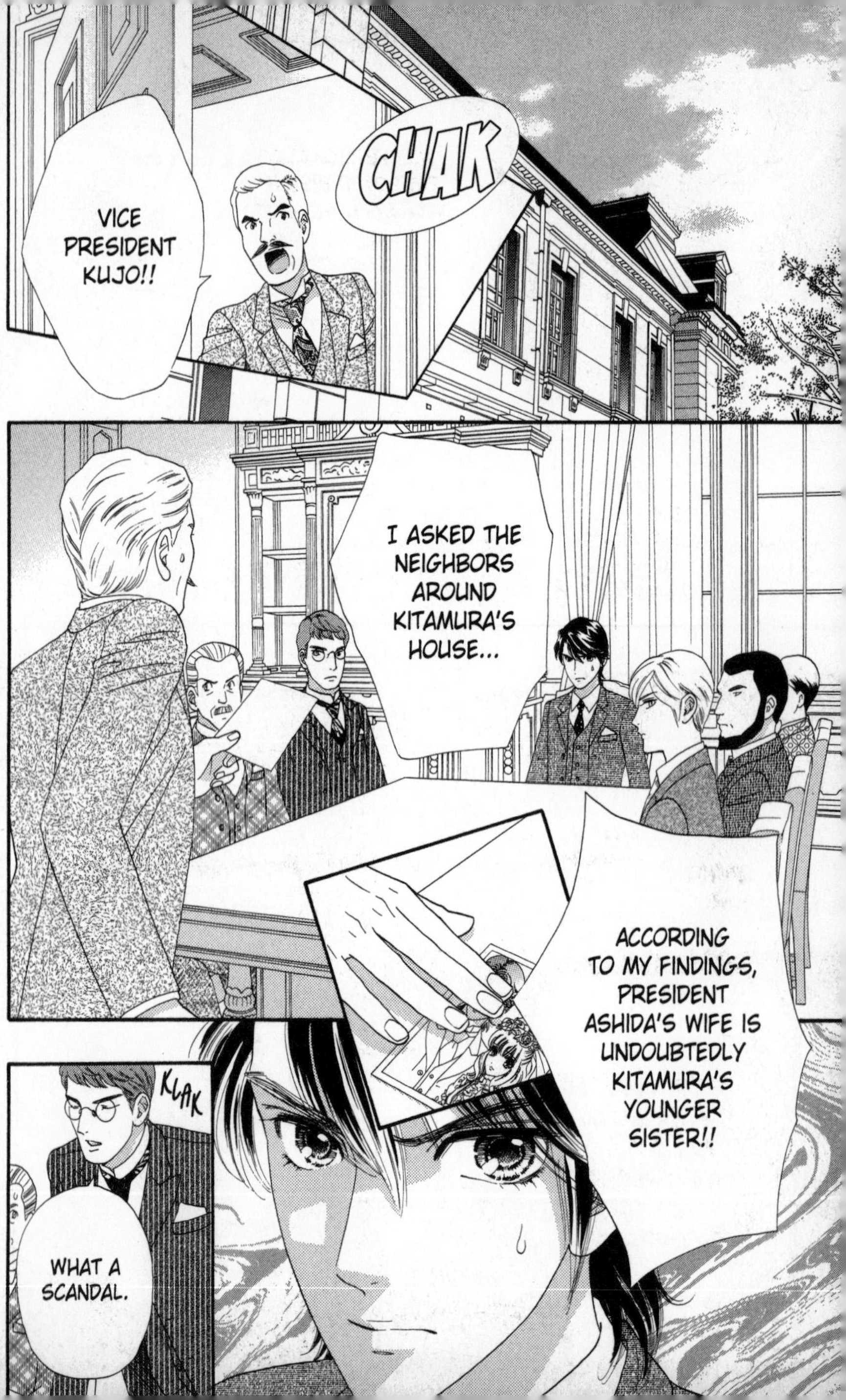
CHAK
VICE PRESIDENT KUJO!!
I ASKED THE NEIGHBORS AROUND KITAMURA'S HOUSE...
ACCORDING TO MY FINDINGS, PRESIDENT ASHIDA'S WIFE IS UNDOUBTEDLY KITAMURA'S YOUNGER SISTER!!
KLAK
WHAT A SCANDAL.

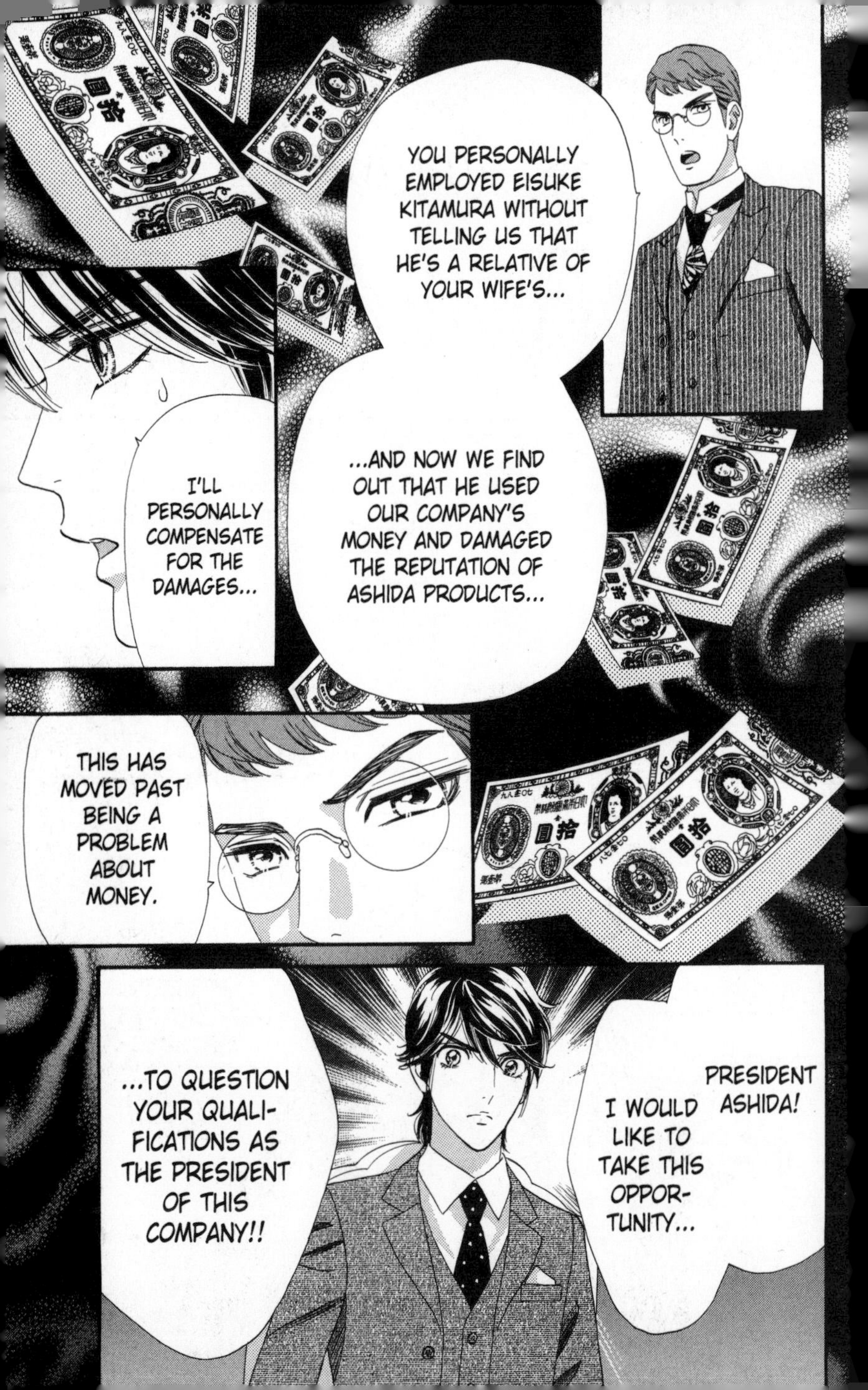
YOU PERSONALLY EMPLOYED EISUKE KITAMURA WITHOUT TELLING US THAT HE'S A RELATIVE OF YOUR WIFE'S...
...AND NOW WE FIND OUT THAT HE USED OUR COMPANY'S MONEY AND DAMAGED THE REPUTATION OF ASHIDA PRODUCTS...
I'LL PERSONALLY COMPENSATE FOR THE DAMAGES...
THIS HAS MOVED PAST BEING A PROBLEM ABOUT MONEY.
PRESIDENT ASHIDA!
I WOULD LIKE TO TAKE THIS OPPORTUNITY...
...TO QUESTION YOUR QUALIFICATIONS AS THE PRESIDENT OF THIS COMPANY!!

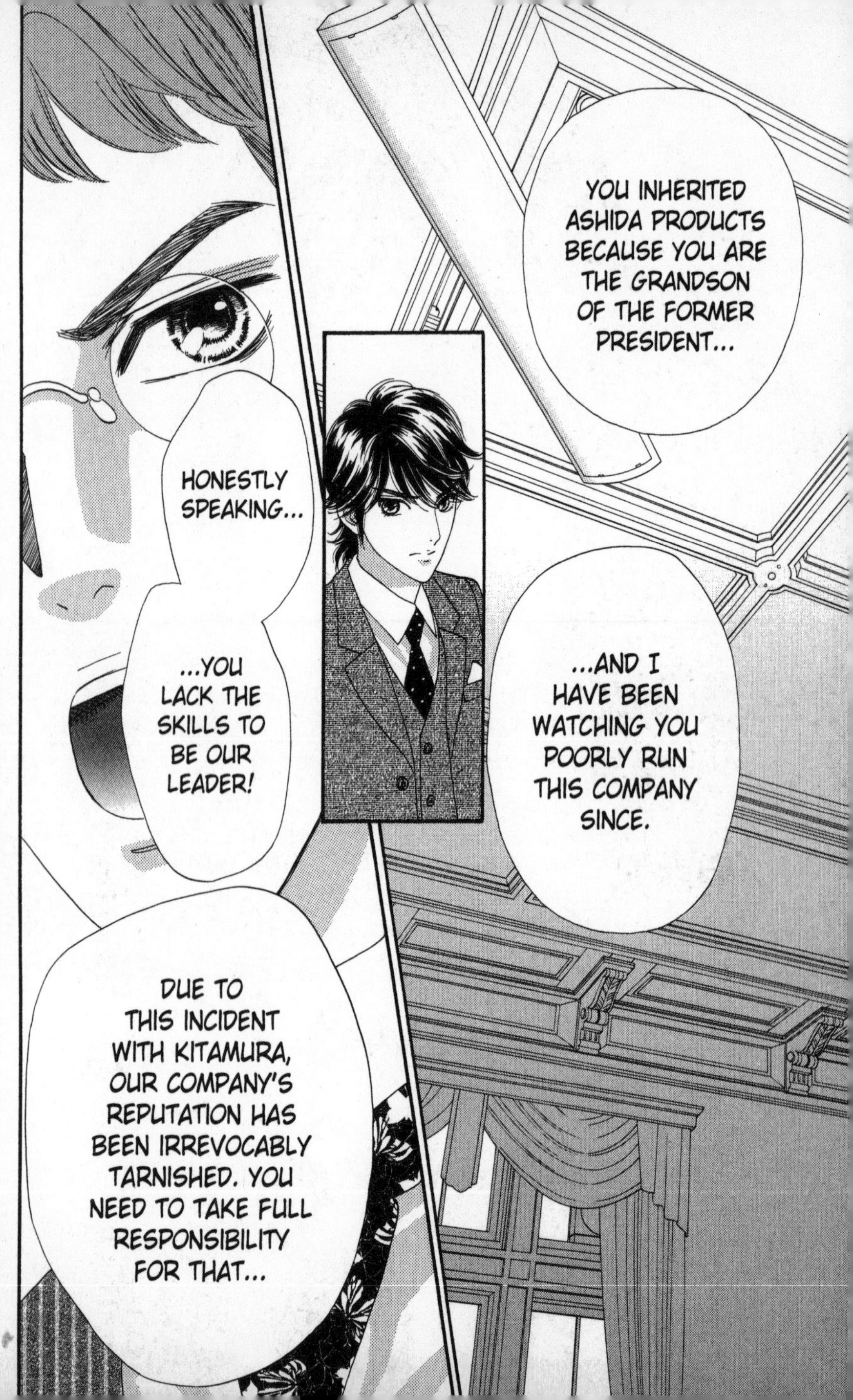
YOU INHERITED ASHIDA PRODUCTS BECAUSE YOU ARE THE GRANDSON OF THE FORMER PRESIDENT...
...AND I HAVE BEEN WATCHING YOU POORLY RUN THIS COMPANY SINCE.
HONESTLY SPEAKING...
...YOU LACK THE SKILLS TO BE OUR LEADER!
DUE TO THIS INCIDENT WITH KITAMURA, OUR COMPANY'S REPUTATION HAS BEEN IRREVOCABLY TARNISHED. YOU NEED TO TAKE FULL RESPONSIBILITY FOR THAT...

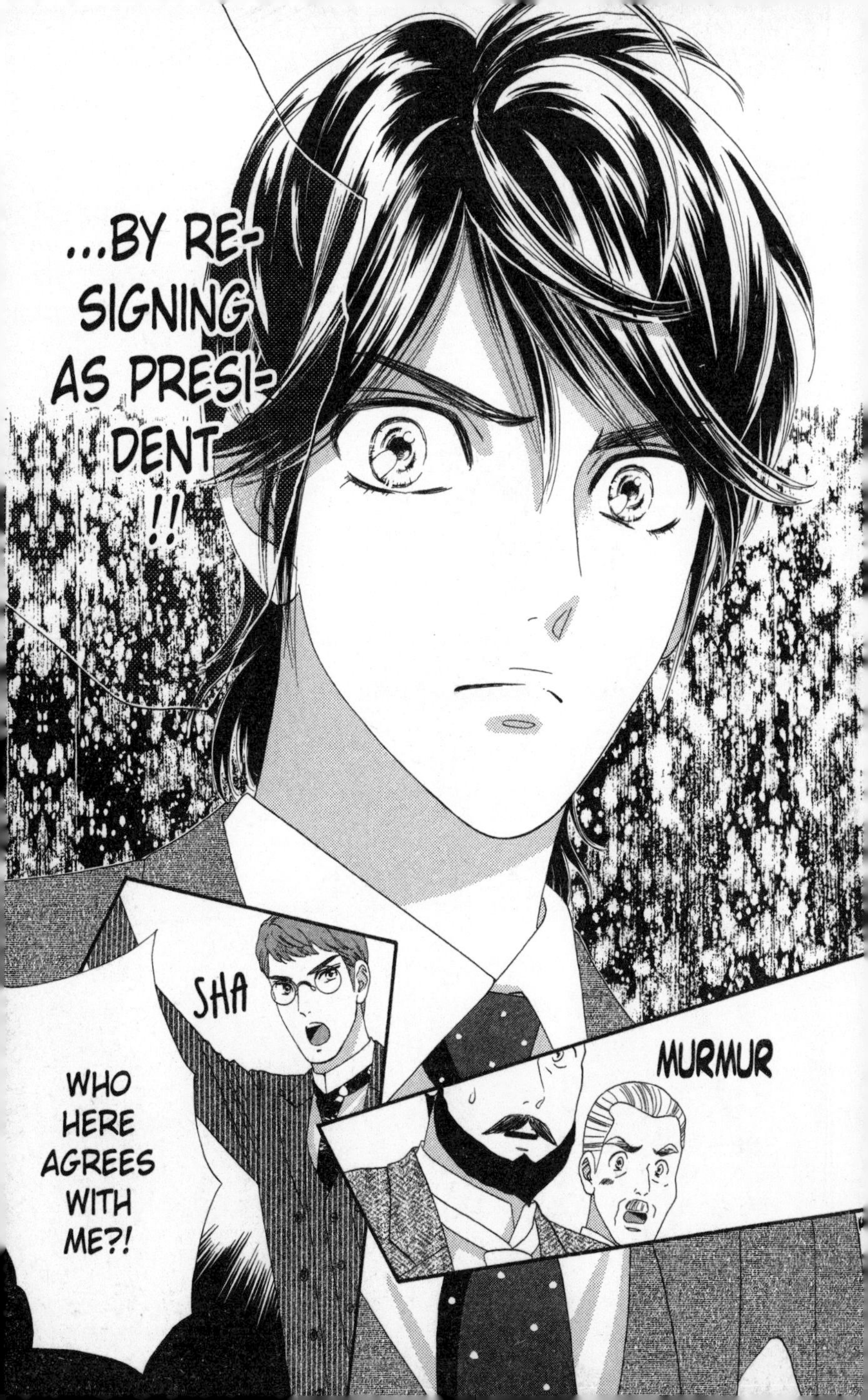
...BY RE-SIGNING AS PRESI-DENT!!
WHO HERE AGREES WITH ME?!
MURMUR
SHA

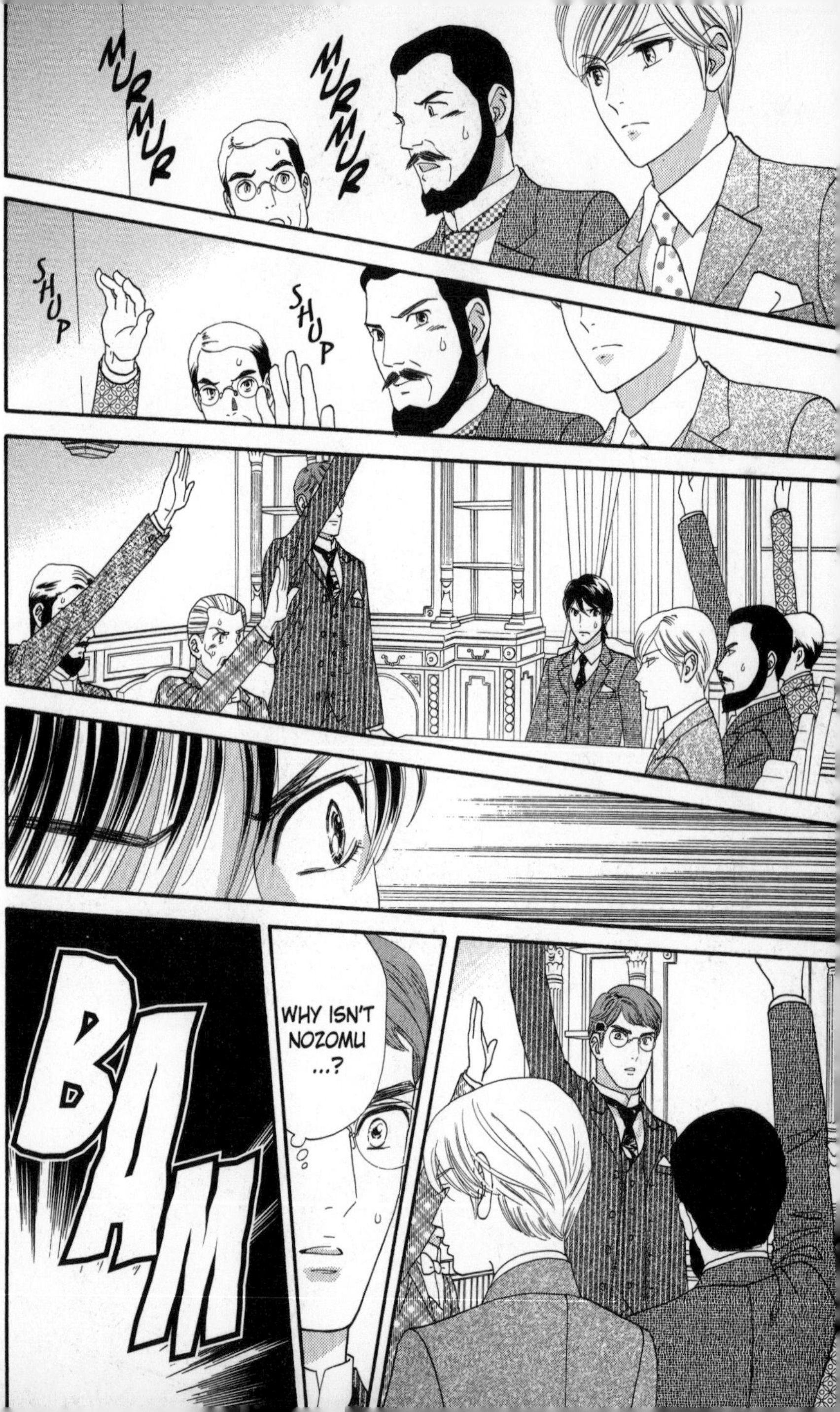
MURMUR
MURMUR
SHUP
SHUP
WHY ISN'T NOZOMU ...?
BAM

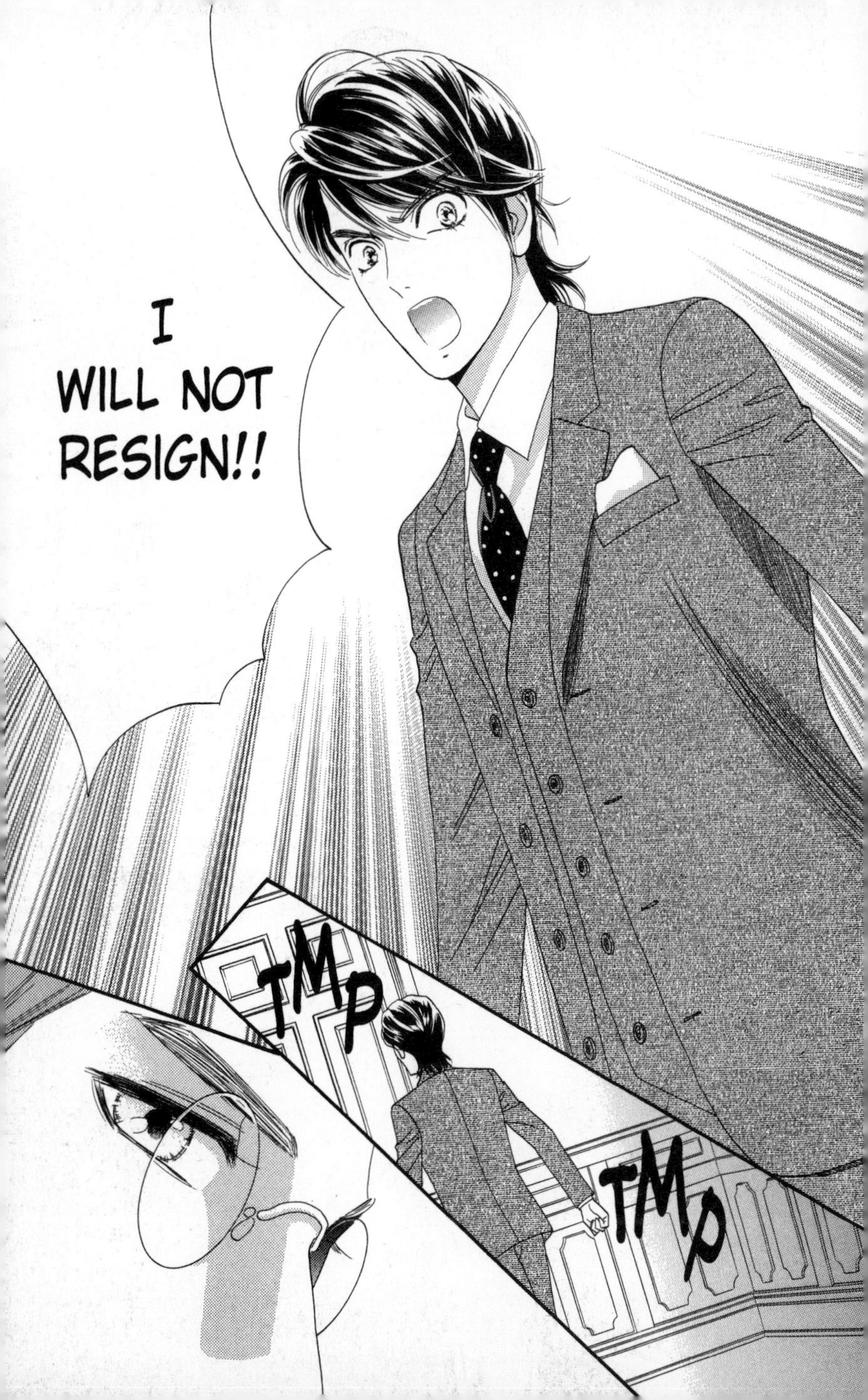
I WILL NOT RESIGN!!
TMP
TMP

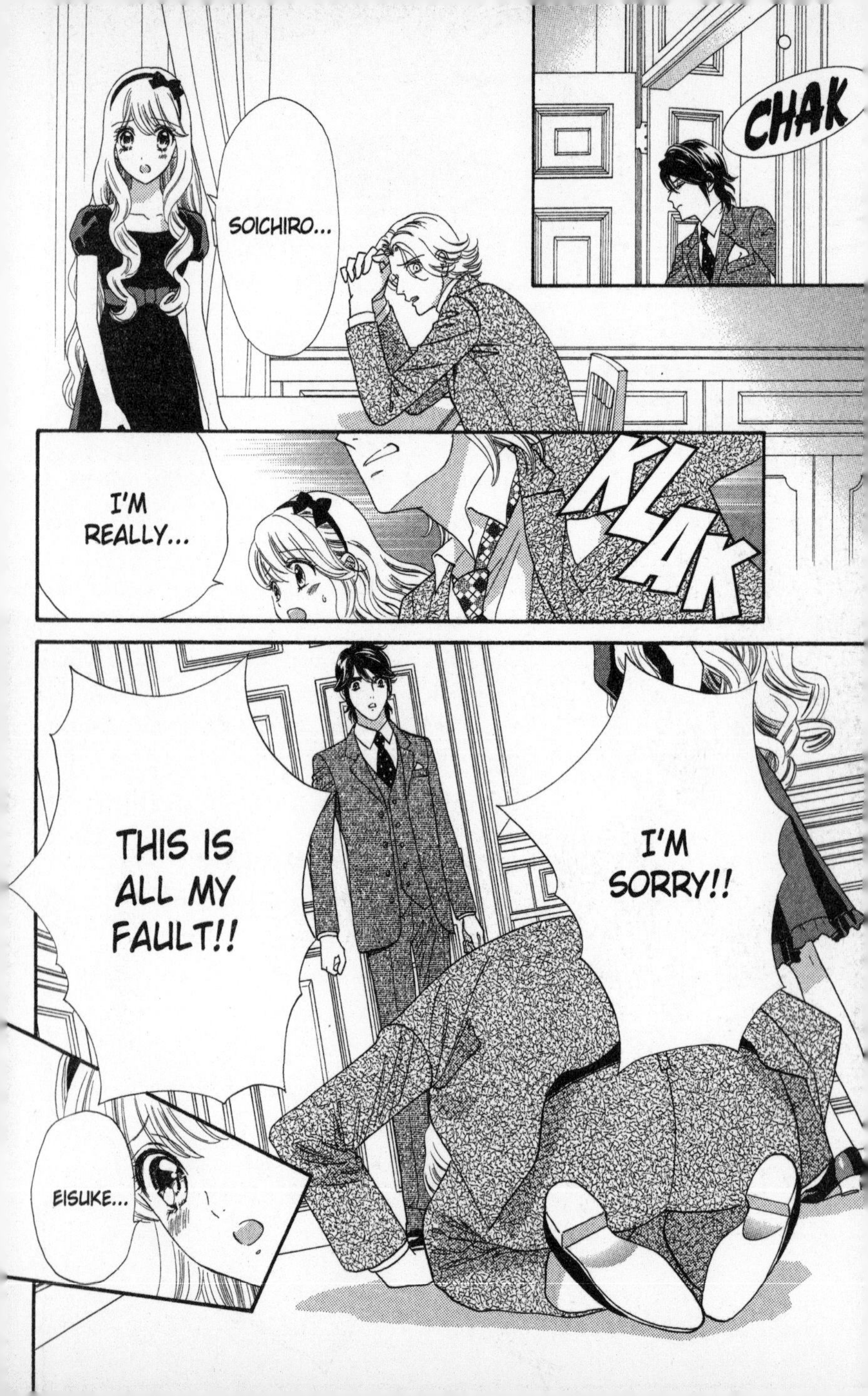
CHAK
SOICHIRO...
KLAK
I'M REALLY...
I'M SORRY!!
THIS IS ALL MY FAULT!!
EISUKE...

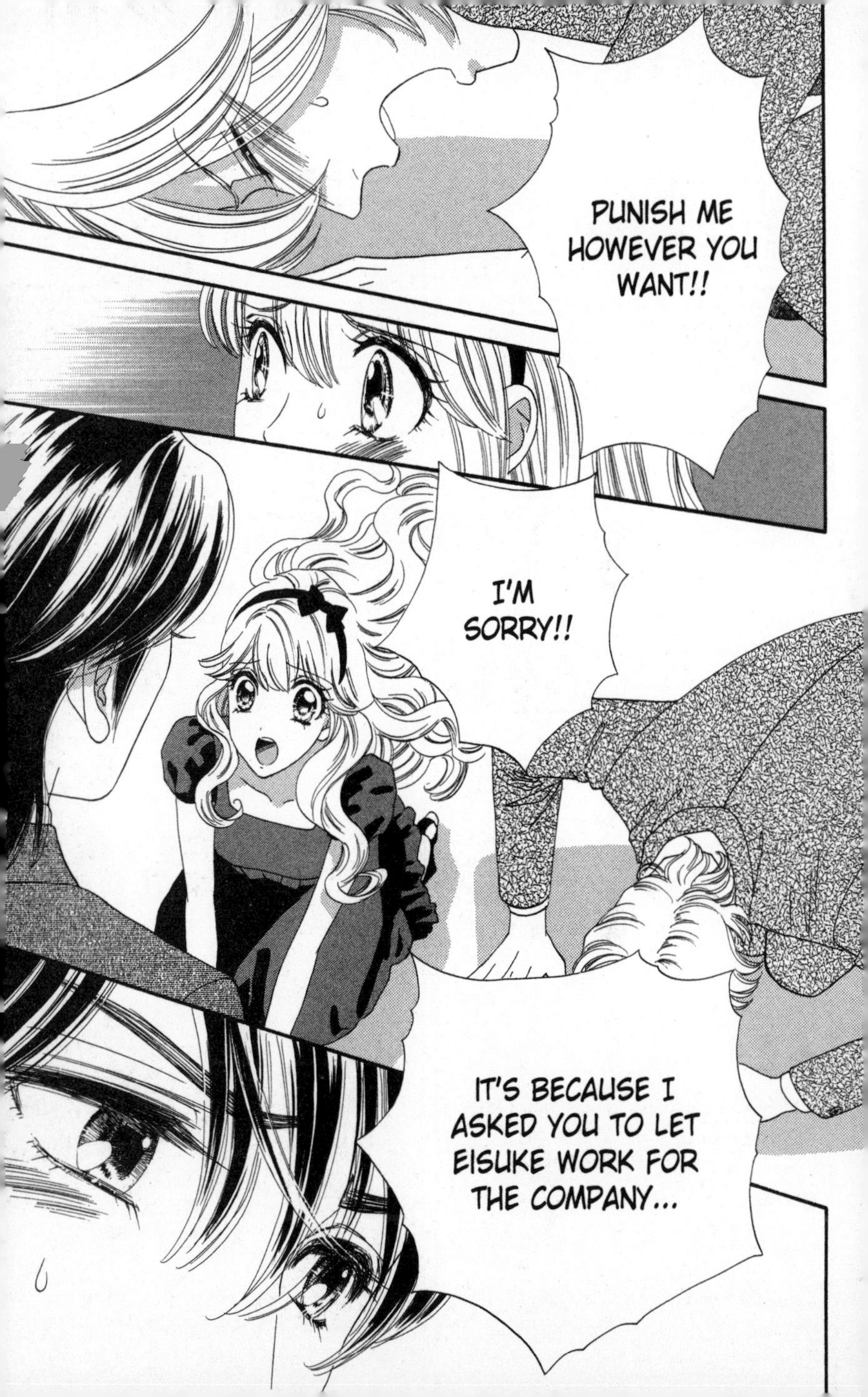
PUNISH ME HOWEVER YOU WANT!!
I'M SORRY!!
IT'S BECAUSE I ASKED YOU TO LET EISUKE WORK FOR THE COMPANY...

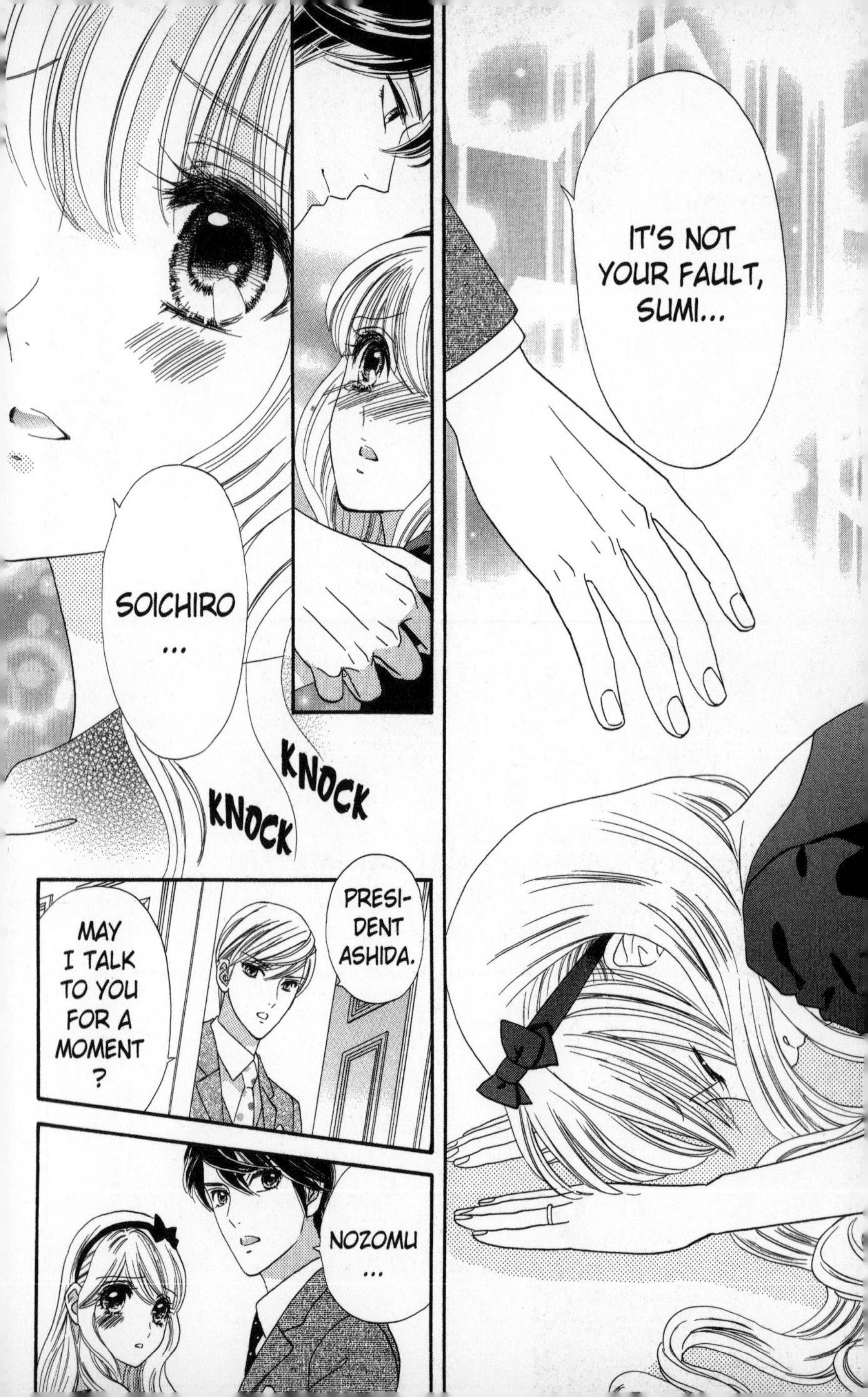
IT'S NOT YOUR FAULT, SUMI...
SOICHIRO...
KNOCK
KNOCK
PRESI-DENT ASHIDA.
MAY I TALK TO YOU FOR A MOMENT?
NOZOMU...

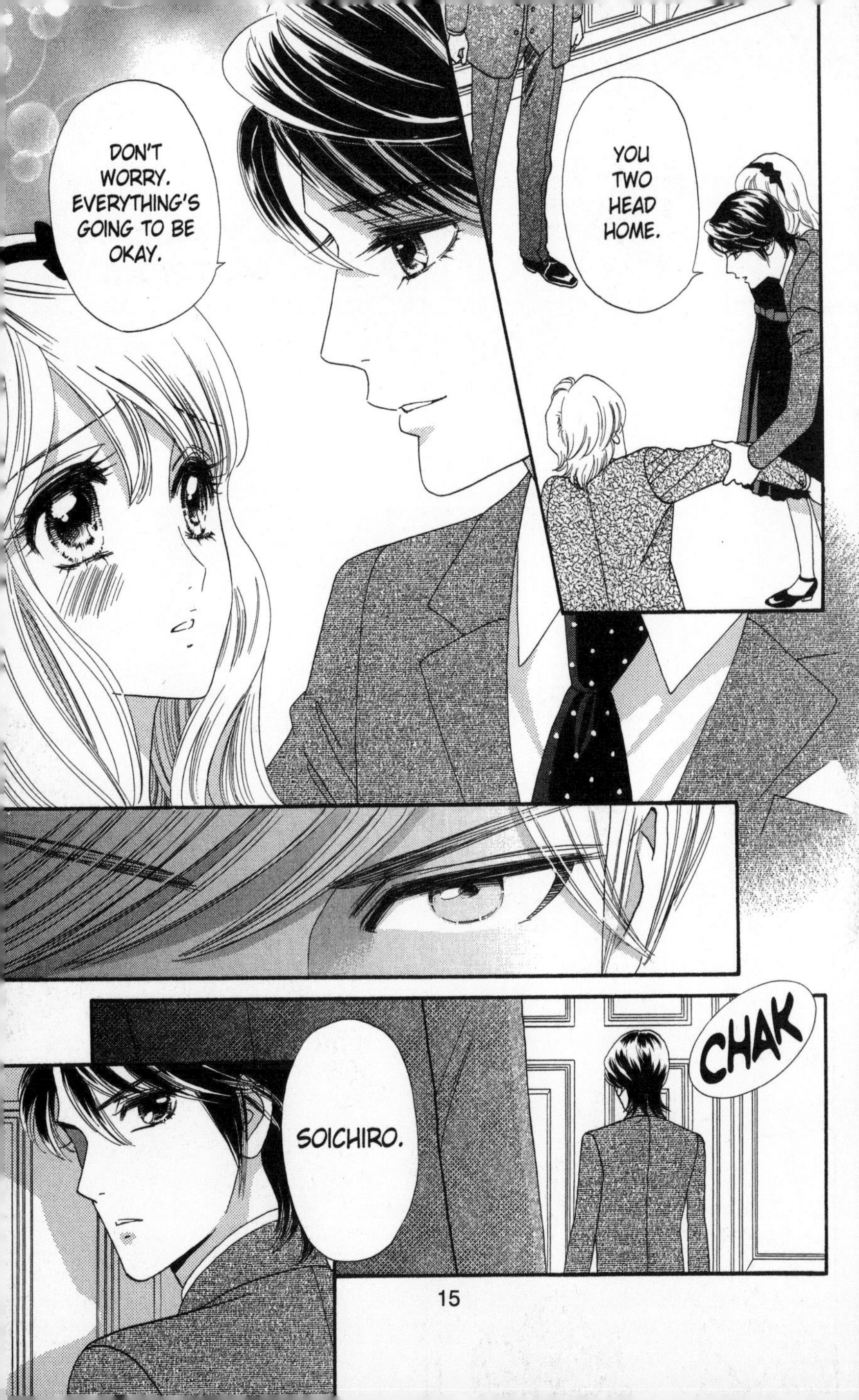
YOU TWO HEAD HOME.
DON'T WORRY. EVERYTHING'S GOING TO BE OKAY.
CHAK
SOICHIRO.

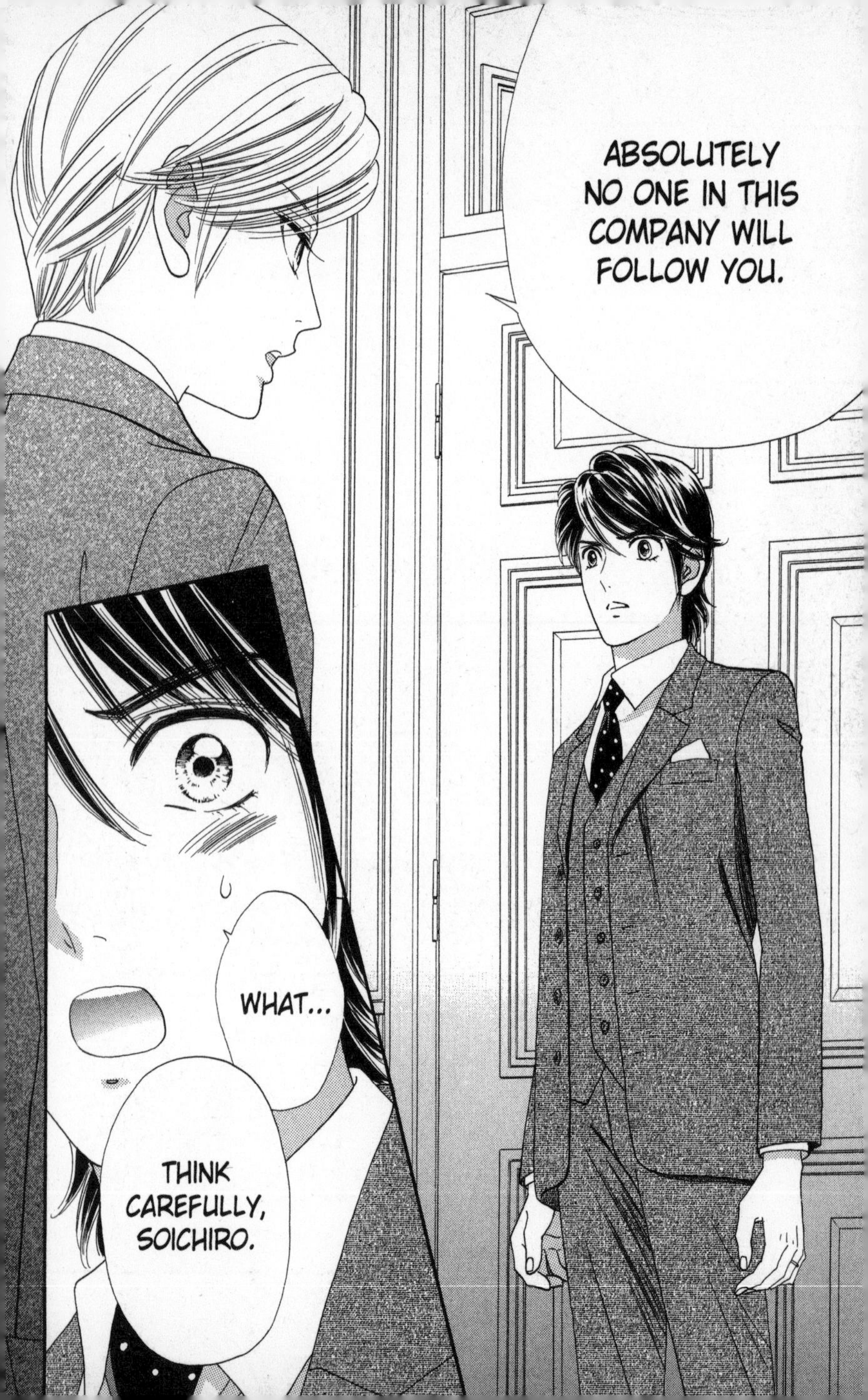
ABSOLUTELY NO ONE IN THIS COMPANY WILL FOLLOW YOU.
WHAT...
THINK CAREFULLY, SOICHIRO.

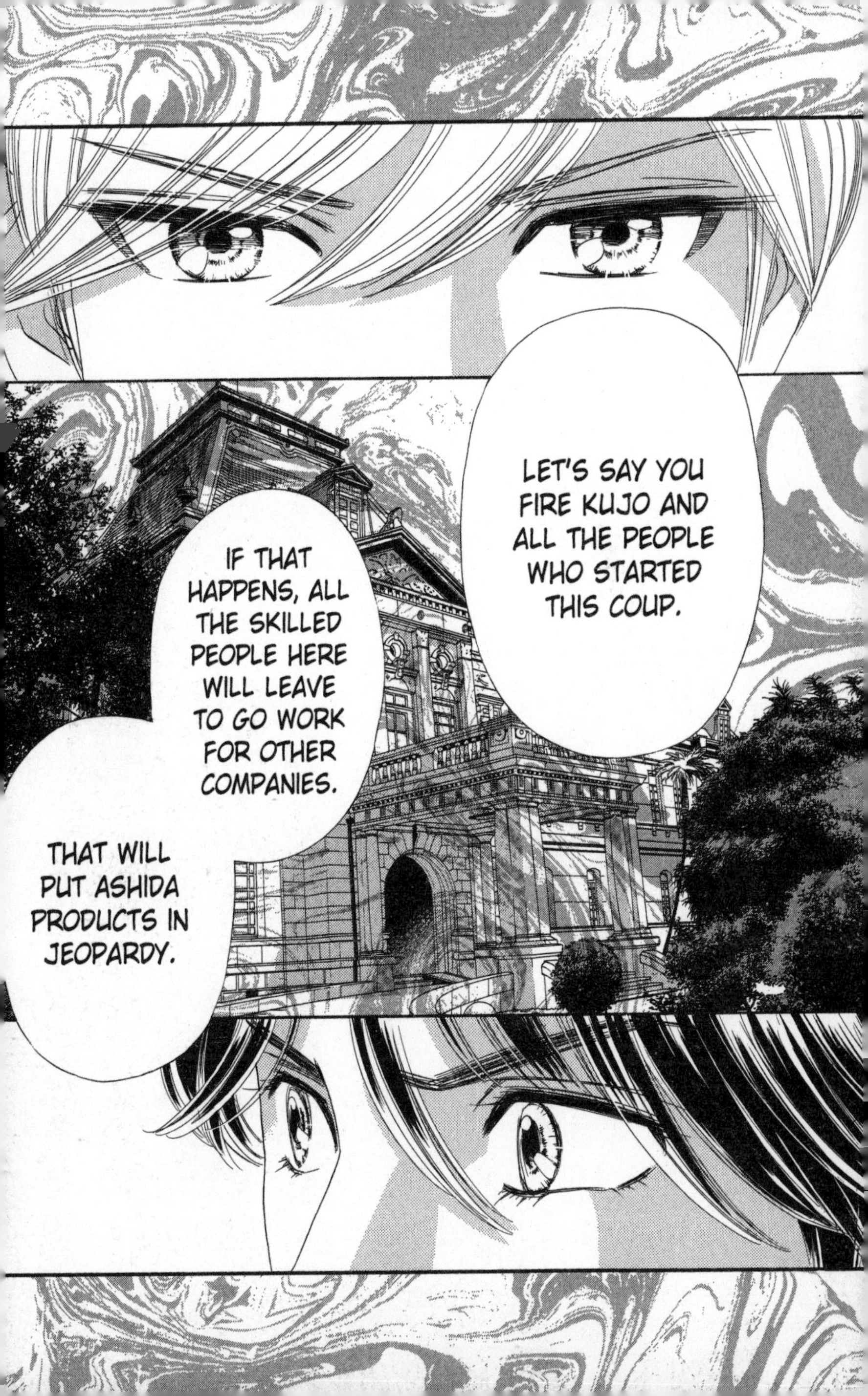
LET'S SAY YOU FIRE KUJO AND ALL THE PEOPLE WHO STARTED THIS COUP.
IF THAT HAPPENS, ALL THE SKILLED PEOPLE HERE WILL LEAVE TO GO WORK FOR OTHER COMPANIES.
THAT WILL PUT ASHIDA PRODUCTS IN JEOPARDY.

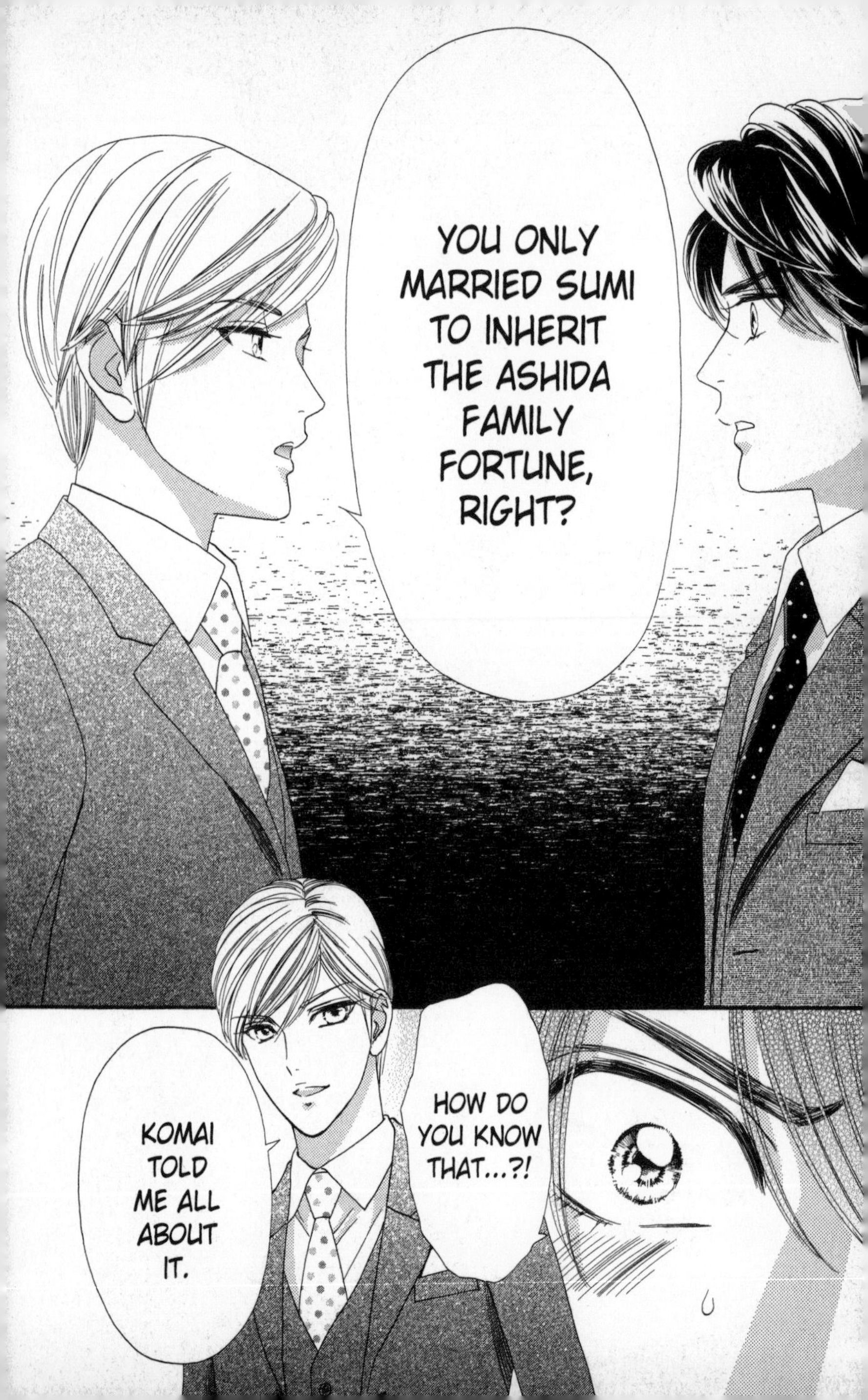
YOU ONLY MARRIED SUMI TO INHERIT THE ASHIDA FAMILY FORTUNE, RIGHT?
HOW DO YOU KNOW THAT...?!
KOMAI TOLD ME ALL ABOUT IT.

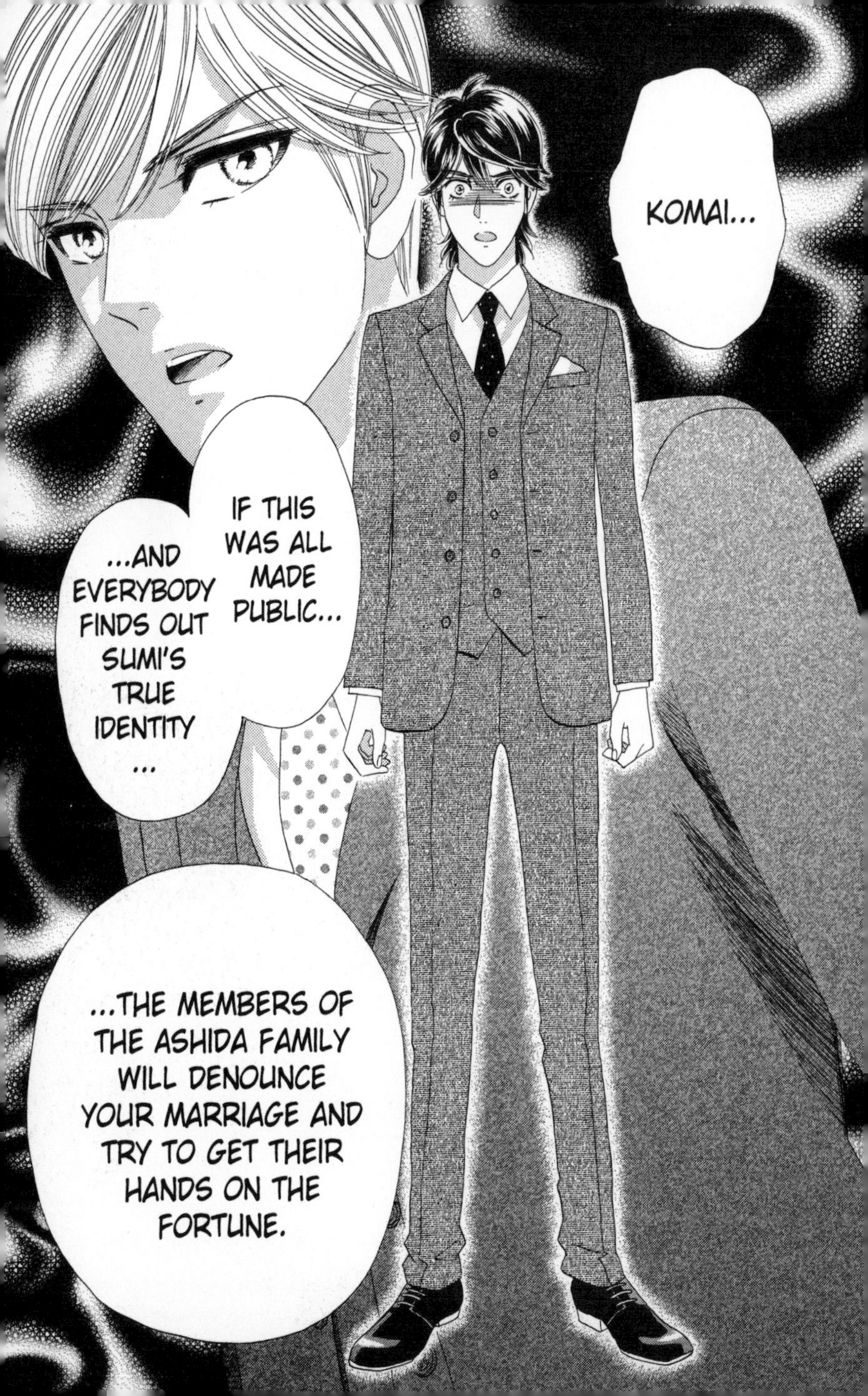
KOMAI...
IF THIS WAS ALL MADE PUBLIC...
...AND EVERYBODY FINDS OUT SUMI'S TRUE IDENTITY ...
...THE MEMBERS OF THE ASHIDA FAMILY WILL DENOUNCE YOUR MARRIAGE AND TRY TO GET THEIR HANDS ON THE FORTUNE.

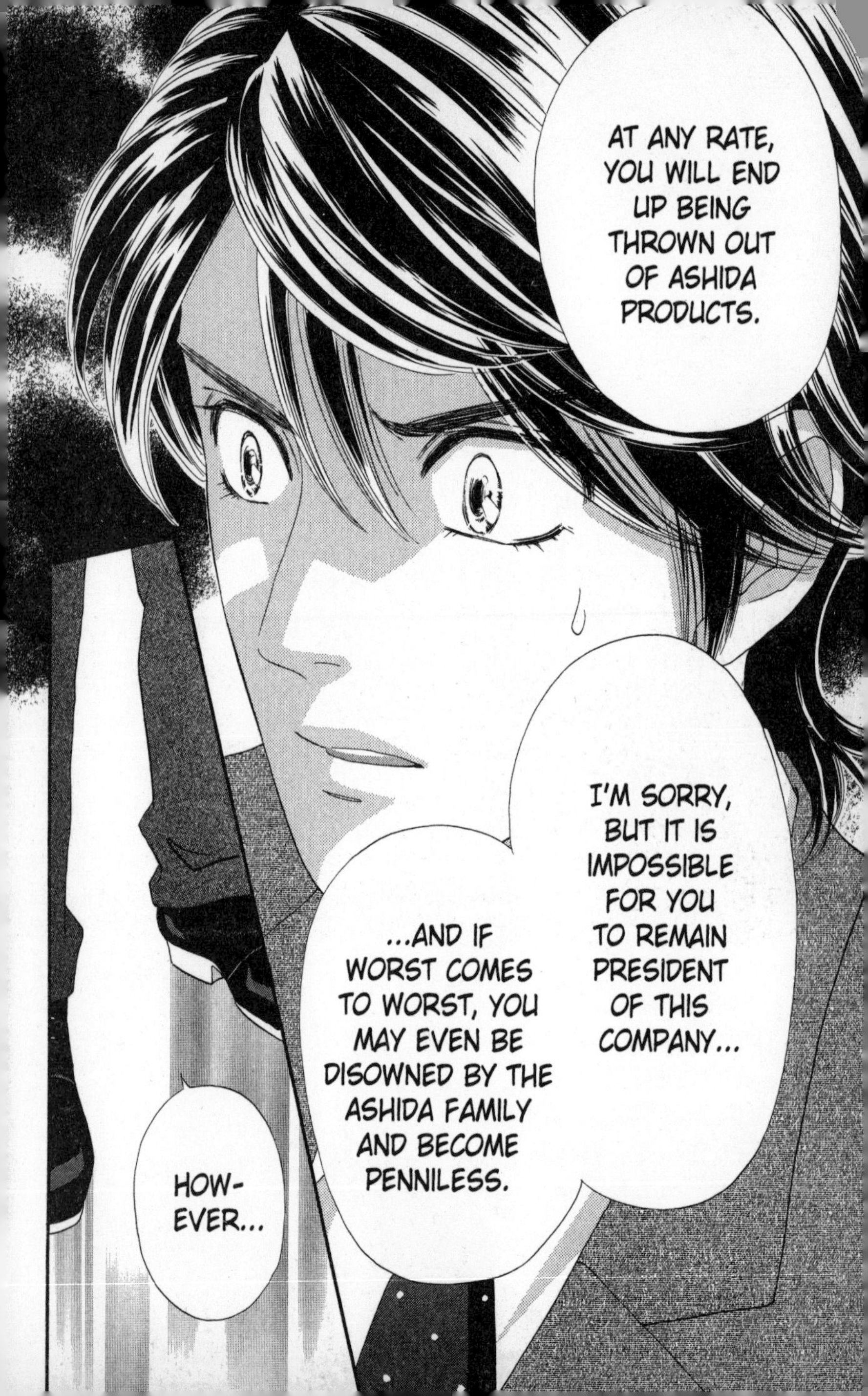
AT ANY RATE, YOU WILL END UP BEING THROWN OUT OF ASHIDA PRODUCTS.
I'M SORRY, BUT IT IS IMPOSSIBLE FOR YOU TO REMAIN PRESIDENT OF THIS COMPANY...
...AND IF WORST COMES TO WORST, YOU MAY EVEN BE DISOWNED BY THE ASHIDA FAMILY AND BECOME PENNILESS.
HOW-EVER...

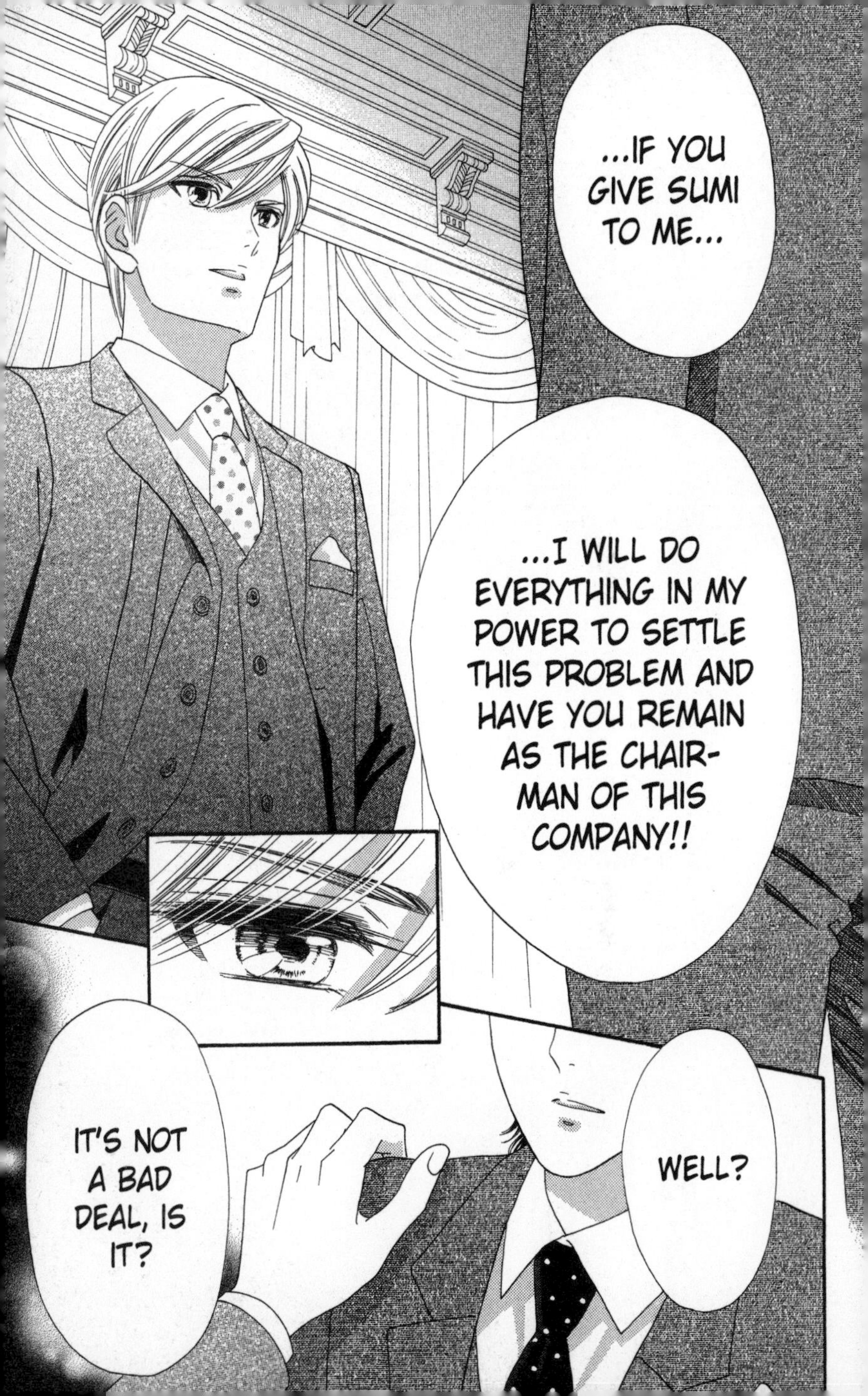
...IF YOU GIVE SUMI TO ME...
...I WILL DO EVERYTHING IN MY POWER TO SETTLE THIS PROBLEM AND HAVE YOU REMAIN AS THE CHAIR-MAN OF THIS COMPANY!!
WELL?
IT'S NOT A BAD DEAL, IS IT?

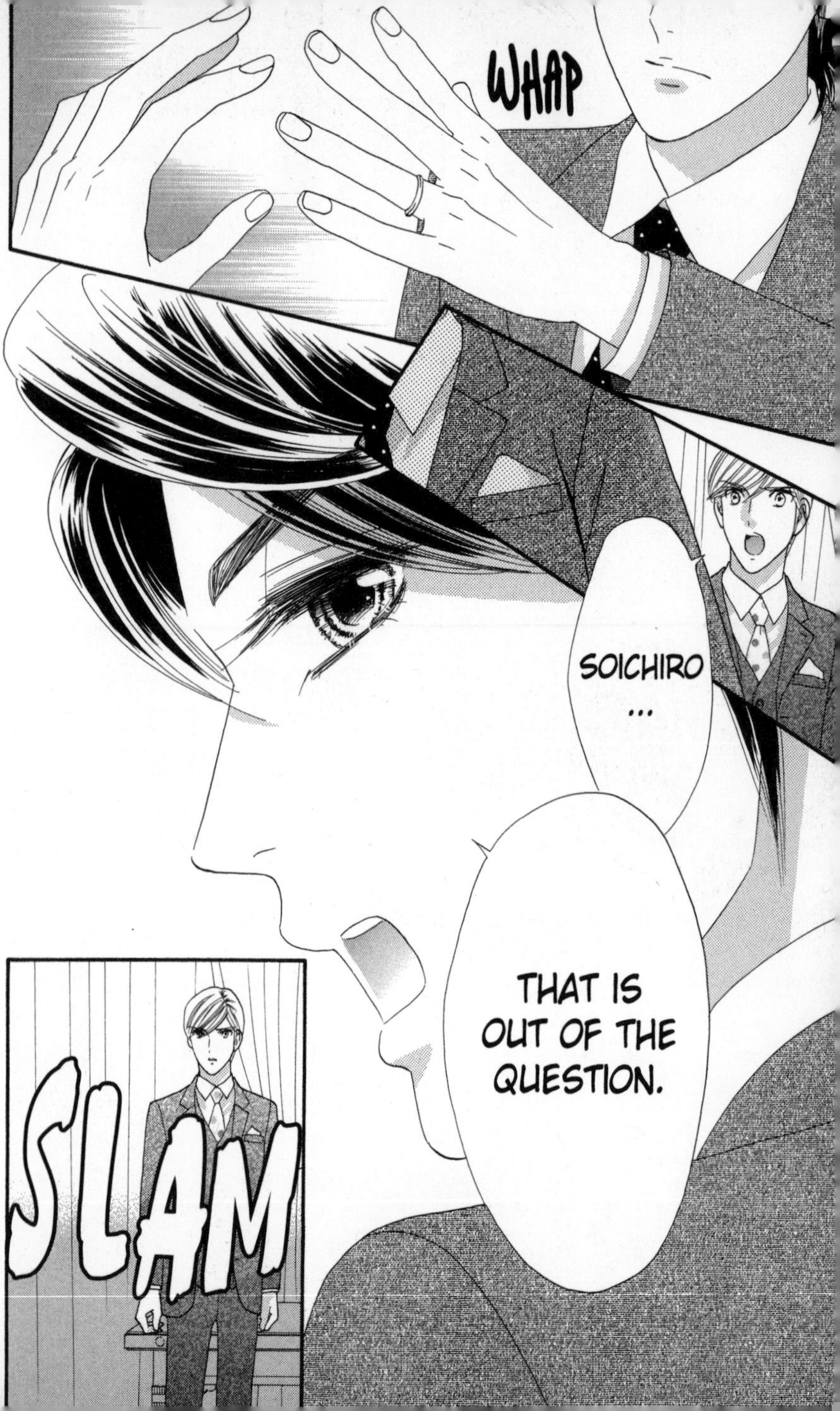
WHAP
SOICHIRO ...
THAT IS OUT OF THE QUESTION.
SLAM

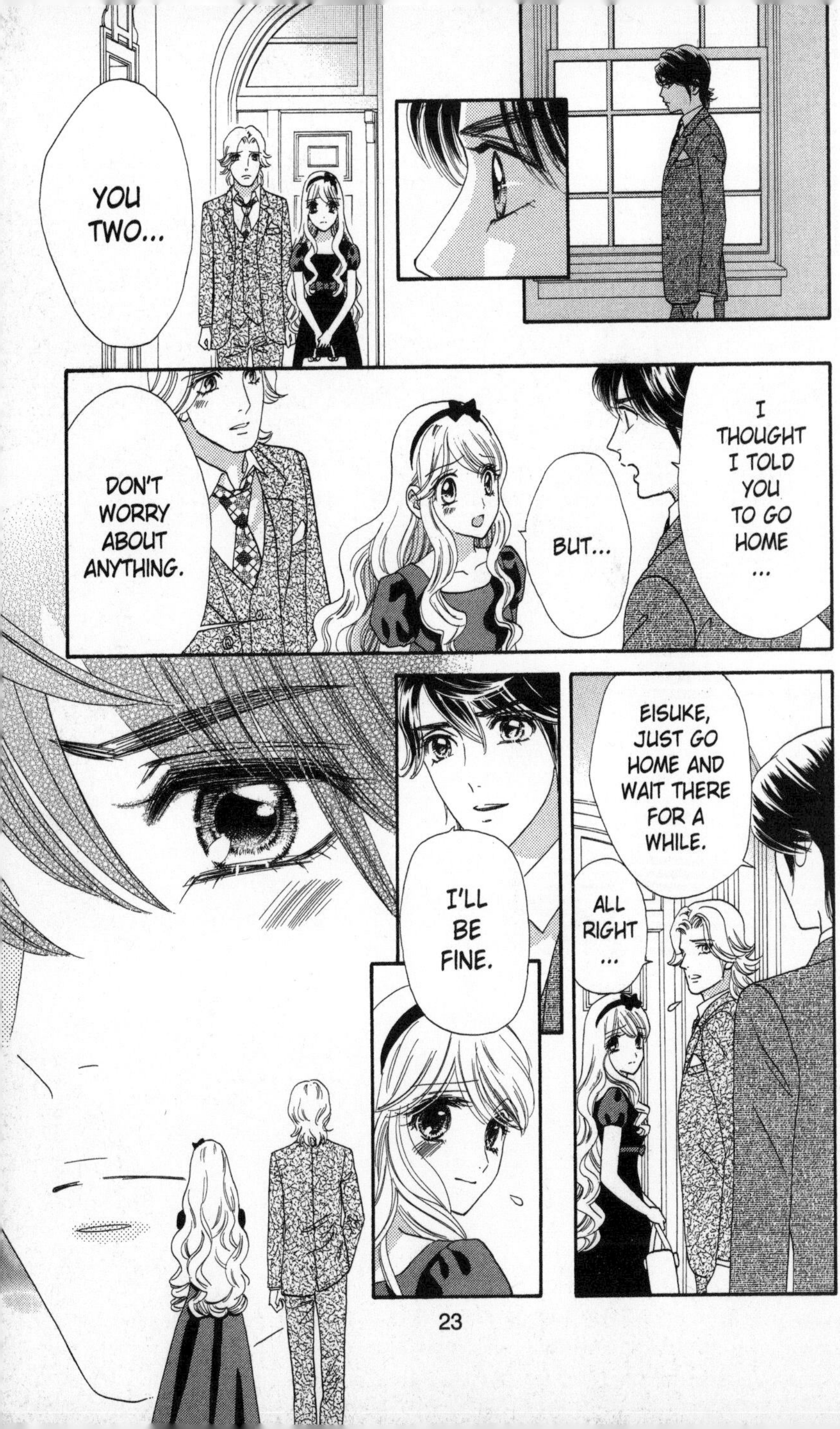
YOU TWO...
I THOUGHT I TOLD YOU TO GO HOME...
BUT...
DON'T WORRY ABOUT ANYTHING.
EISUKE, JUST GO HOME AND WAIT THERE FOR A WHILE.
ALL RIGHT...
I'LL BE FINE.

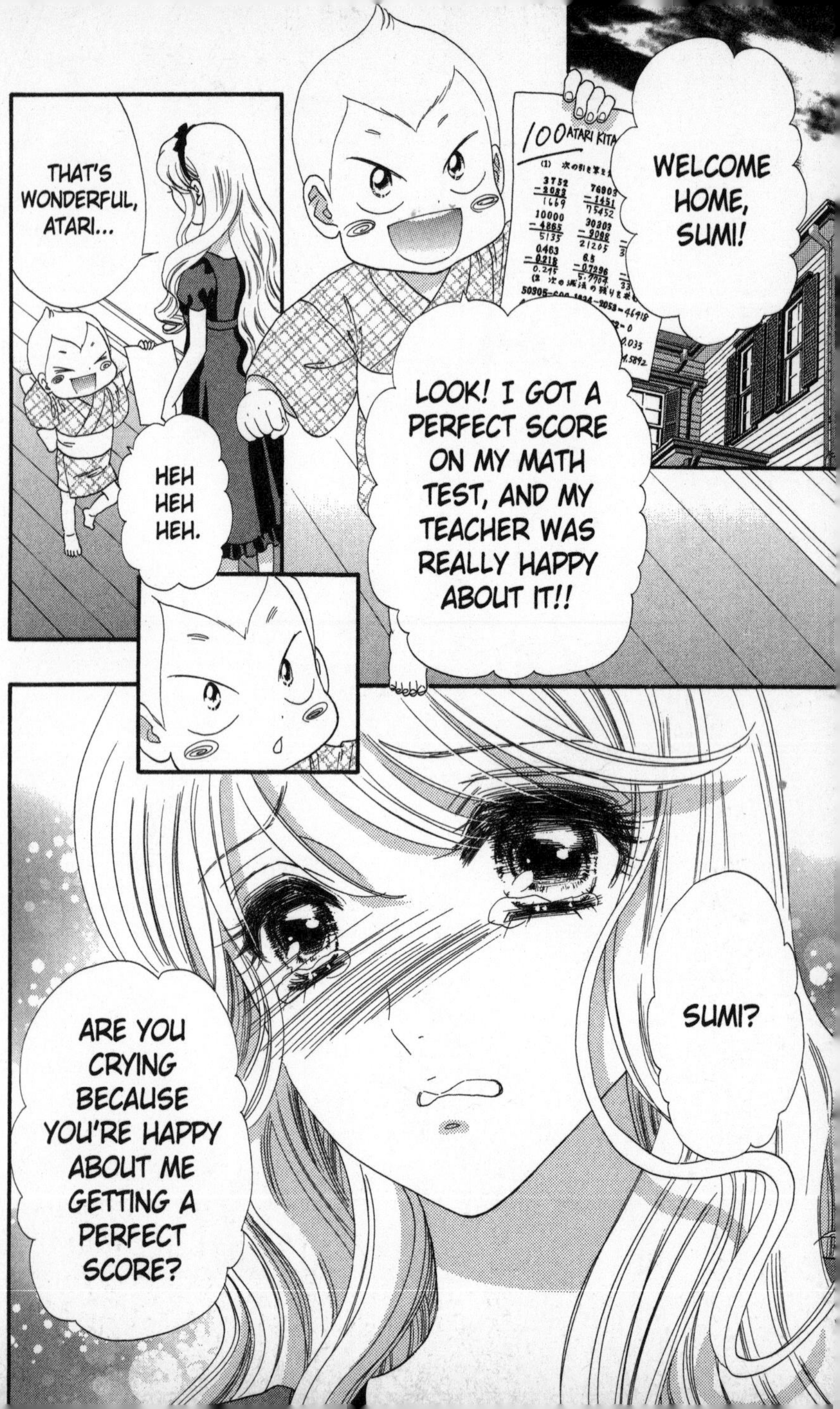
WELCOME HOME, SUMI!
LOOK! I GOT A PERFECT SCORE ON MY MATH TEST, AND MY TEACHER WAS REALLY HAPPY ABOUT IT!!
THAT'S WONDERFUL, ATARI...
HEH HEH HEH.
SUMI?
ARE YOU CRYING BECAUSE YOU'RE HAPPY ABOUT ME GETTING A PERFECT SCORE?

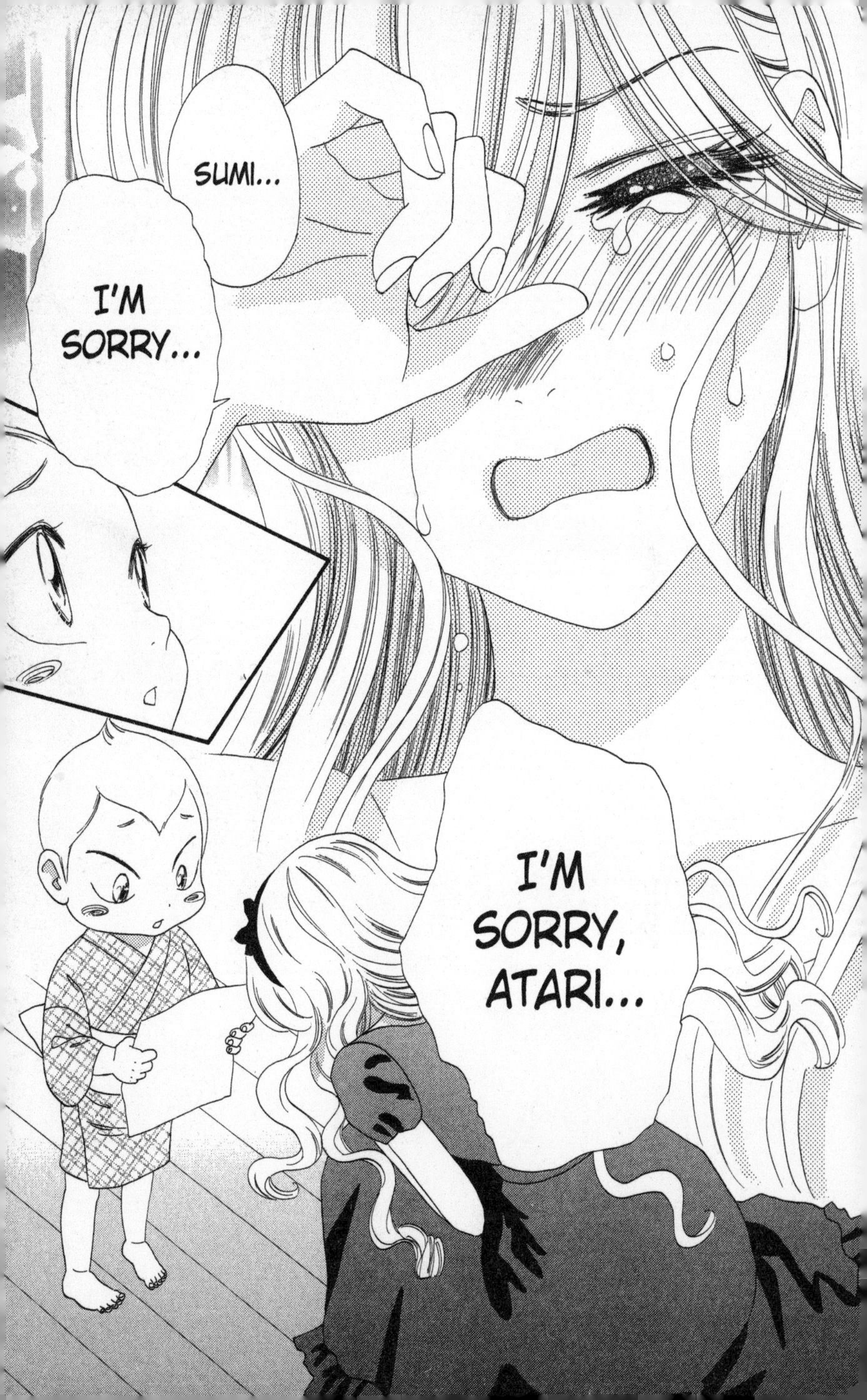
SUMI...
I'M SORRY...
I'M SORRY, ATARI...

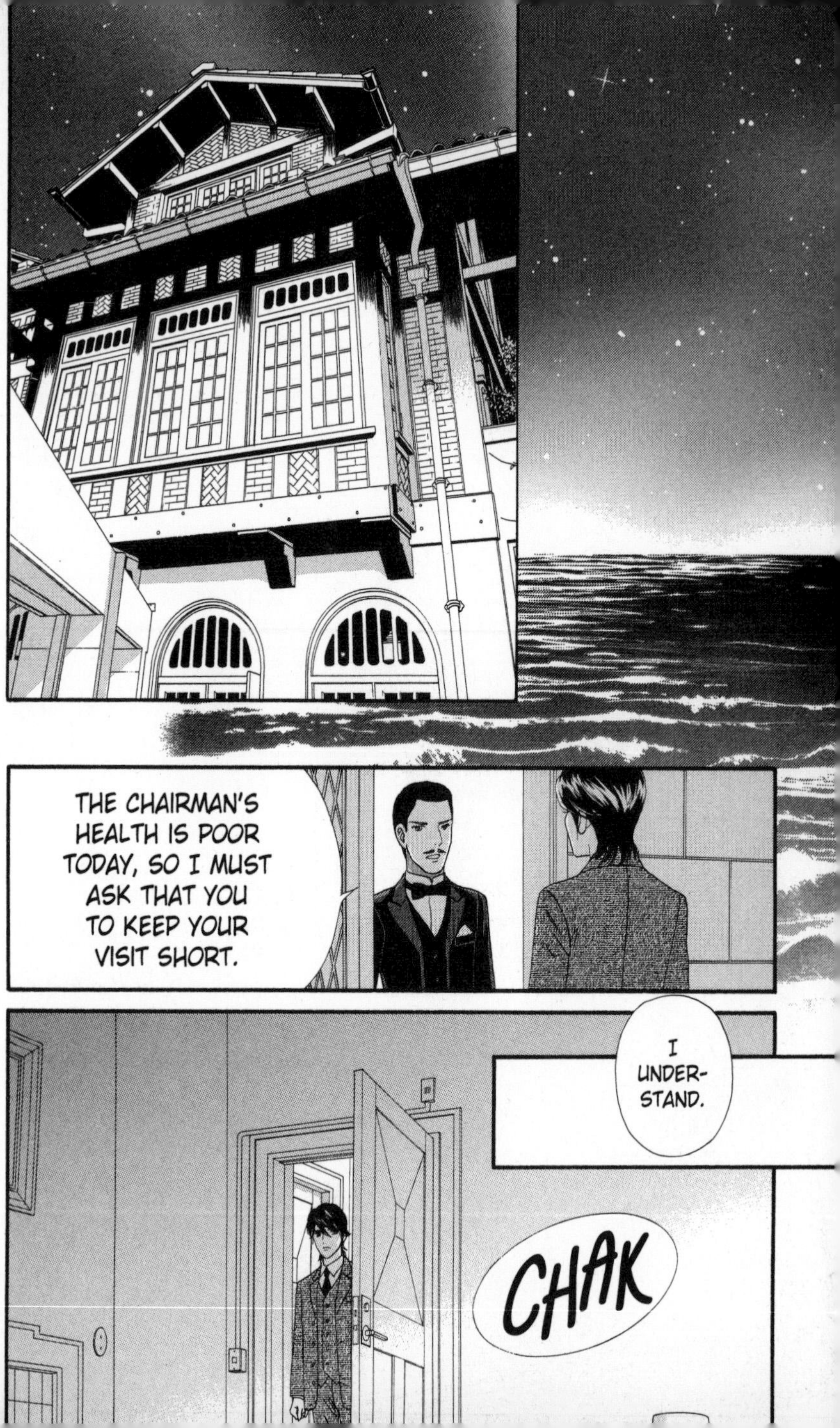
THE CHAIRMAN'S HEALTH IS POOR TODAY, SO I MUST ASK THAT YOU TO KEEP YOUR VISIT SHORT.
I UNDER-STAND.
CHAK

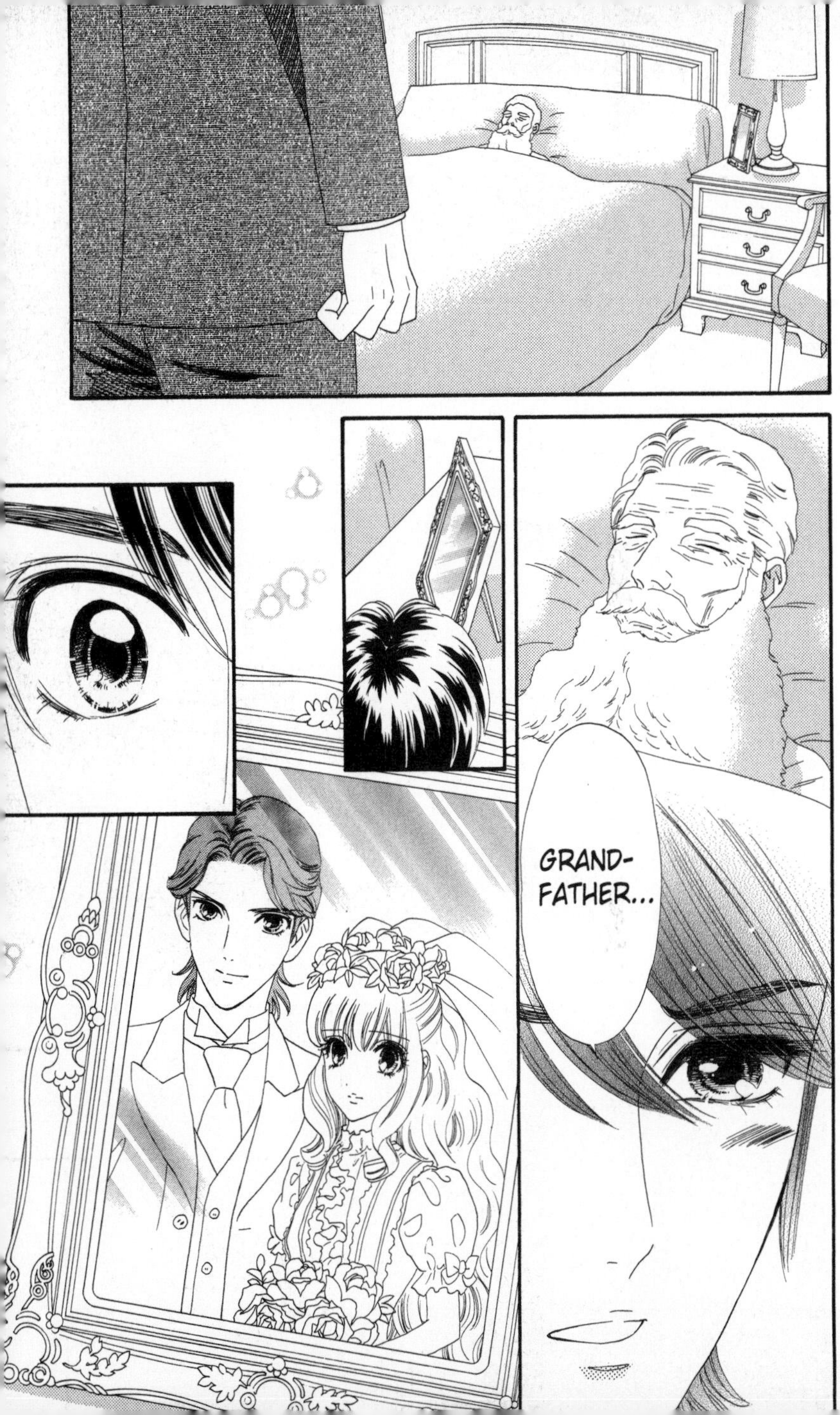
GRAND-
FATHER...

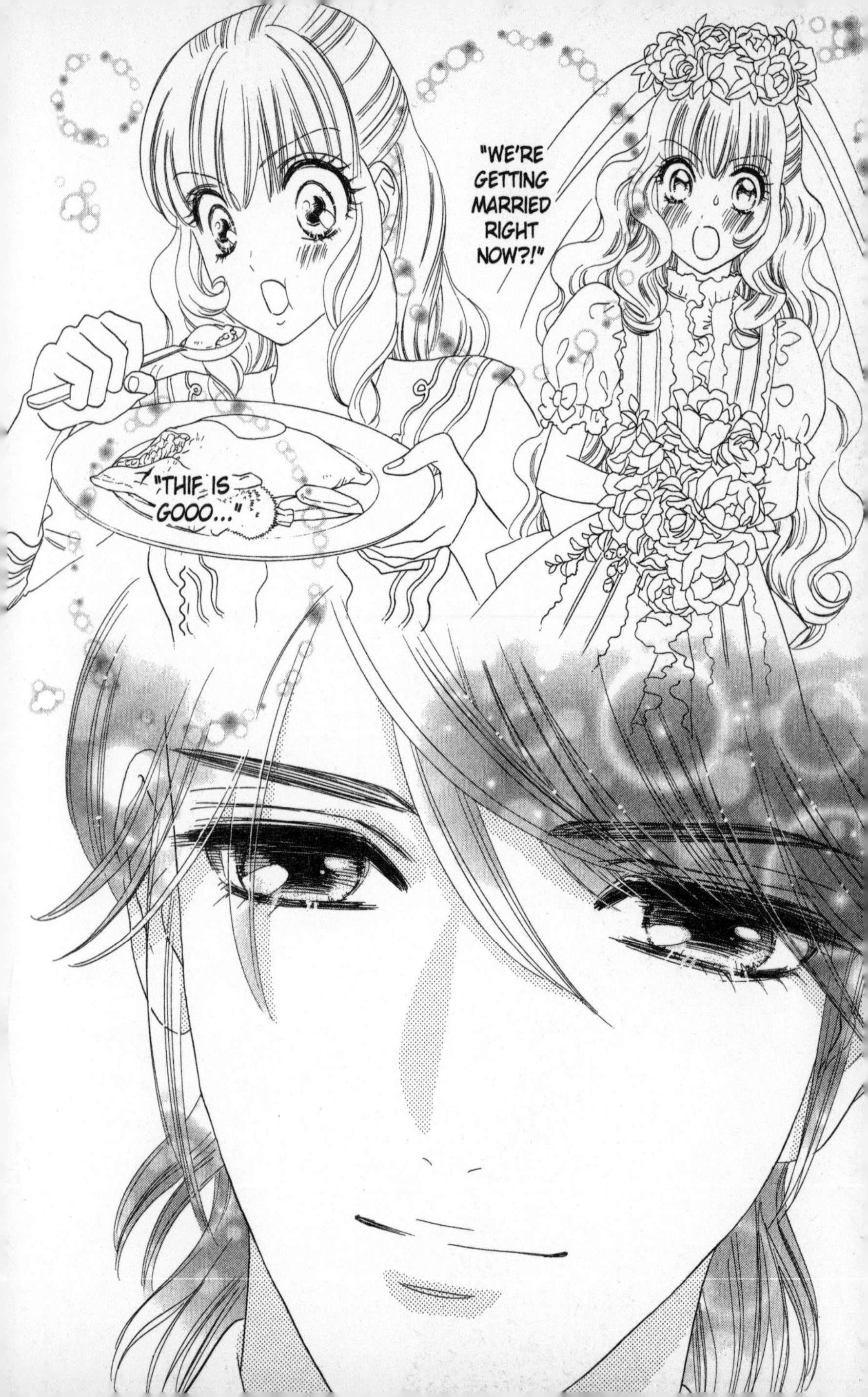
"WE'RE GETTING MARRIED RIGHT NOW?!"
"THIF IS GOOO..."

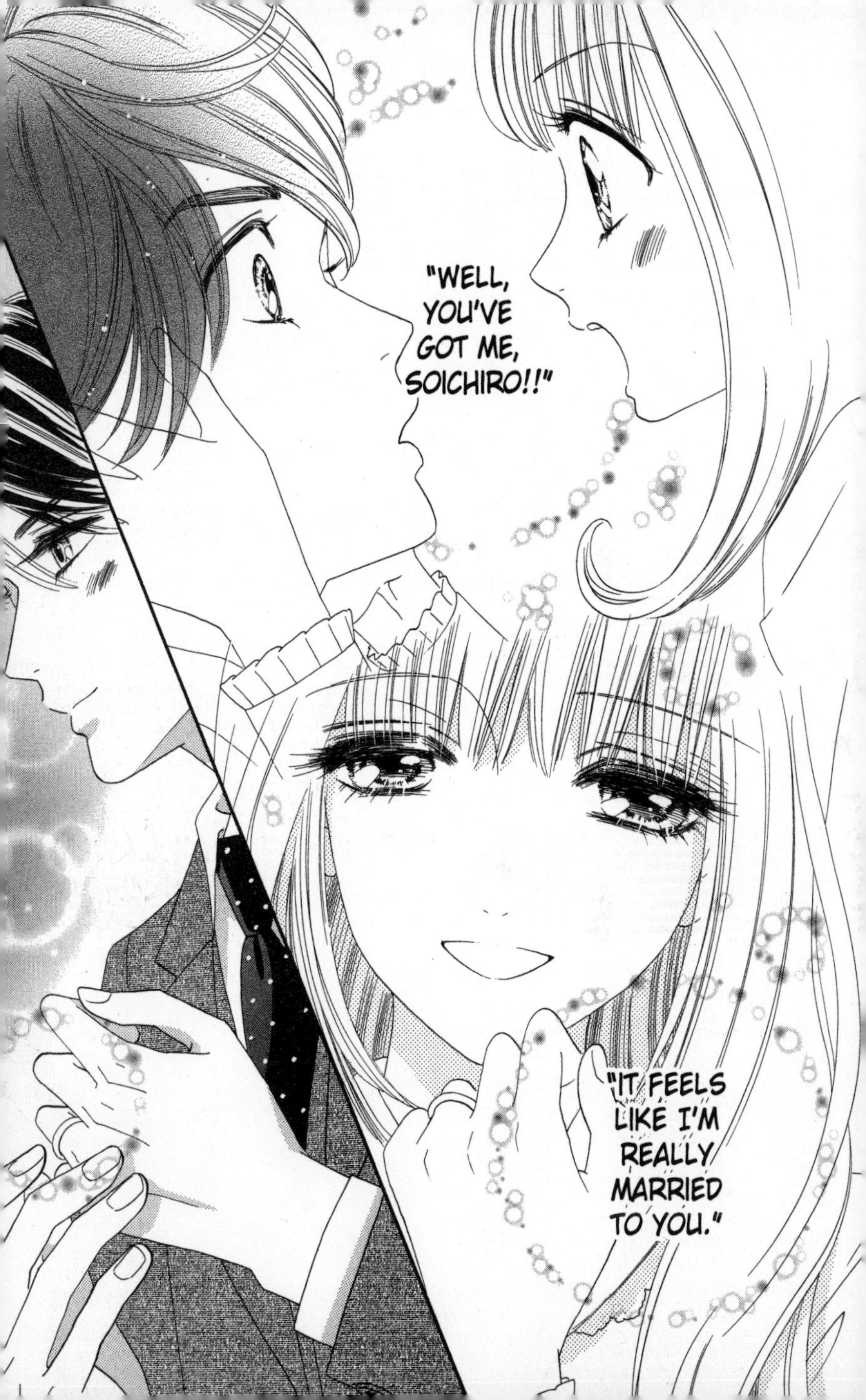
"WELL, YOU'VE GOT ME, SOICHIRO!!"
"IT FEELS LIKE I'M REALLY MARRIED TO YOU."

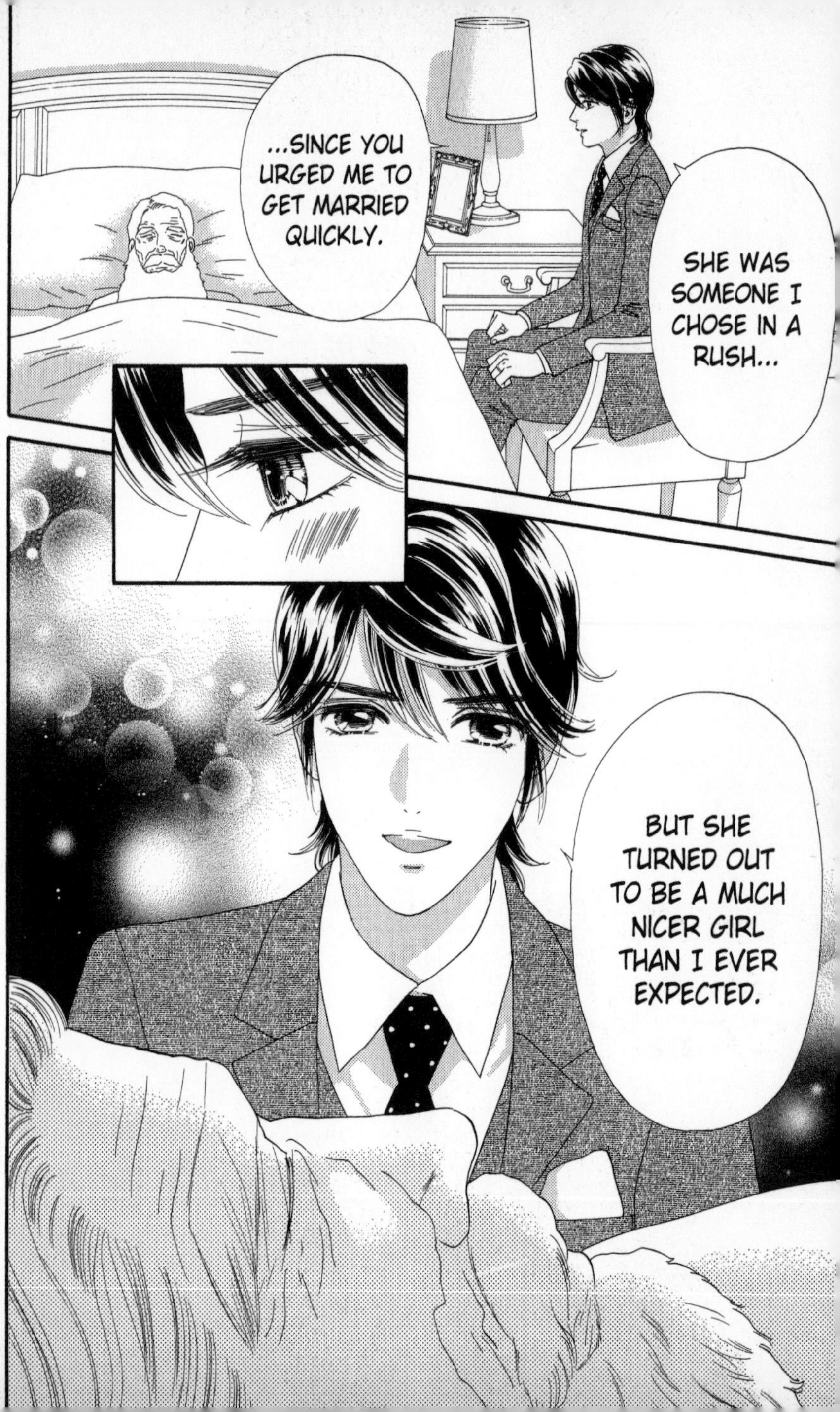
SHE WAS SOMEONE I CHOSE IN A RUSH...
...SINCE YOU URGED ME TO GET MARRIED QUICKLY.
BUT SHE TURNED OUT TO BE A MUCH NICER GIRL THAN I EVER EXPECTED.

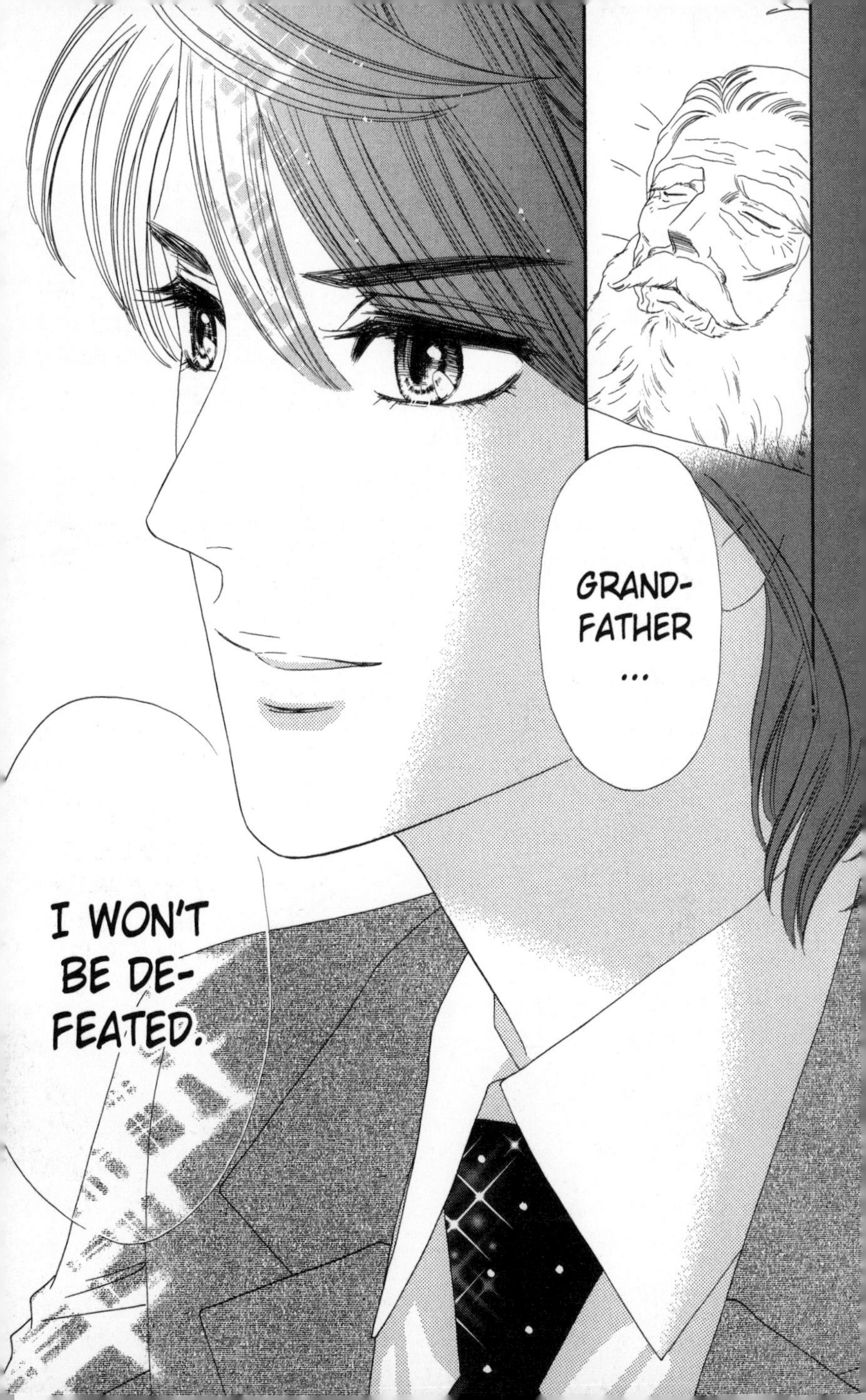
GRAND-FATHER...
I WON'T BE DE-FEATED.

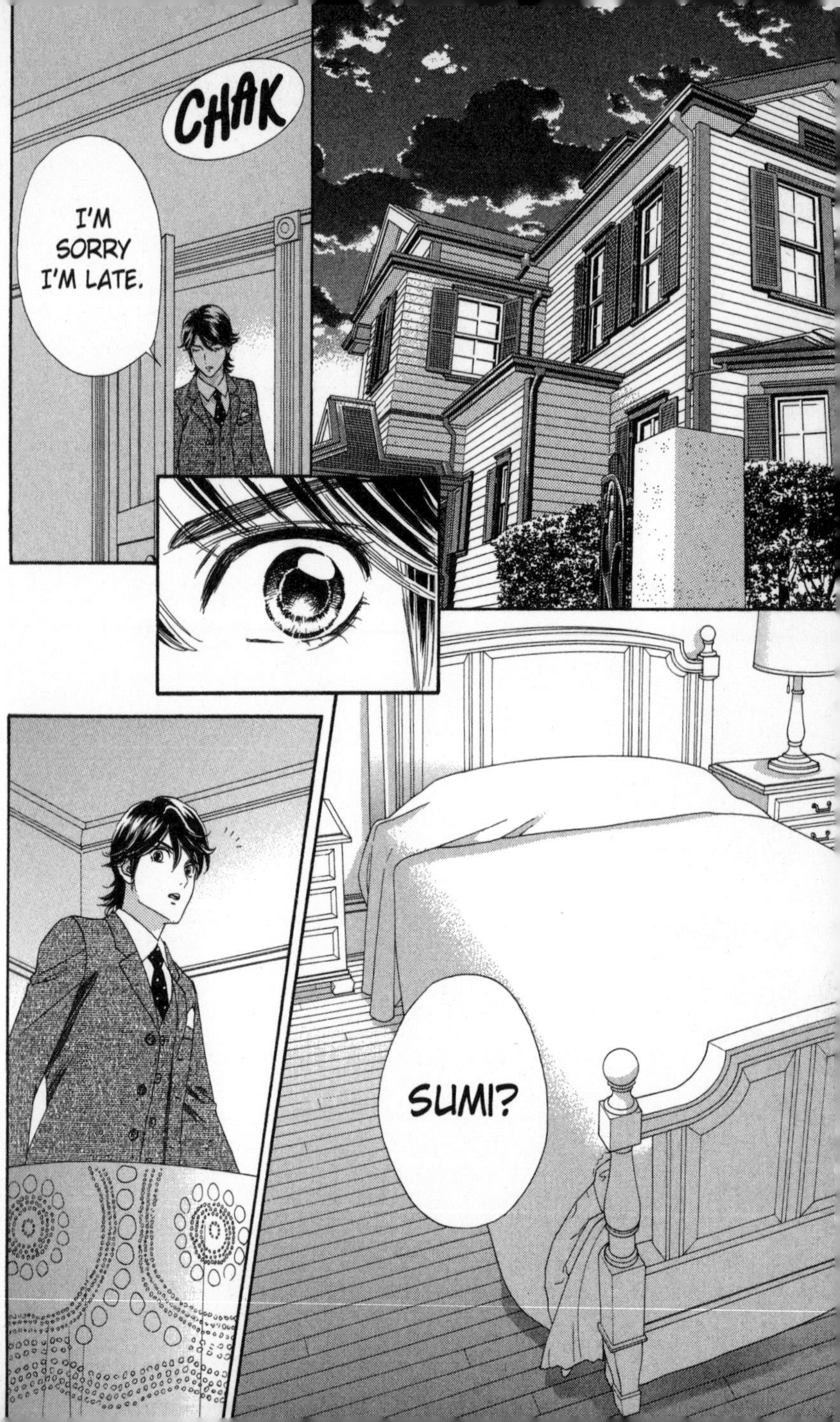
CHAK
I'M SORRY I'M LATE.
SUMI?

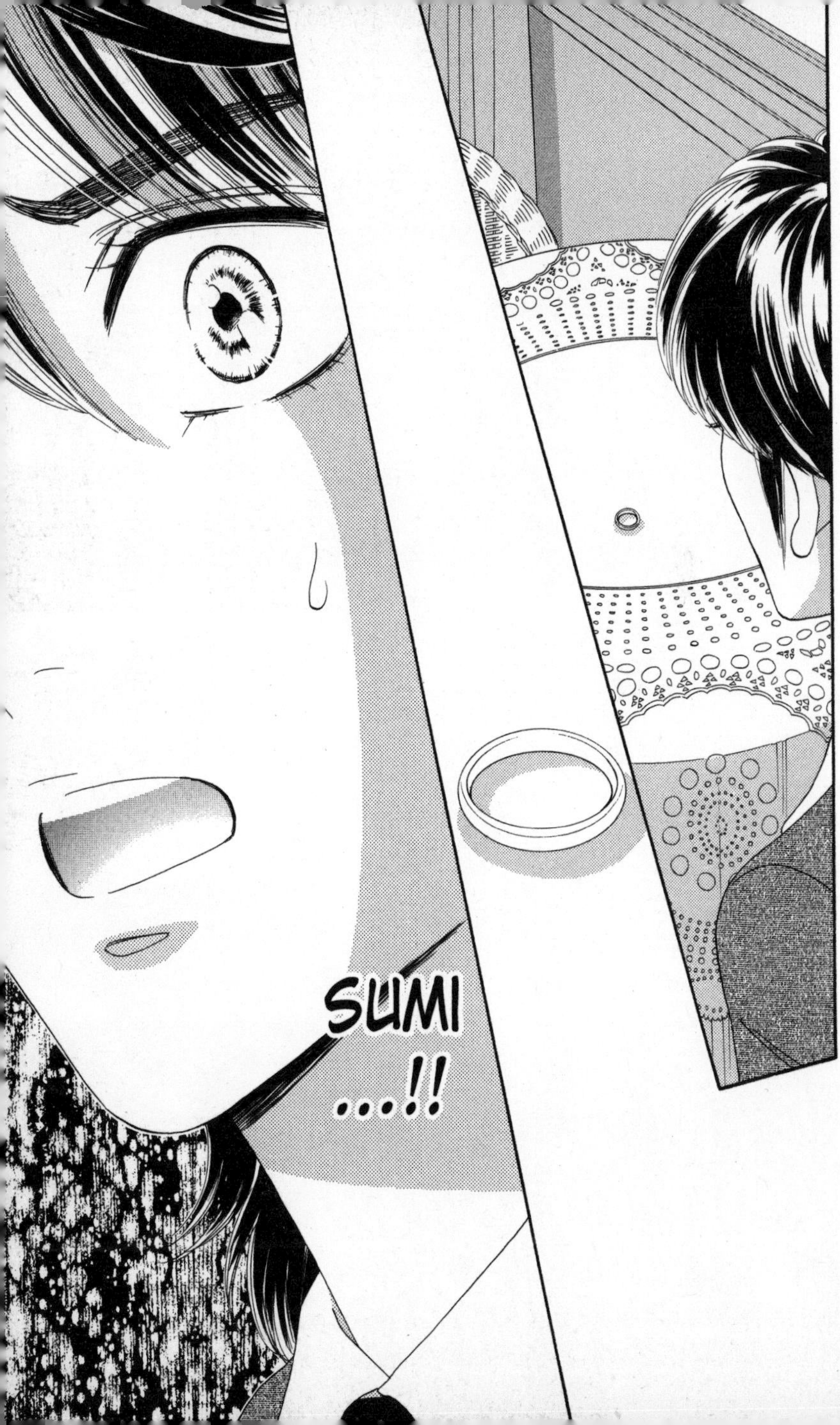
SUMI ...!!

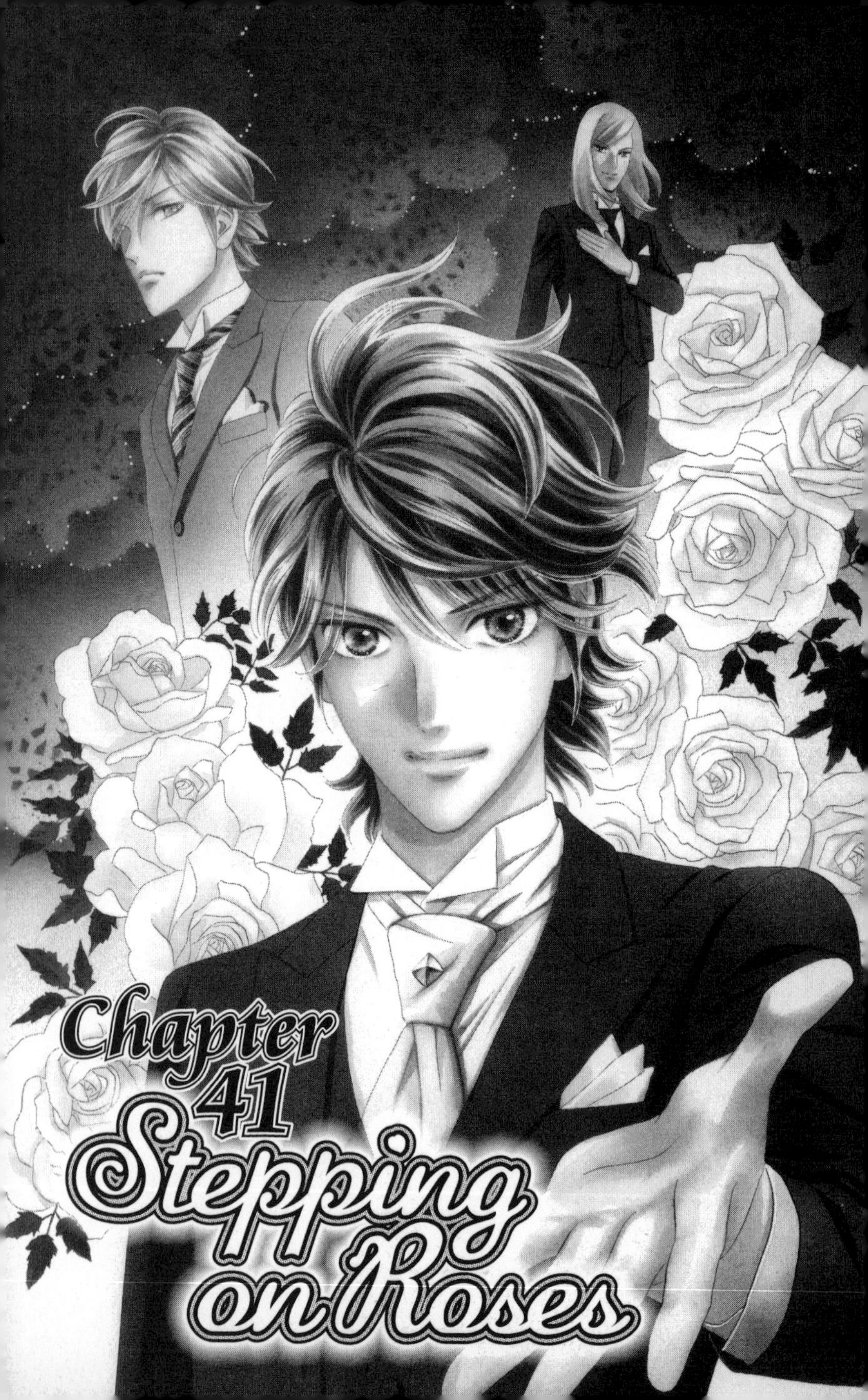
Chapter 41
Stepping on Roses

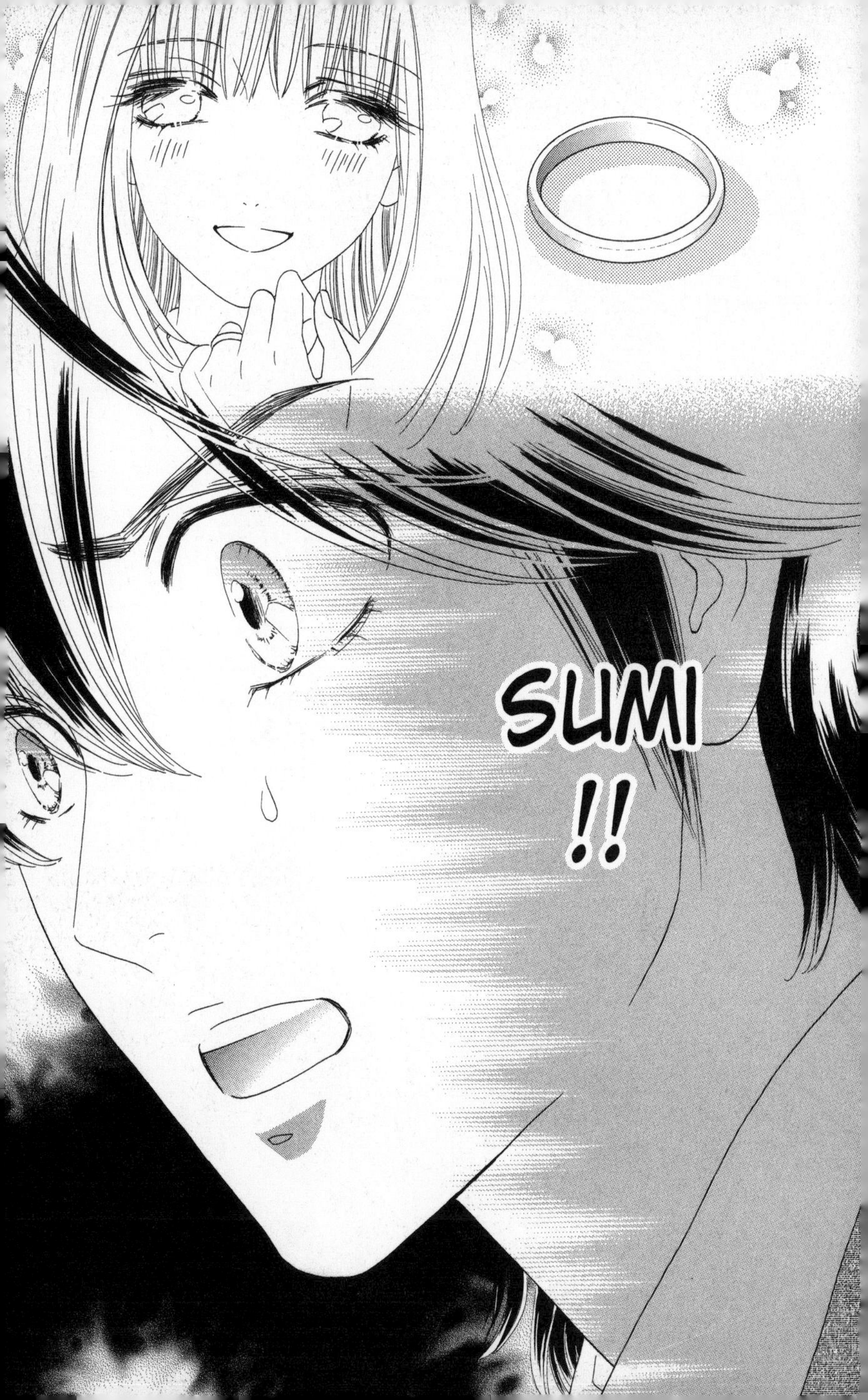
SUMI !!

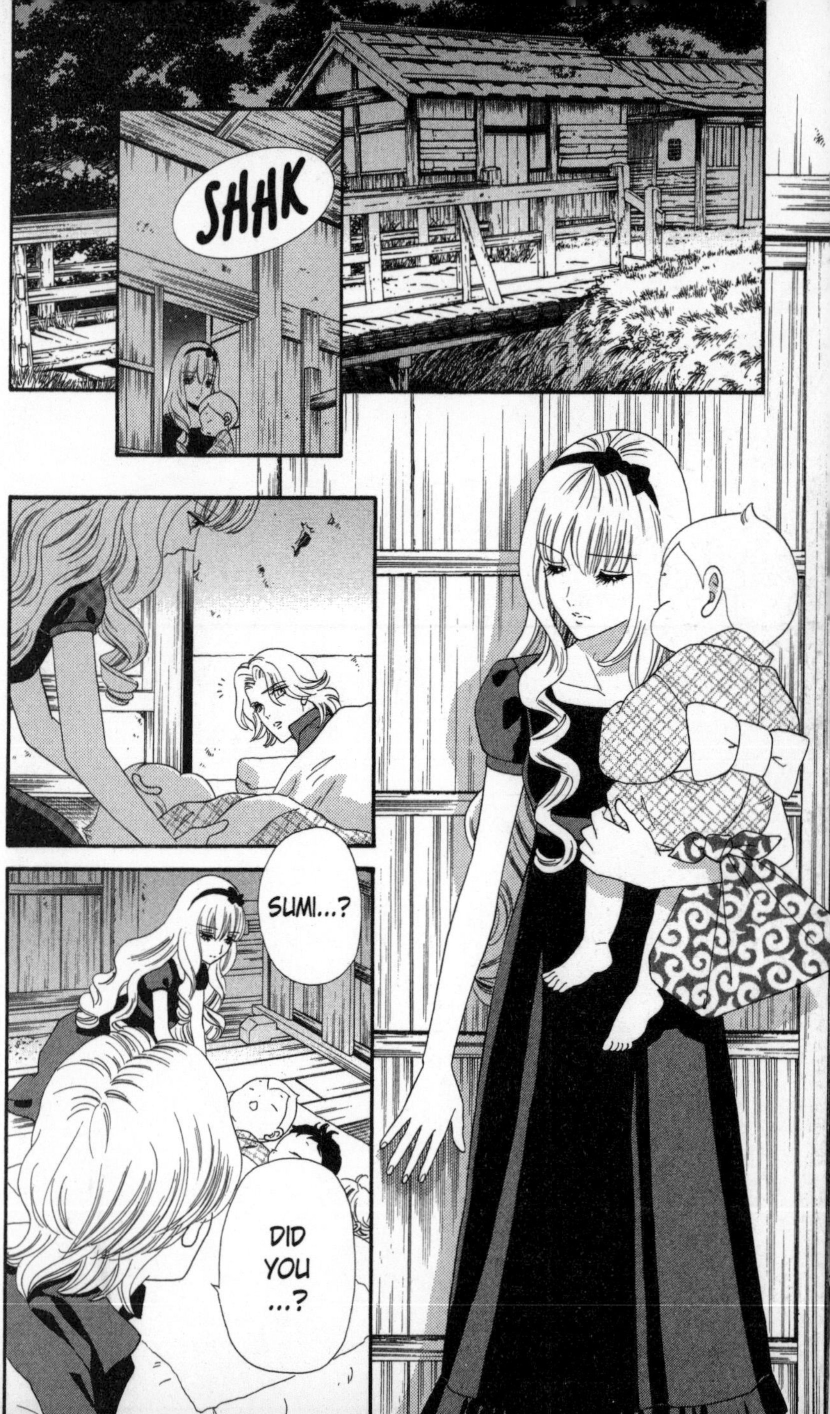
SHHK
SUMI...?
DID YOU ...?

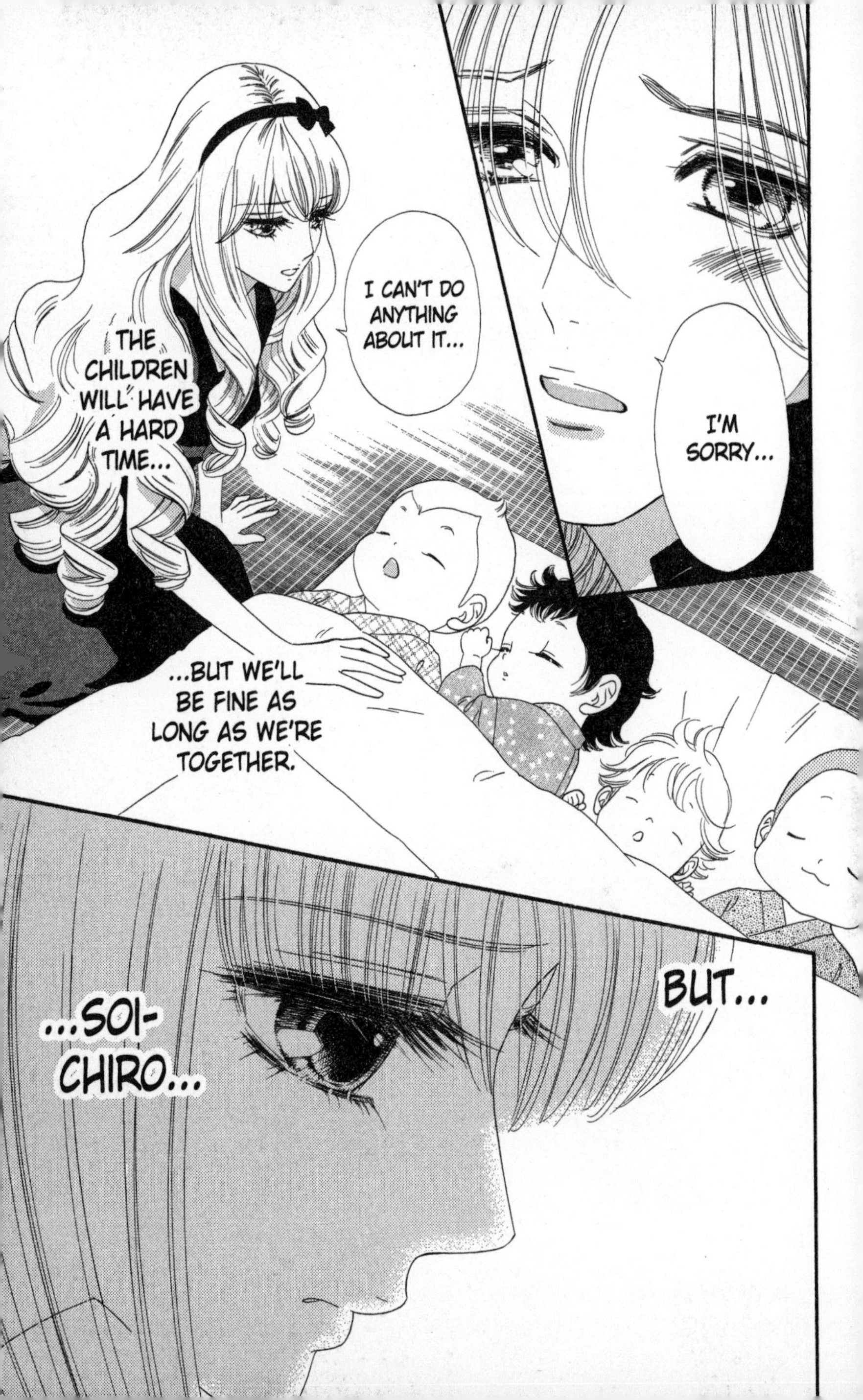
I'M SORRY...
I CAN'T DO ANYTHING ABOUT IT...
THE CHILDREN WILL HAVE A HARD TIME...
...BUT WE'LL BE FINE AS LONG AS WE'RE TOGETHER.
BUT...
...SOI-CHIRO...

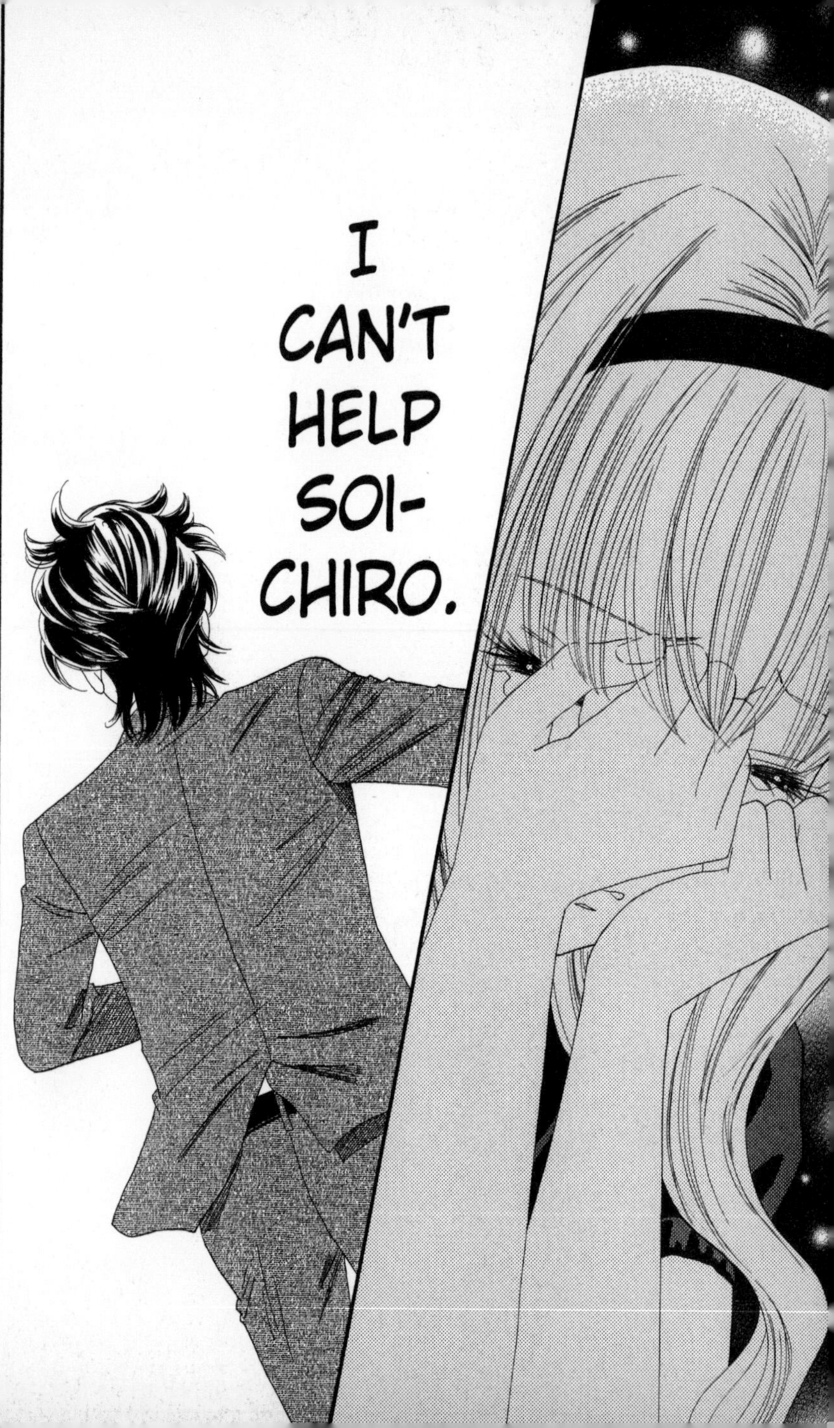
I CAN'T HELP SOI-CHIRO.

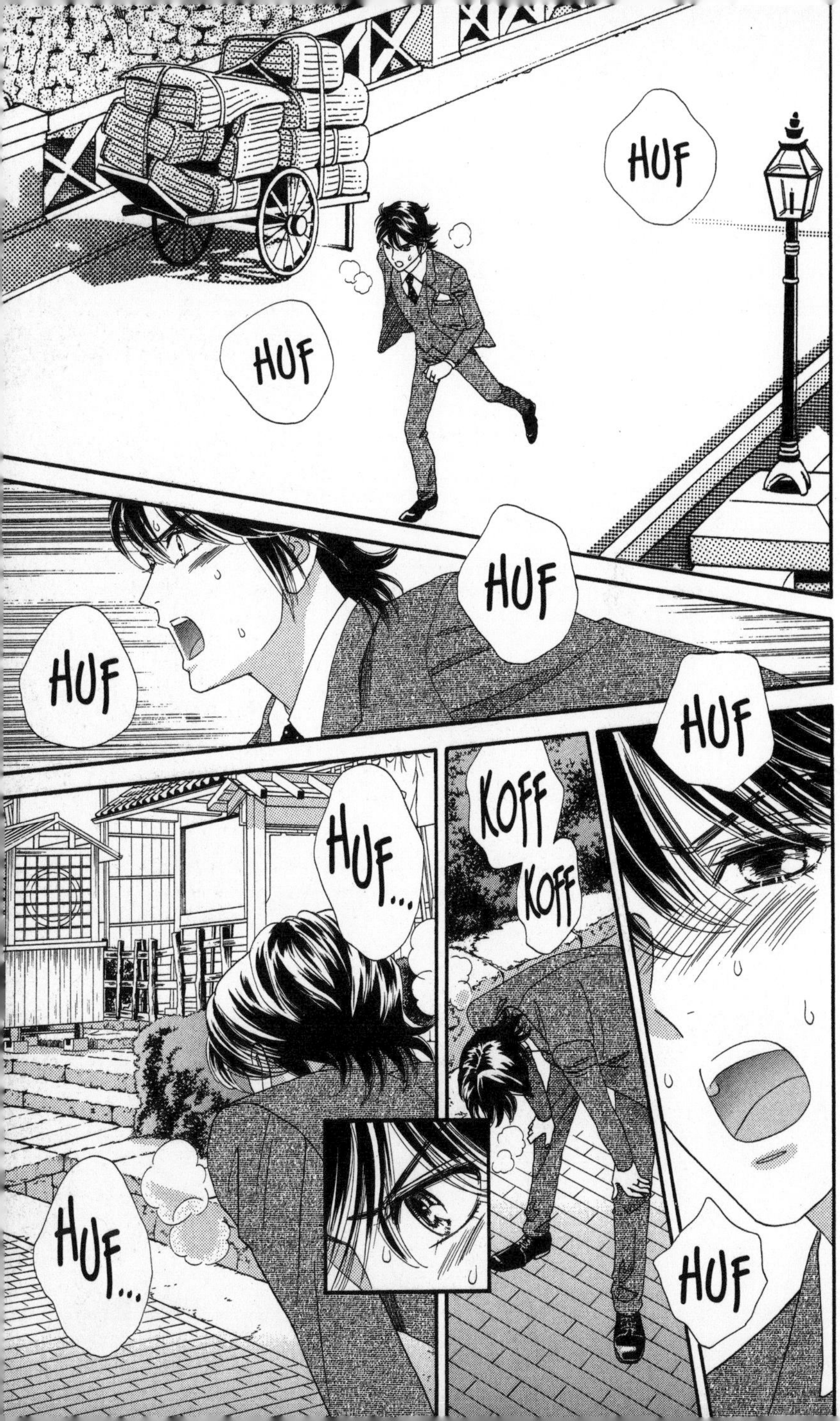

HUF
HUF
HUF
HUF
HUF
HUF
KOFF
KOFF
HUF...
HUF...

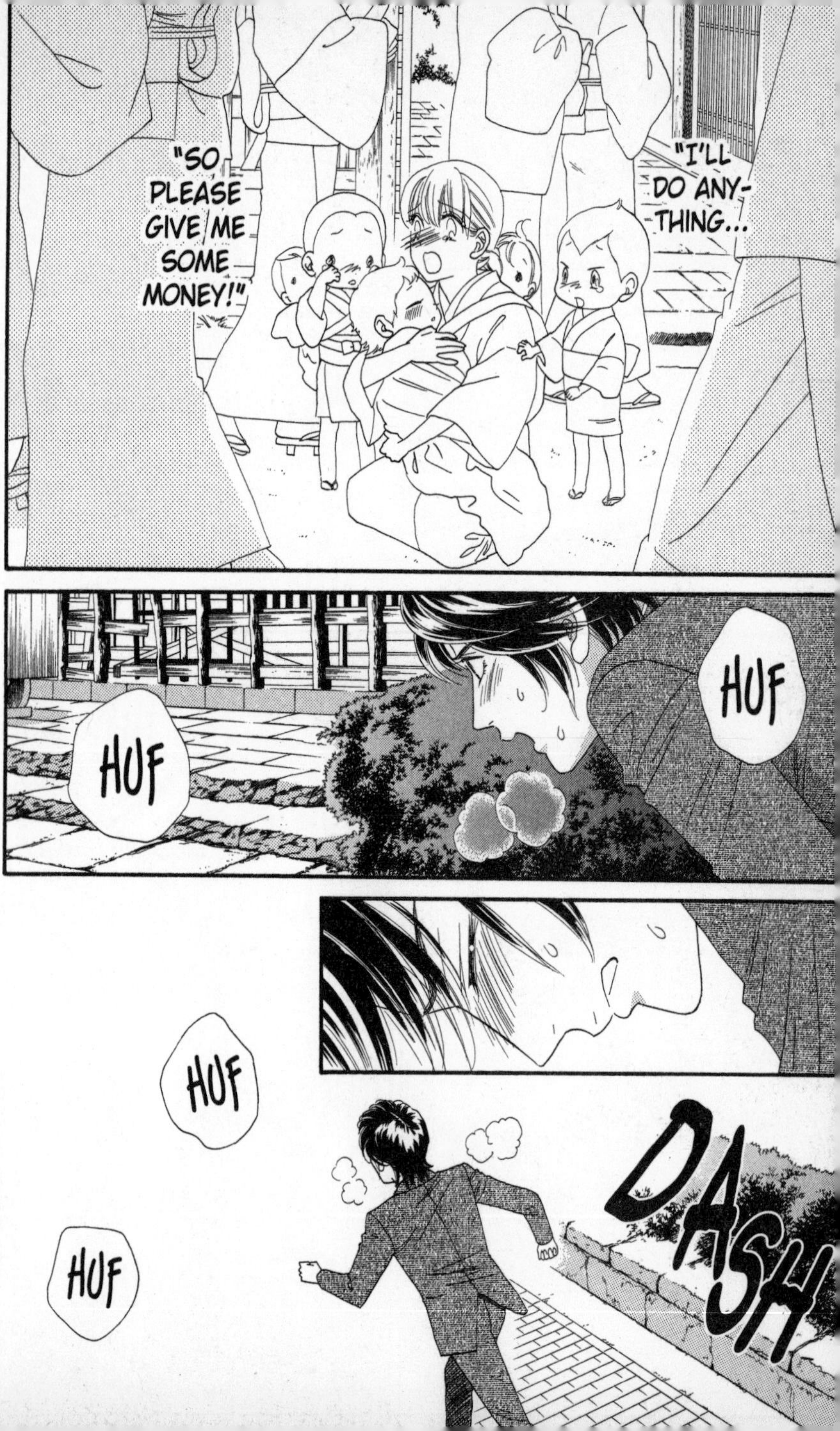
"I'LL DO ANY-THING...
"SO PLEASE GIVE ME SOME MONEY!"
HUF
HUF
DASH
HUF
HUF

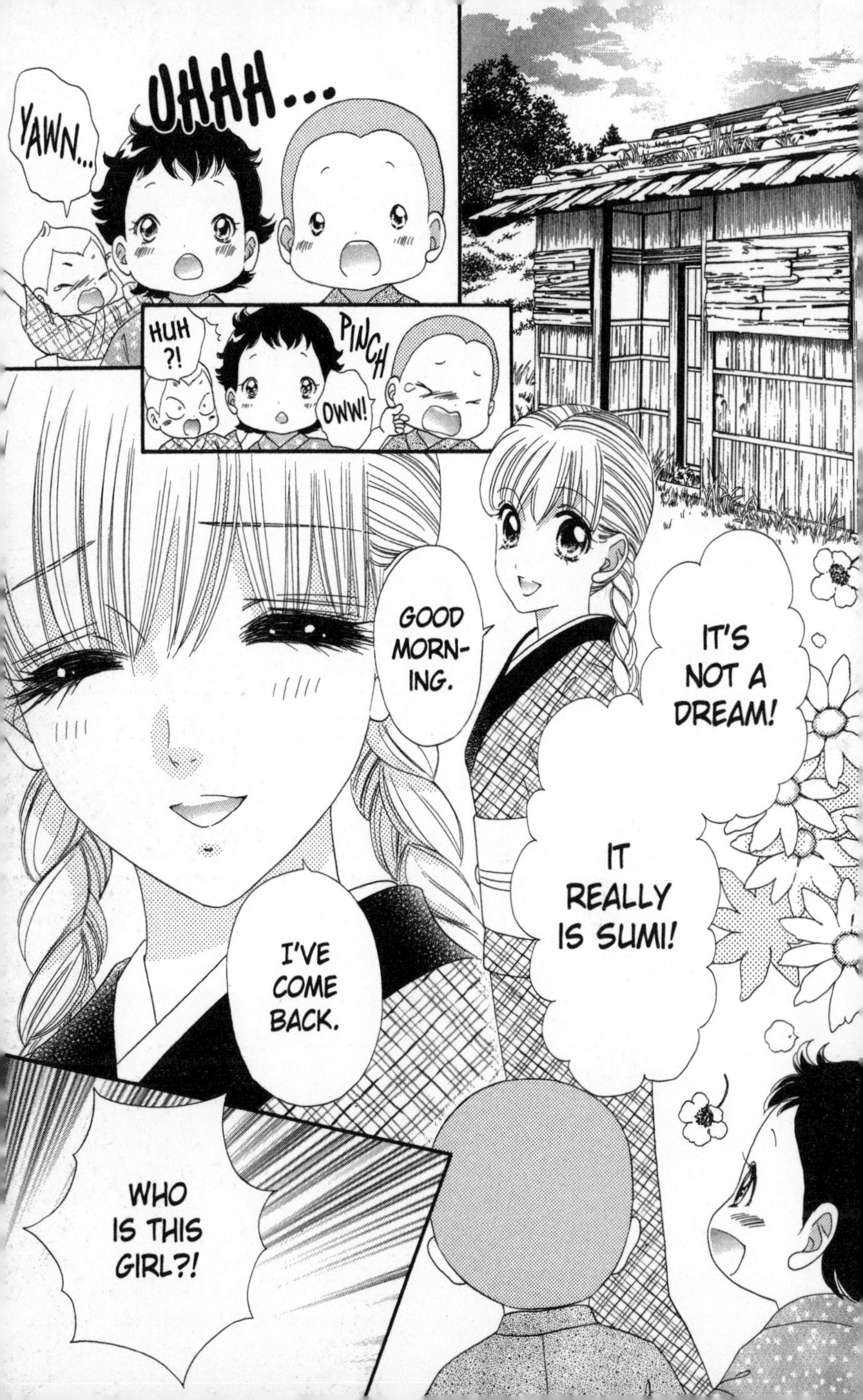
UHHH...
YAWN...
PINCH
OWW!
HUH ?!
GOOD MORN-ING.
IT'S NOT A DREAM!
IT REALLY IS SUMI!
I'VE COME BACK.
WHO IS THIS GIRL?!

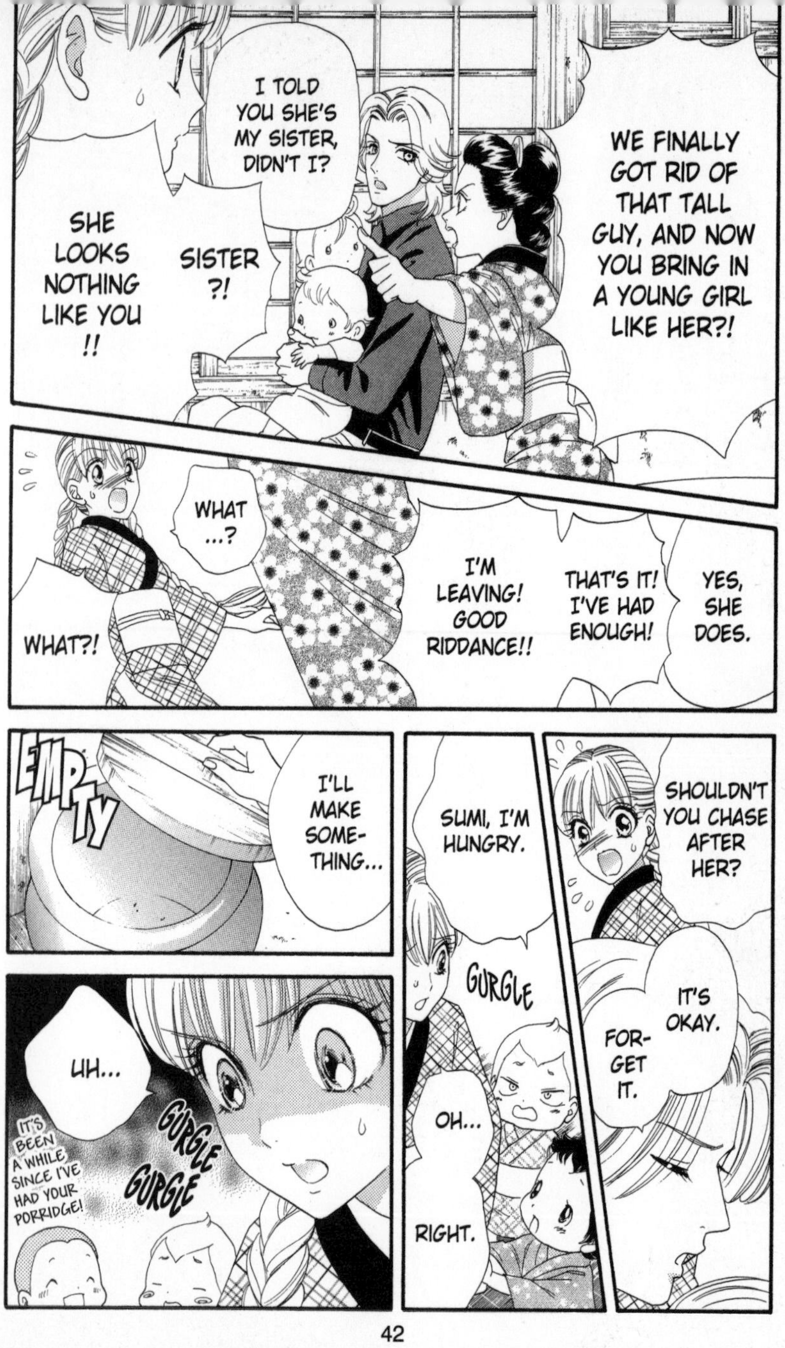
WE FINALLY GOT RID OF THAT TALL GUY, AND NOW YOU BRING IN A YOUNG GIRL LIKE HER?!
I TOLD YOU SHE'S MY SISTER, DIDN'T I?
SISTER ?!
SHE LOOKS NOTHING LIKE YOU !!
YES, SHE DOES.
THAT'S IT! I'VE HAD ENOUGH!
I'M LEAVING! GOOD RIDDANCE!!
WHAT ...?
WHAT?!
SHOULDN'T YOU CHASE AFTER HER?
IT'S OKAY.
FOR-GET IT.
SUMI, I'M HUNGRY.
GURGLE
OH...
RIGHT.
I'LL MAKE SOME-THING...
EMPTY
UH...
GURGLE GURGLE
IT'S BEEN A WHILE SINCE I'VE HAD YOUR PORRIDGE!

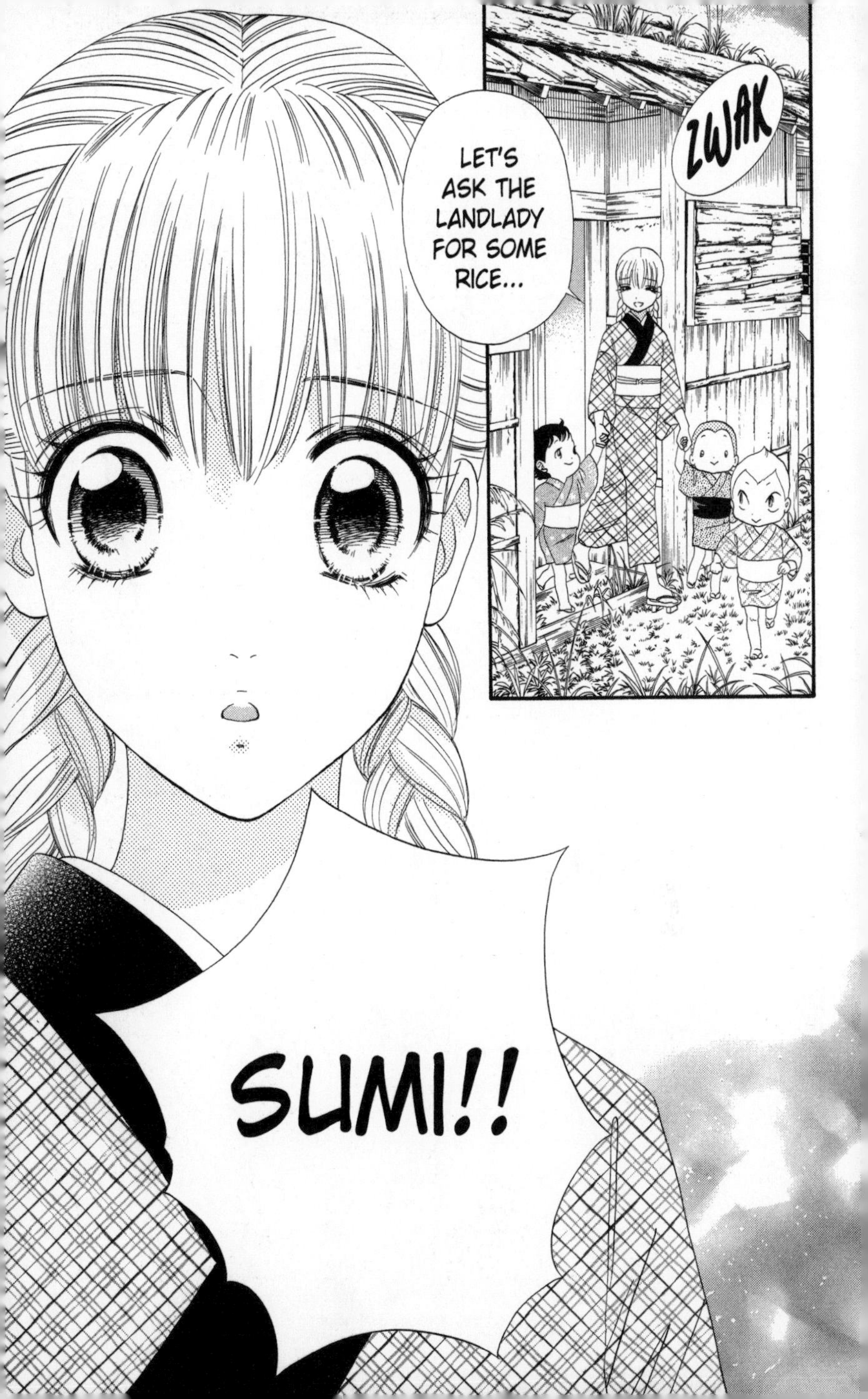
ZWAK
LET'S ASK THE LANDLADY FOR SOME RICE...
SUMI!!

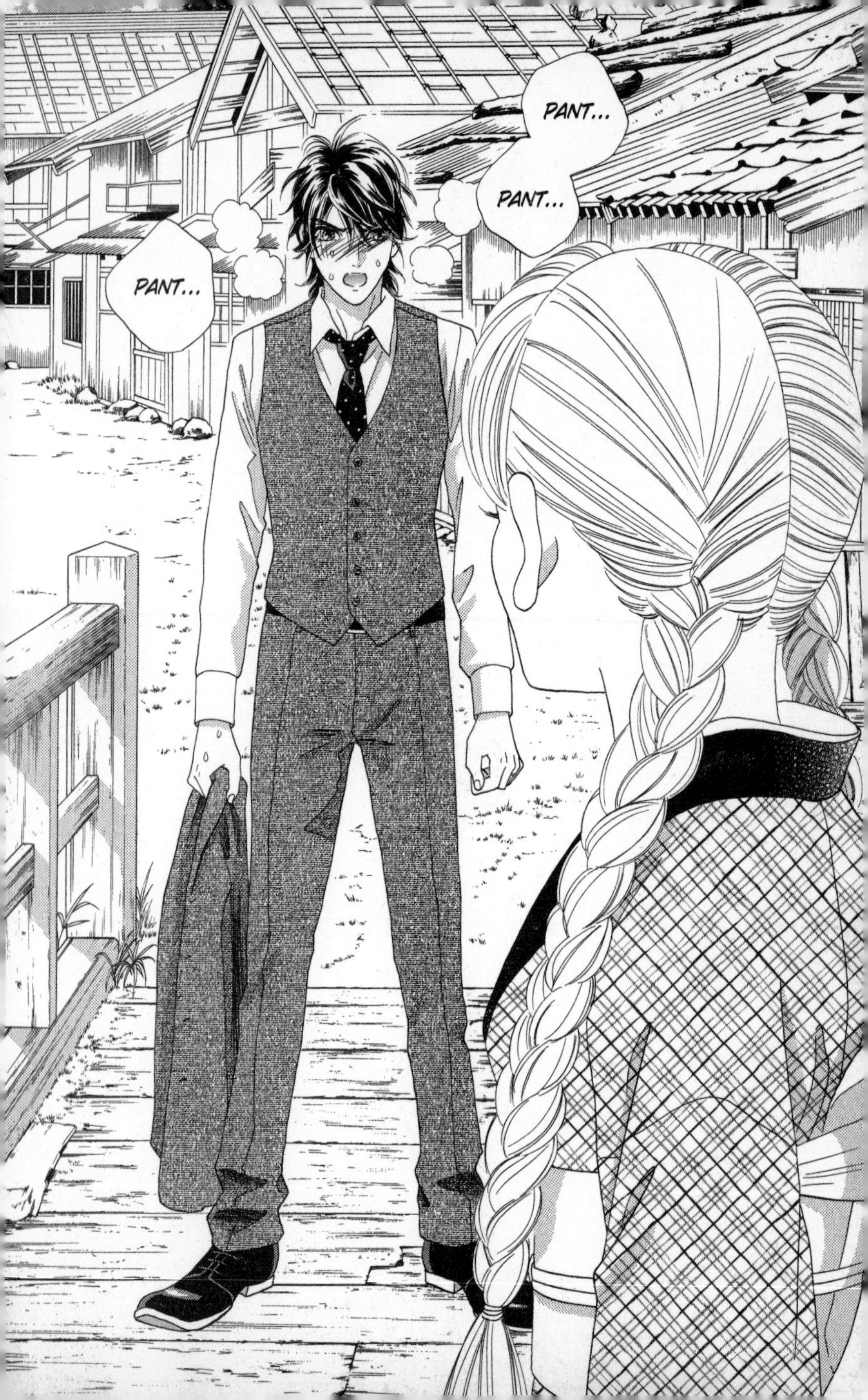
PANT...
PANT...
PANT...

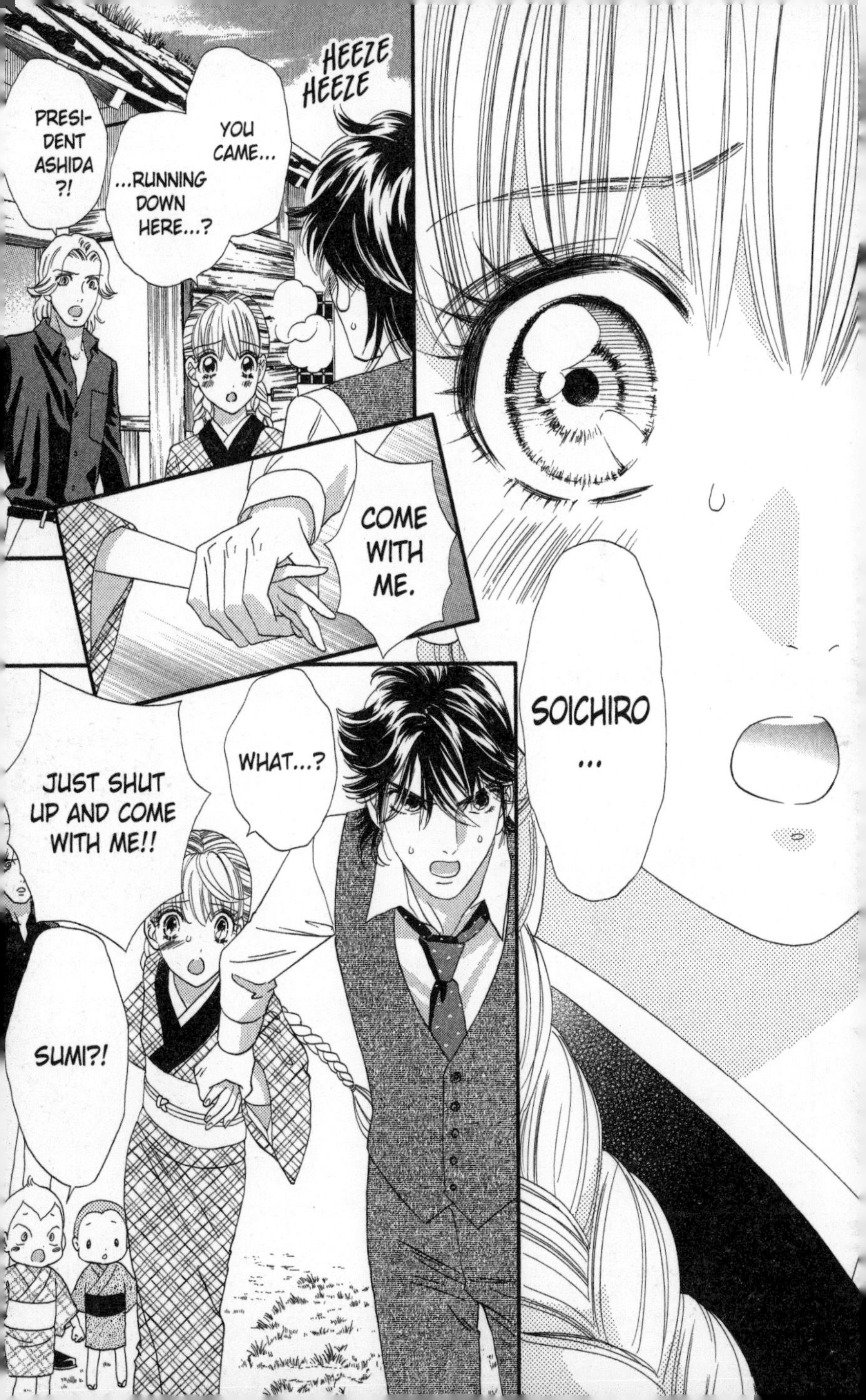
SOICHIRO ...
HEEZE HEEZE
YOU CAME...
...RUNNING DOWN HERE...?
PRESI-DENT ASHIDA ?!
COME WITH ME.
WHAT...?
JUST SHUT UP AND COME WITH ME!!
SUMI?!

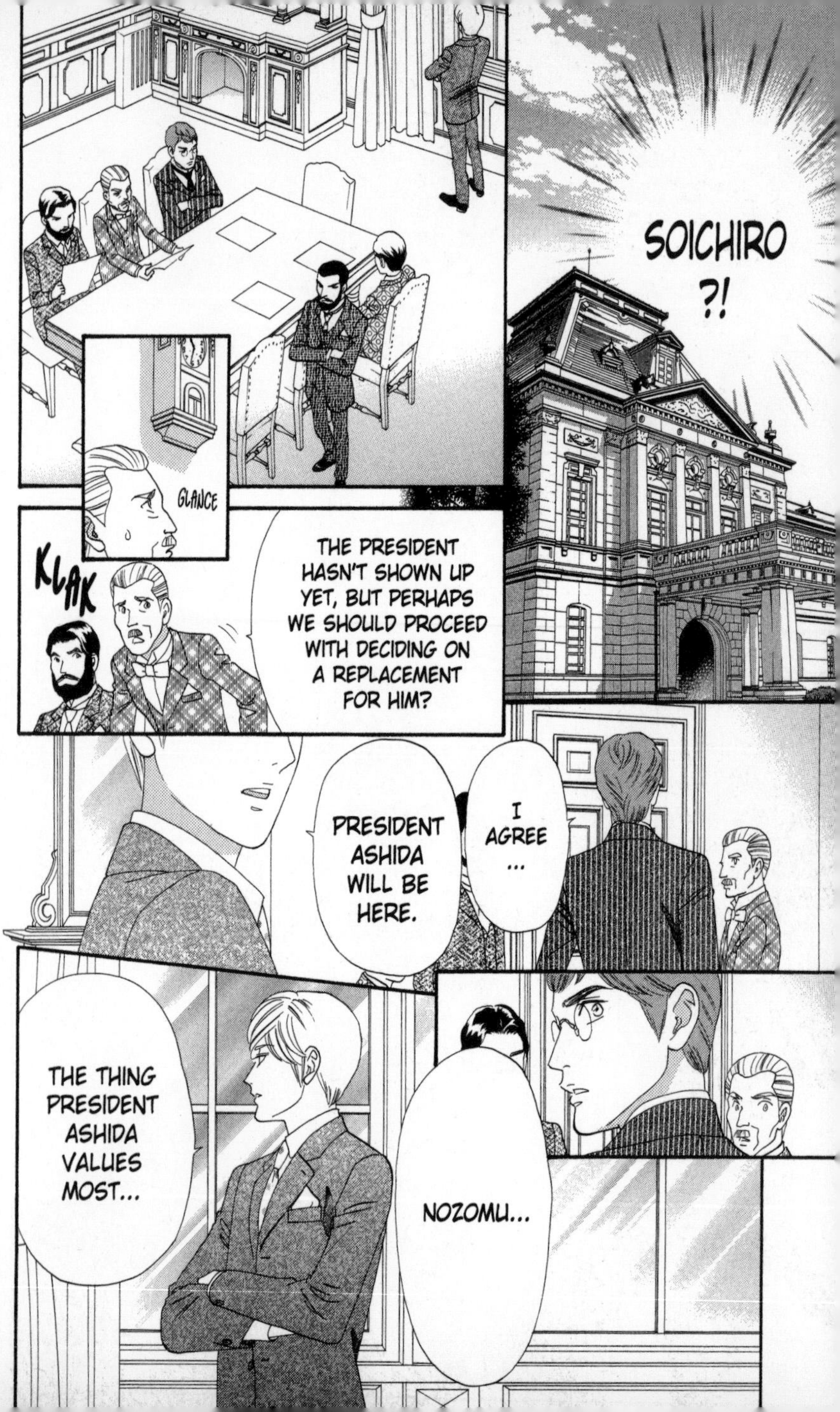
SOICHIRO ?!
GLANCE
KLAK
THE PRESIDENT HASN'T SHOWN UP YET, BUT PERHAPS WE SHOULD PROCEED WITH DECIDING ON A REPLACEMENT FOR HIM?
I AGREE ...
PRESIDENT ASHIDA WILL BE HERE.
NOZOMU...
THE THING PRESIDENT ASHIDA VALUES MOST...

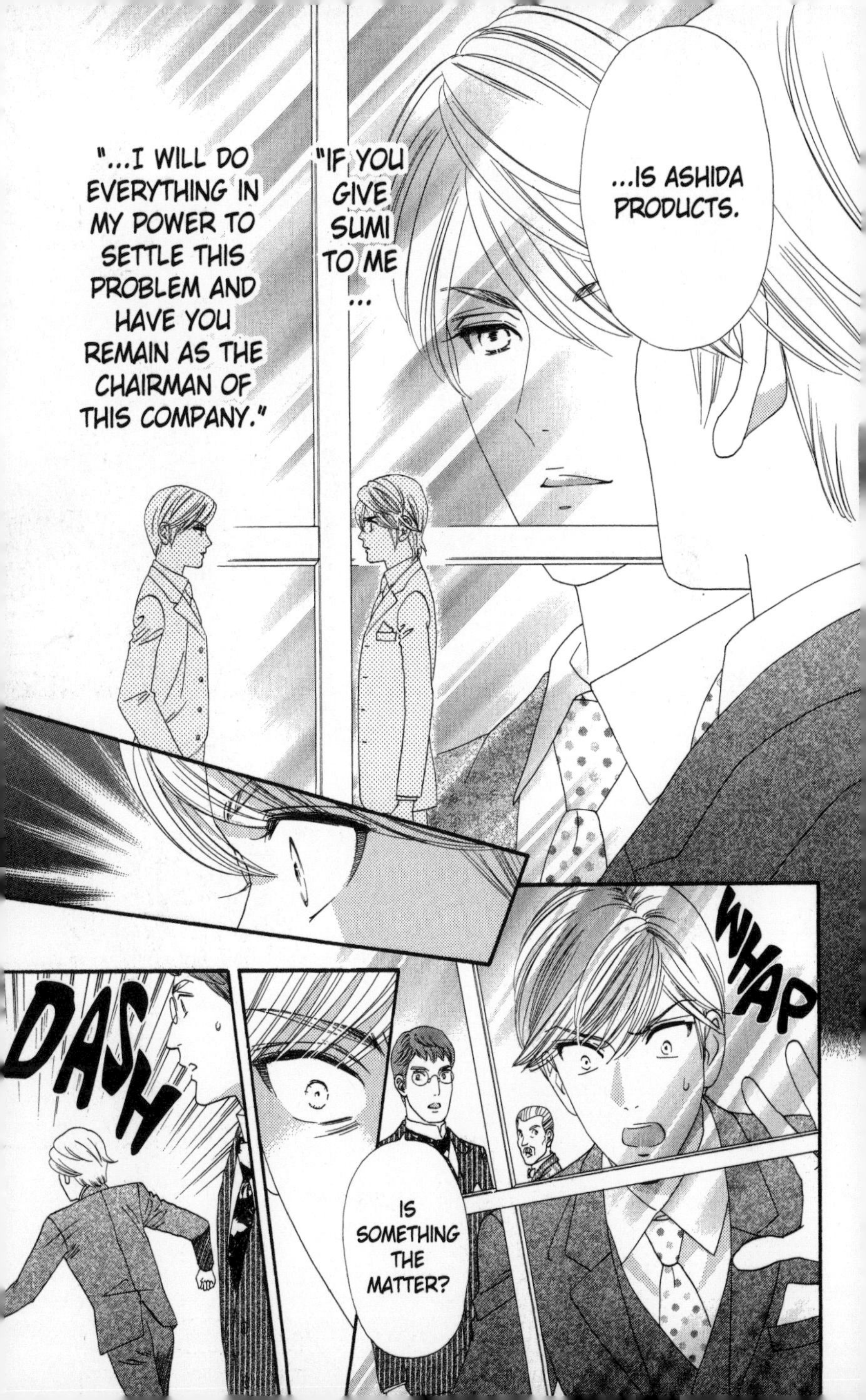
...IS ASHIDA PRODUCTS.
"IF YOU GIVE SUMI TO ME ...
"...I WILL DO EVERYTHING IN MY POWER TO SETTLE THIS PROBLEM AND HAVE YOU REMAIN AS THE CHAIRMAN OF THIS COMPANY."
WHAP
IS SOMETHING THE MATTER?
DASH

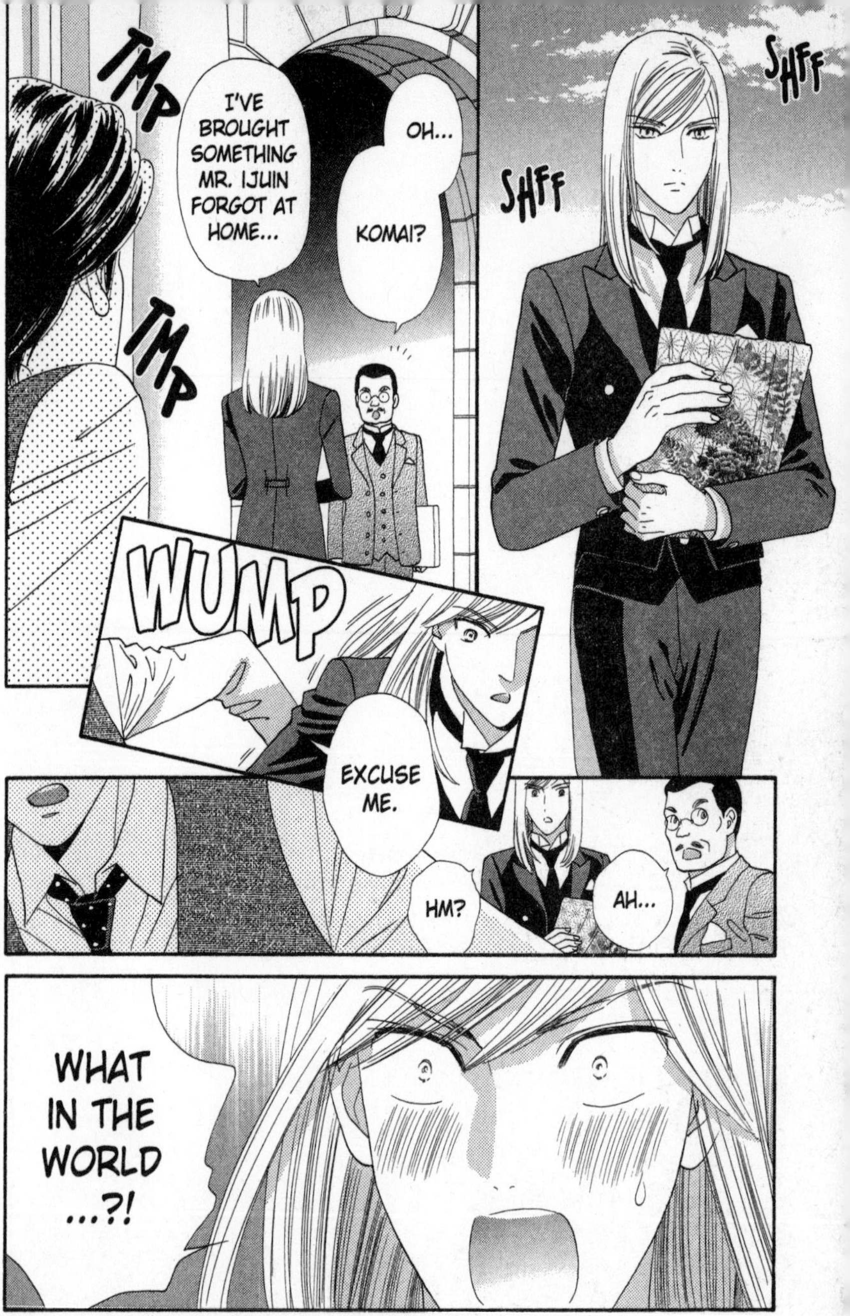
SHFF
SHFF
OH...
KOMAI?
I'VE BROUGHT SOMETHING MR. IJUIN FORGOT AT HOME...
TMP
TMP
WUMP
EXCUSE ME.
AH...
HM?
WHAT IN THE WORLD ...?!

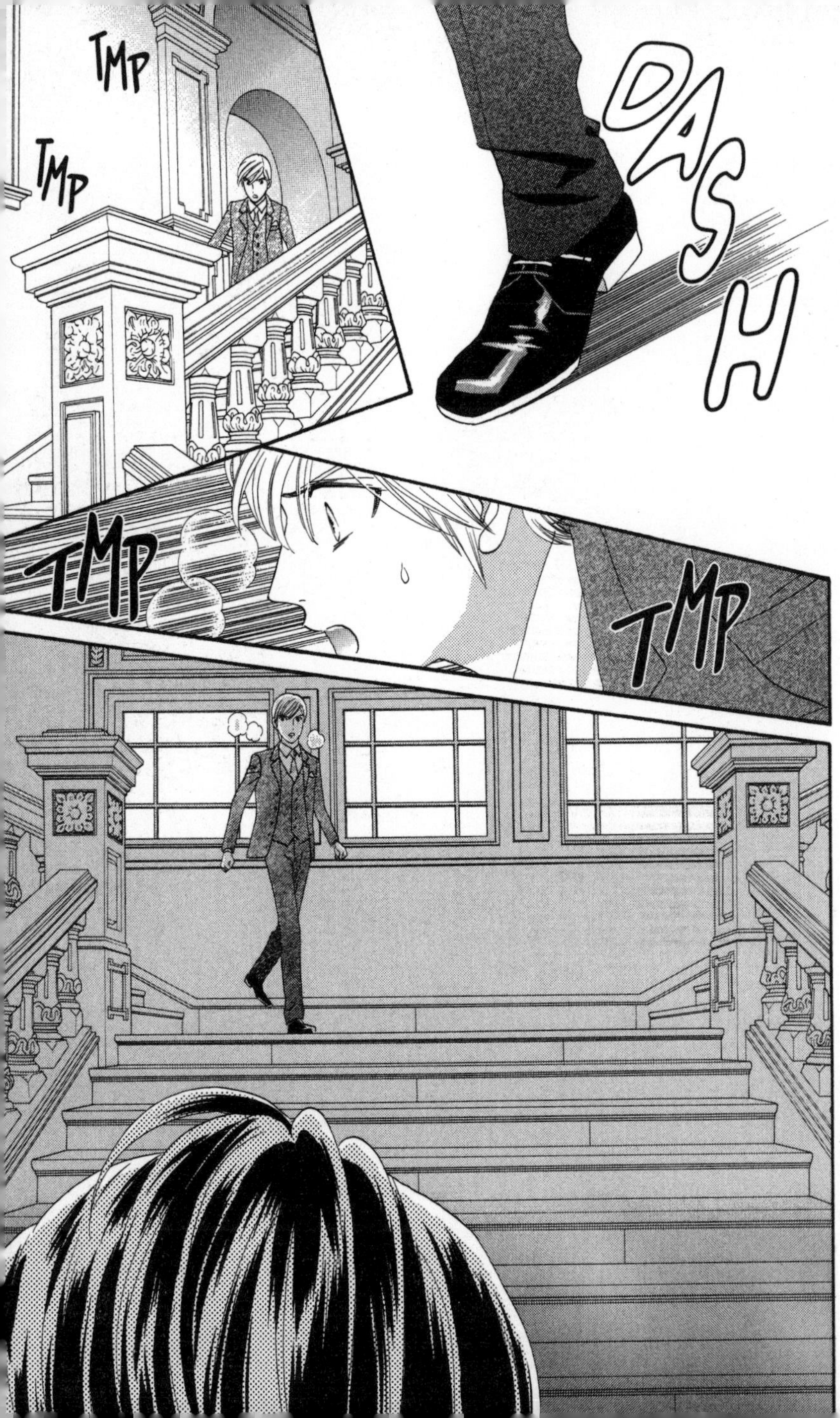
DASH
TMP
TMP
TMP
TMP

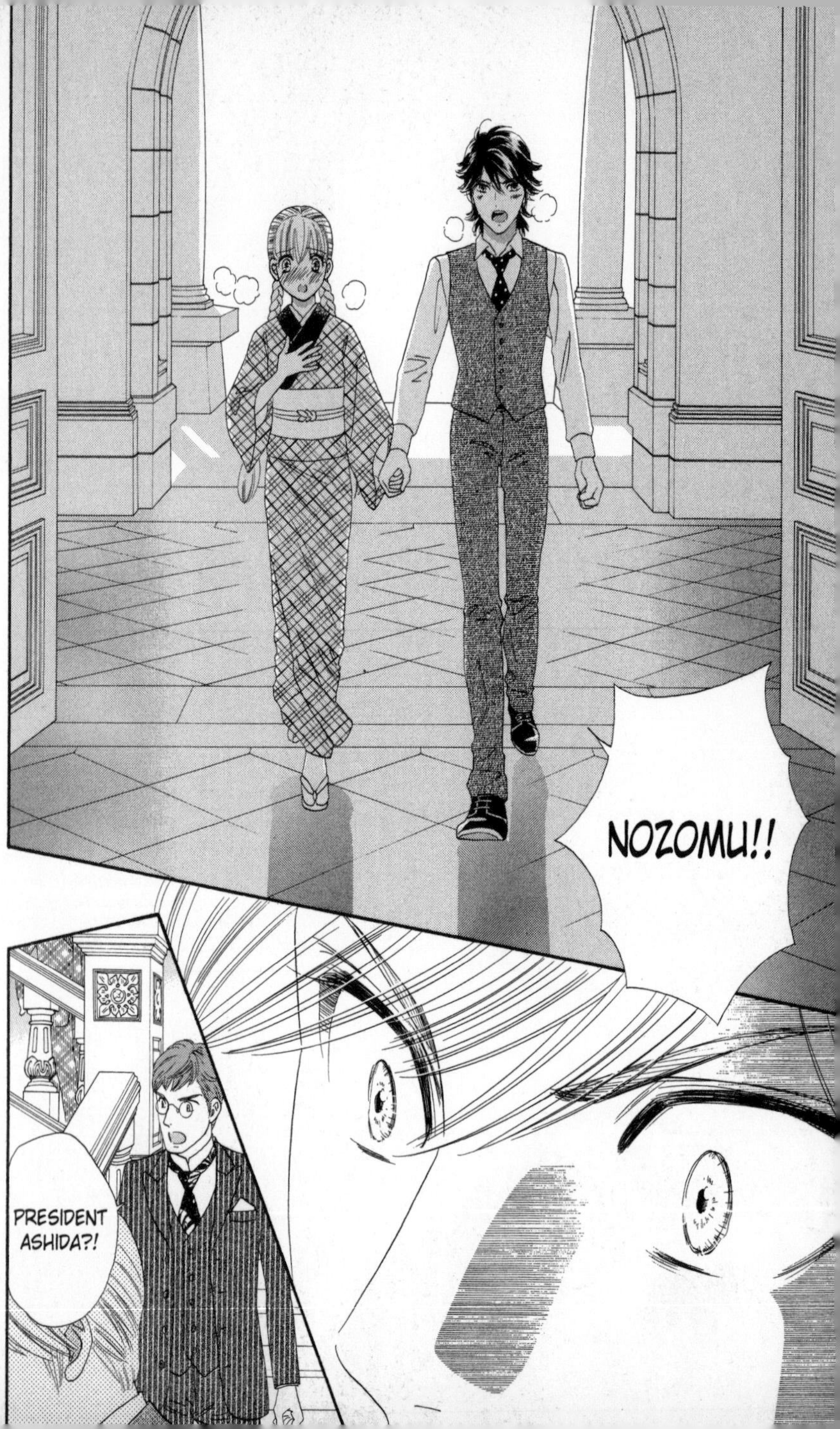
NOZOMU!!
PRESIDENT ASHIDA?!

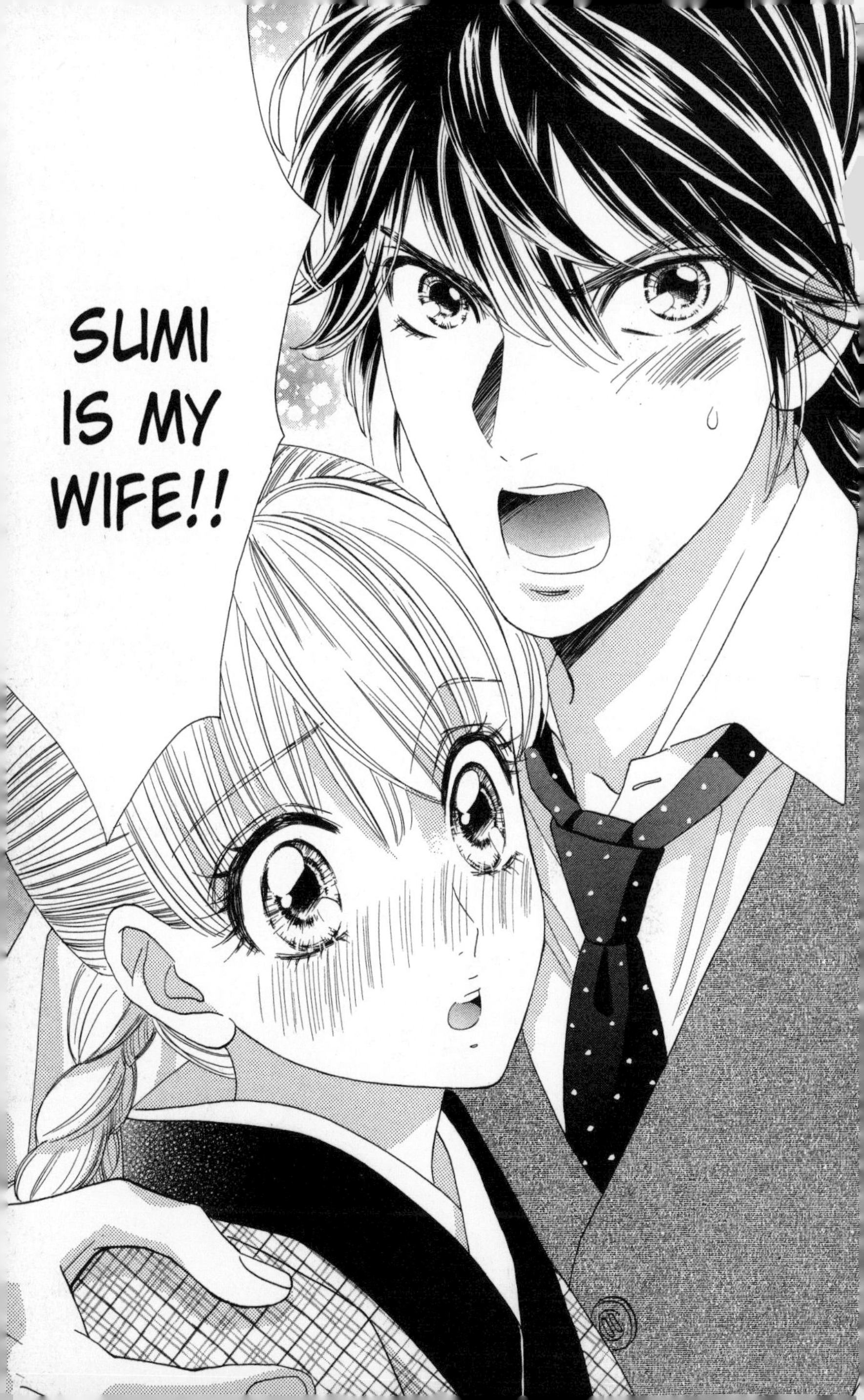
SUMI IS MY WIFE!!

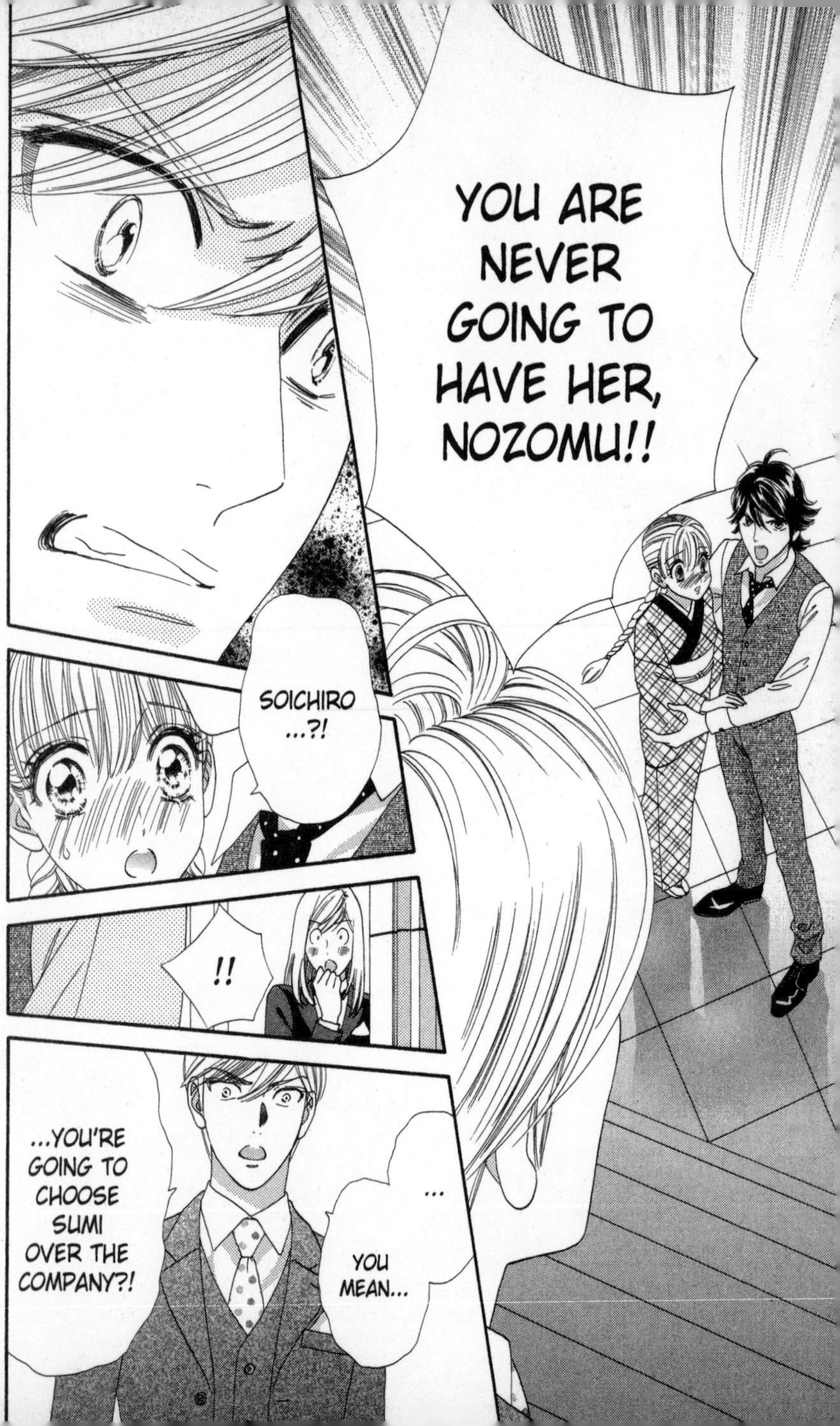
YOU ARE NEVER GOING TO HAVE HER, NOZOMU!!
SOICHIRO ...?!
!!
...
YOU MEAN...
...YOU'RE GOING TO CHOOSE SUMI OVER THE COMPANY?!

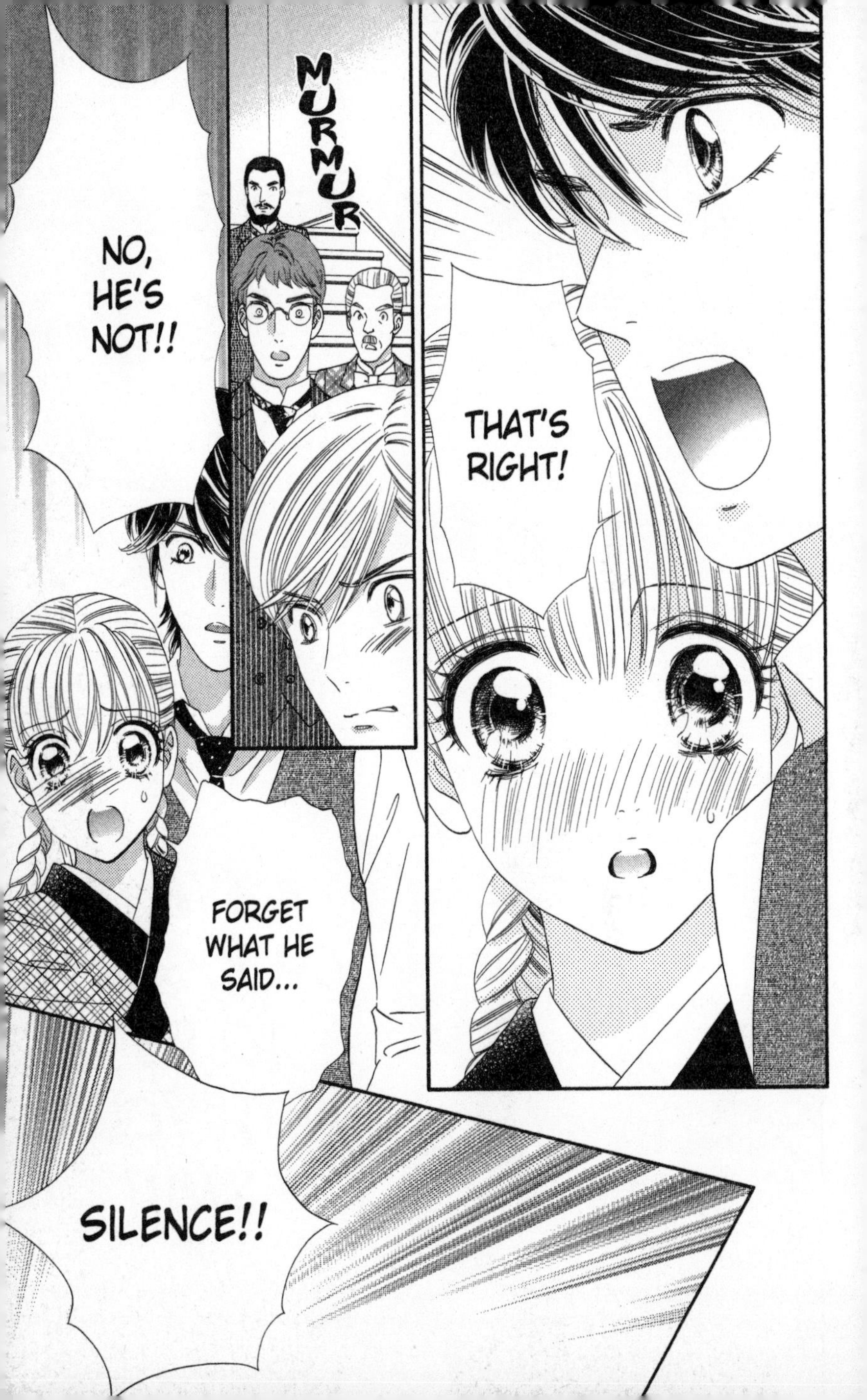
THAT'S RIGHT!
MURMUR
NO, HE'S NOT!!
FORGET WHAT HE SAID...
SILENCE!!

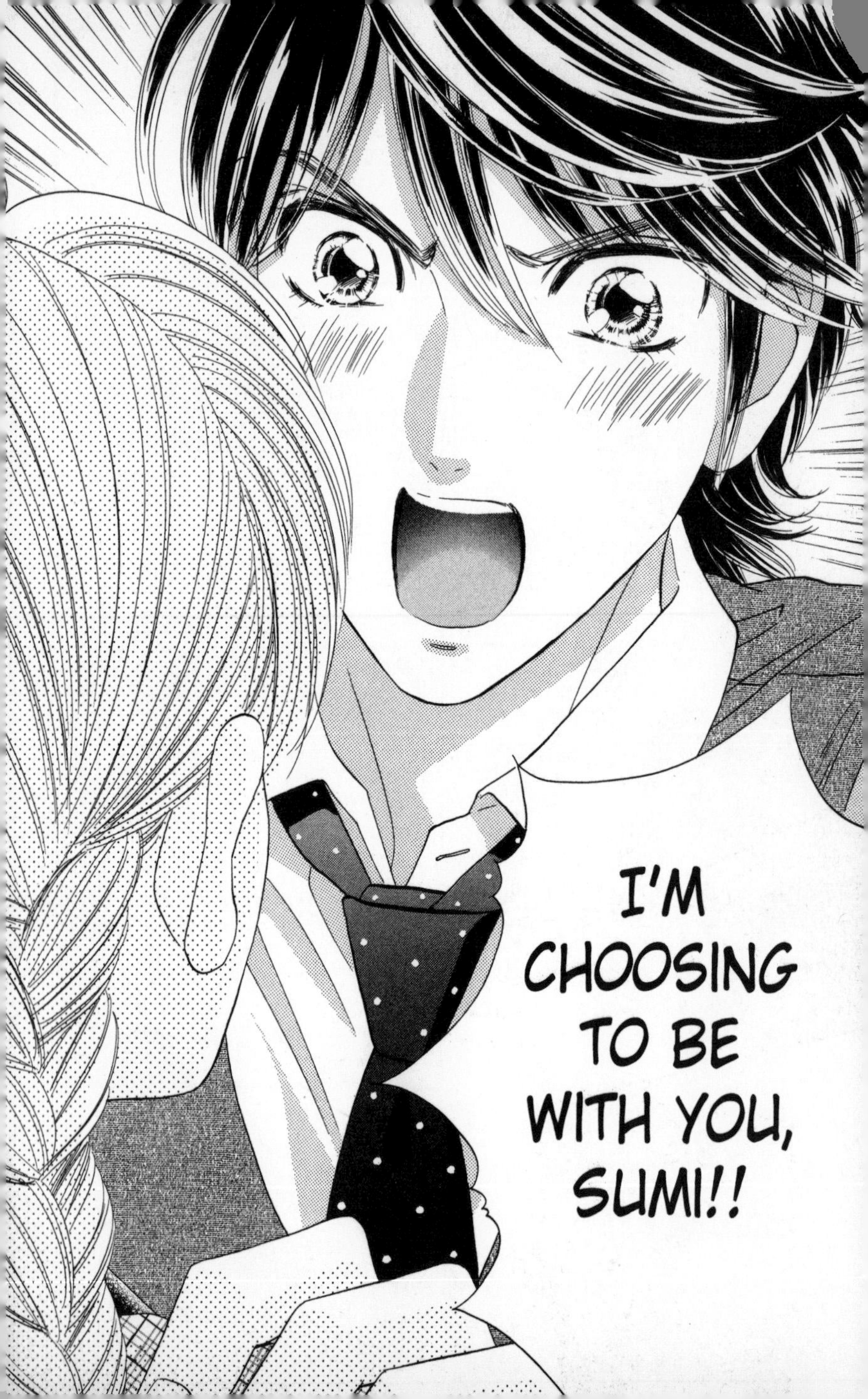
I'M CHOOSING TO BE WITH YOU, SUMI!!

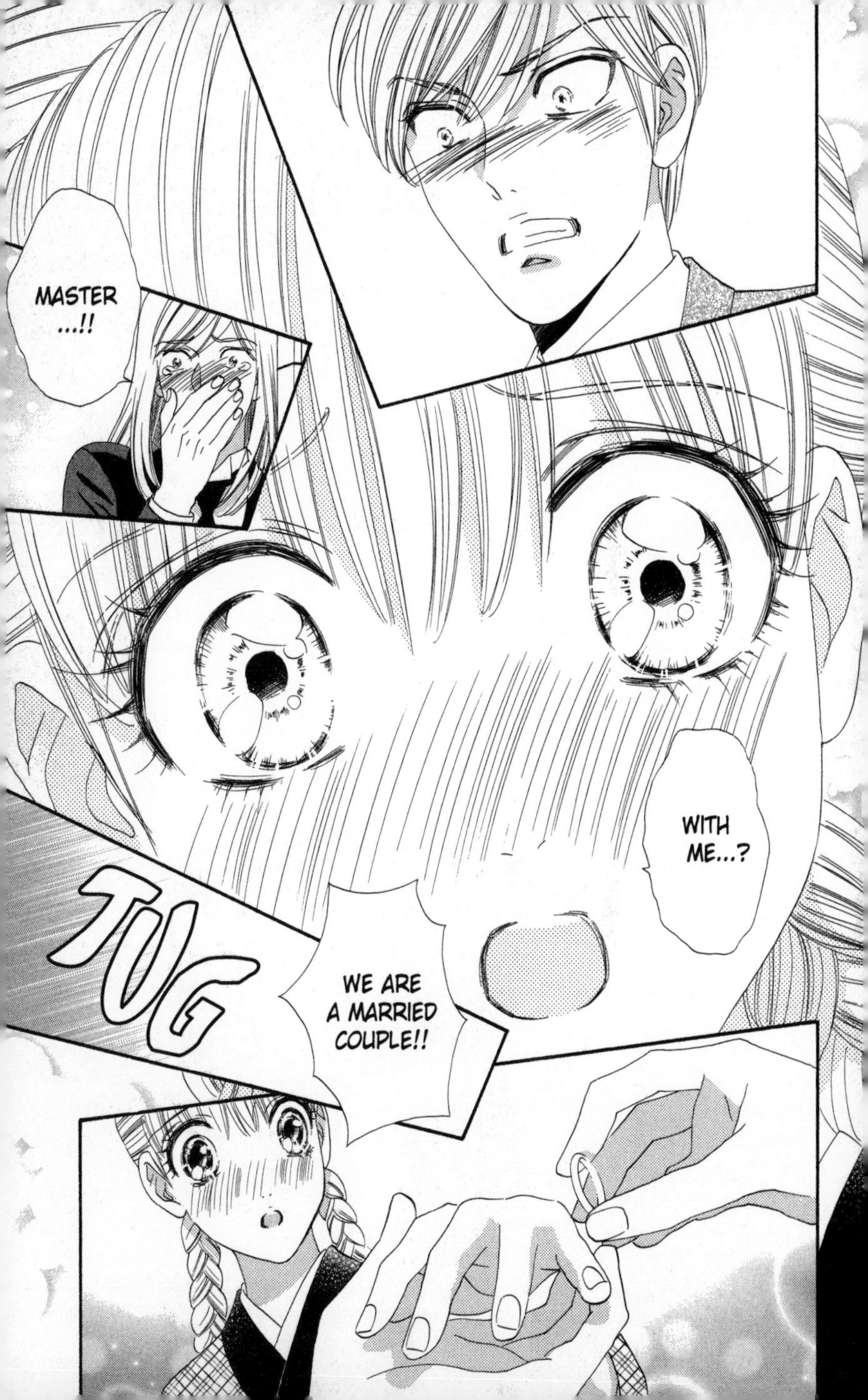
MASTER ...!!
WITH ME...?
WE ARE A MARRIED COUPLE!!
TUG

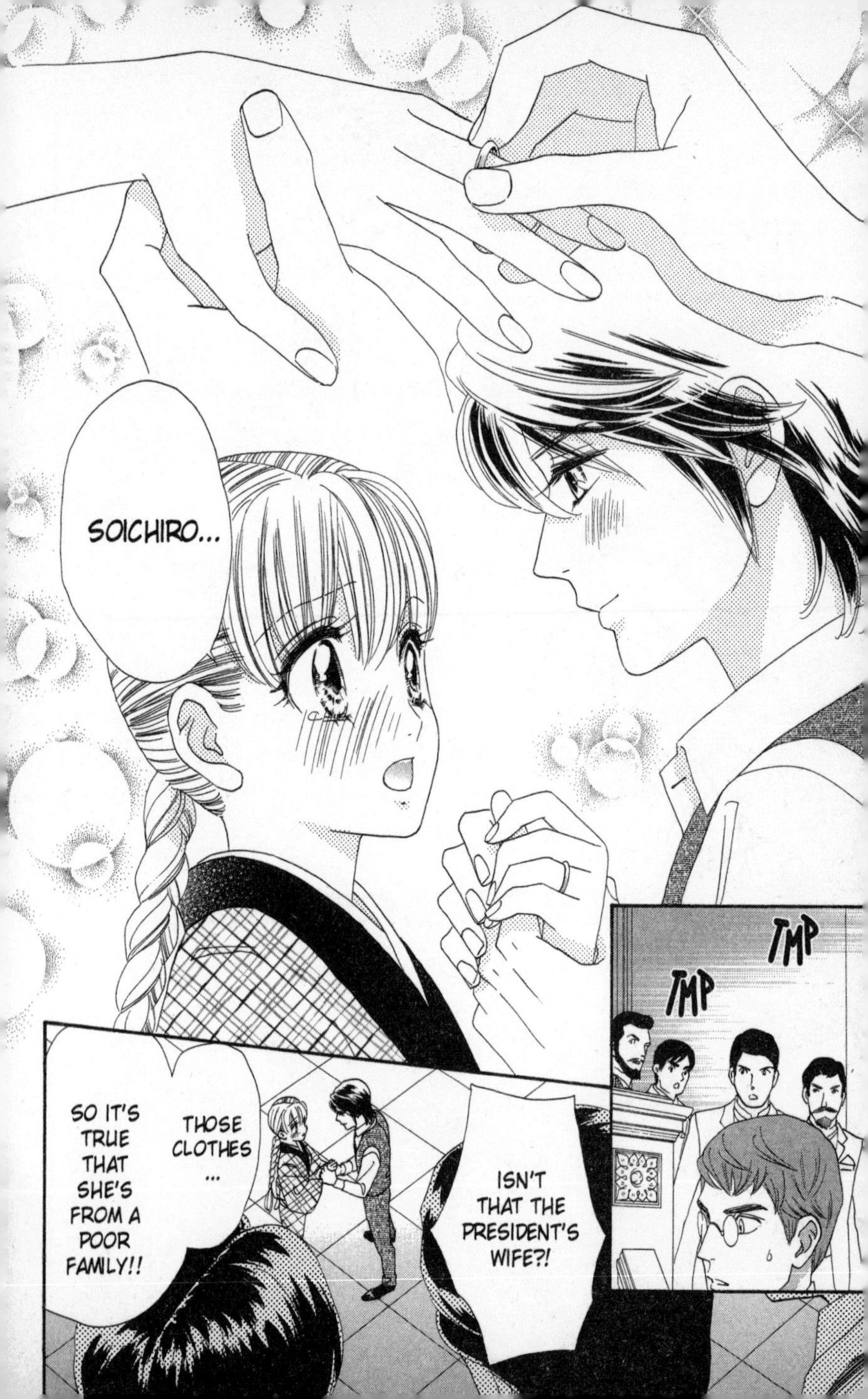
SOICHIRO...
TMP
TMP
ISN'T THAT THE PRESIDENT'S WIFE?!
THOSE CLOTHES ...
SO IT'S TRUE THAT SHE'S FROM A POOR FAMILY!!

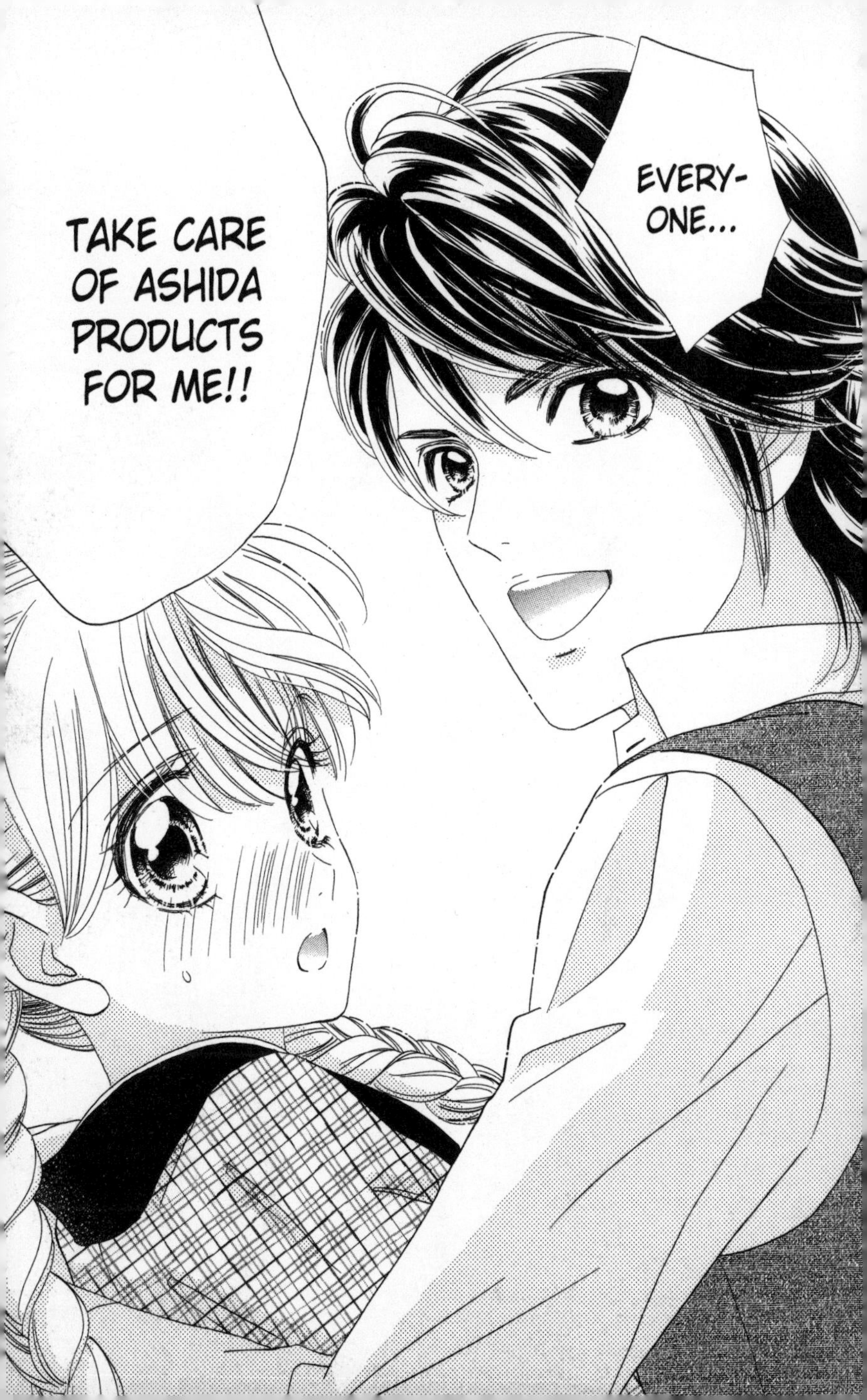
EVERY-ONE...
TAKE CARE OF ASHIDA PRODUCTS FOR ME!!

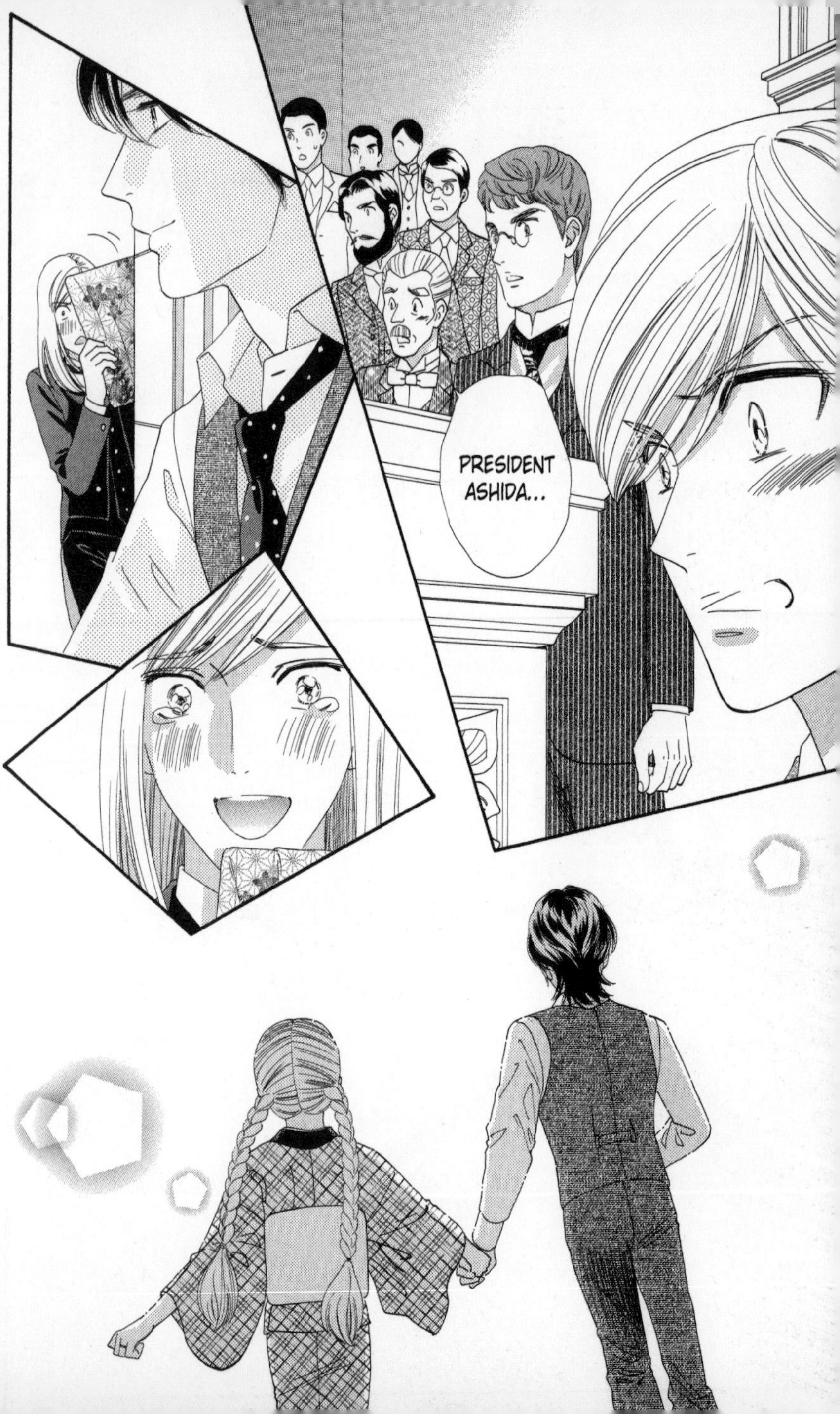
PRESIDENT ASHIDA...

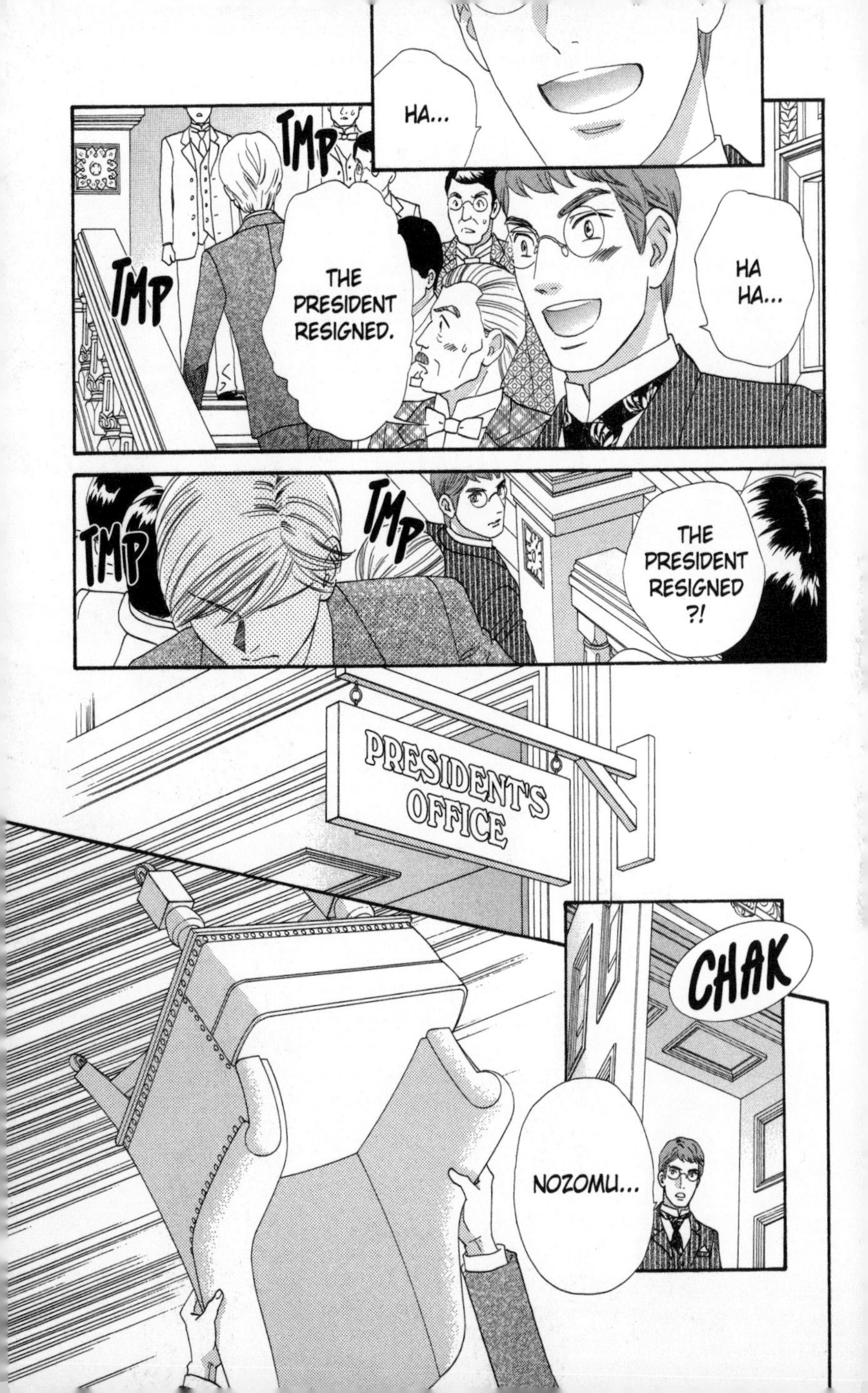
HA...
HA HA...
THE PRESIDENT RESIGNED.
TMP
TMP
THE PRESIDENT RESIGNED ?!
TMP
TMP
CHAK
NOZOMU...
PRESIDENT'S OFFICE

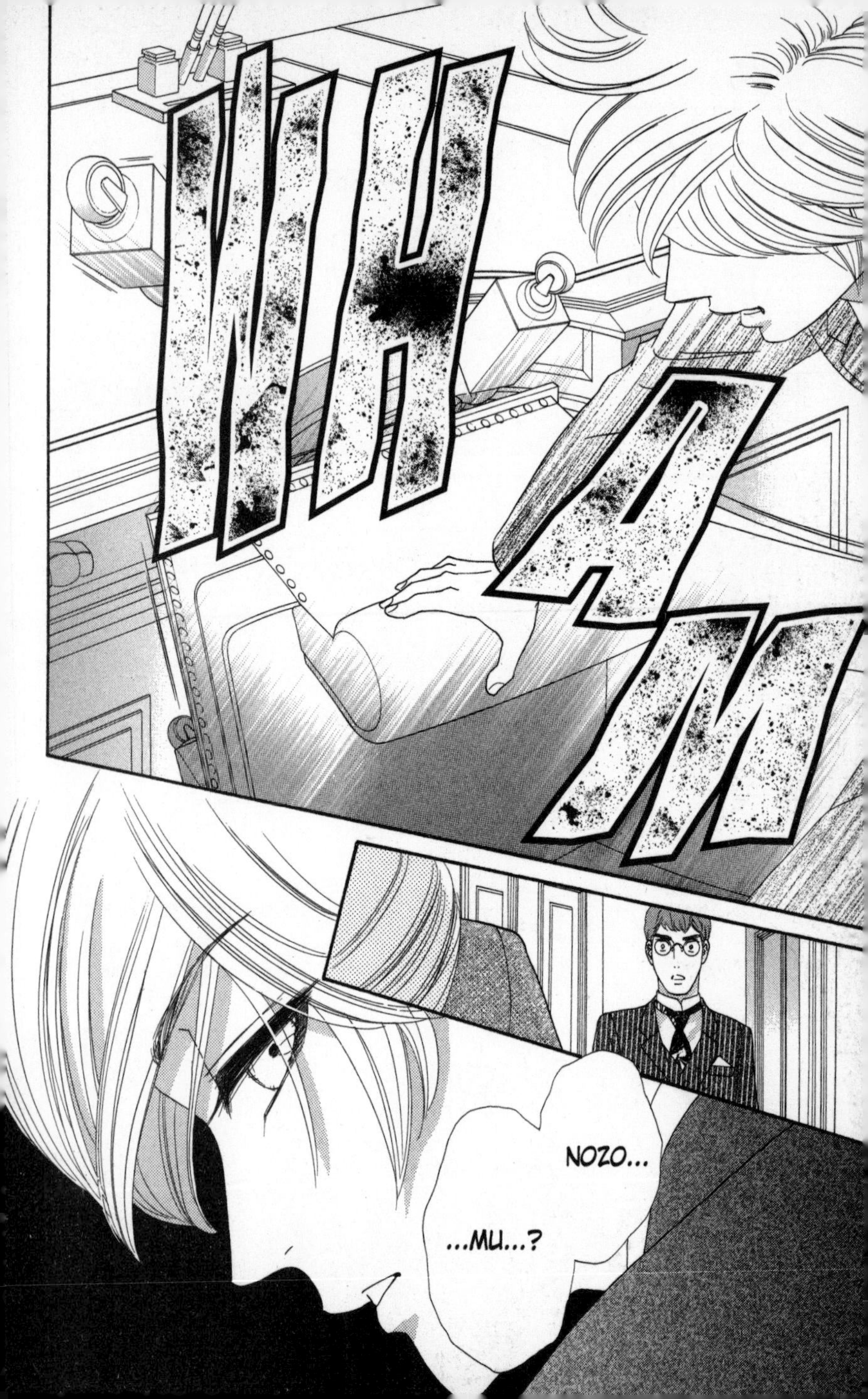
WHAM
NOZO...
...MU...?

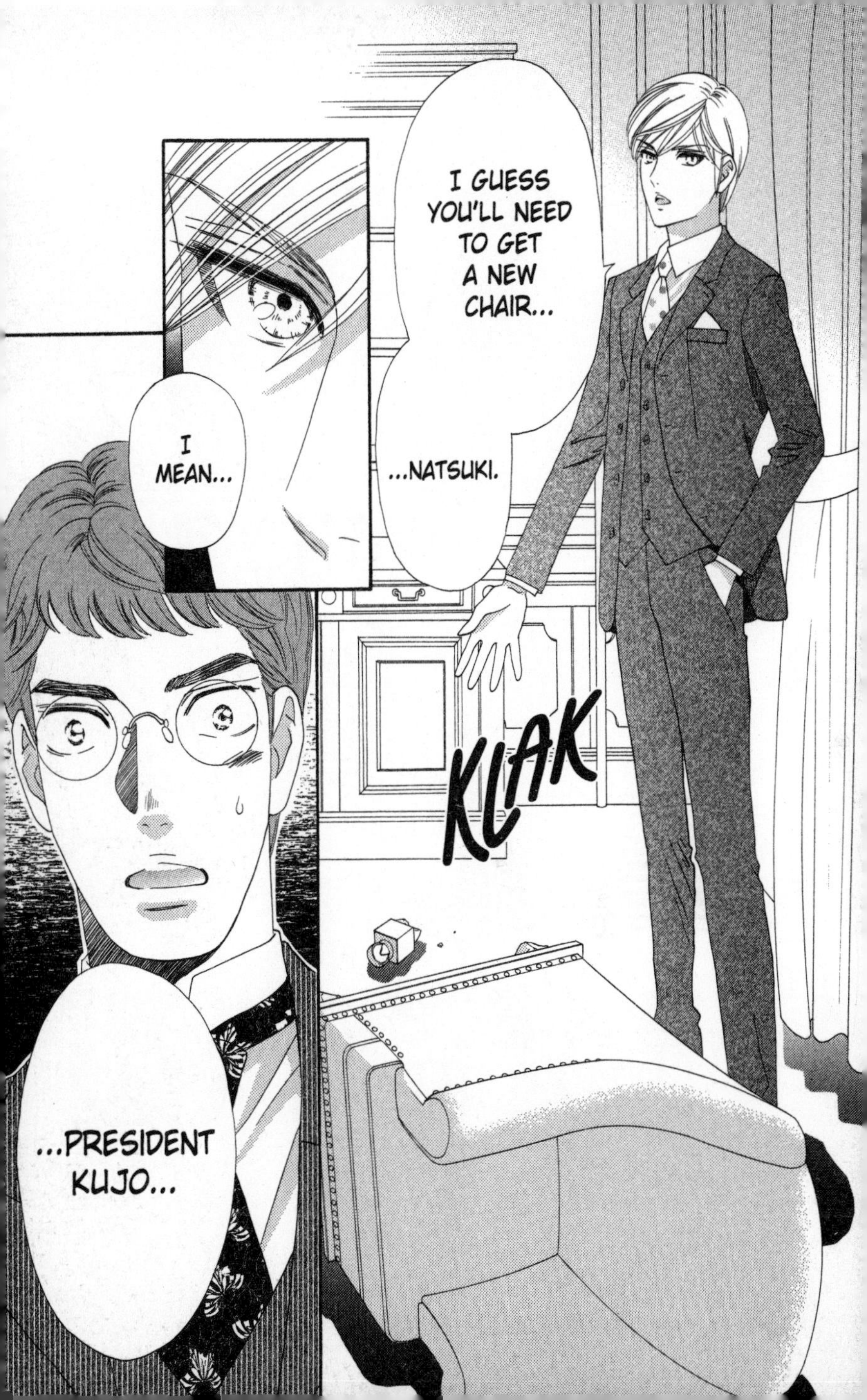
I GUESS YOU'LL NEED TO GET A NEW CHAIR...
...NATSUKI.
KLAK
I MEAN...
...PRESIDENT KUJO...

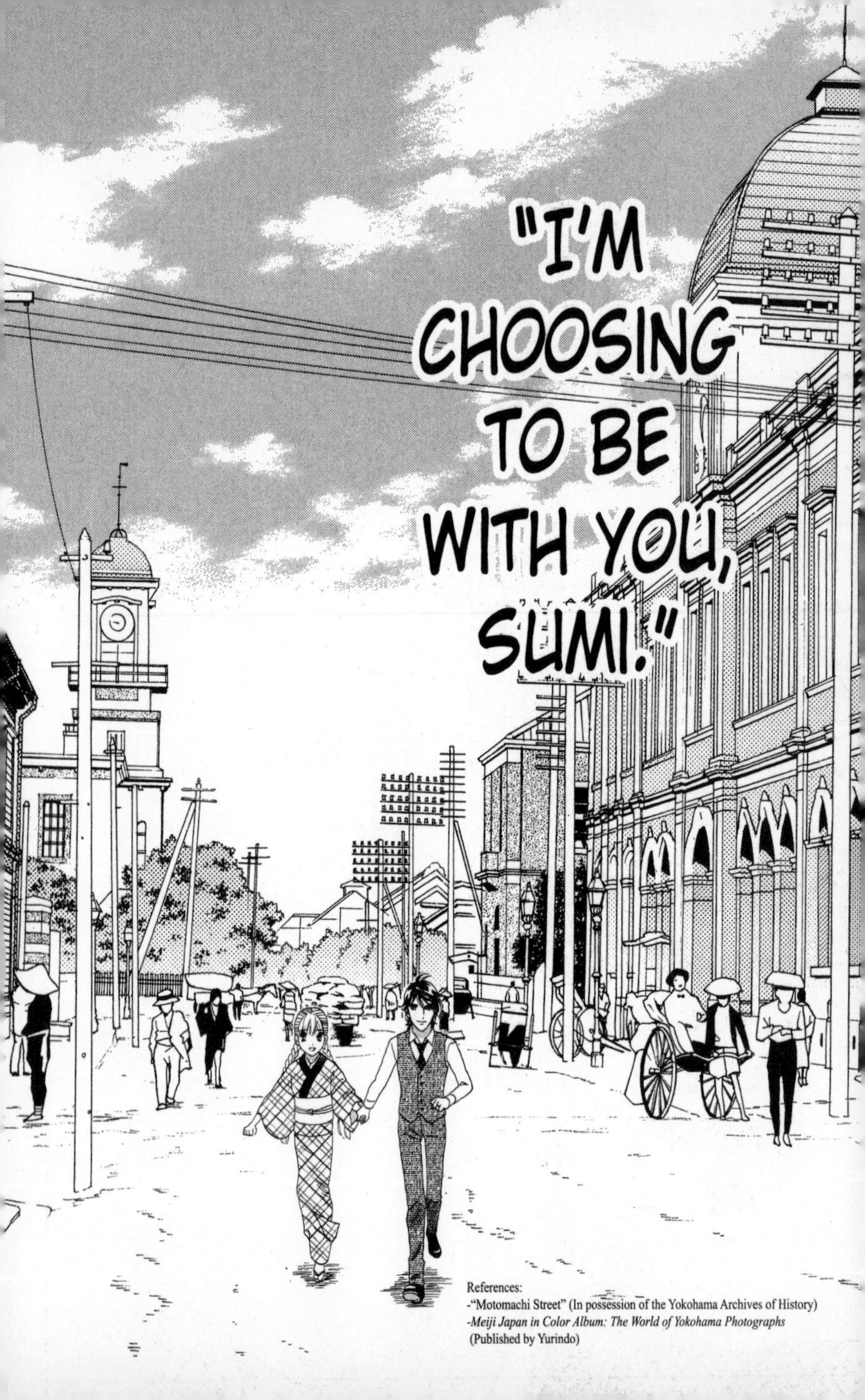
"I'M CHOOSING TO BE WITH YOU, SUMI."

References:
-"Motomachi Street" (In possession of the Yokohama Archives of History)
-*Meiji Japan in Color Album: The World of Yokohama Photographs* (Published by Yurindo)

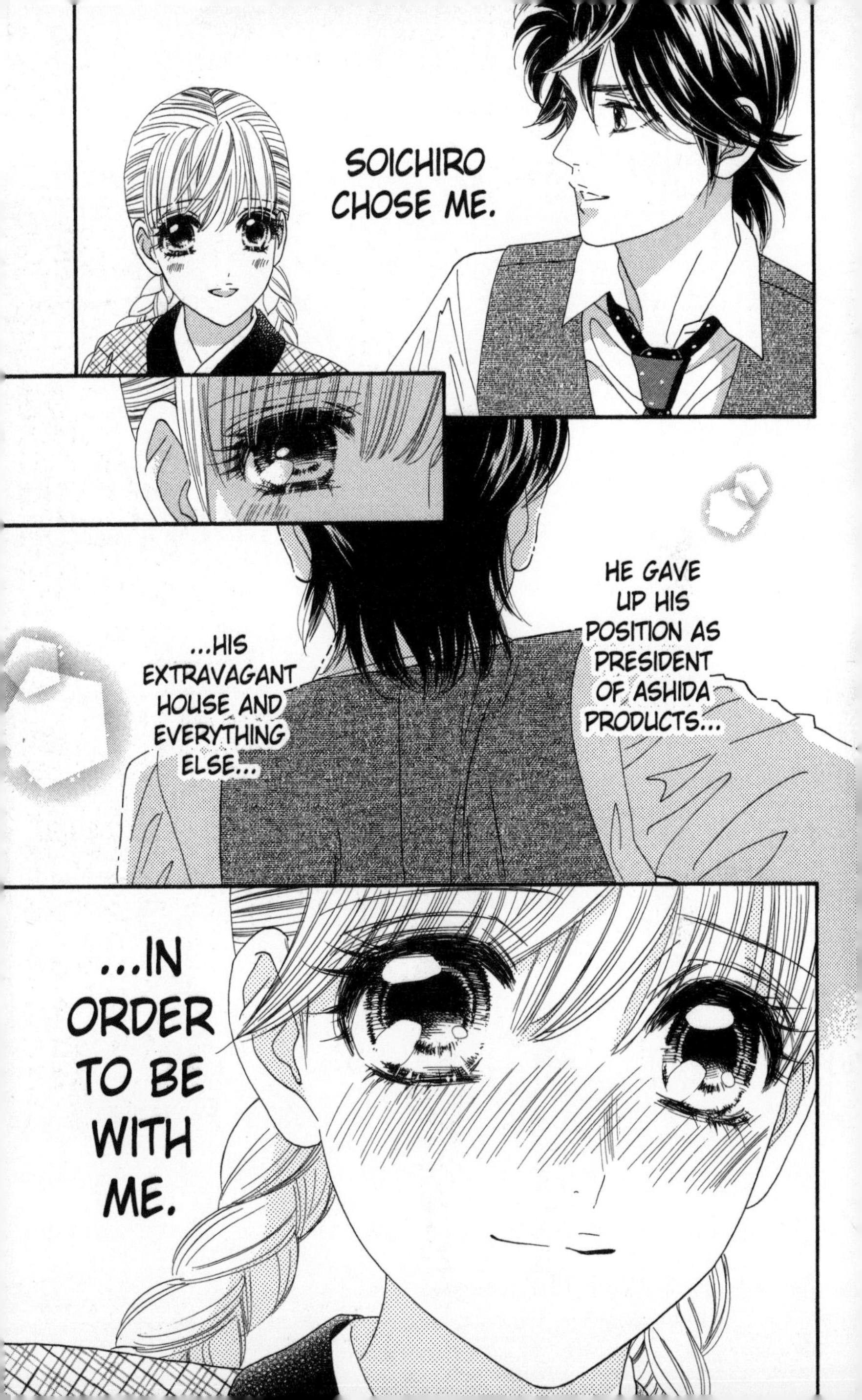
SOICHIRO CHOSE ME.
HE GAVE UP HIS POSITION AS PRESIDENT OF ASHIDA PRODUCTS...
...HIS EXTRAVAGANT HOUSE AND EVERYTHING ELSE...
...IN ORDER TO BE WITH ME.

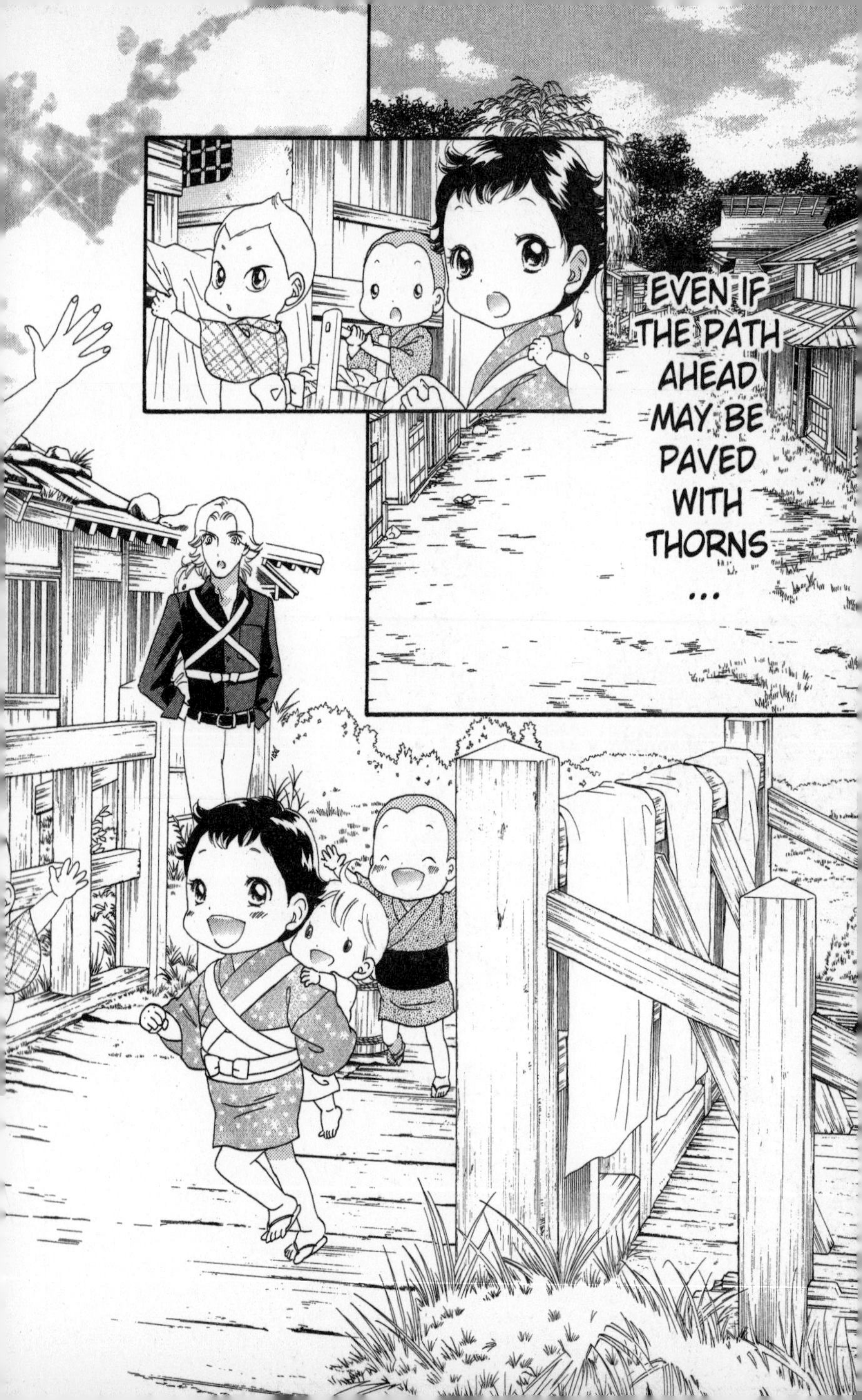
EVEN IF THE PATH AHEAD MAY BE PAVED WITH THORNS ...

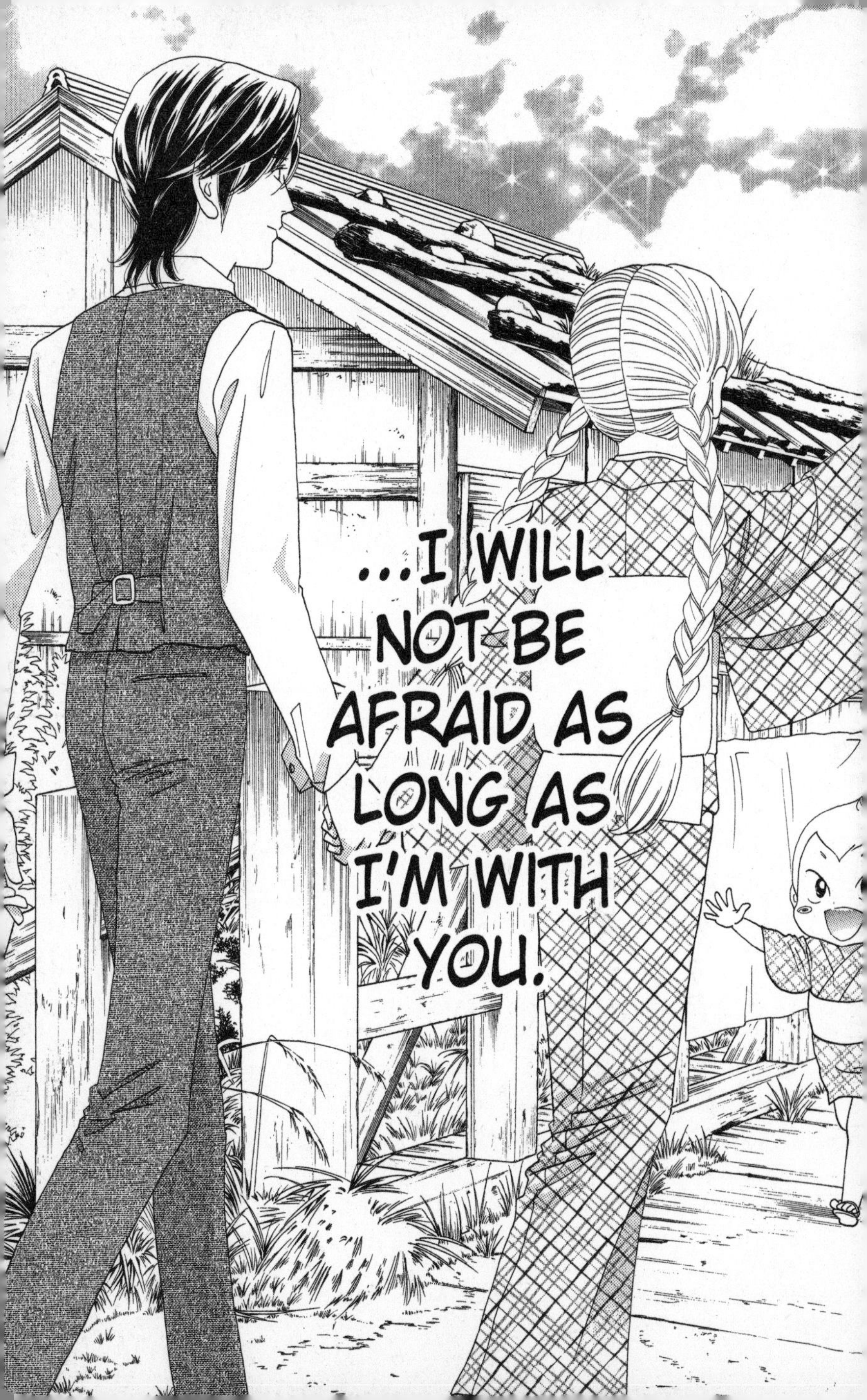
...I WILL NOT BE AFRAID AS LONG AS I'M WITH YOU.

GREETINGS ~~

HELLO, IT'S ME, UE-RIN!! I WAS FINALLY ABLE TO PUBLISH A NEW VOLUME AFTER SIX MONTHS!! HURRAY!

THIS IS ON THE PERSONAL SIDE, BUT MY DAUGHTER STARTED NURSERY SCHOOL DURING THE END OF LAST YEAR. FOR THE FIRST TWO WEEKS, SHE CRIED WHENEVER I DROPPED HER OFF. BUT THESE DAYS, SHE'LL GO RUNNING IN THERE HERSELF. I'M SOOOO GLAD!

JUST WHEN I THOUGHT I CAN FINALLY CONCENTRATE ON MY MANGA, ♪ THE WHOLE FAMILY CAUGHT A COLD AND THE FLU FROM MY DAUGHTER... WE'VE BEEN HAVING QUITE A TOUGH TIME! (*TEARS*) I JUST CAN'T WAIT FOR SPRING TO COME!!

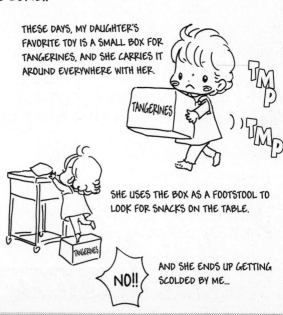

THESE DAYS, MY DAUGHTER'S FAVORITE TOY IS A SMALL BOX FOR TANGERINES, AND SHE CARRIES IT AROUND EVERYWHERE WITH HER.

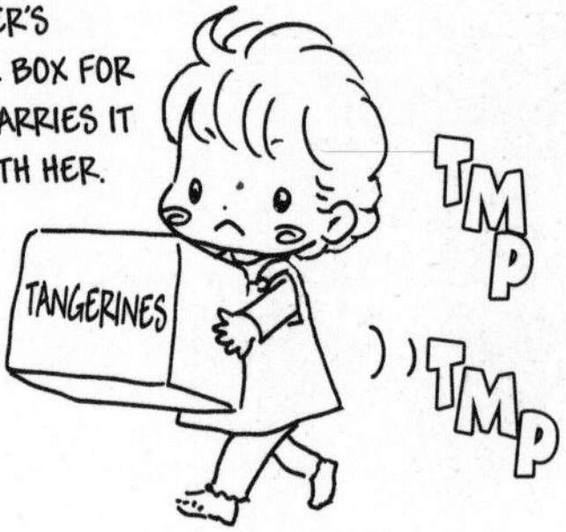
TANGERINES
TMP
TMP

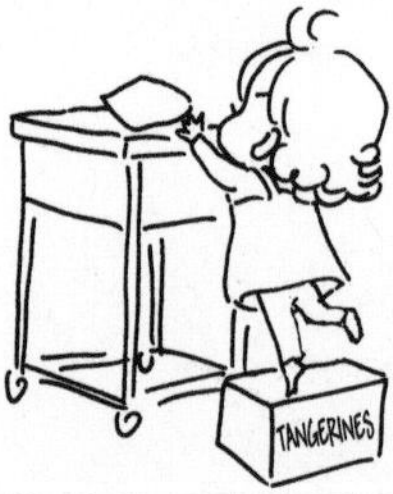
TANGERINES

SHE USES THE BOX AS A FOOTSTOOL TO LOOK FOR SNACKS ON THE TABLE.

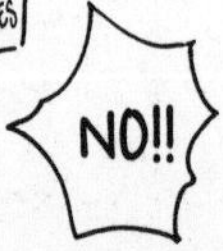
NO!!

AND SHE ENDS UP GETTING SCOLDED BY ME...

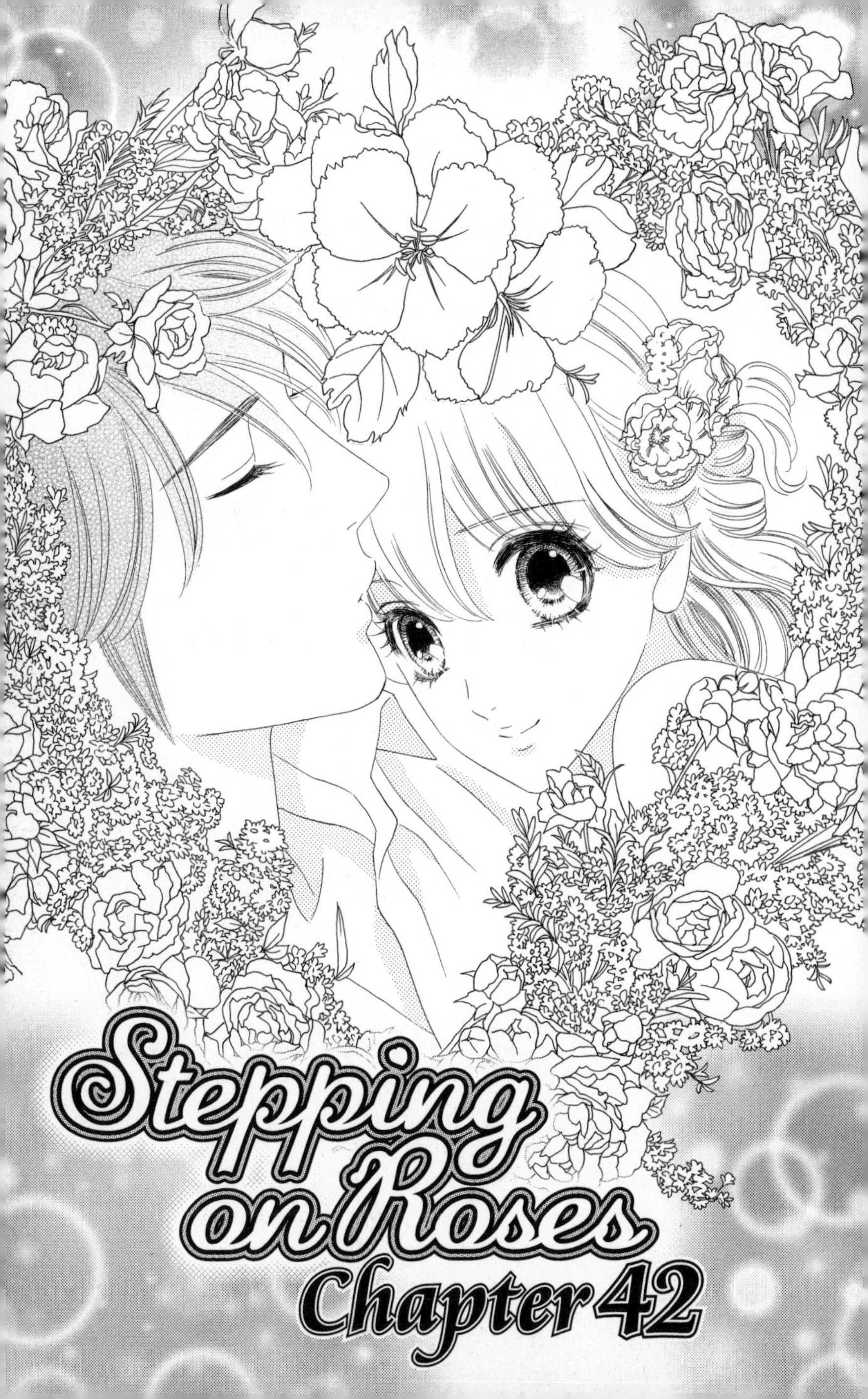
Stepping on Roses
Chapter 42

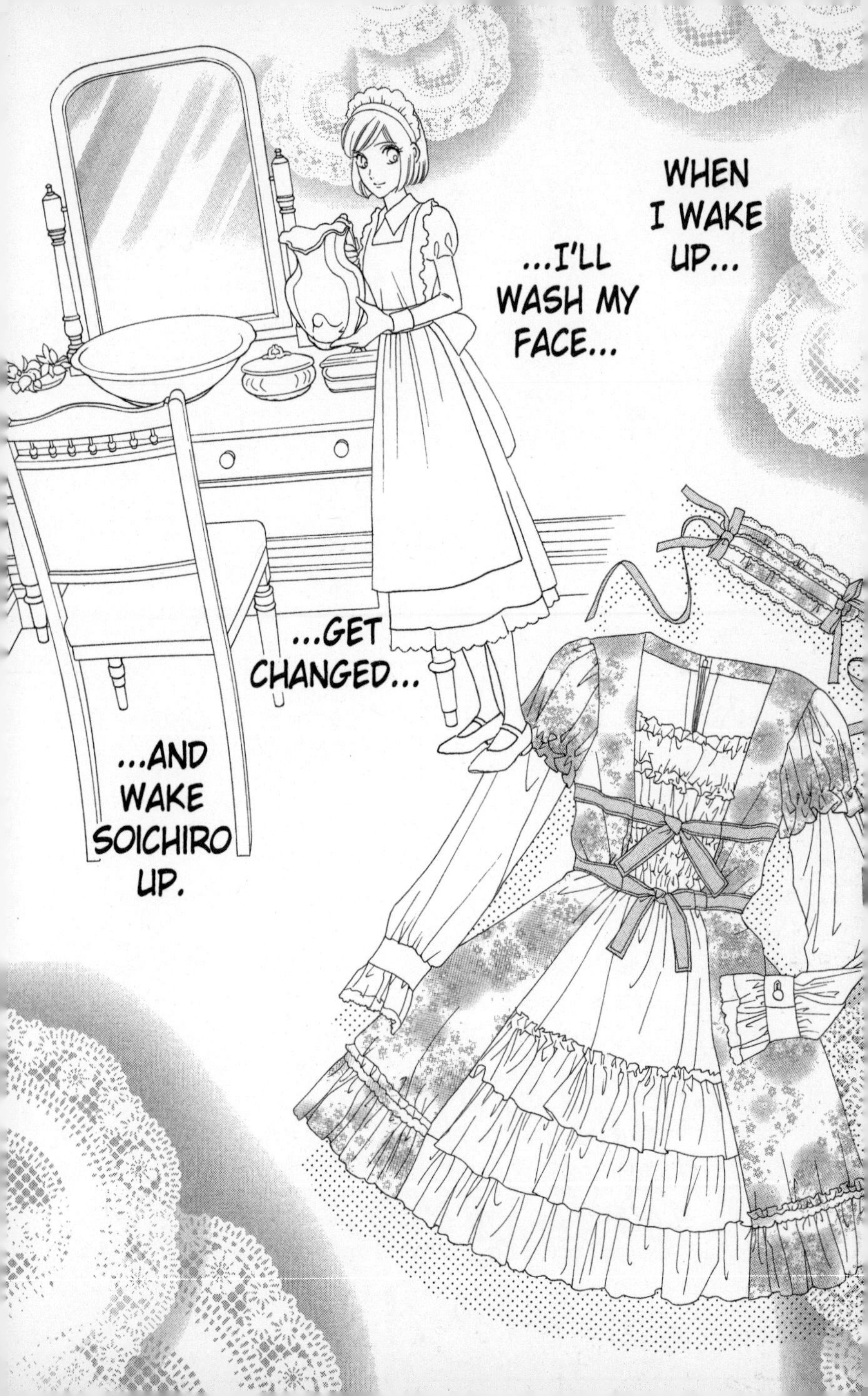
WHEN I WAKE UP...
...I'LL WASH MY FACE...
...GET CHANGED...
...AND WAKE SOICHIRO UP.

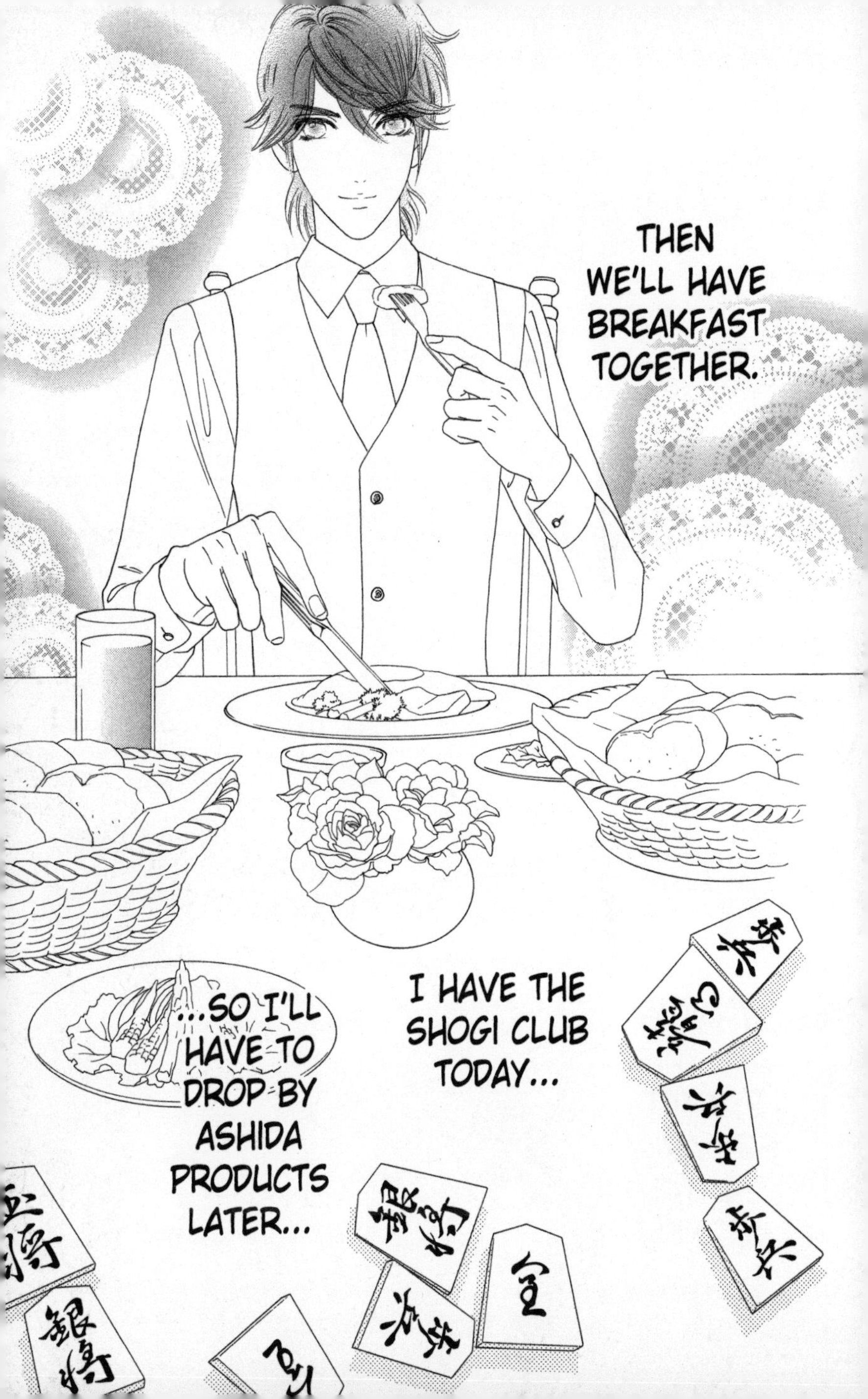
THEN WE'LL HAVE BREAKFAST TOGETHER.
I HAVE THE SHOGI CLUB TODAY...
...SO I'LL HAVE TO DROP BY ASHIDA PRODUCTS LATER...

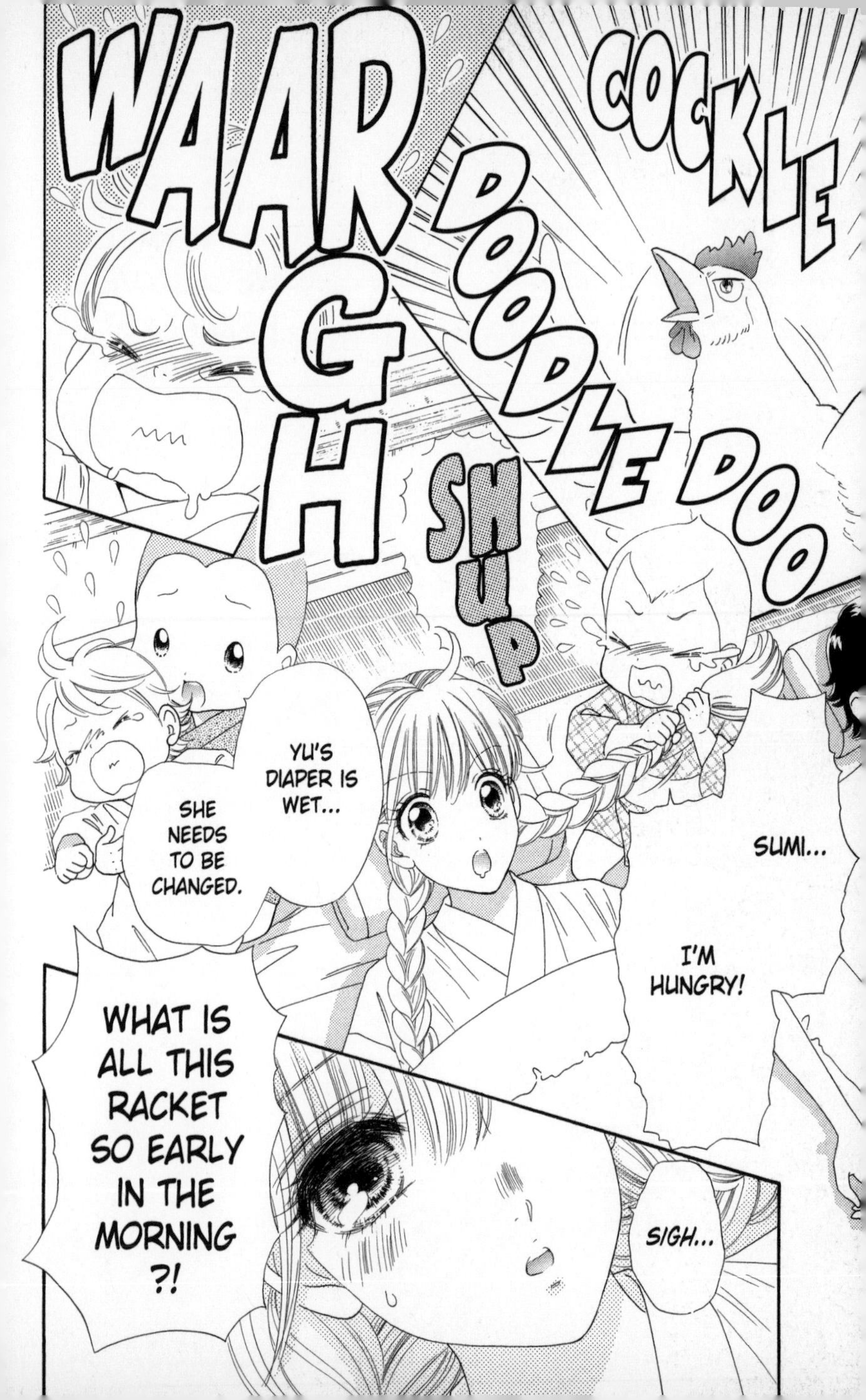
COCKLE DOODLE DOO
WAARGH
SHUP
SUMI...
I'M HUNGRY!
YU'S DIAPER IS WET...
SHE NEEDS TO BE CHANGED.
SIGH...
WHAT IS ALL THIS RACKET SO EARLY IN THE MORNING?!

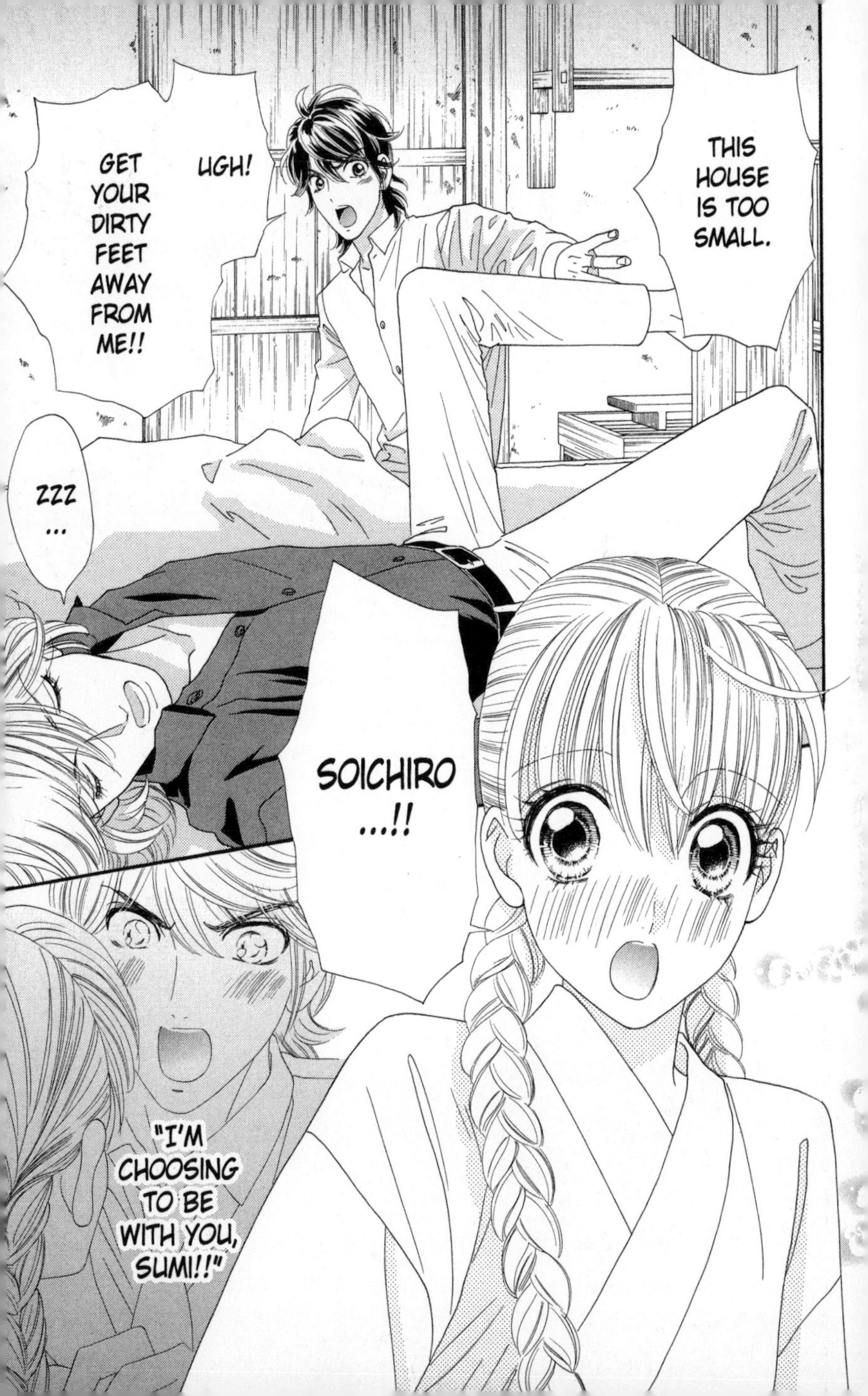
THIS HOUSE IS TOO SMALL.
UGH!
GET YOUR DIRTY FEET AWAY FROM ME!!
ZZZ ...
SOICHIRO ...!!
"I'M CHOOSING TO BE WITH YOU, SUMI!!"

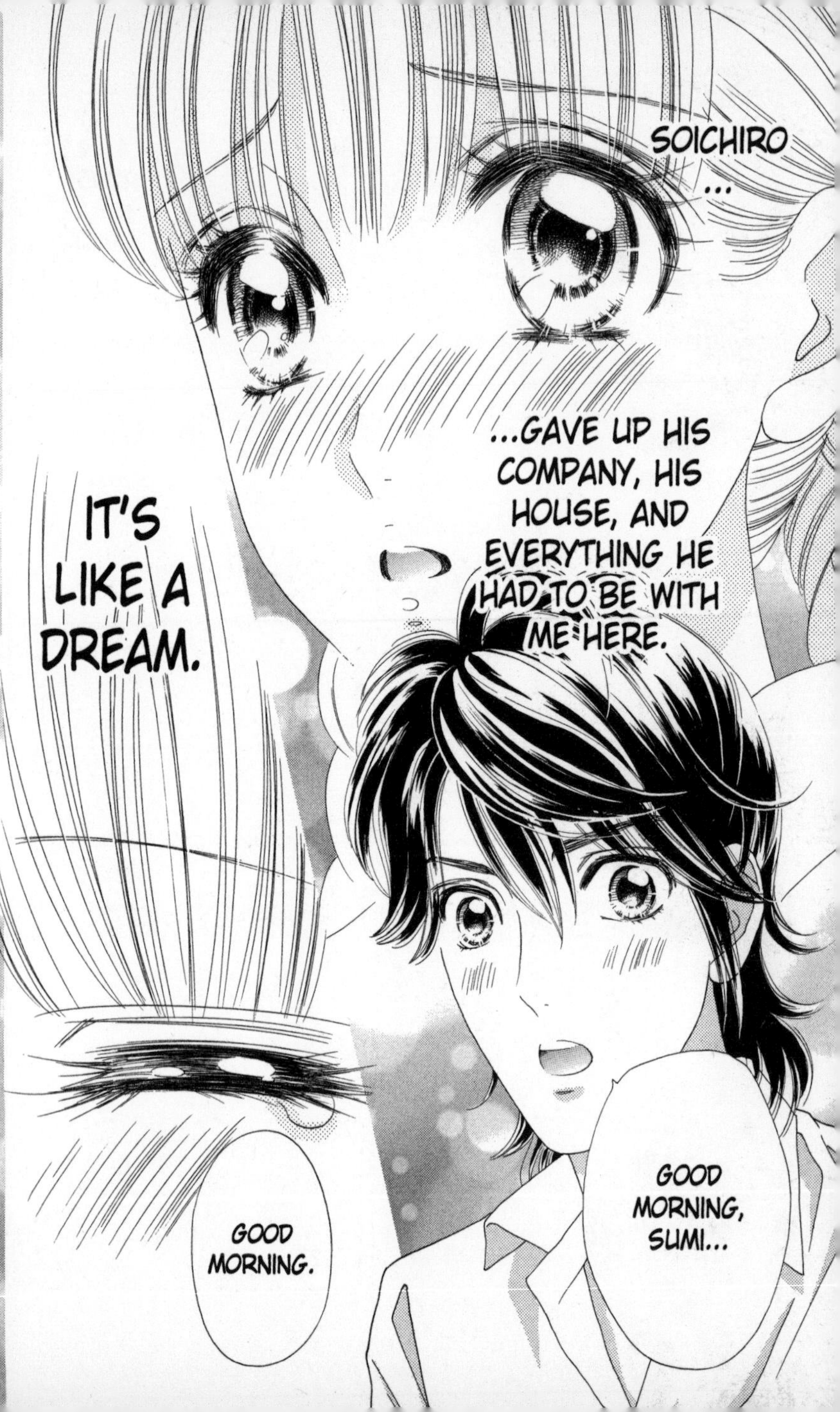
SOICHIRO ...
...GAVE UP HIS COMPANY, HIS HOUSE, AND EVERYTHING HE HAD TO BE WITH ME HERE.
IT'S LIKE A DREAM.
GOOD MORNING, SUMI...
GOOD MORNING.

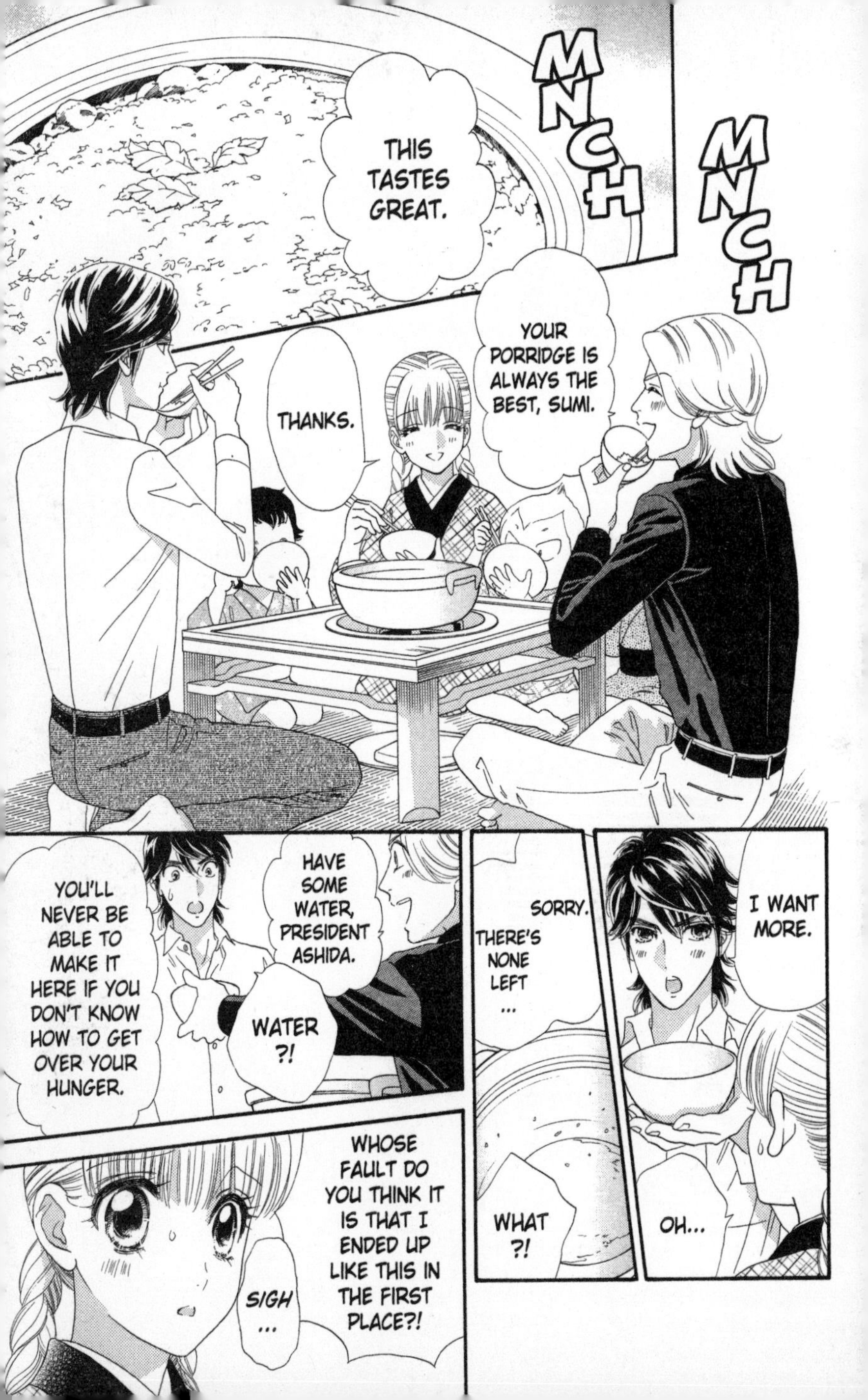
MNCH
MNCH
THIS TASTES GREAT.
YOUR PORRIDGE IS ALWAYS THE BEST, SUMI.
THANKS.
I WANT MORE.
OH...
SORRY. THERE'S NONE LEFT ...
WHAT ?!
HAVE SOME WATER, PRESIDENT ASHIDA.
WATER ?!
YOU'LL NEVER BE ABLE TO MAKE IT HERE IF YOU DON'T KNOW HOW TO GET OVER YOUR HUNGER.
WHOSE FAULT DO YOU THINK IT IS THAT I ENDED UP LIKE THIS IN THE FIRST PLACE?!
SIGH ...

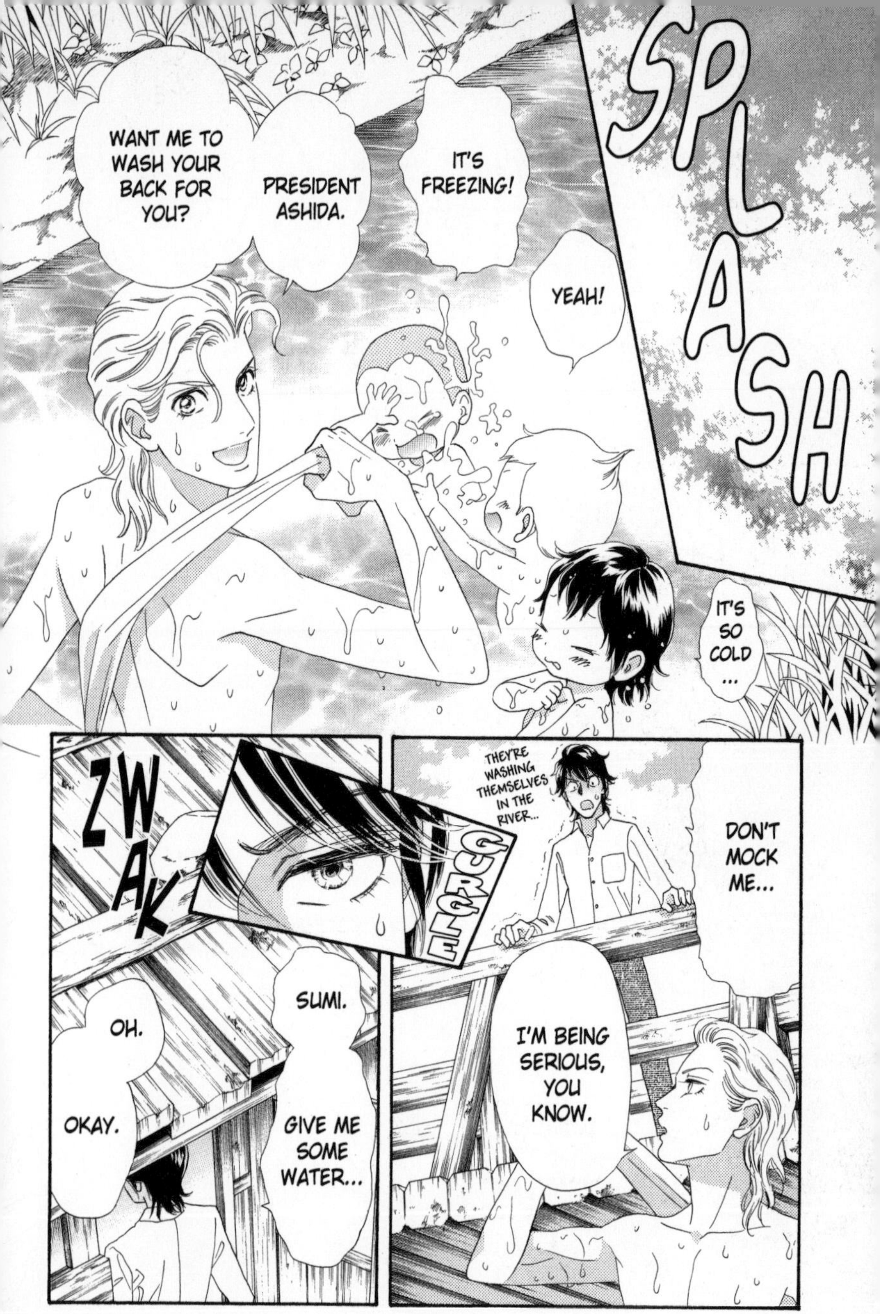
SPLASH
IT'S FREEZING!
PRESIDENT ASHIDA.
WANT ME TO WASH YOUR BACK FOR YOU?
YEAH!
IT'S SO COLD ...
DON'T MOCK ME...
THEY'RE WASHING THEMSELVES IN THE RIVER...
I'M BEING SERIOUS, YOU KNOW.
GURGLE
ZWAK
SUMI.
GIVE ME SOME WATER...
OH.
OKAY.

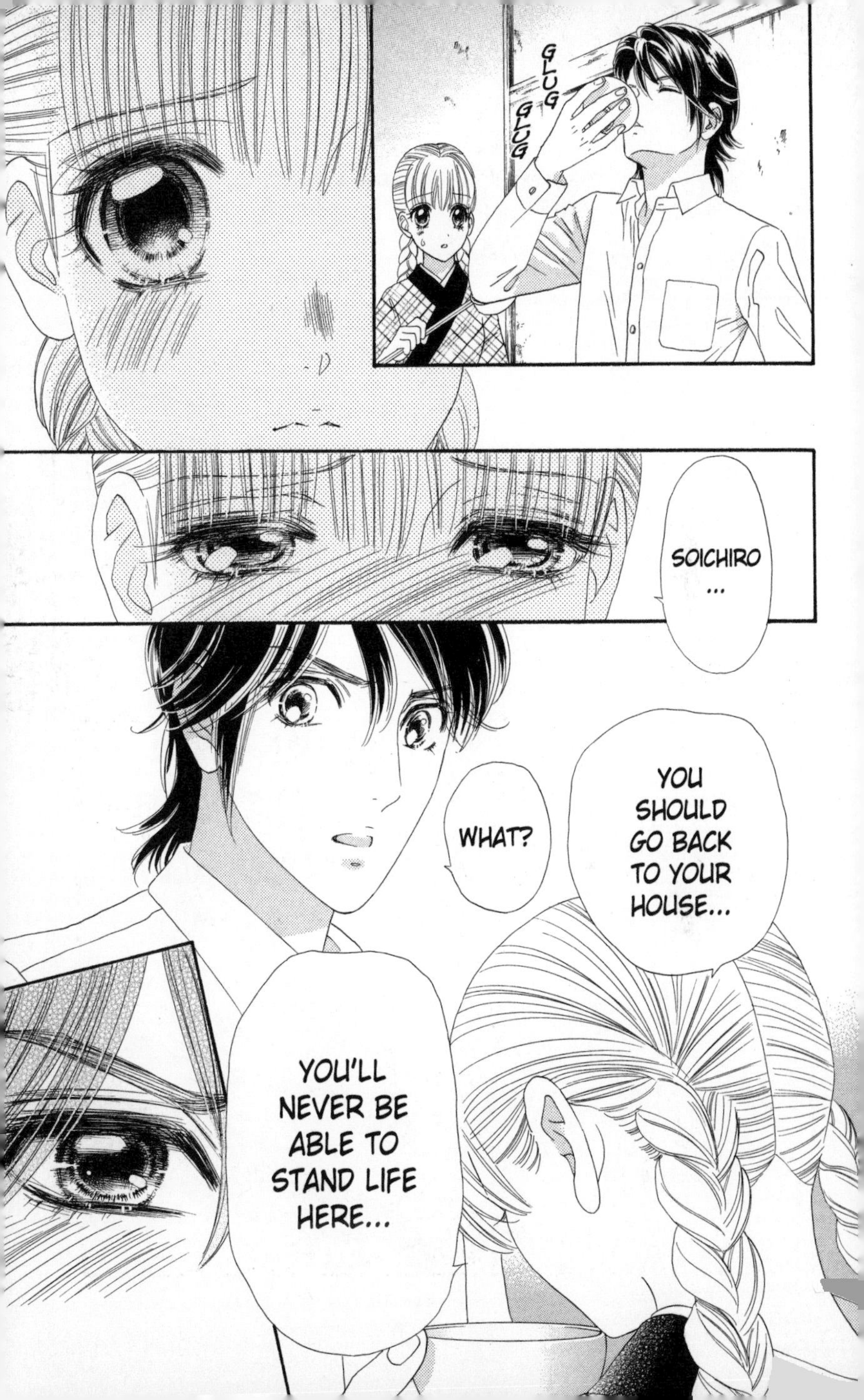
GLUG GLUG
SOICHIRO...
YOU SHOULD GO BACK TO YOUR HOUSE...
WHAT?
YOU'LL NEVER BE ABLE TO STAND LIFE HERE...

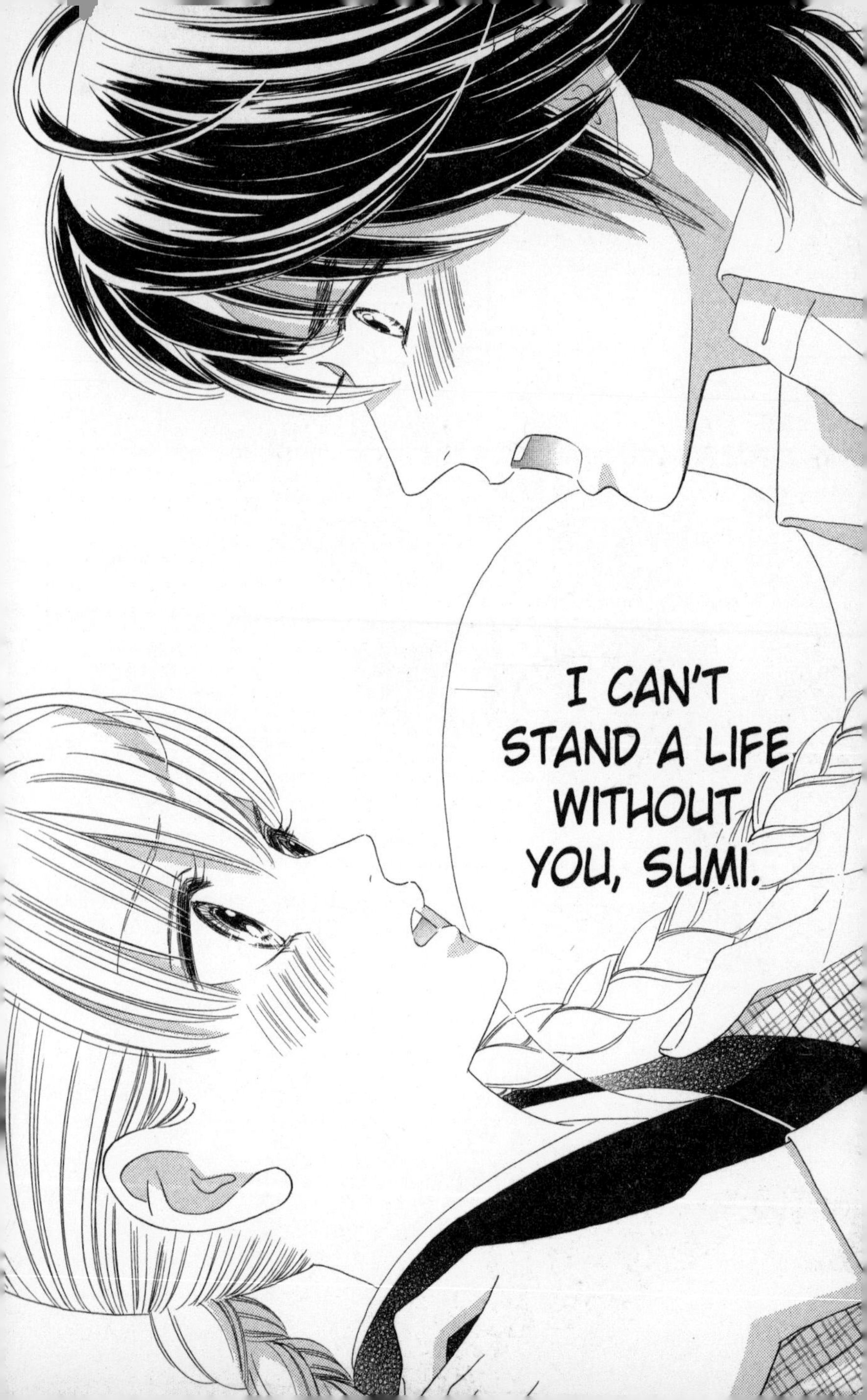
I CAN'T STAND A LIFE WITHOUT YOU, SUMI.

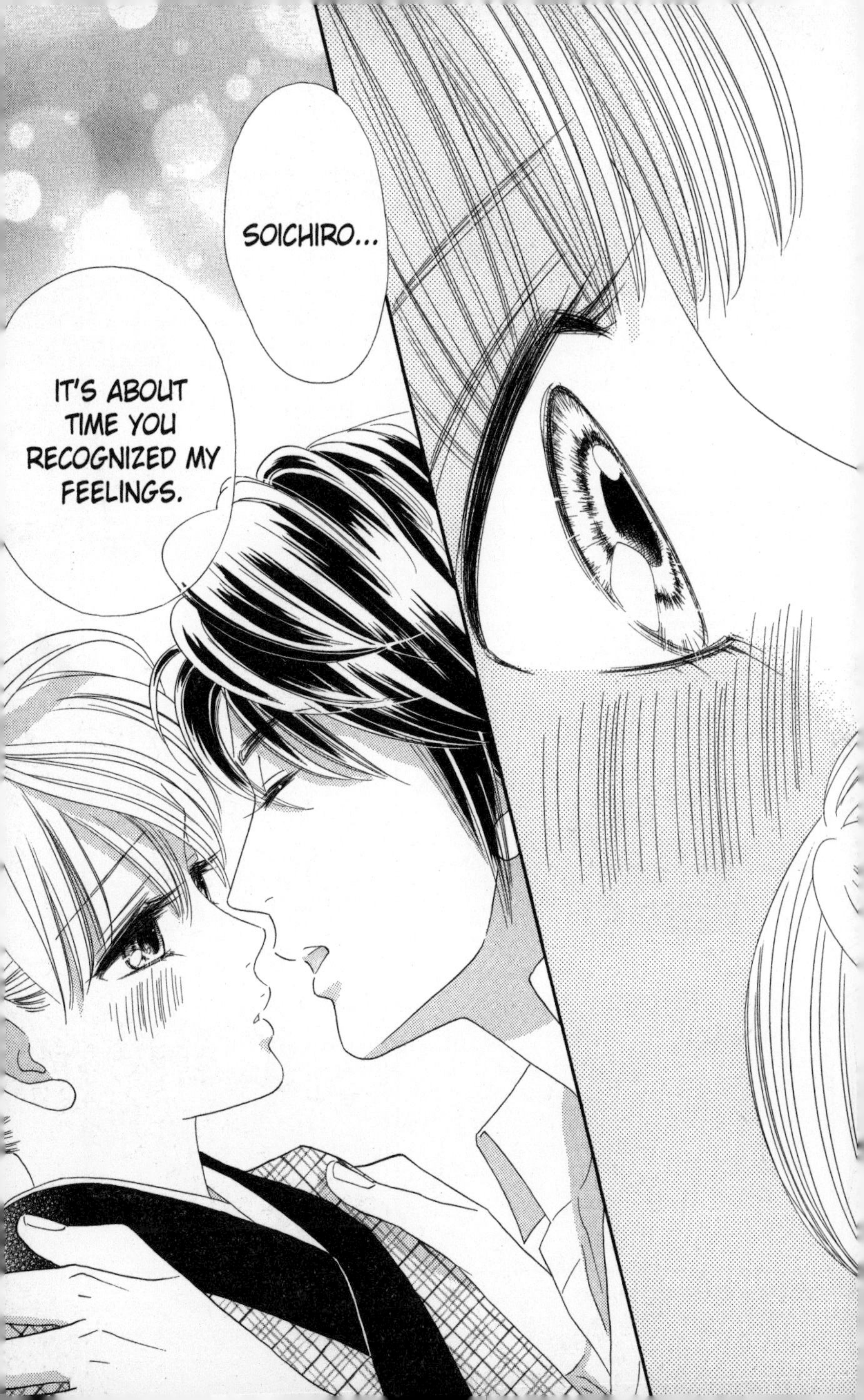
SOICHIRO...
IT'S ABOUT TIME YOU RECOGNIZED MY FEELINGS.

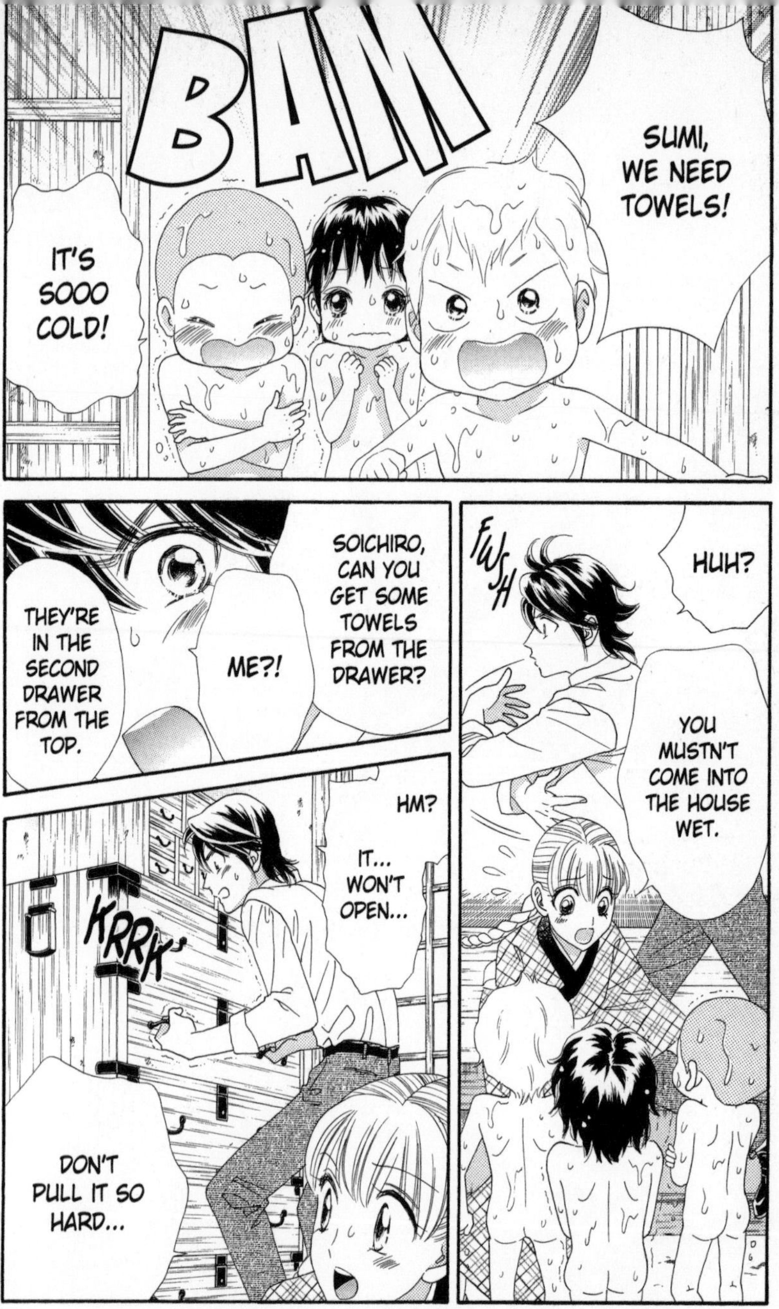
BAM
SUMI, WE NEED TOWELS!
IT'S SOOO COLD!
HUH?
FWSH
YOU MUSTN'T COME INTO THE HOUSE WET.
SOICHIRO, CAN YOU GET SOME TOWELS FROM THE DRAWER?
ME?!
THEY'RE IN THE SECOND DRAWER FROM THE TOP.
HM?
IT... WON'T OPEN...
KRRK
DON'T PULL IT SO HARD...

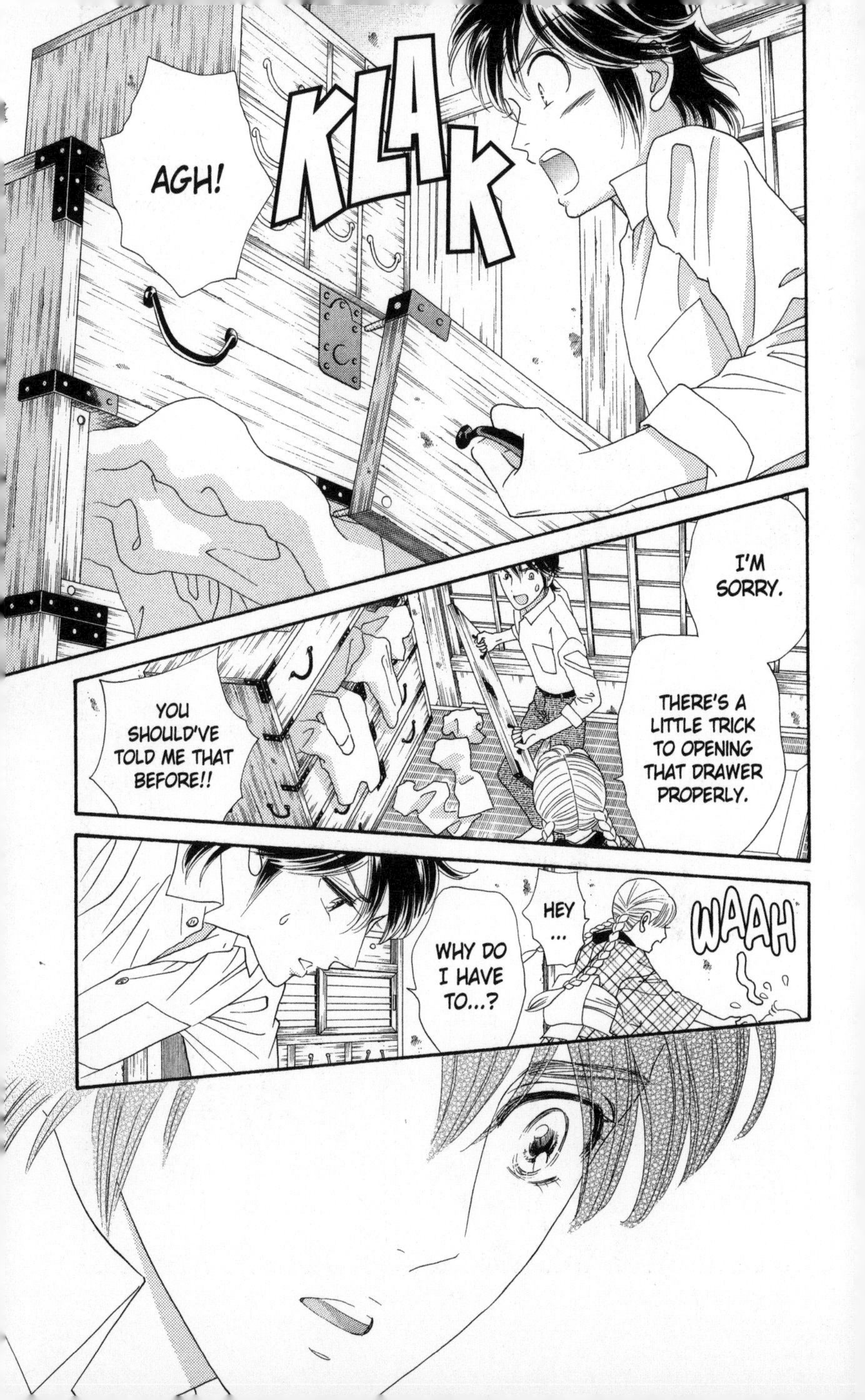
KLAK
AGH!
I'M SORRY.
THERE'S A LITTLE TRICK TO OPENING THAT DRAWER PROPERLY.
YOU SHOULD'VE TOLD ME THAT BEFORE!!
WAAH
HEY ...
WHY DO I HAVE TO...?

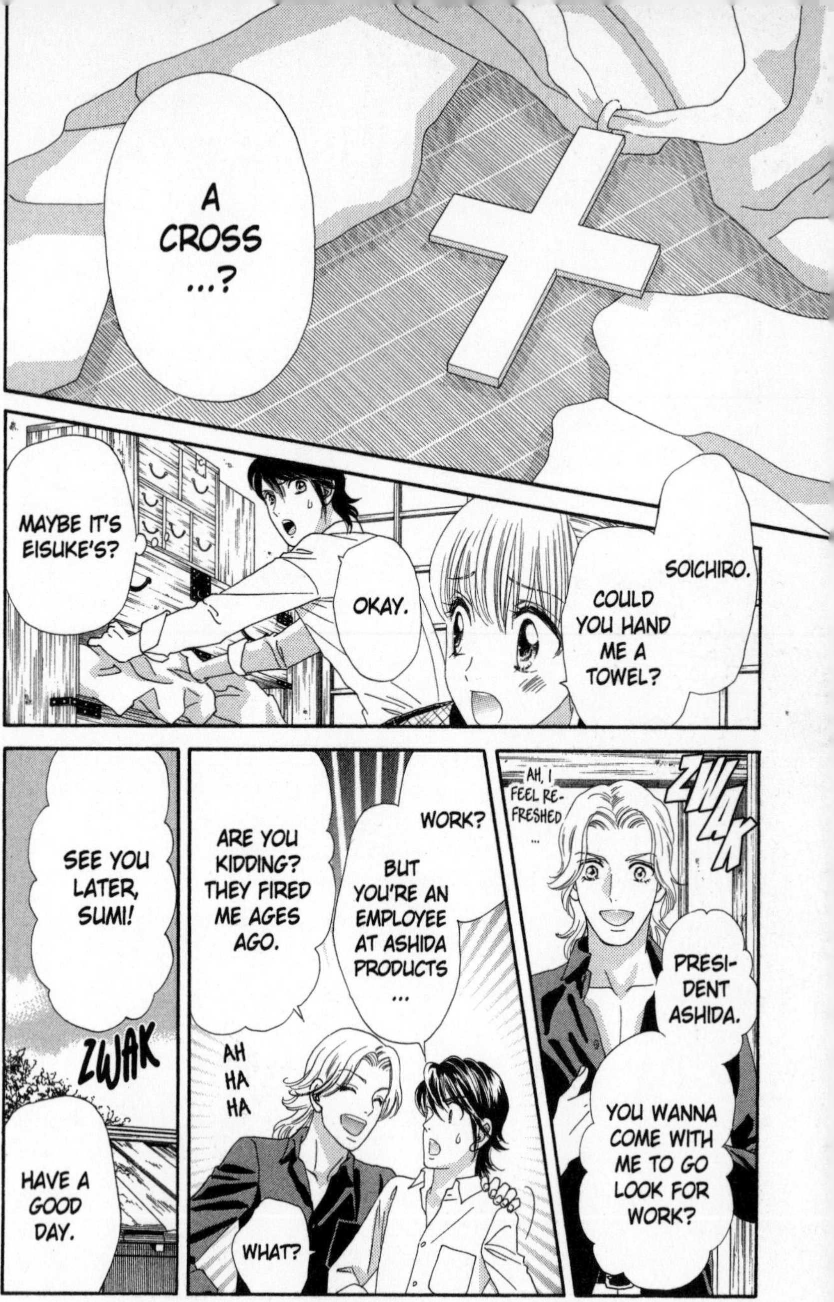
A CROSS ...?
SOICHIRO.
COULD YOU HAND ME A TOWEL?
OKAY.
MAYBE IT'S EISUKE'S?
ZWAK
AH, I FEEL REFRESHED ...
PRESIDENT ASHIDA.
YOU WANNA COME WITH ME TO GO LOOK FOR WORK?
WORK?
BUT YOU'RE AN EMPLOYEE AT ASHIDA PRODUCTS ...
ARE YOU KIDDING? THEY FIRED ME AGES AGO.
AH HA HA
WHAT?
SEE YOU LATER, SUMI!
ZWAK
HAVE A GOOD DAY.

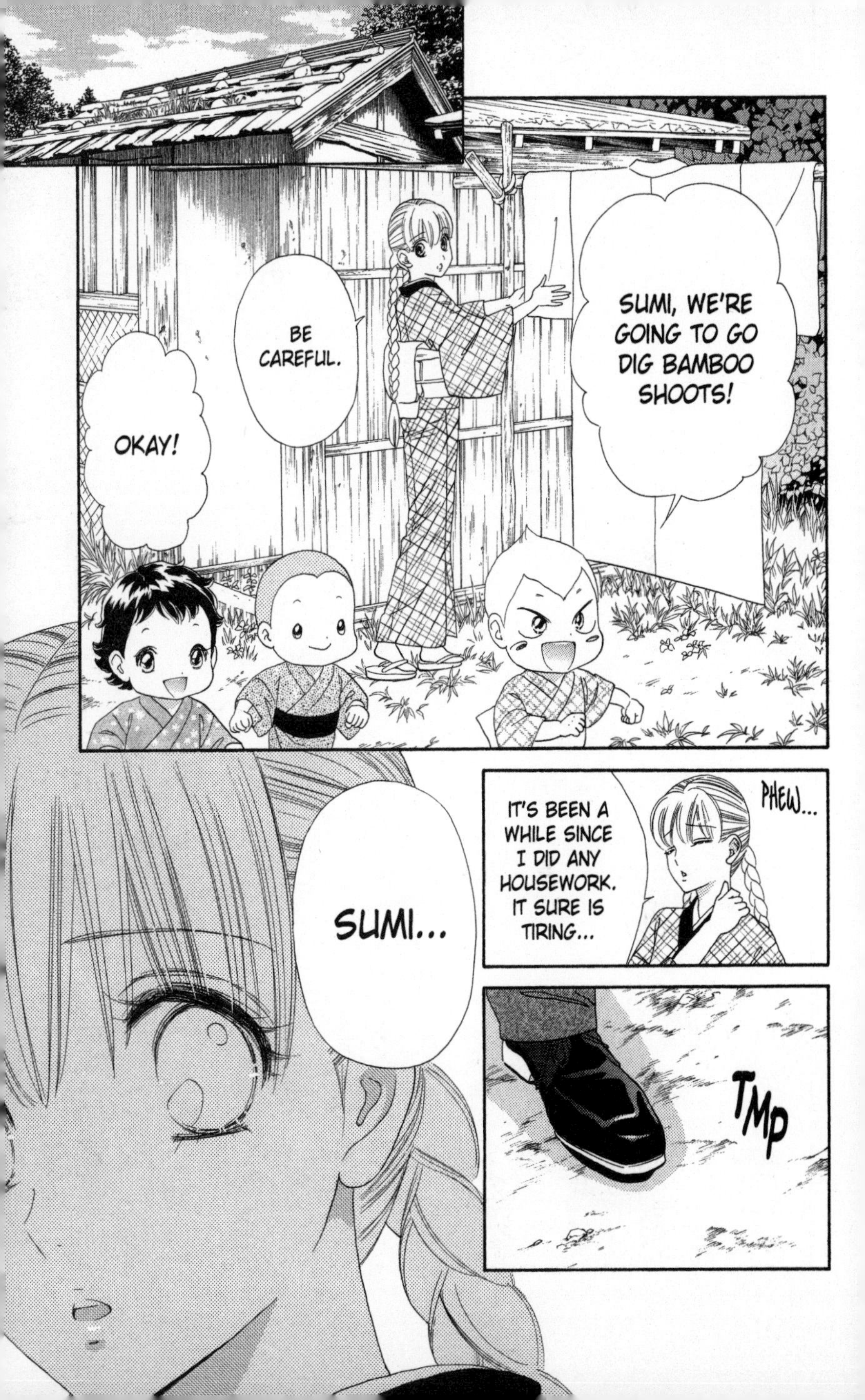
SUMI, WE'RE GOING TO GO DIG BAMBOO SHOOTS!
BE CAREFUL.
OKAY!
PHEW...
IT'S BEEN A WHILE SINCE I DID ANY HOUSEWORK. IT SURE IS TIRING...
TMP
SUMI...

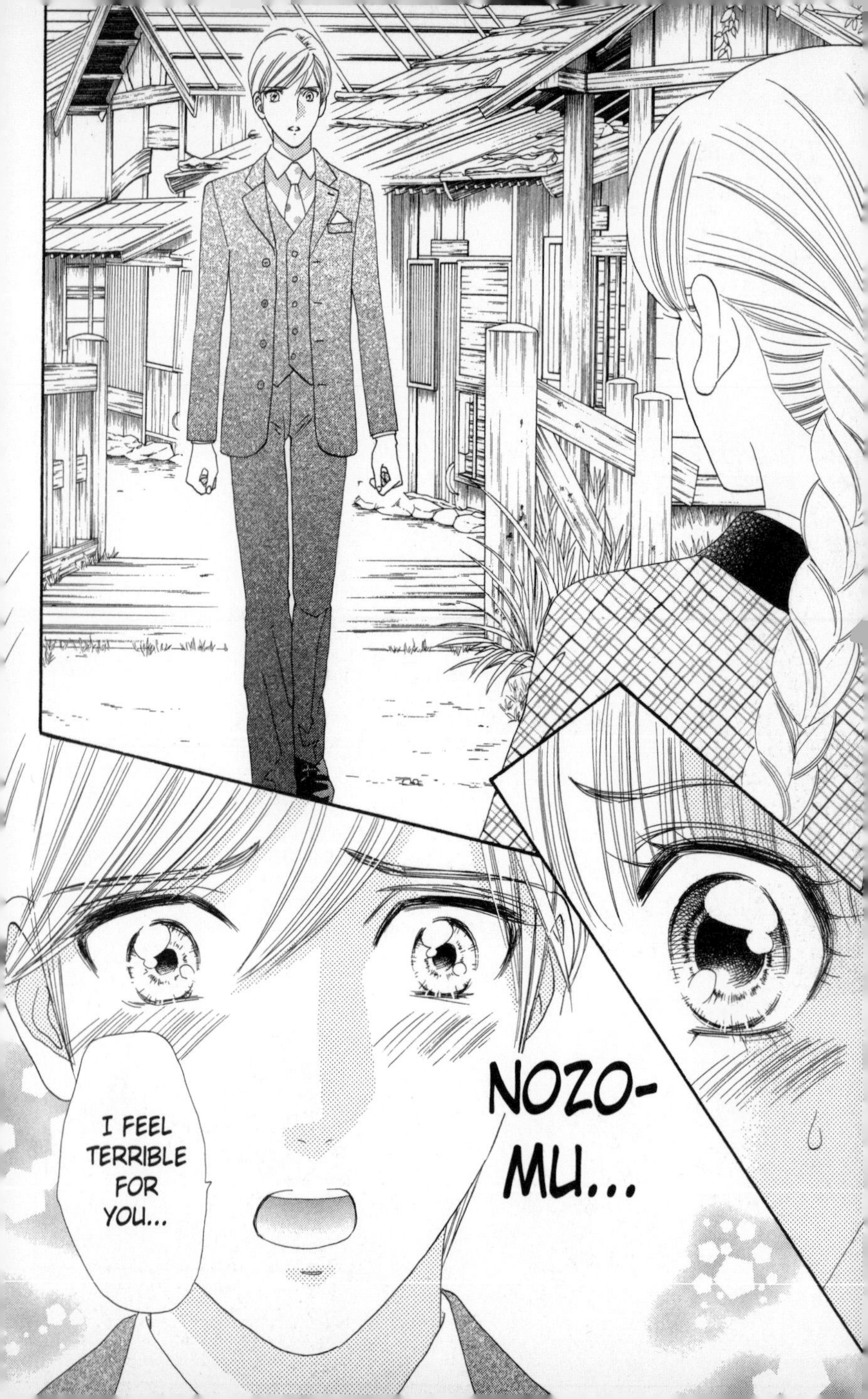
NOZO-MU...
I FEEL TERRIBLE FOR YOU...

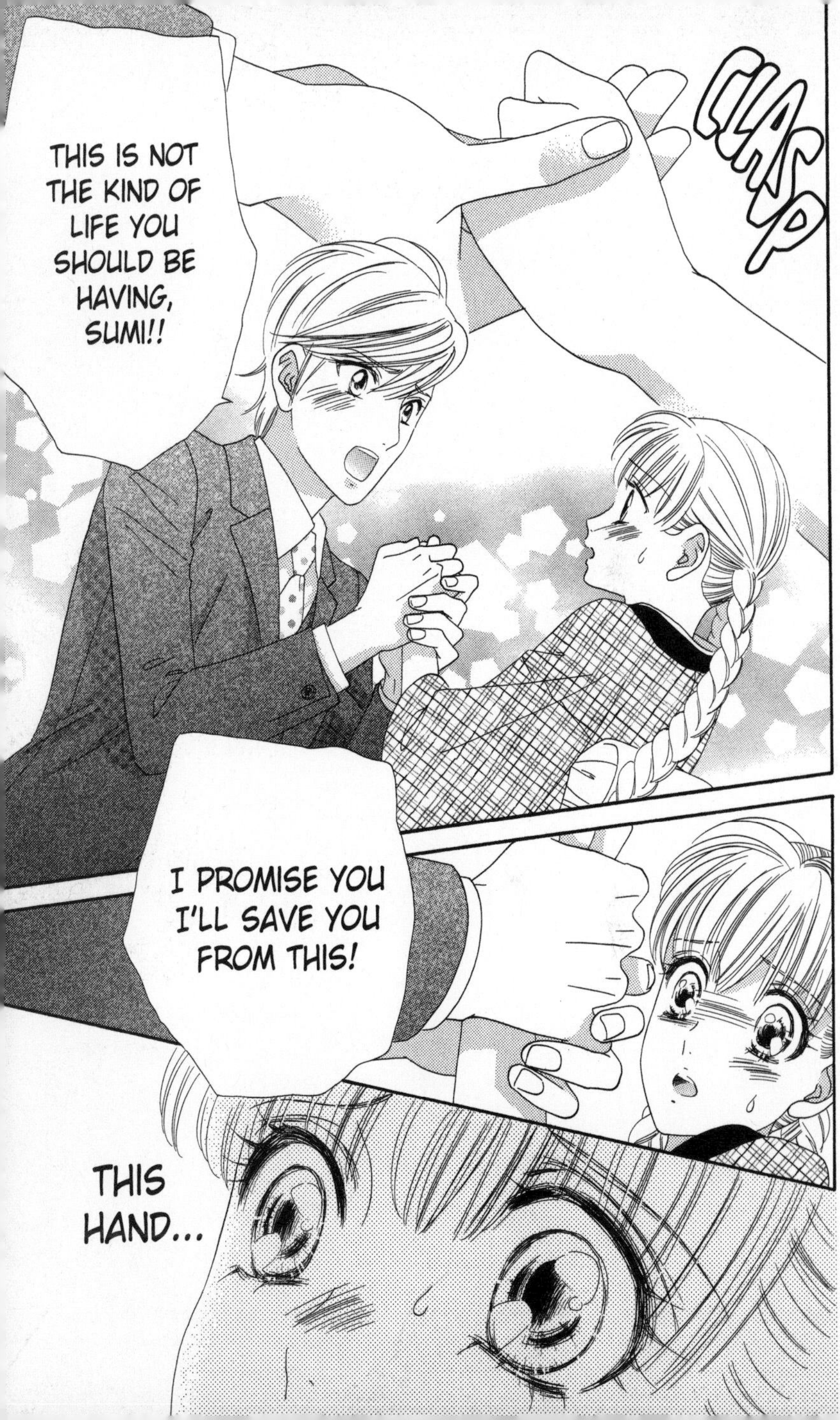
CLASP
THIS IS NOT THE KIND OF LIFE YOU SHOULD BE HAVING, SUMI!!
I PROMISE YOU I'LL SAVE YOU FROM THIS!
THIS HAND...

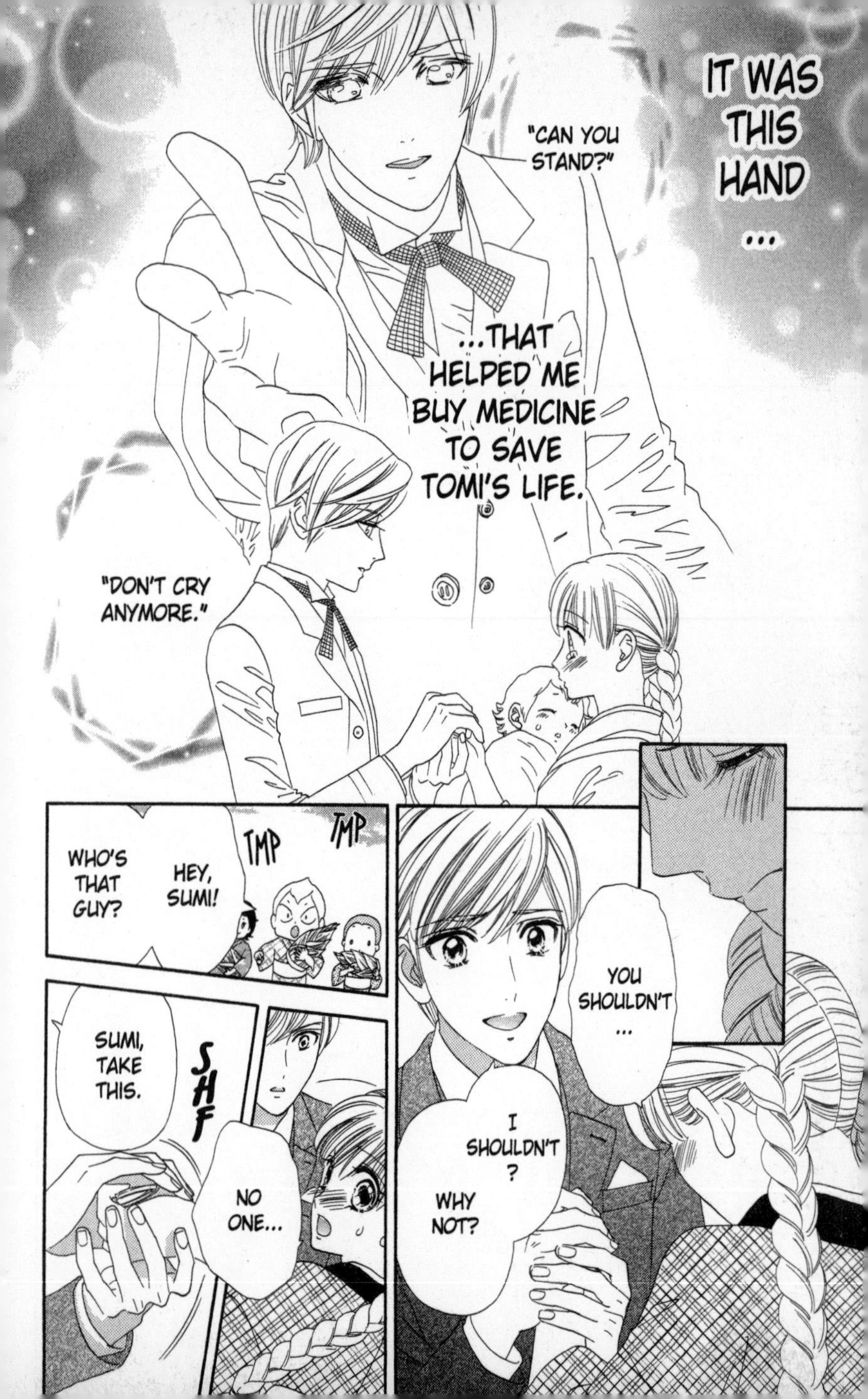
IT WAS THIS HAND...
"CAN YOU STAND?"
...THAT HELPED ME BUY MEDICINE TO SAVE TOMI'S LIFE.
"DON'T CRY ANYMORE."
YOU SHOULDN'T...
I SHOULDN'T?
WHY NOT?
TMP
TMP
HEY, SUMI!
WHO'S THAT GUY?
NO ONE...
SHF
SUMI, TAKE THIS.

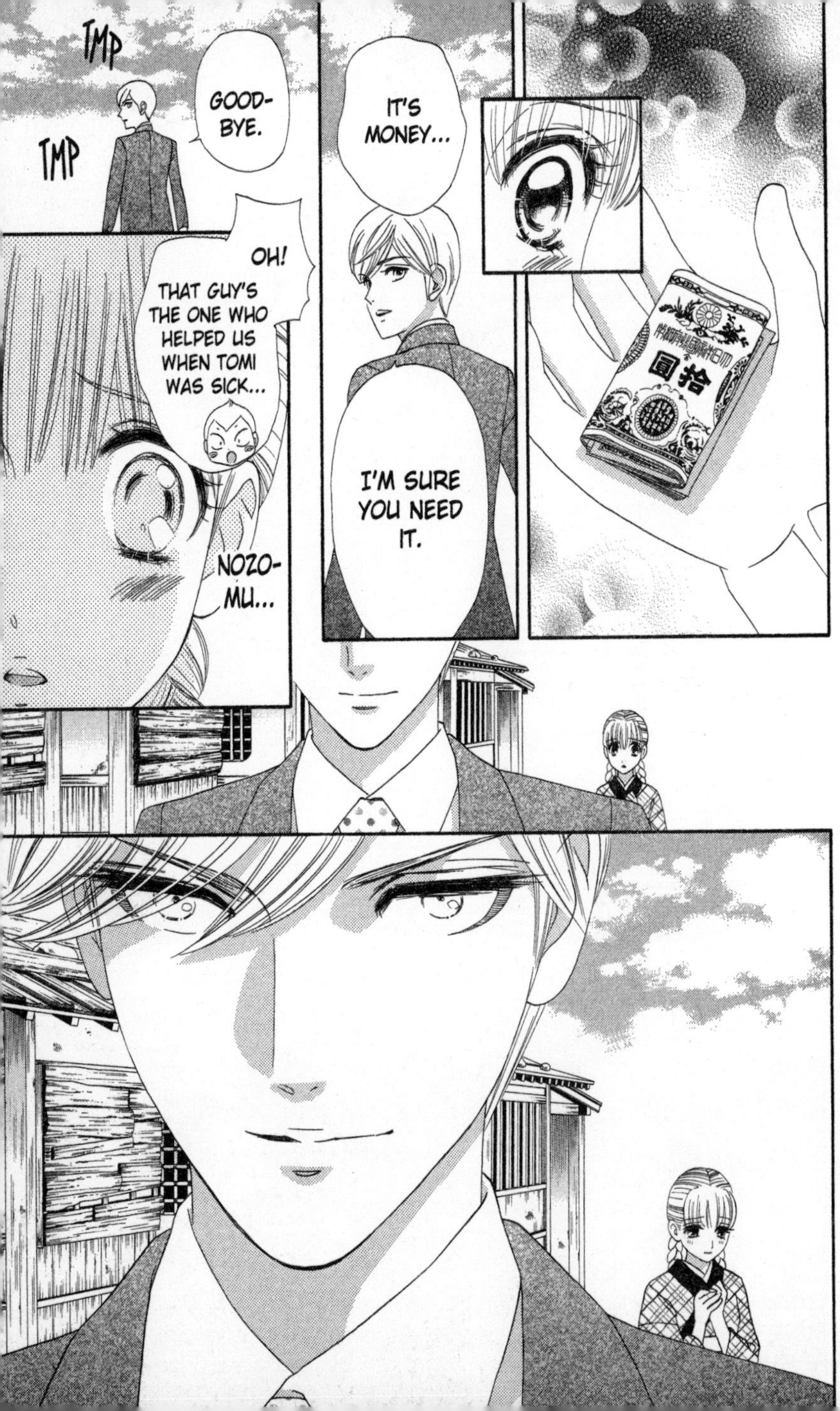
IT'S MONEY...
I'M SURE YOU NEED IT.
TMP
TMP
GOOD-BYE.
OH!
THAT GUY'S THE ONE WHO HELPED US WHEN TOMI WAS SICK...
NOZO-MU...

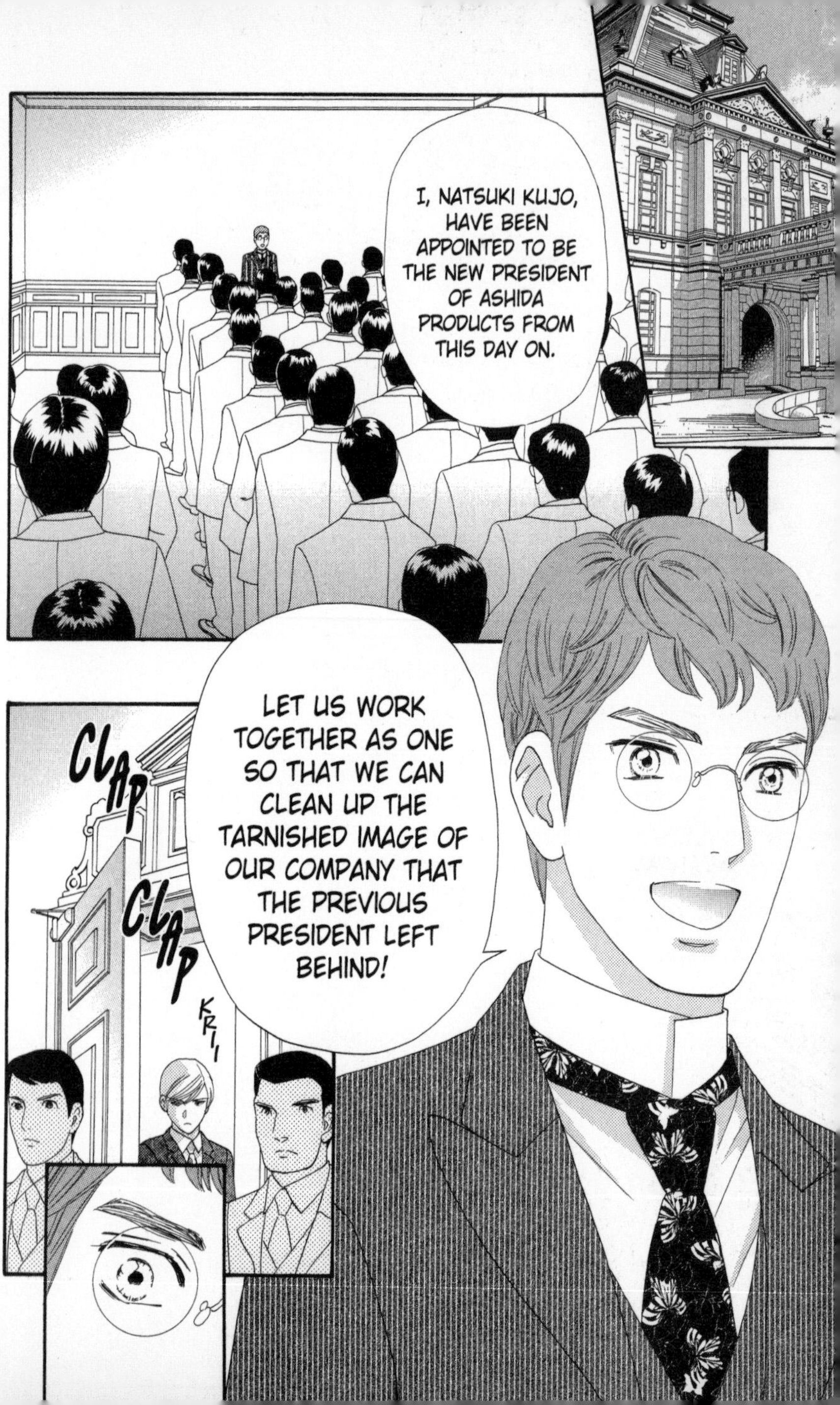

I, NATSUKI KUJO, HAVE BEEN APPOINTED TO BE THE NEW PRESIDENT OF ASHIDA PRODUCTS FROM THIS DAY ON.
LET US WORK TOGETHER AS ONE SO THAT WE CAN CLEAN UP THE TARNISHED IMAGE OF OUR COMPANY THAT THE PREVIOUS PRESIDENT LEFT BEHIND!
CLAP
CLAP
KRIII

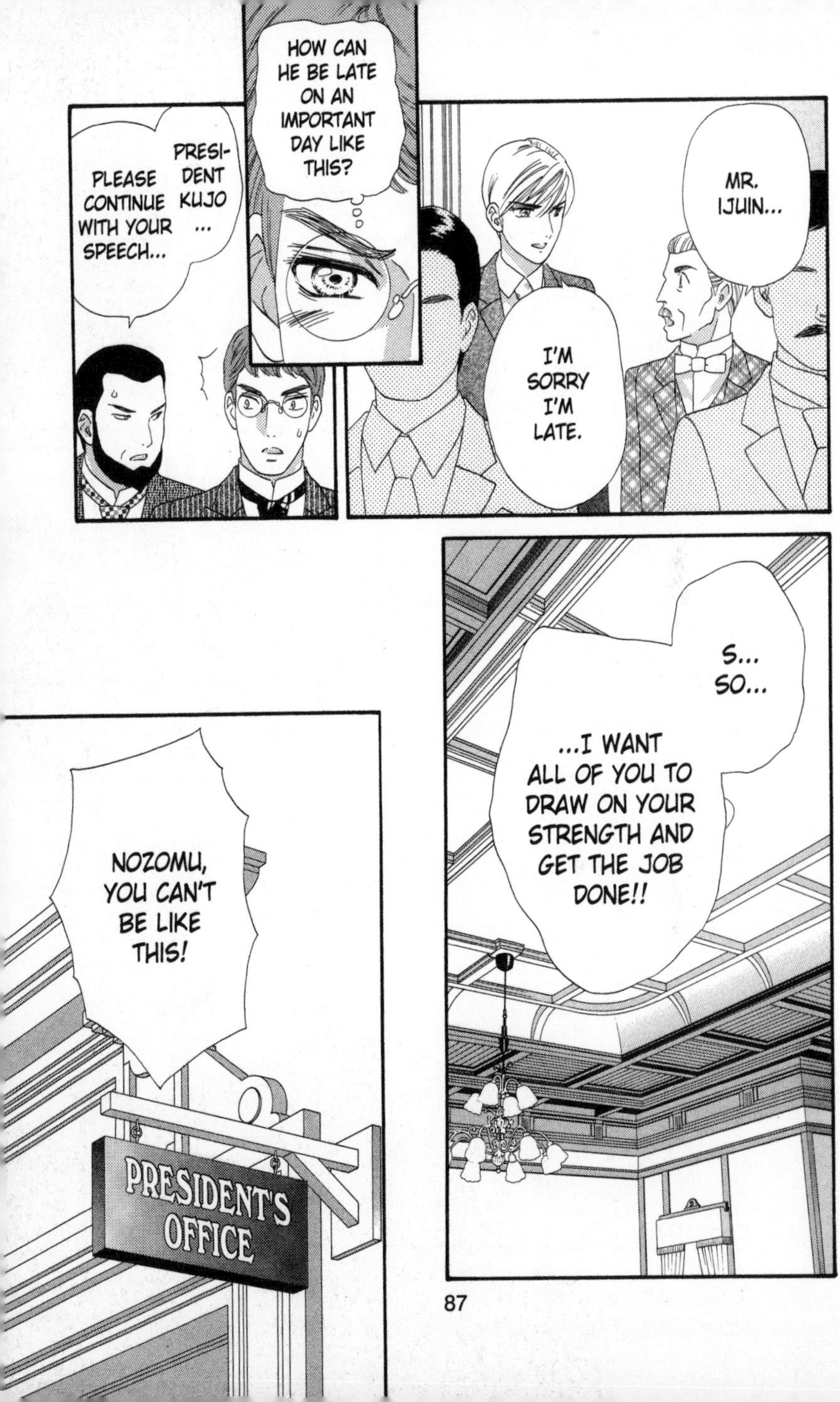
MR. IJUIN...
I'M SORRY I'M LATE.
HOW CAN HE BE LATE ON AN IMPORTANT DAY LIKE THIS?
PRESIDENT KUJO... PLEASE CONTINUE WITH YOUR SPEECH...
S... SO... ...I WANT ALL OF YOU TO DRAW ON YOUR STRENGTH AND GET THE JOB DONE!!
NOZOMU, YOU CAN'T BE LIKE THIS!
PRESIDENT'S OFFICE

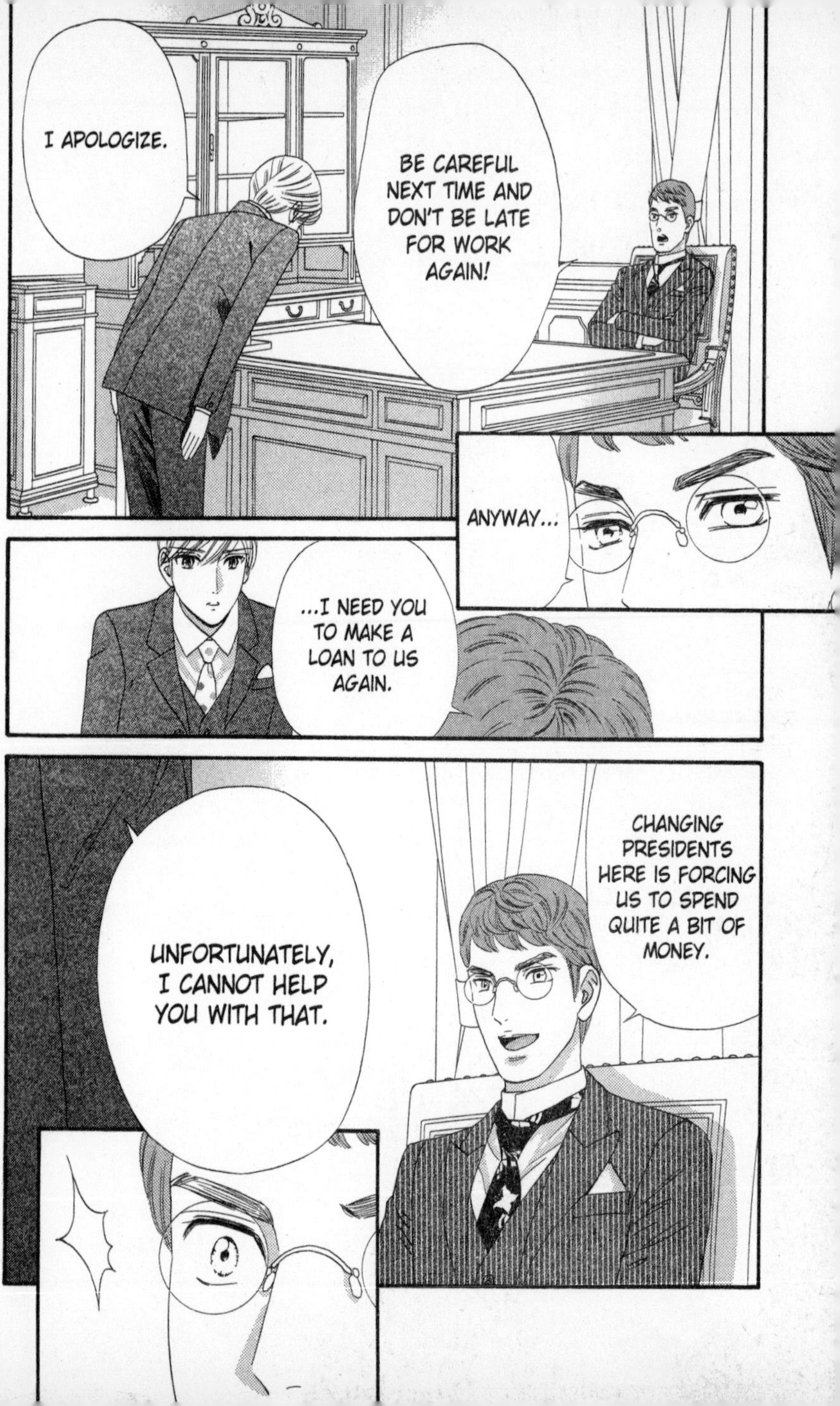
BE CAREFUL NEXT TIME AND DON'T BE LATE FOR WORK AGAIN!
I APOLOGIZE.
ANYWAY...
...I NEED YOU TO MAKE A LOAN TO US AGAIN.
CHANGING PRESIDENTS HERE IS FORCING US TO SPEND QUITE A BIT OF MONEY.
UNFORTUNATELY, I CANNOT HELP YOU WITH THAT.

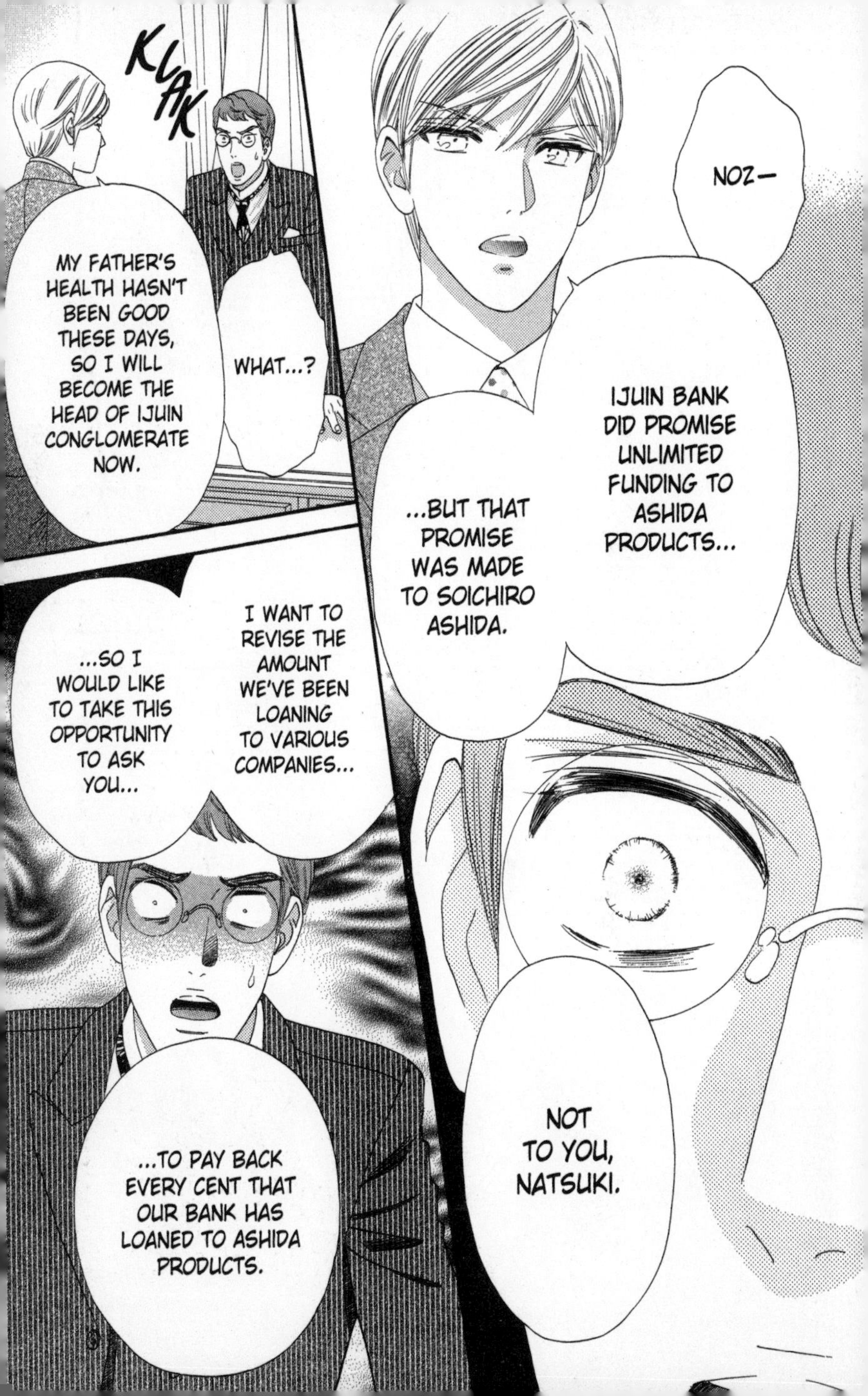
NOZ—
IJUIN BANK DID PROMISE UNLIMITED FUNDING TO ASHIDA PRODUCTS...
...BUT THAT PROMISE WAS MADE TO SOICHIRO ASHIDA.
NOT TO YOU, NATSUKI.
KLAK
WHAT...?
MY FATHER'S HEALTH HASN'T BEEN GOOD THESE DAYS, SO I WILL BECOME THE HEAD OF IJUIN CONGLOMERATE NOW.
I WANT TO REVISE THE AMOUNT WE'VE BEEN LOANING TO VARIOUS COMPANIES...
...SO I WOULD LIKE TO TAKE THIS OPPORTUNITY TO ASK YOU...
...TO PAY BACK EVERY CENT THAT OUR BANK HAS LOANED TO ASHIDA PRODUCTS.

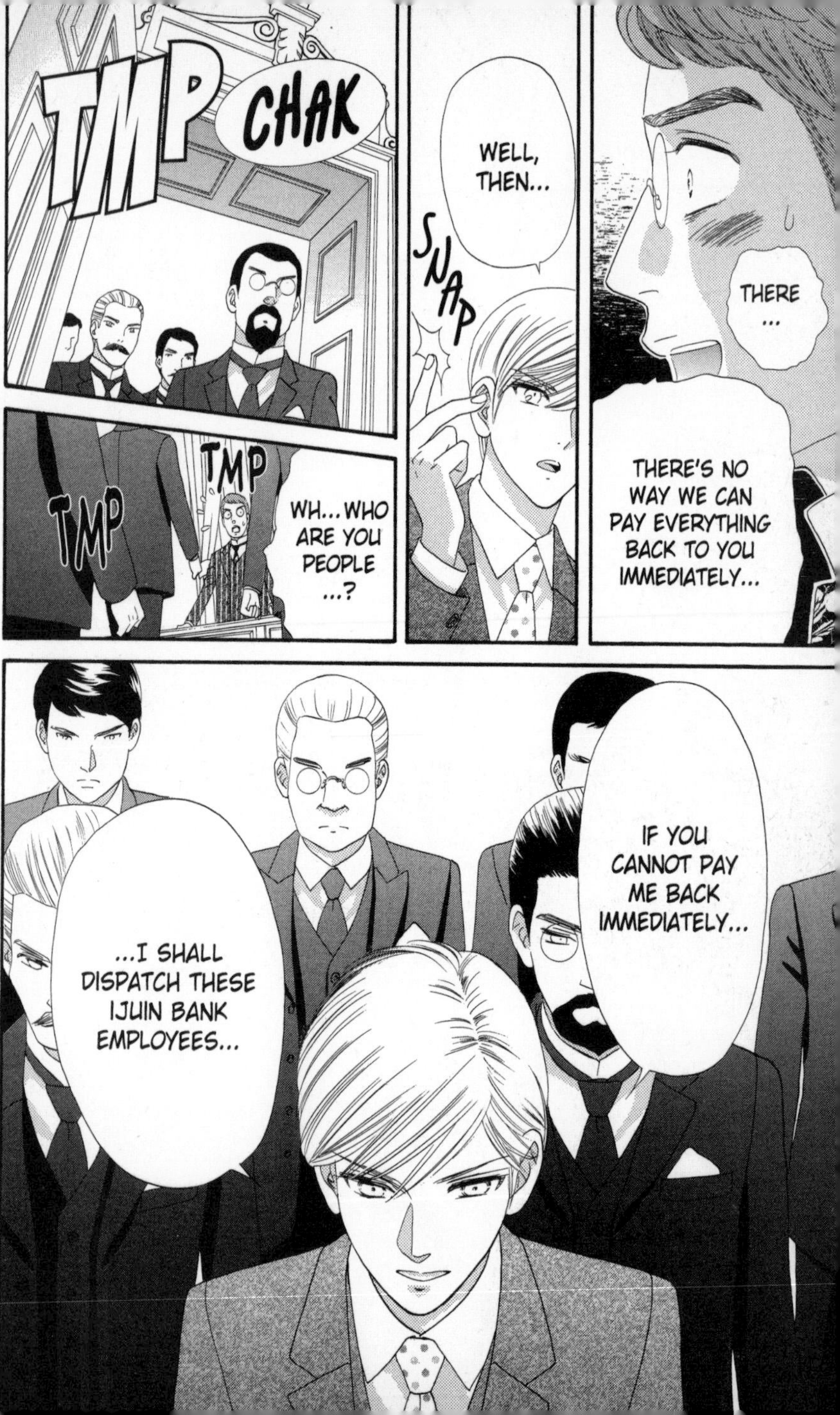
THERE ...
THERE'S NO WAY WE CAN PAY EVERYTHING BACK TO YOU IMMEDIATELY...
WELL, THEN...
SNAP
CHAK
TMP
WH...WHO ARE YOU PEOPLE ...?
TMP
TMP
IF YOU CANNOT PAY ME BACK IMMEDIATELY...
...I SHALL DISPATCH THESE IJUIN BANK EMPLOYEES...

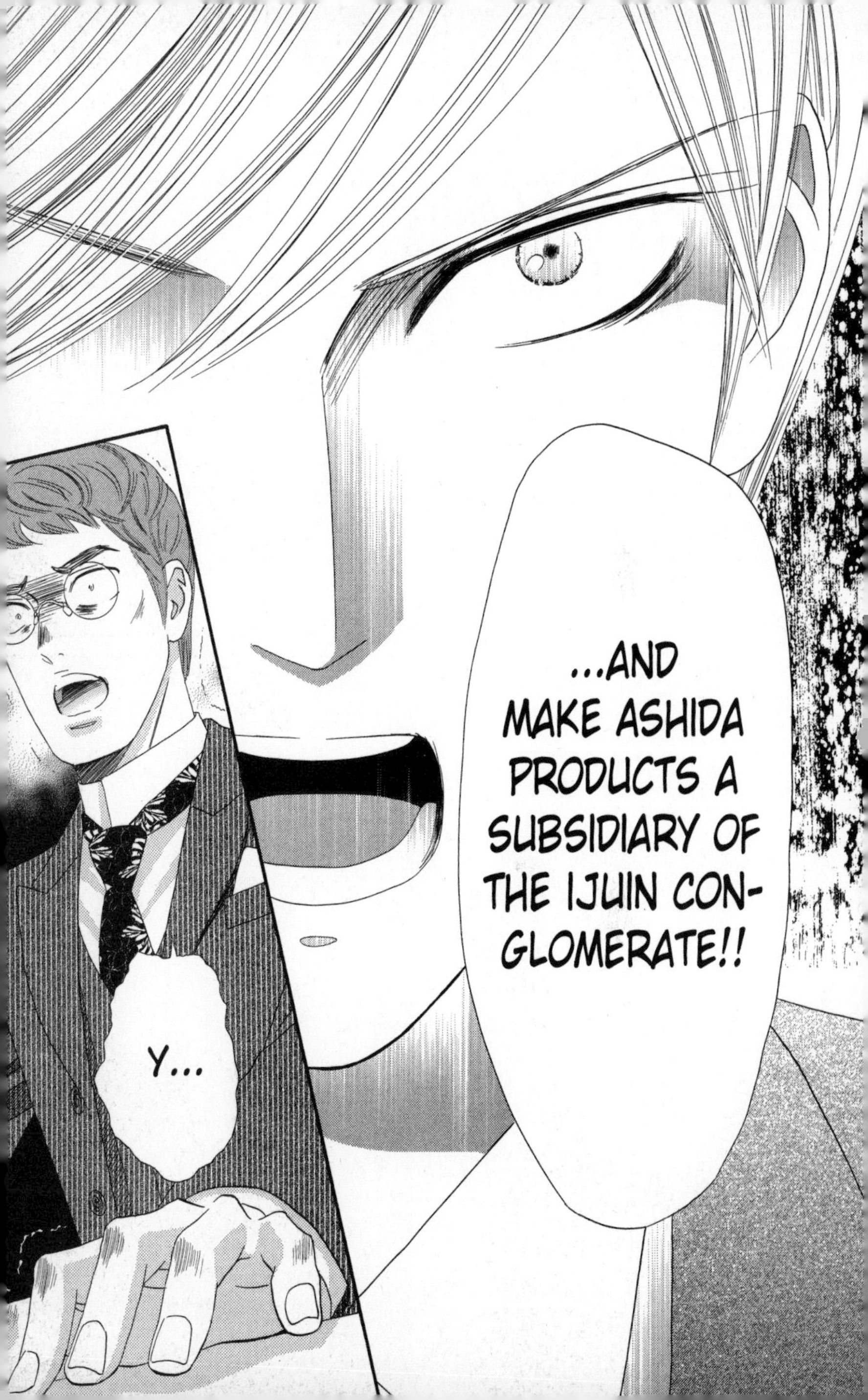
...AND MAKE ASHIDA PRODUCTS A SUBSIDIARY OF THE IJUIN CON-GLOMERATE!!
Y...

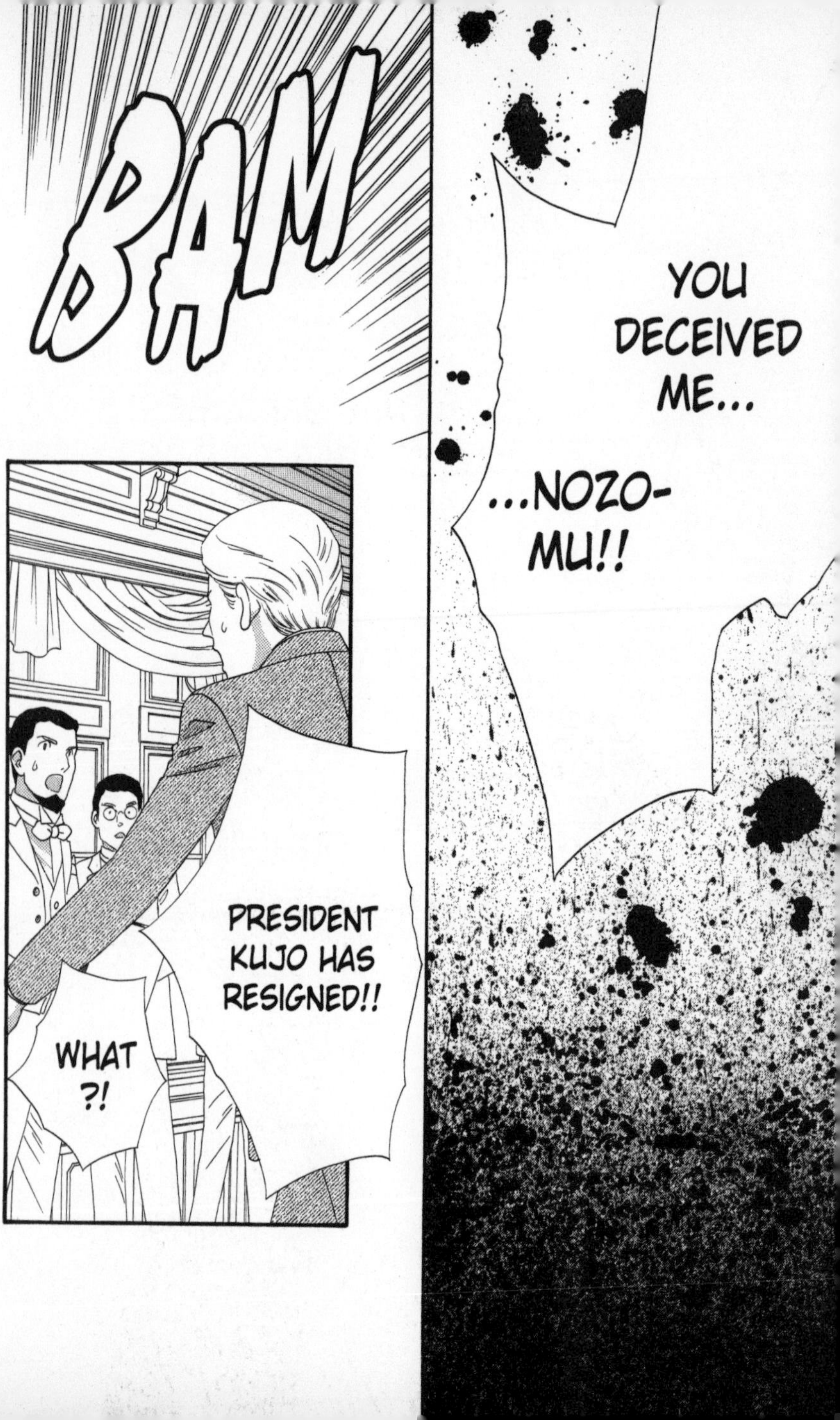
YOU DECEIVED ME...
...NOZO-MU!!
BAM
PRESIDENT KUJO HAS RESIGNED!!
WHAT ?!

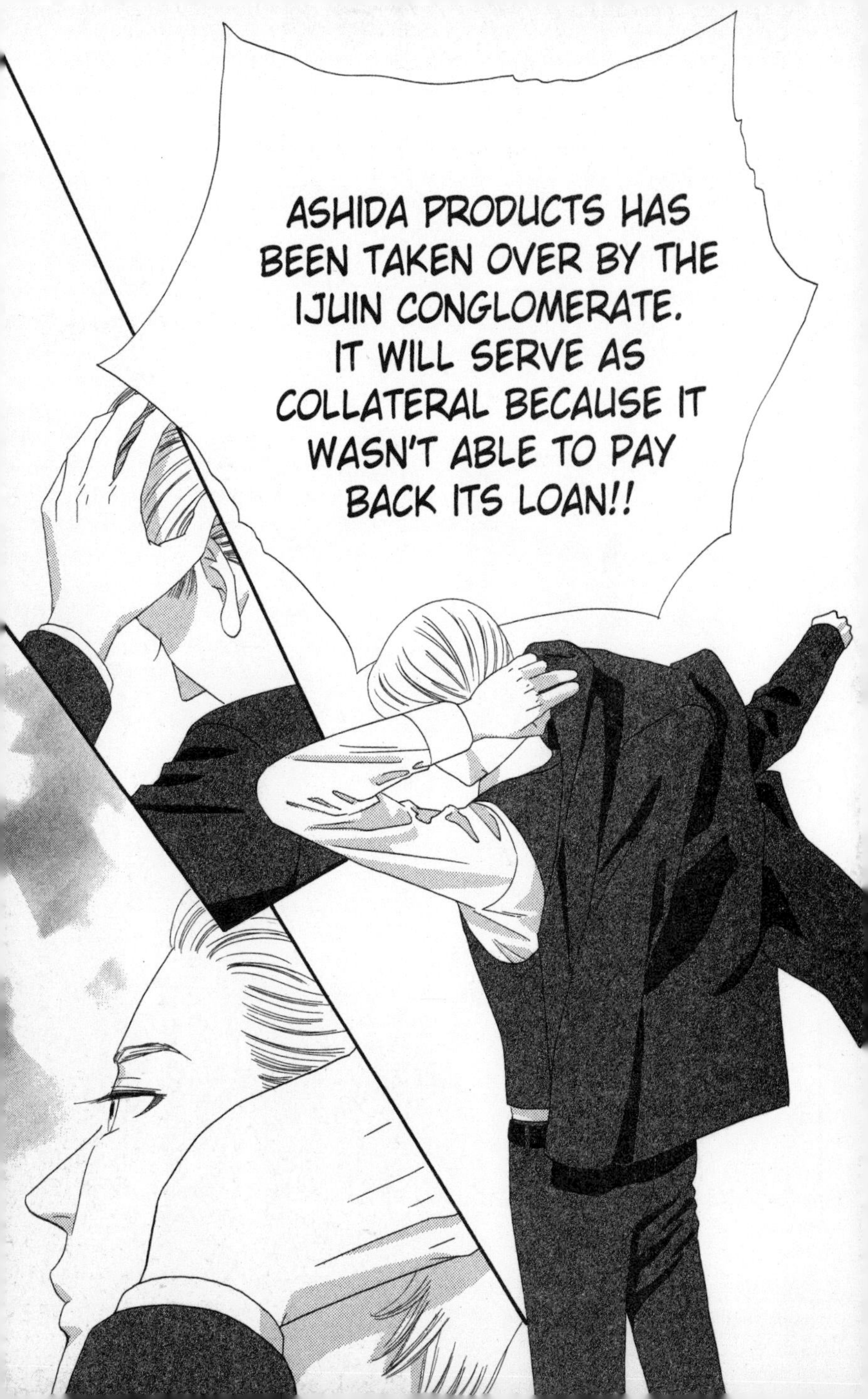
ASHIDA PRODUCTS HAS BEEN TAKEN OVER BY THE IJUIN CONGLOMERATE. IT WILL SERVE AS COLLATERAL BECAUSE IT WASN'T ABLE TO PAY BACK ITS LOAN!!

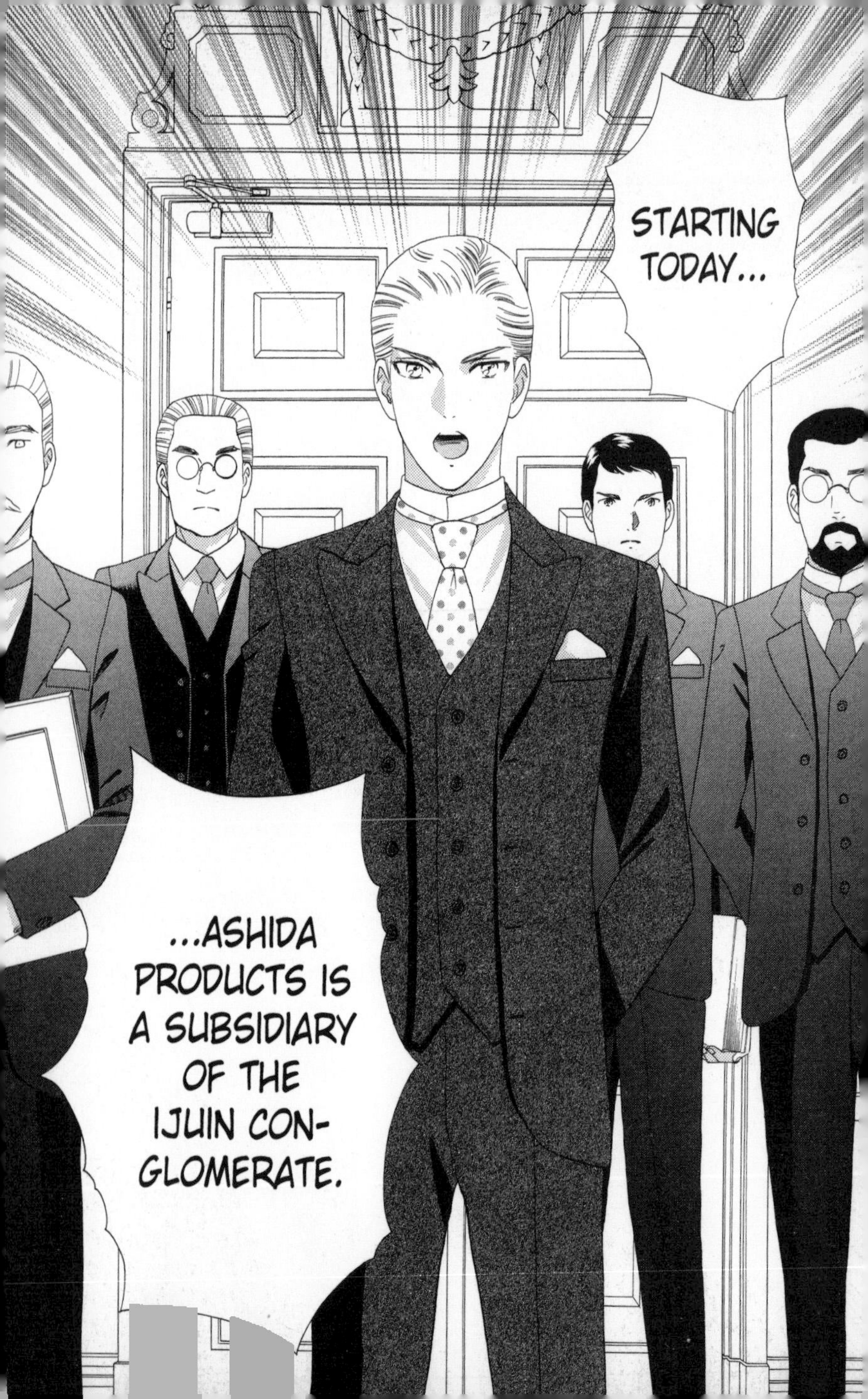
STARTING TODAY...
...ASHIDA PRODUCTS IS A SUBSIDIARY OF THE IJUIN CON-GLOMERATE.

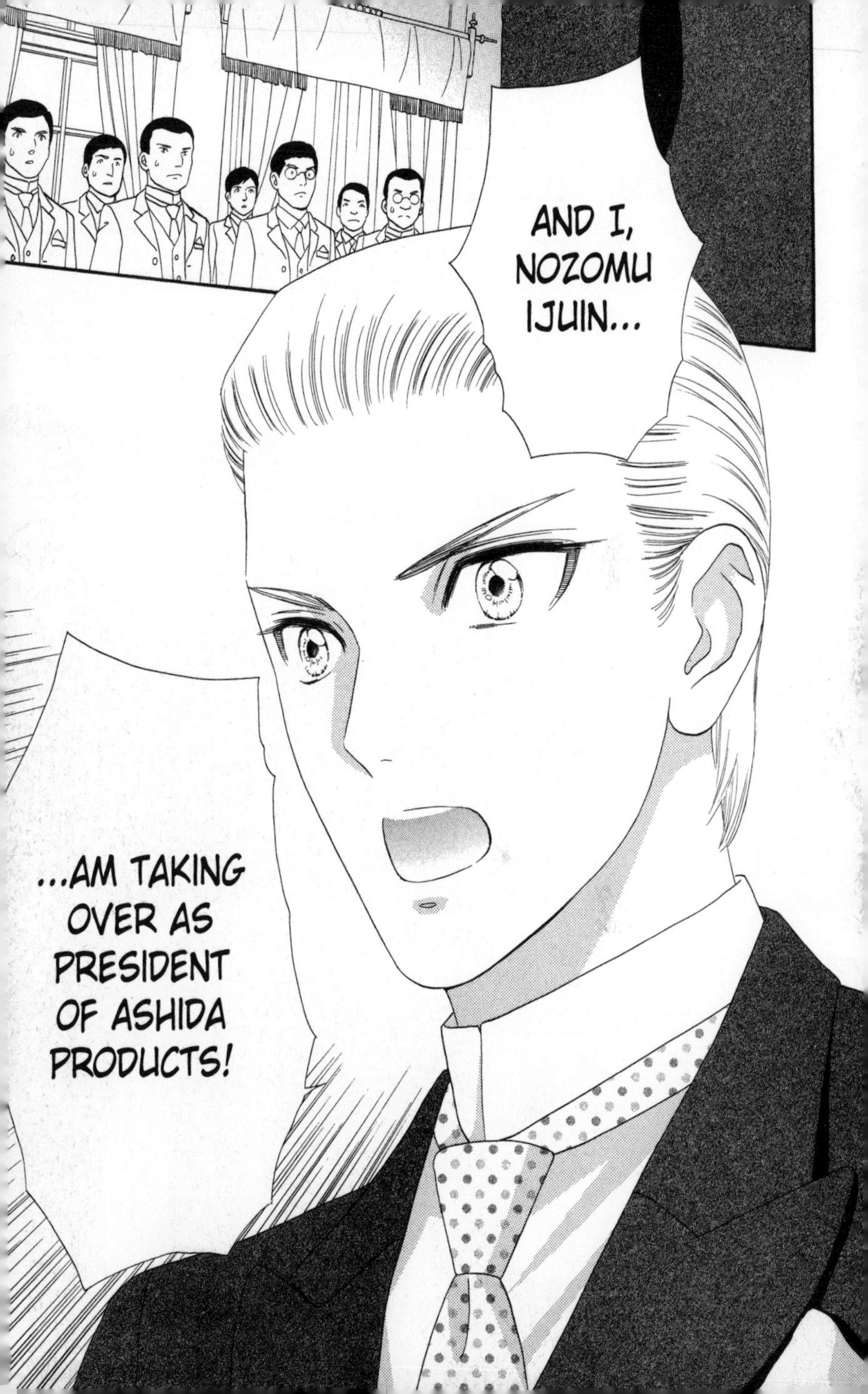
AND I, NOZOMU IJUIN...
...AM TAKING OVER AS PRESIDENT OF ASHIDA PRODUCTS!

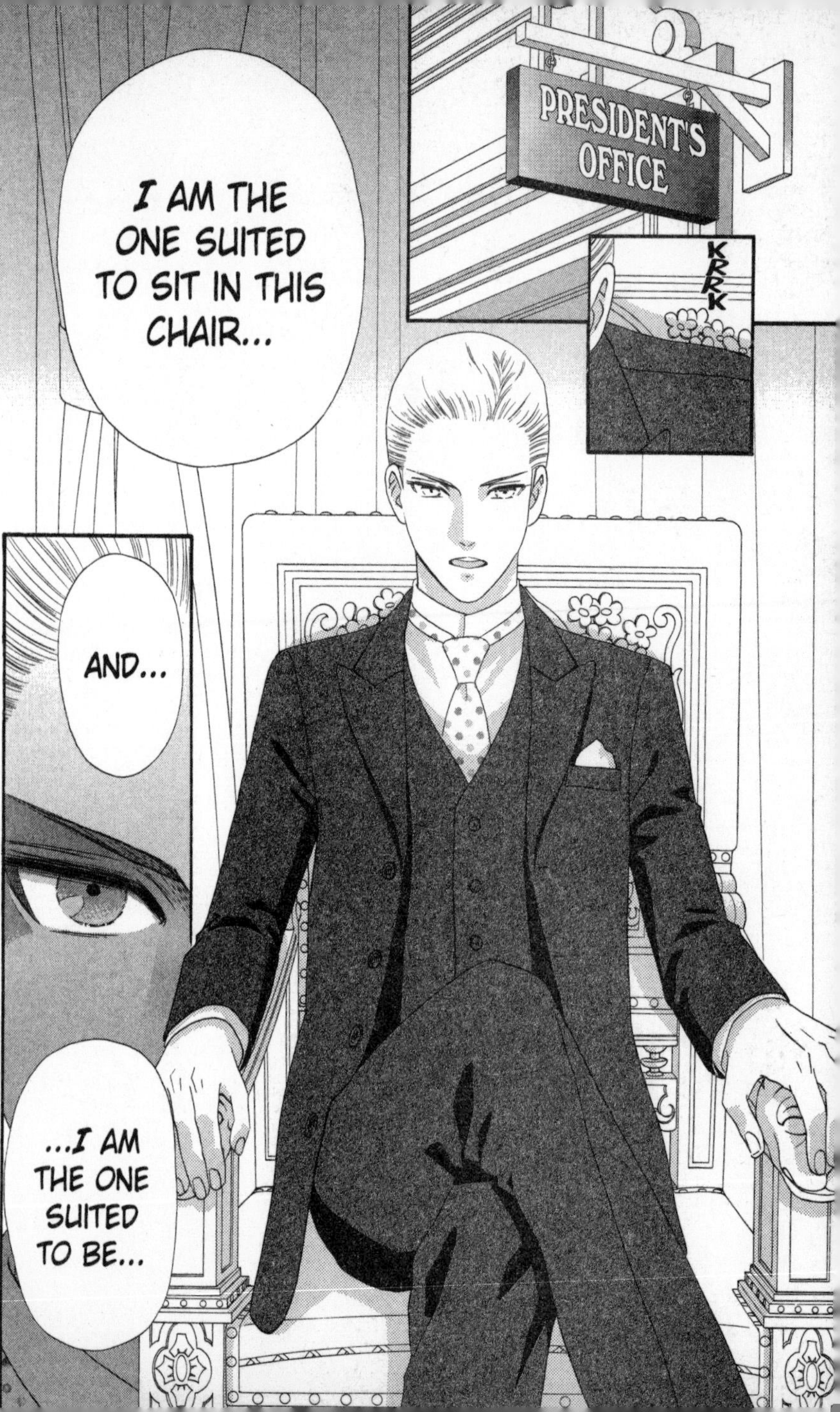
PRESIDENT'S OFFICE
KRRK
I AM THE ONE SUITED TO SIT IN THIS CHAIR...
AND...
...I AM THE ONE SUITED TO BE...

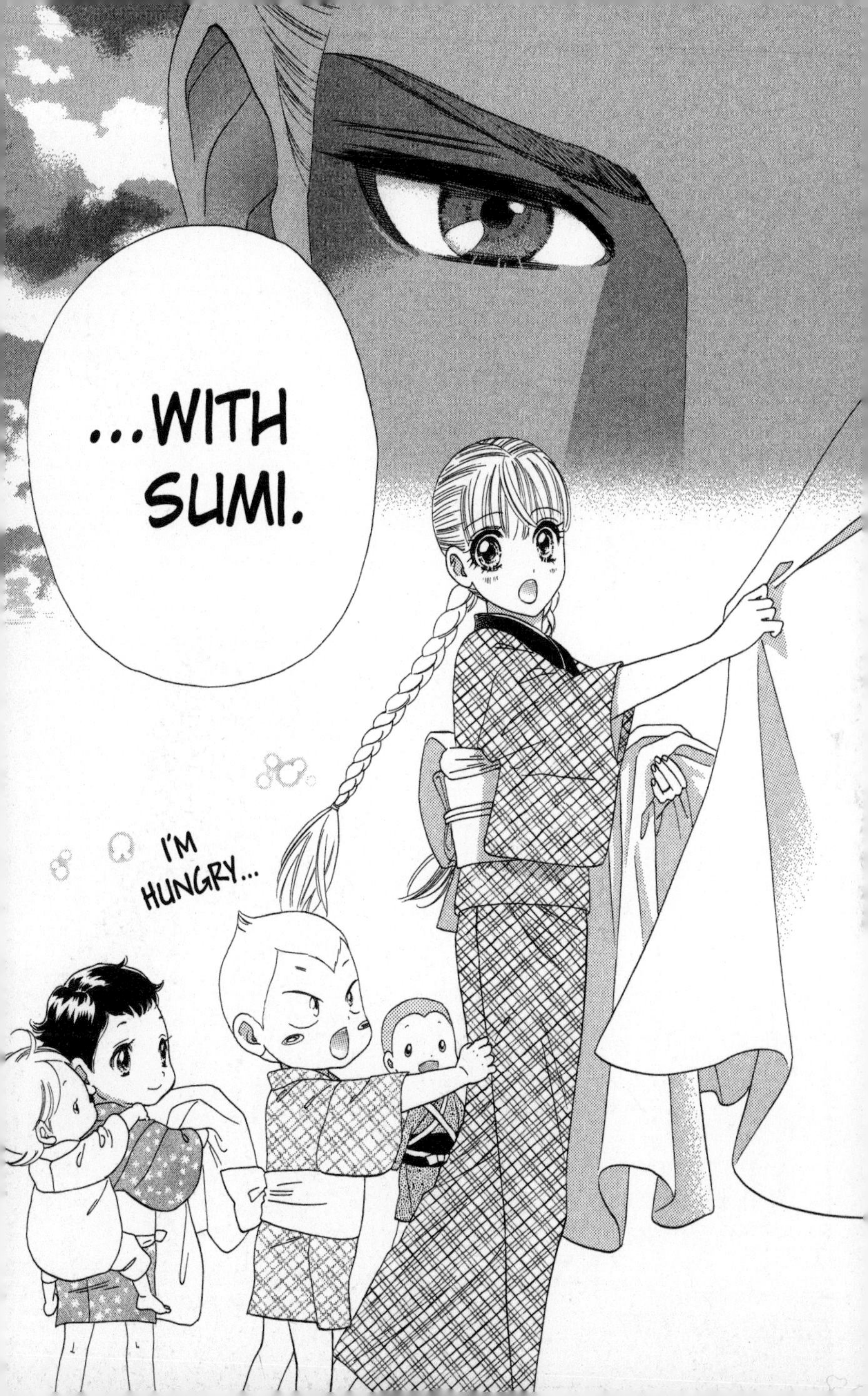
...WITH SUMI.
I'M HUNGRY...

RAISING A CHILD AND WORKING ON MANGA IS MUCH TOUGHER THAN YOU'D IMAGINE.

THIS IS THE DAILY SCHEDULE THAT I CURRENTLY WORK UNDER SO THAT I CAN SOMEHOW DO THEM BOTH!!

3:00 WAKE UP. MAKE SOME COFFEE AND DO WORK.

7:00 WAKE UP THE FAMILY AND LET MY PARAKEET OUT. MAKE BREAKFAST, DO MORNING CHORES.

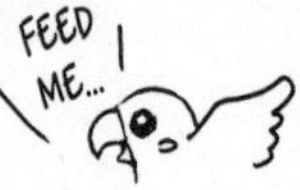
FEED ME...

9:00 TAKE MY DAUGHTER TO NURSERY SCHOOL AND RETURN TO WORK.

13:00 LUNCH.

17:00 GO PICK UP MY DAUGHTER FROM SCHOOL.

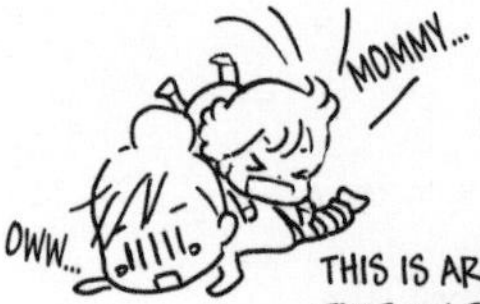
MOMMY...
OWW...

18:00 TAKE A BATH RIGHT AFTER GETTING HOME.

THIS IS AROUND THE TIME MY FATIGUE IS AT ITS PEAK...

19:00 MAKE & EAT DINNER.

20:30 GET READY FOR TOMORROW AND LET MY PARAKEET OUT ONE MORE TIME. PLAY AROUND A BIT.

21:30 ROLL AROUND IN MY FUTON AND EVENTUALLY GO TO SLEEP.

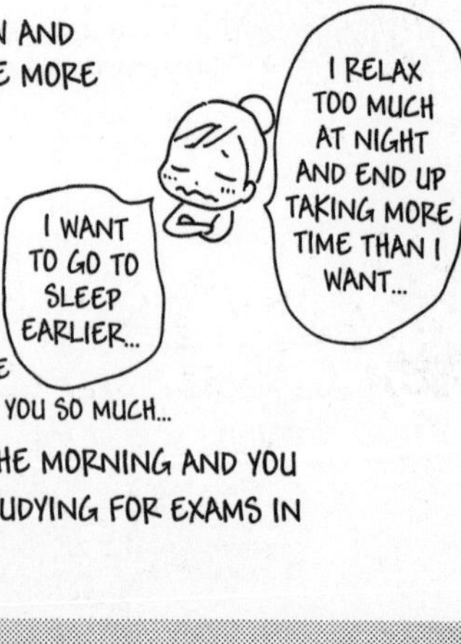
I RELAX TOO MUCH AT NIGHT AND END UP TAKING MORE TIME THAN I WANT...
I WANT TO GO TO SLEEP EARLIER...

*MY HUSBAND HANGS UP THE LAUNDRY AT NIGHT. THANK YOU SO MUCH...

IT'S EASY TO CONCENTRATE EARLY IN THE MORNING AND YOU FEEL REFRESHED, SO I RECOMMEND STUDYING FOR EXAMS IN THIS SAME MANNER TOO. ☆

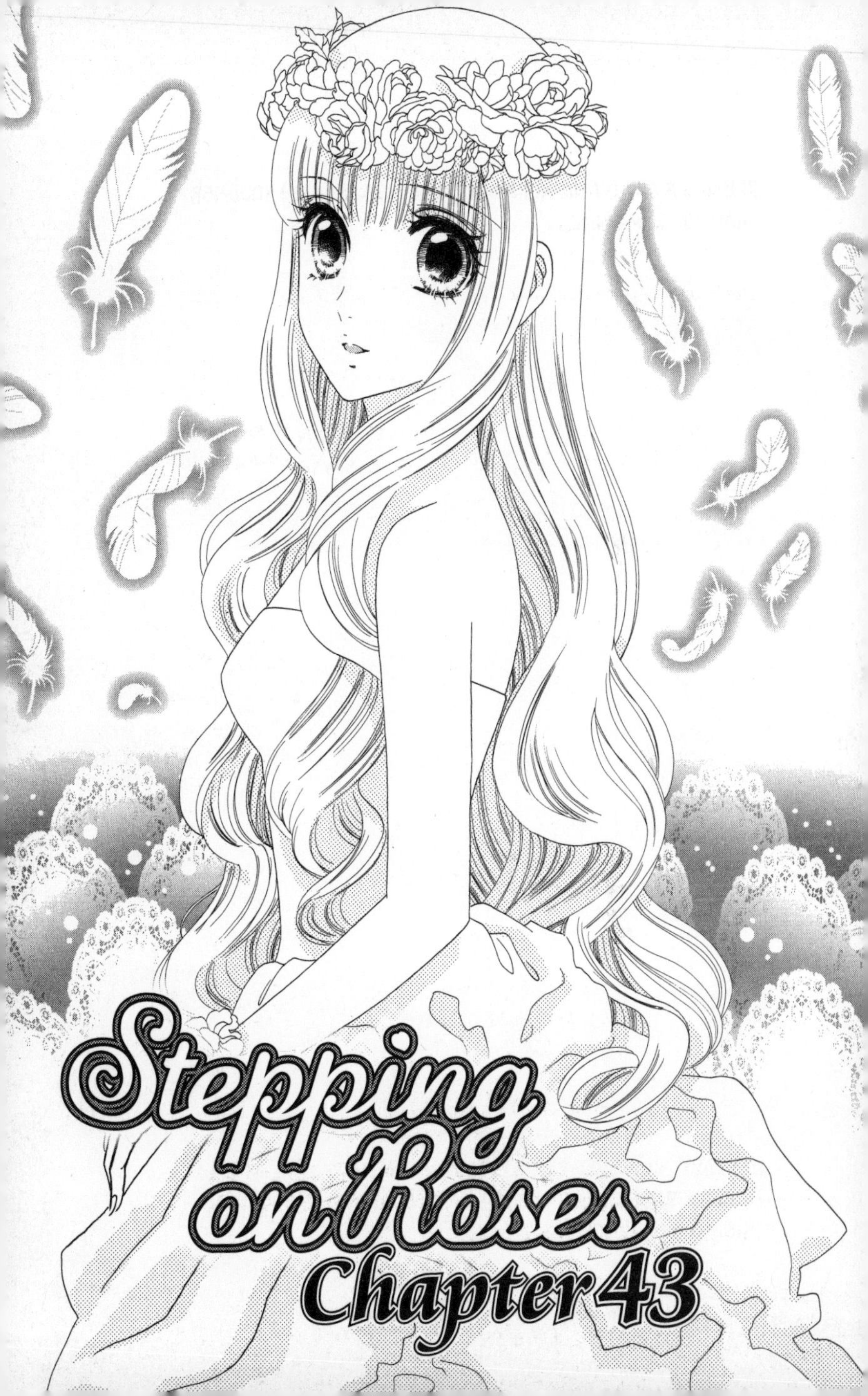
Stepping on Roses
Chapter 43

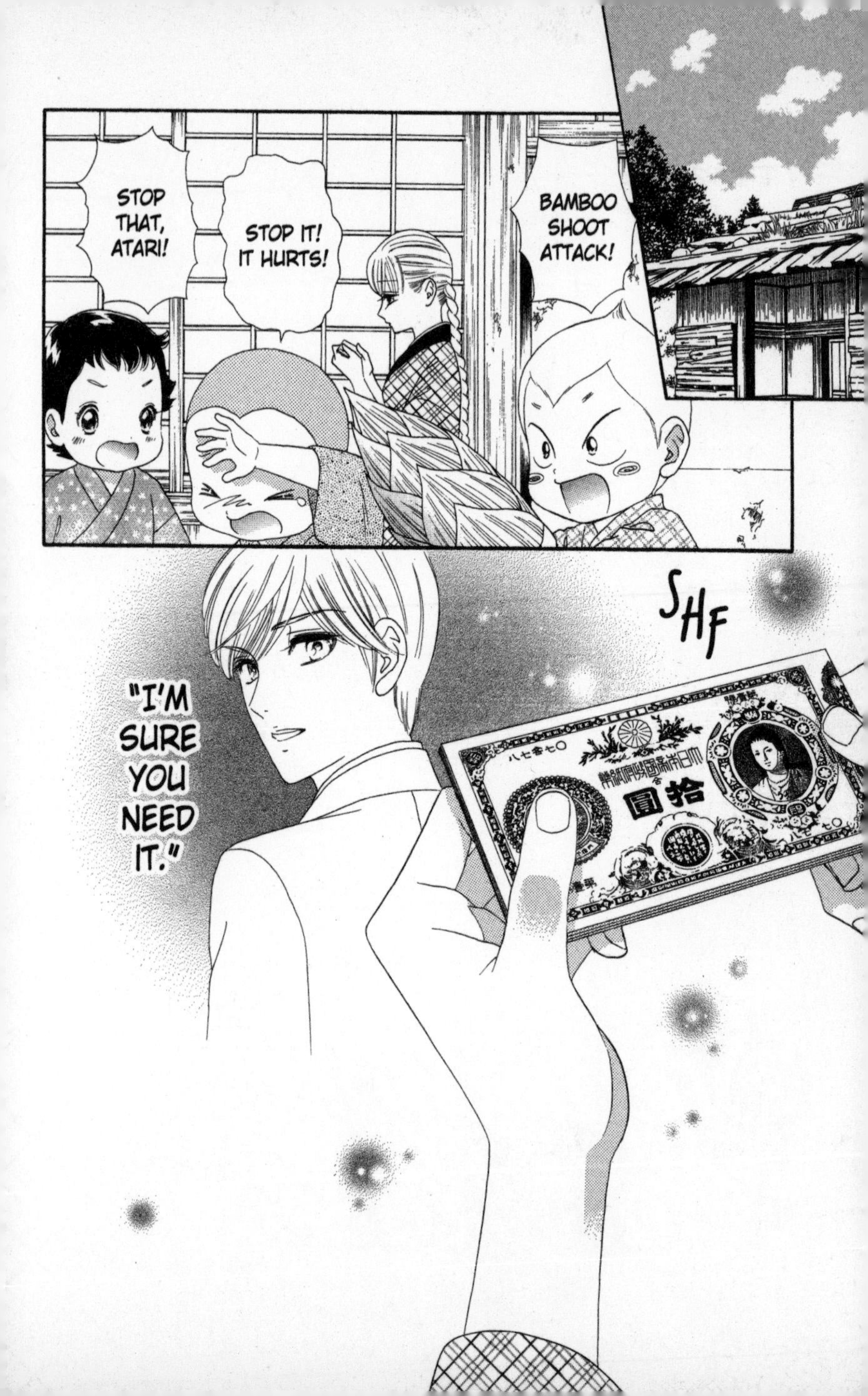
BAMBOO SHOOT ATTACK!
STOP IT! IT HURTS!
STOP THAT, ATARI!
SHF
"I'M SURE YOU NEED IT."

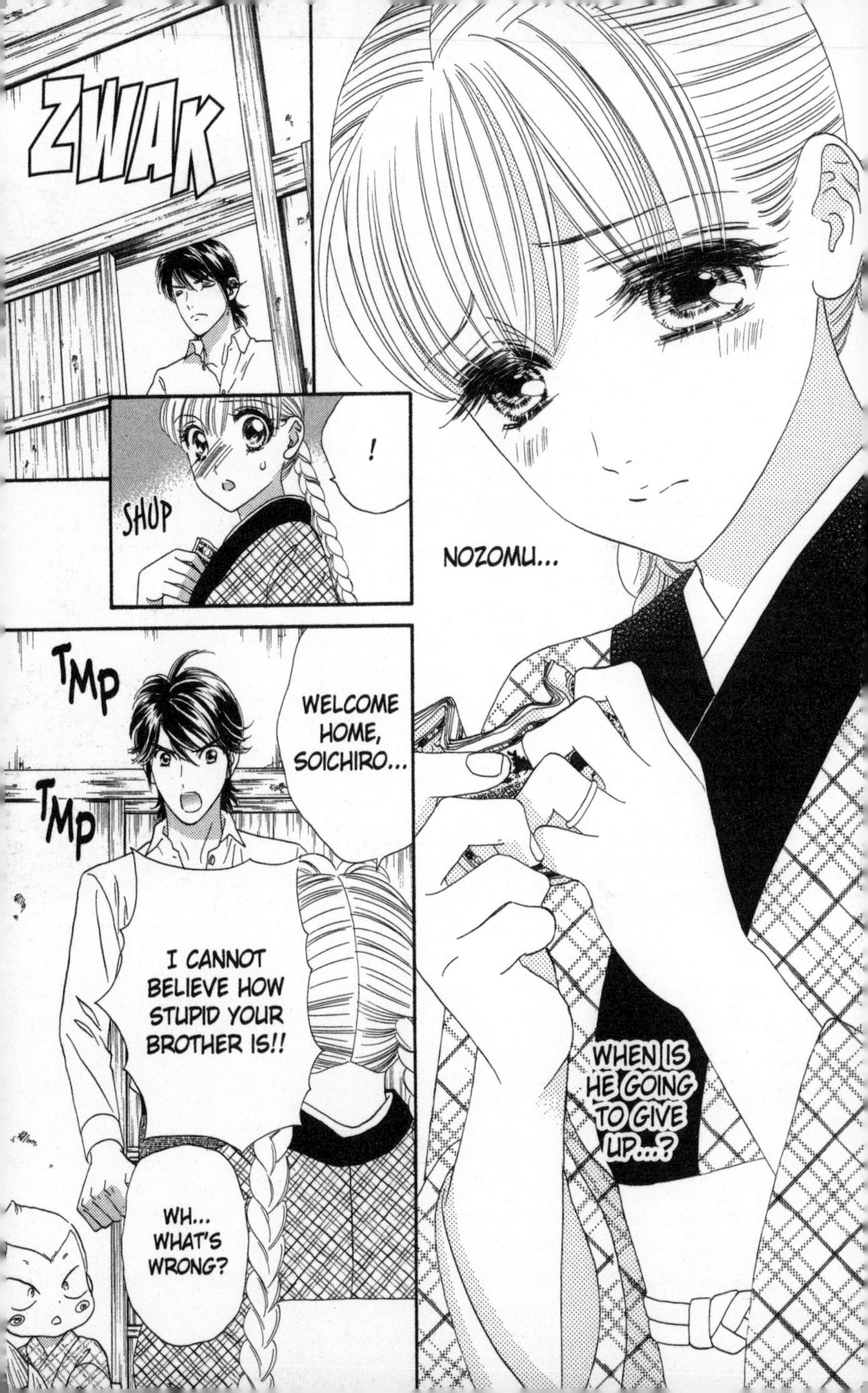
NOZOMU...
WHEN IS HE GOING TO GIVE UP...?
ZWAK
!
SHUP
WELCOME HOME, SOICHIRO...
TMP
TMP
I CANNOT BELIEVE HOW STUPID YOUR BROTHER IS!!
WH... WHAT'S WRONG?

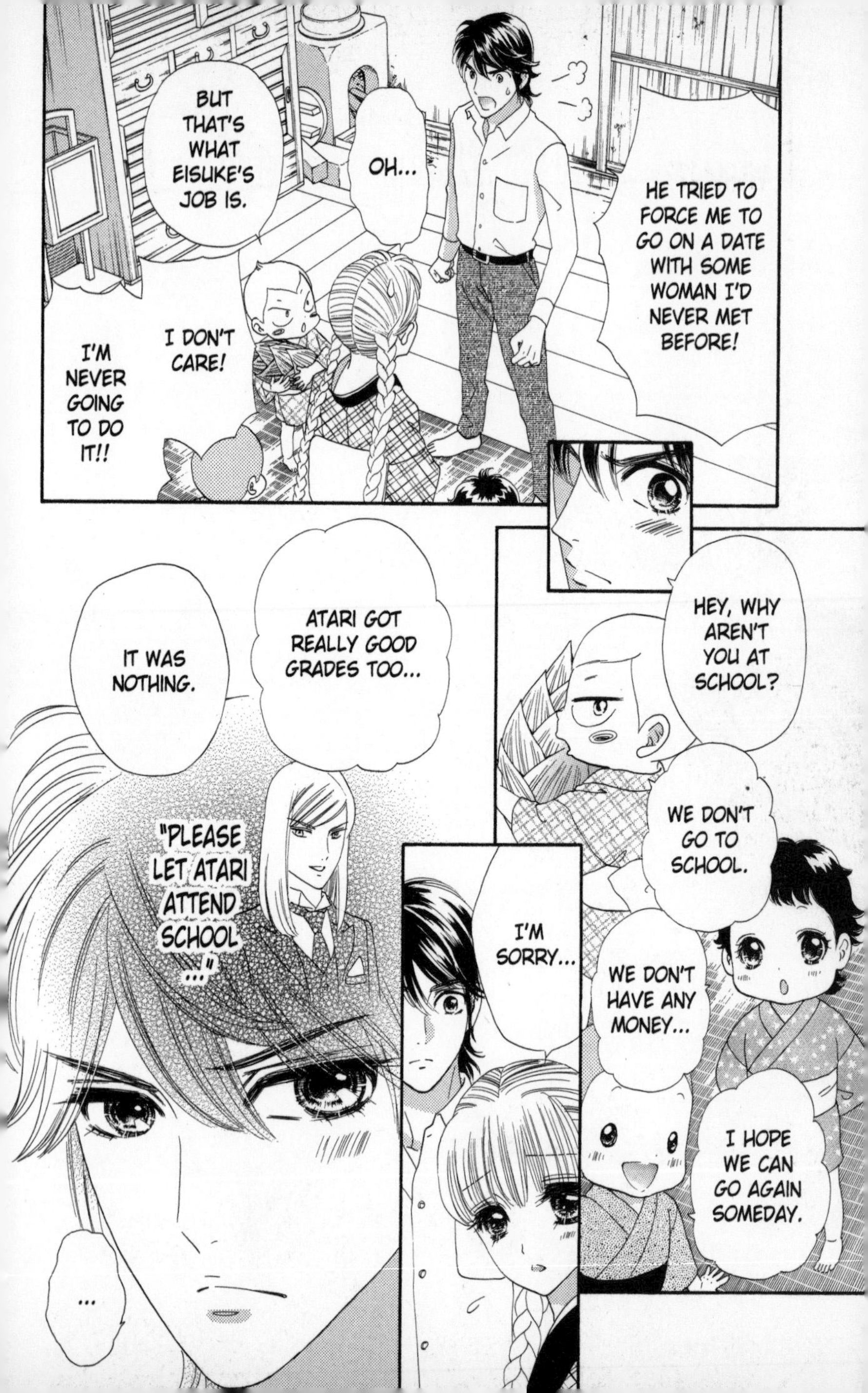
HE TRIED TO FORCE ME TO GO ON A DATE WITH SOME WOMAN I'D NEVER MET BEFORE!
OH...
BUT THAT'S WHAT EISUKE'S JOB IS.
I DON'T CARE!
I'M NEVER GOING TO DO IT!!
HEY, WHY AREN'T YOU AT SCHOOL?
WE DON'T GO TO SCHOOL.
WE DON'T HAVE ANY MONEY...
I HOPE WE CAN GO AGAIN SOMEDAY.
I'M SORRY...
ATARI GOT REALLY GOOD GRADES TOO...
IT WAS NOTHING.
"PLEASE LET ATARI ATTEND SCHOOL..."
...

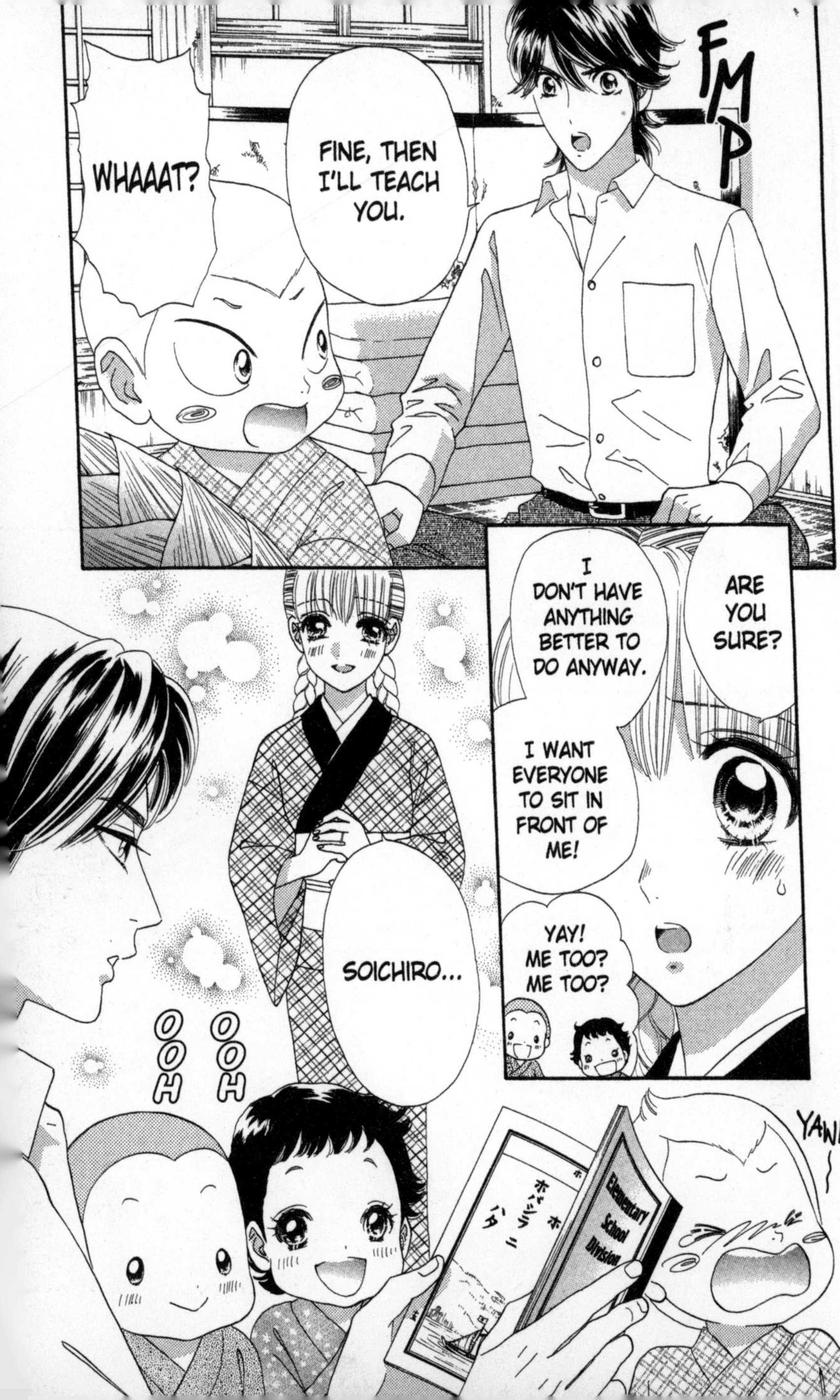
FMP
FINE, THEN I'LL TEACH YOU.
WHAAAT?
ARE YOU SURE?
I DON'T HAVE ANYTHING BETTER TO DO ANYWAY.
I WANT EVERYONE TO SIT IN FRONT OF ME!
YAY! ME TOO? ME TOO?
SOICHIRO...
OOH
OOH
YAWN
Elementary School Division
ホバシラ ニ ハタ

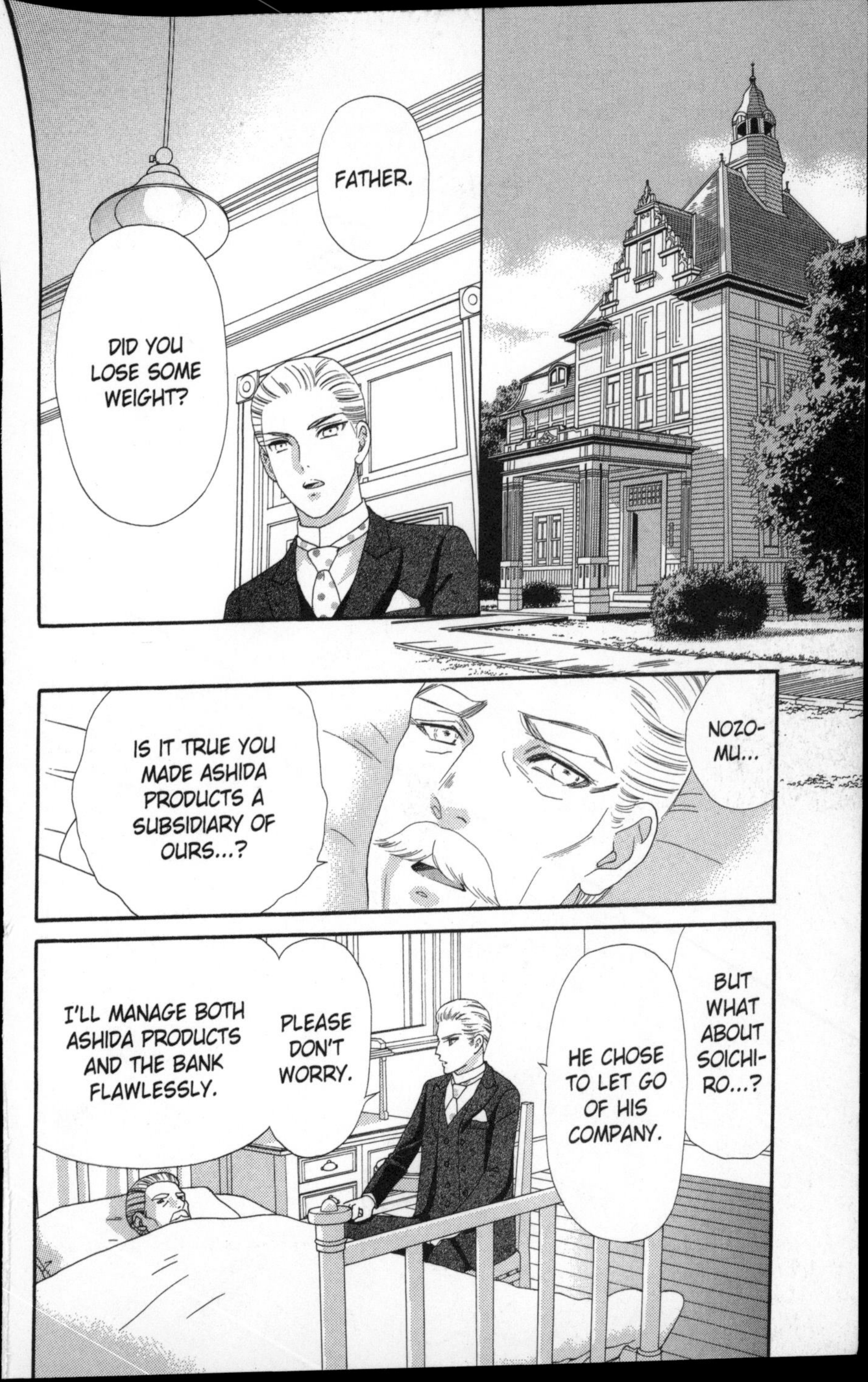
FATHER.
DID YOU LOSE SOME WEIGHT?
NOZO-MU...
IS IT TRUE YOU MADE ASHIDA PRODUCTS A SUBSIDIARY OF OURS...?
BUT WHAT ABOUT SOICHI-RO...?
HE CHOSE TO LET GO OF HIS COMPANY.
PLEASE DON'T WORRY.
I'LL MANAGE BOTH ASHIDA PRODUCTS AND THE BANK FLAWLESSLY.

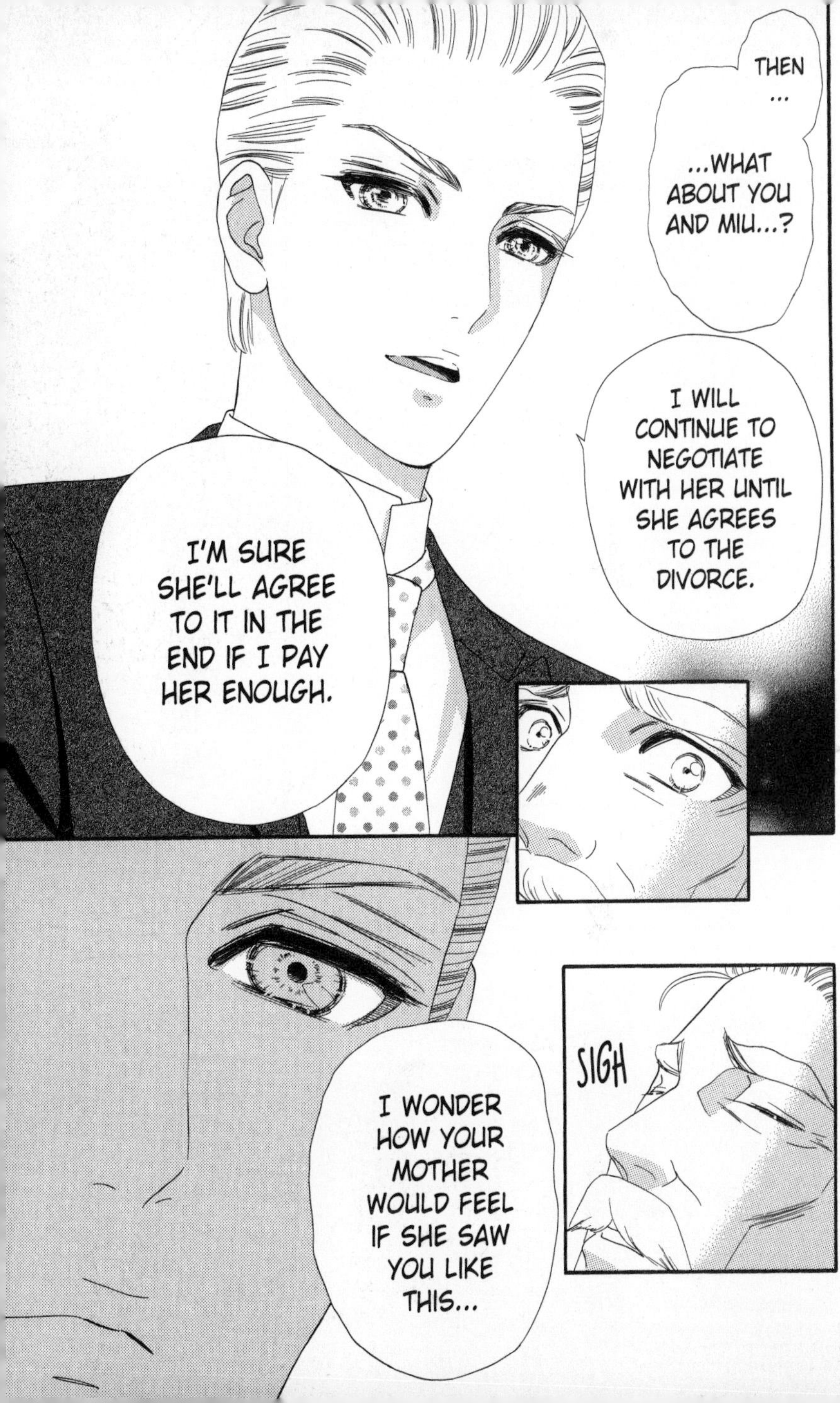
THEN ...
...WHAT ABOUT YOU AND MIU...?
I WILL CONTINUE TO NEGOTIATE WITH HER UNTIL SHE AGREES TO THE DIVORCE.
I'M SURE SHE'LL AGREE TO IT IN THE END IF I PAY HER ENOUGH.
SIGH
I WONDER HOW YOUR MOTHER WOULD FEEL IF SHE SAW YOU LIKE THIS...

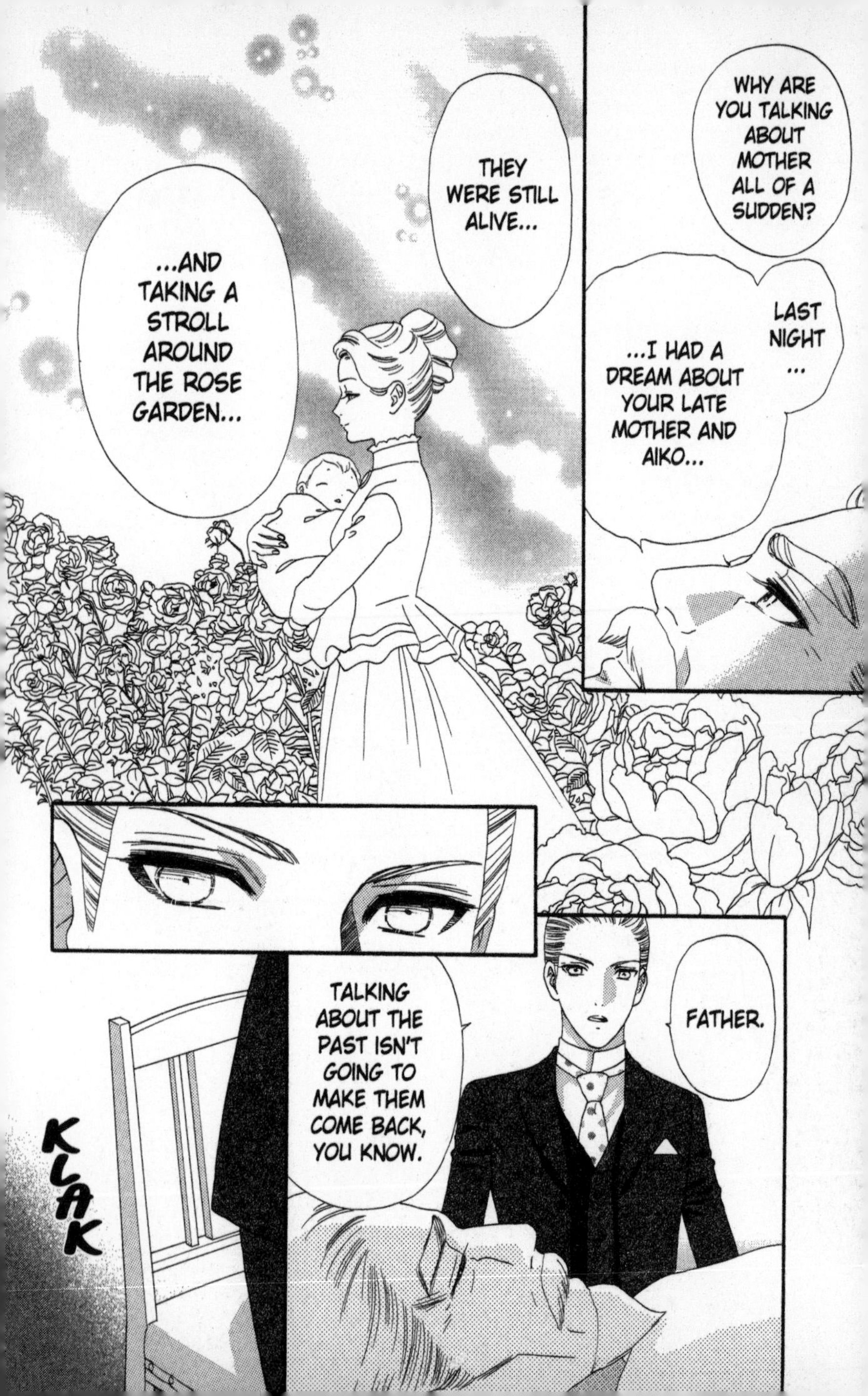
WHY ARE YOU TALKING ABOUT MOTHER ALL OF A SUDDEN?
LAST NIGHT ...
...I HAD A DREAM ABOUT YOUR LATE MOTHER AND AIKO...
THEY WERE STILL ALIVE...
...AND TAKING A STROLL AROUND THE ROSE GARDEN...
FATHER.
TALKING ABOUT THE PAST ISN'T GOING TO MAKE THEM COME BACK, YOU KNOW.
KLAK

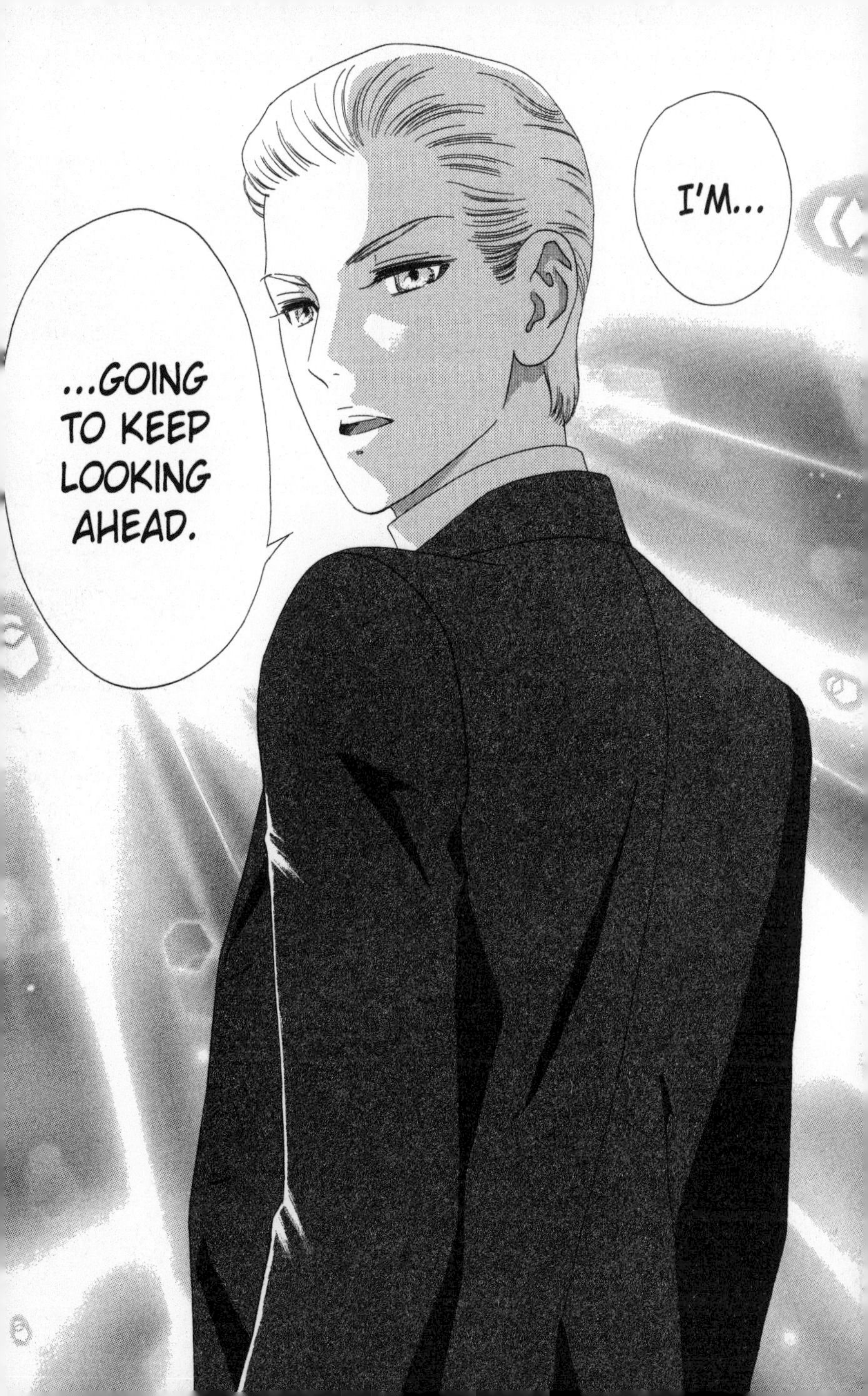
I'M...
...GOING TO KEEP LOOKING AHEAD.

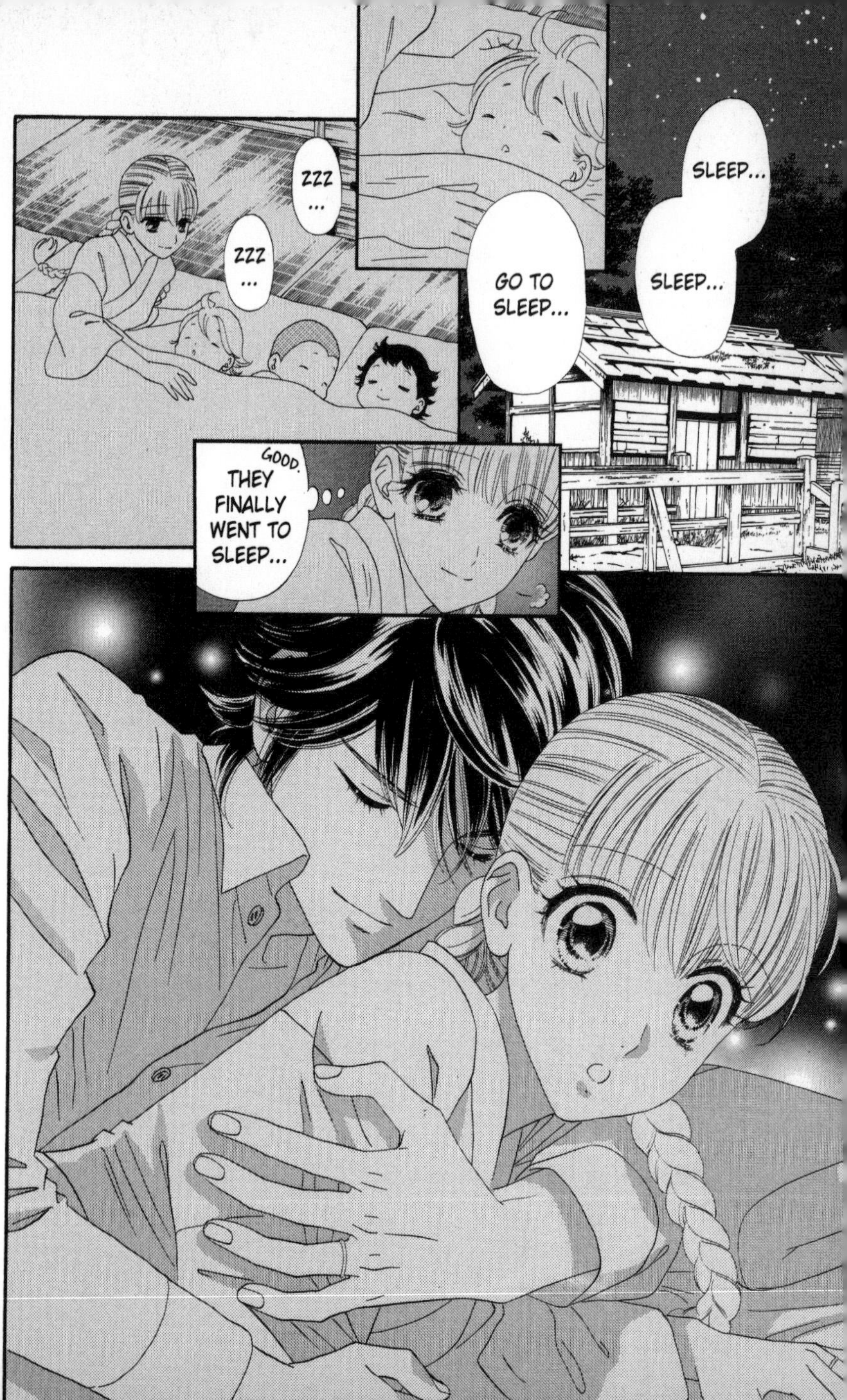
SLEEP...
SLEEP...
GO TO SLEEP...
ZZZ ...
ZZZ ...
GOOD. THEY FINALLY WENT TO SLEEP...

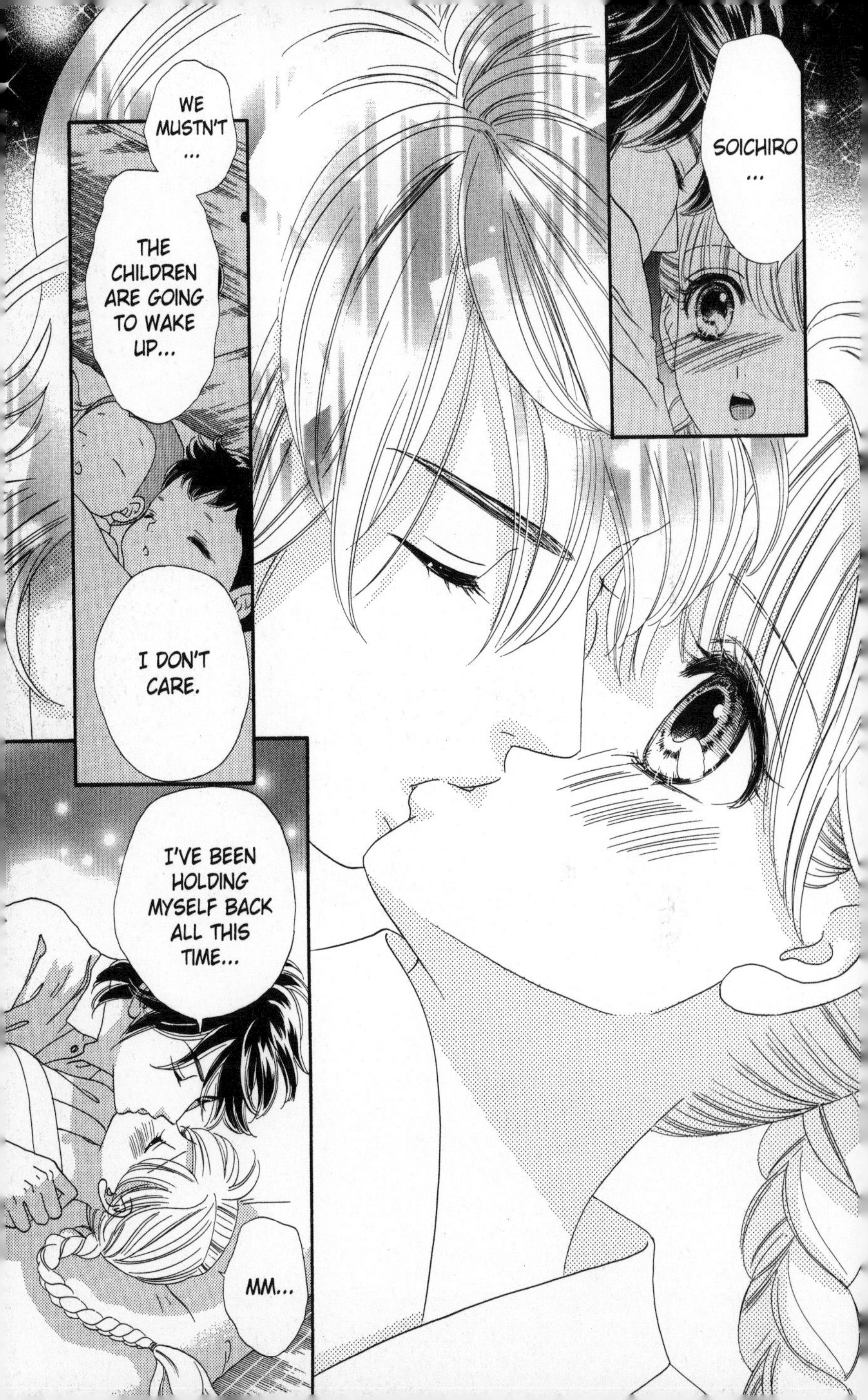
SOICHIRO ...
WE MUSTN'T ...
THE CHILDREN ARE GOING TO WAKE UP...
I DON'T CARE.
I'VE BEEN HOLDING MYSELF BACK ALL THIS TIME...
MM...

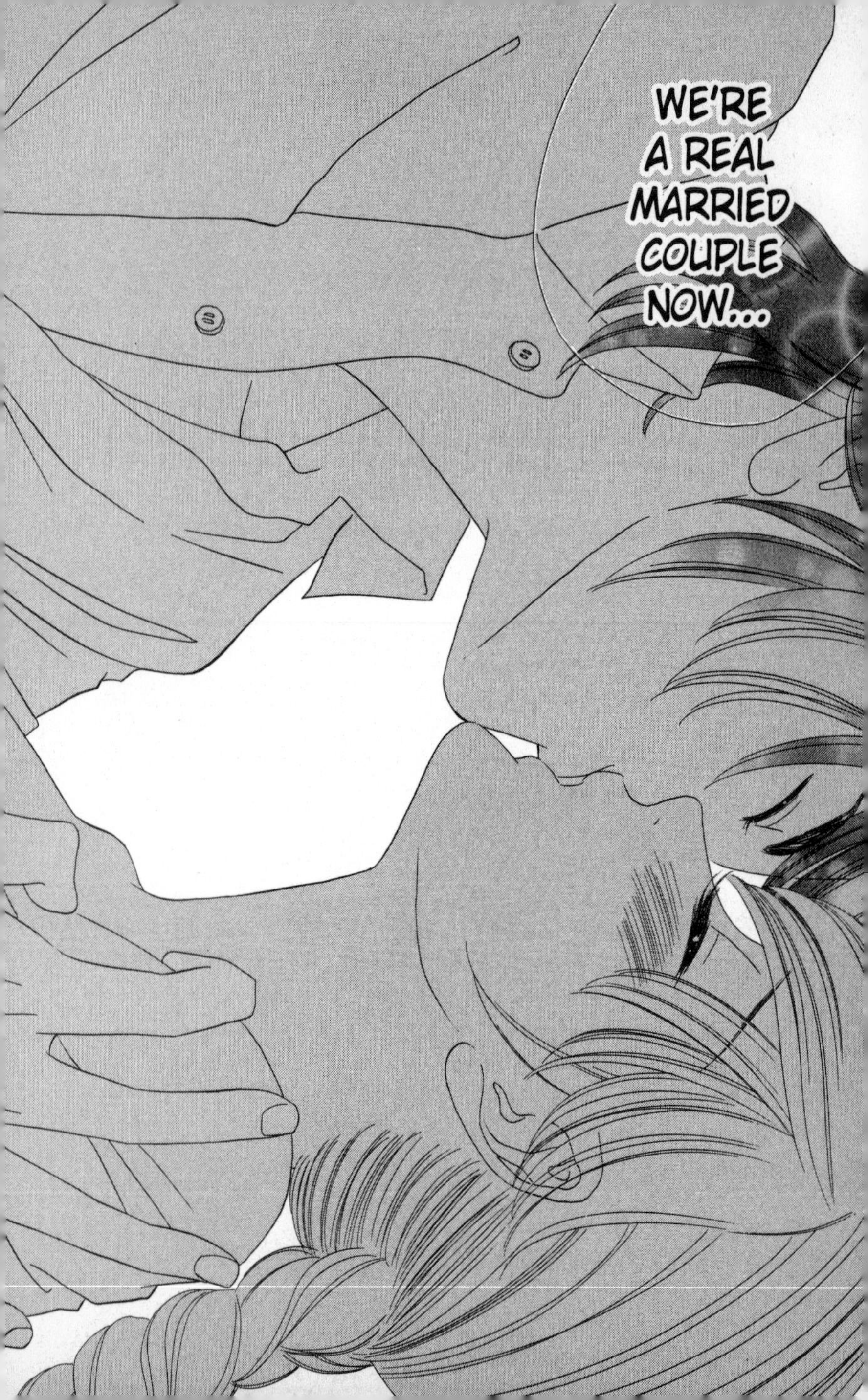
WE'RE A REAL MARRIED COUPLE NOW...

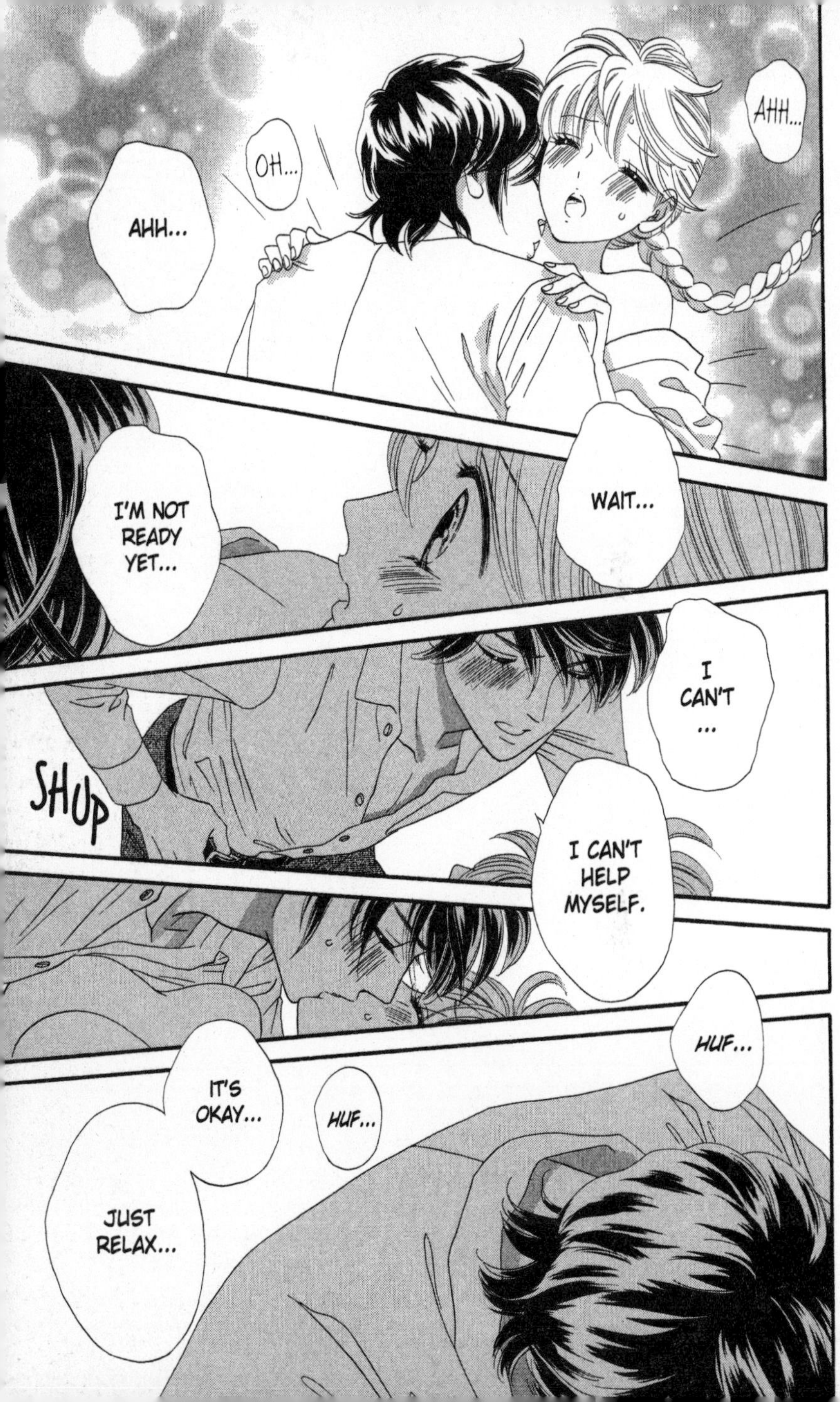
AHH...
OH...
AHH...
WAIT...
I'M NOT READY YET...
I CAN'T ...
SHUP
I CAN'T HELP MYSELF.
HUF...
HUF...
IT'S OKAY...
JUST RELAX...

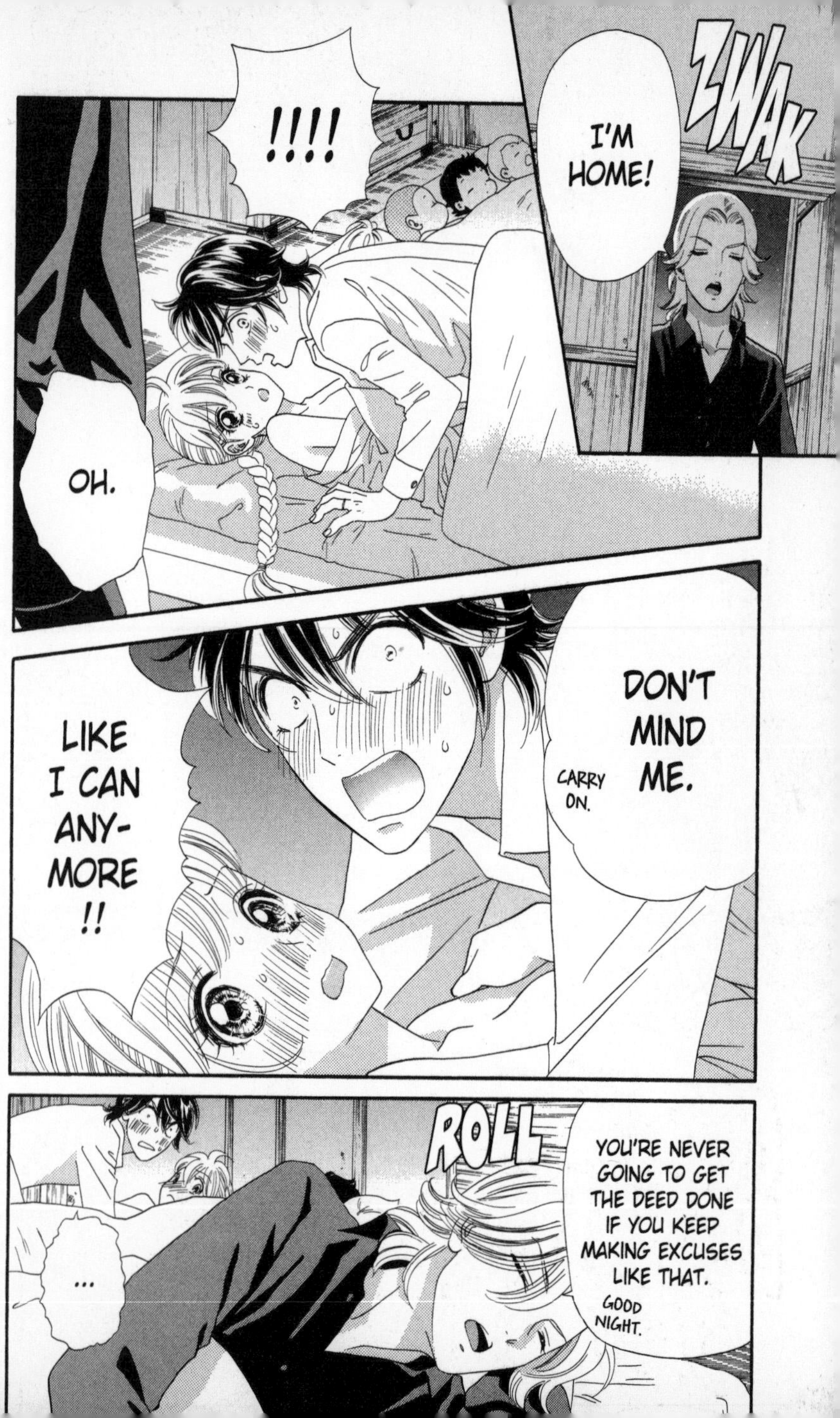
ZWAK
I'M HOME!
!!!!
OH.
DON'T MIND ME.
CARRY ON.
LIKE I CAN ANY-MORE!!
ROLL
YOU'RE NEVER GOING TO GET THE DEED DONE IF YOU KEEP MAKING EXCUSES LIKE THAT.
GOOD NIGHT.
...

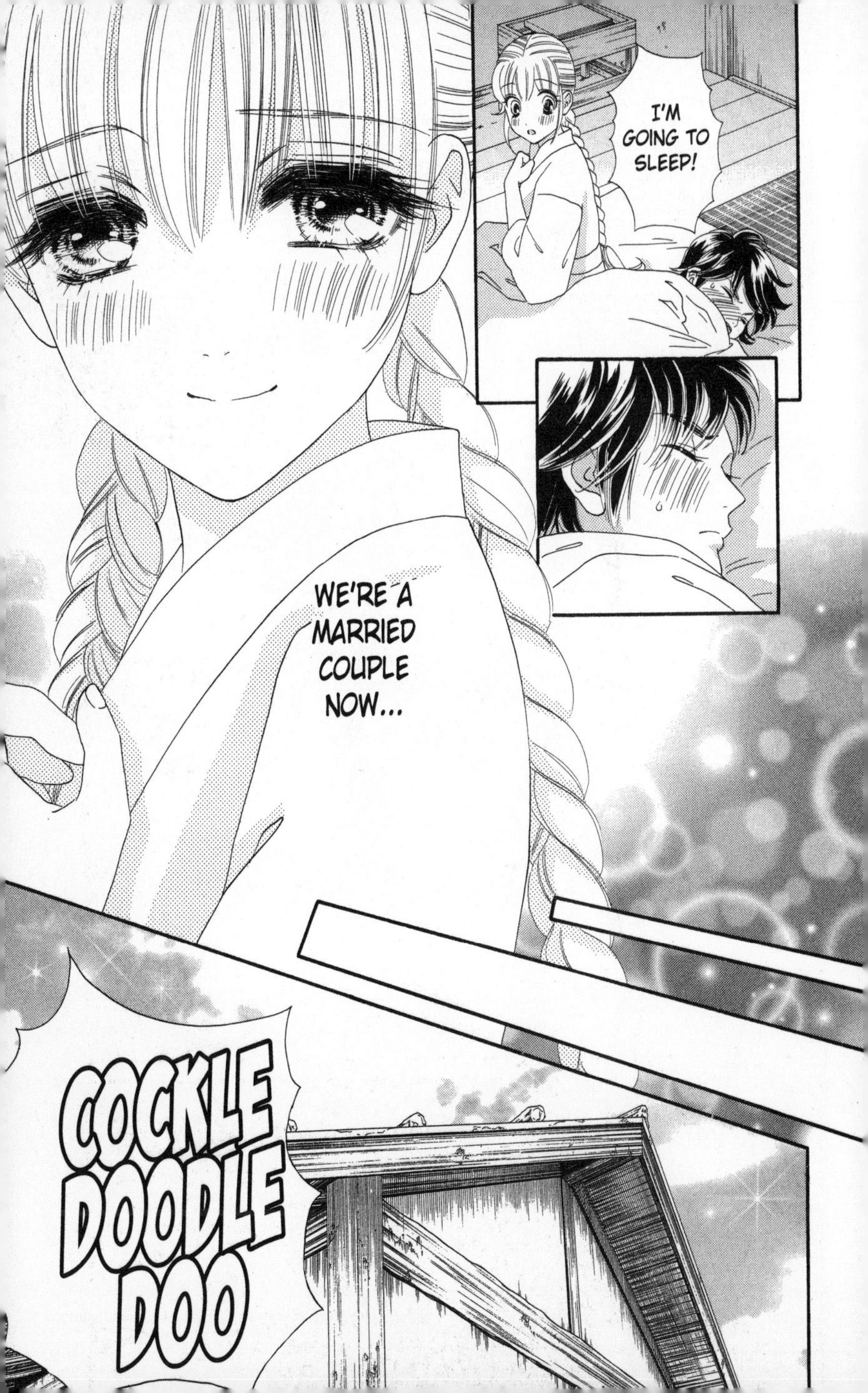
I'M GOING TO SLEEP!
WE'RE A MARRIED COUPLE NOW...
COCKLE DOODLE DOO

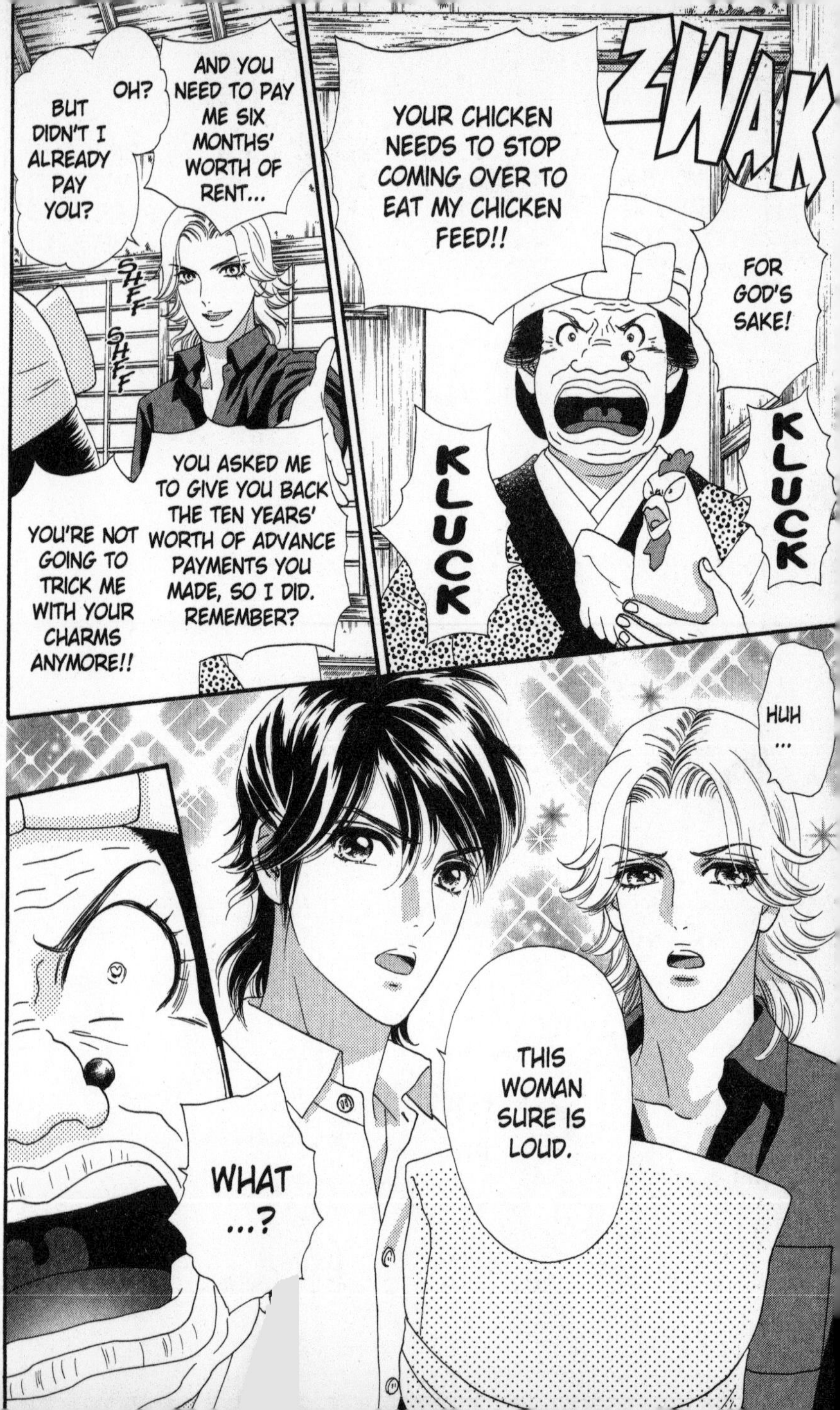
ZWAK
YOUR CHICKEN NEEDS TO STOP COMING OVER TO EAT MY CHICKEN FEED!!
FOR GOD'S SAKE!
KLUCK
KLUCK
AND YOU NEED TO PAY ME SIX MONTHS' WORTH OF RENT...
OH? BUT DIDN'T I ALREADY PAY YOU?
SHFF SHFF
YOU ASKED ME TO GIVE YOU BACK THE TEN YEARS' WORTH OF ADVANCE PAYMENTS YOU MADE, SO I DID. REMEMBER?
YOU'RE NOT GOING TO TRICK ME WITH YOUR CHARMS ANYMORE!!
HUH ...
THIS WOMAN SURE IS LOUD.
WHAT ...?

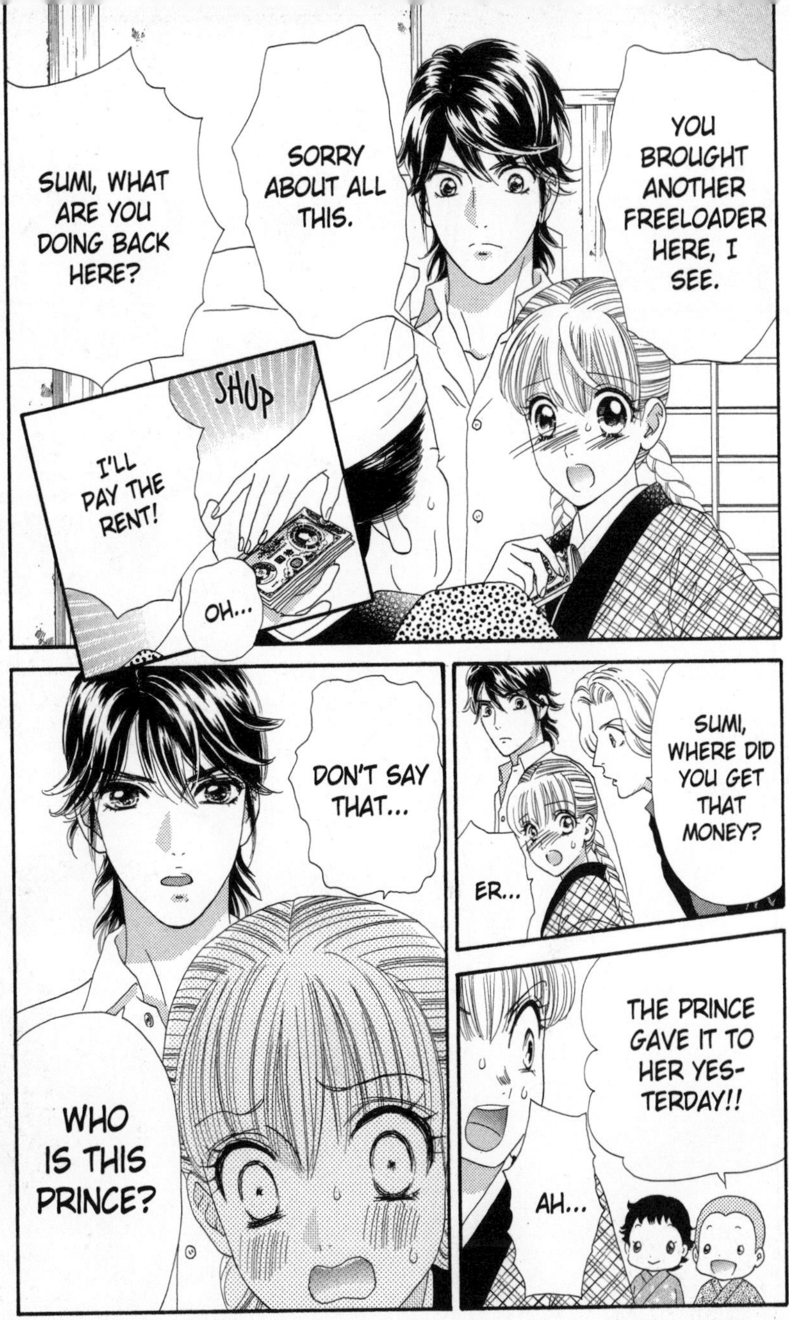
YOU BROUGHT ANOTHER FREELOADER HERE, I SEE.
SORRY ABOUT ALL THIS.
SUMI, WHAT ARE YOU DOING BACK HERE?
SHUP
I'LL PAY THE RENT!
OH...
SUMI, WHERE DID YOU GET THAT MONEY?
ER...
THE PRINCE GAVE IT TO HER YES-TERDAY!!
AH...
DON'T SAY THAT...
WHO IS THIS PRINCE?

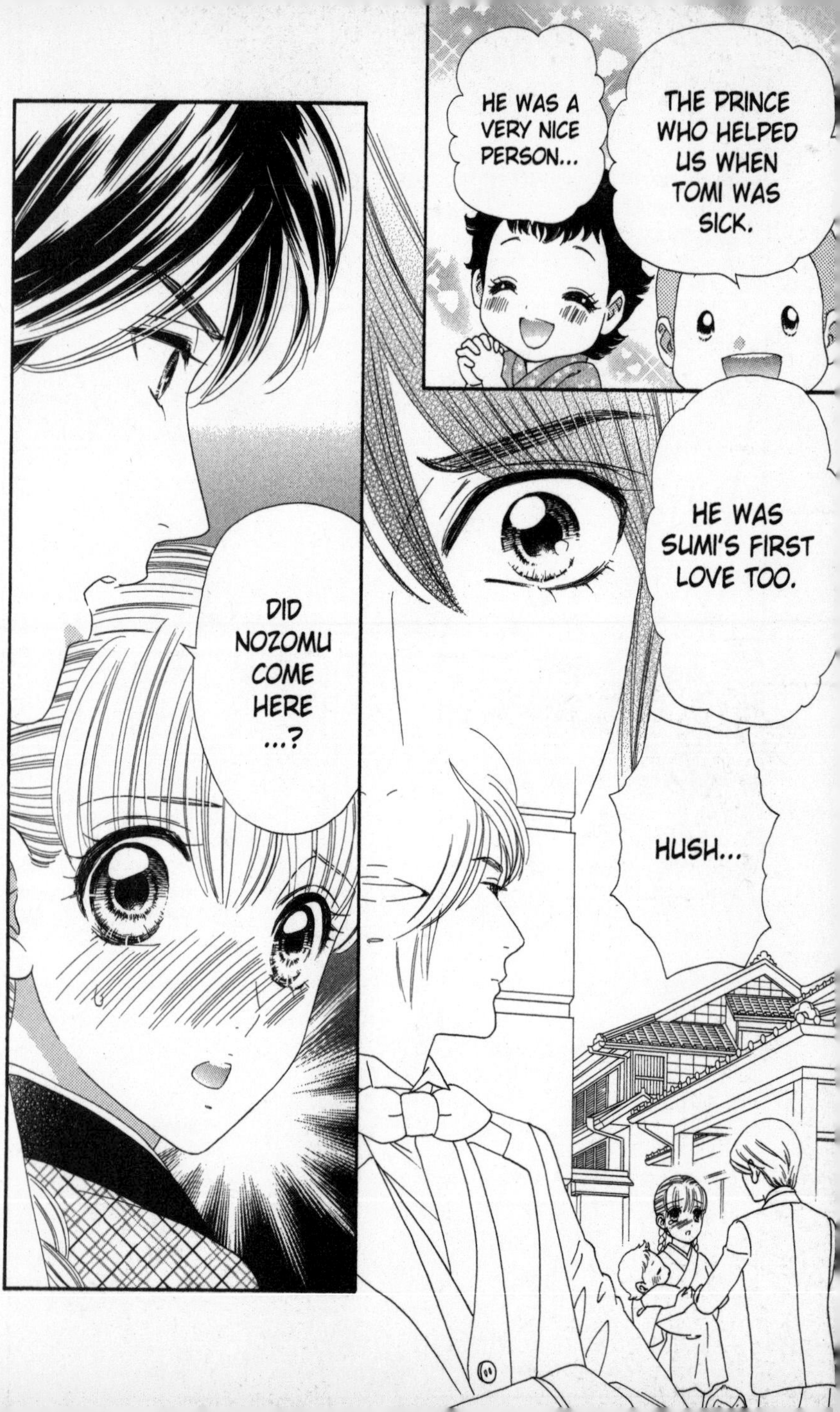
THE PRINCE WHO HELPED US WHEN TOMI WAS SICK.
HE WAS A VERY NICE PERSON...
HE WAS SUMI'S FIRST LOVE TOO.
HUSH...
DID NOZOMU COME HERE ...?

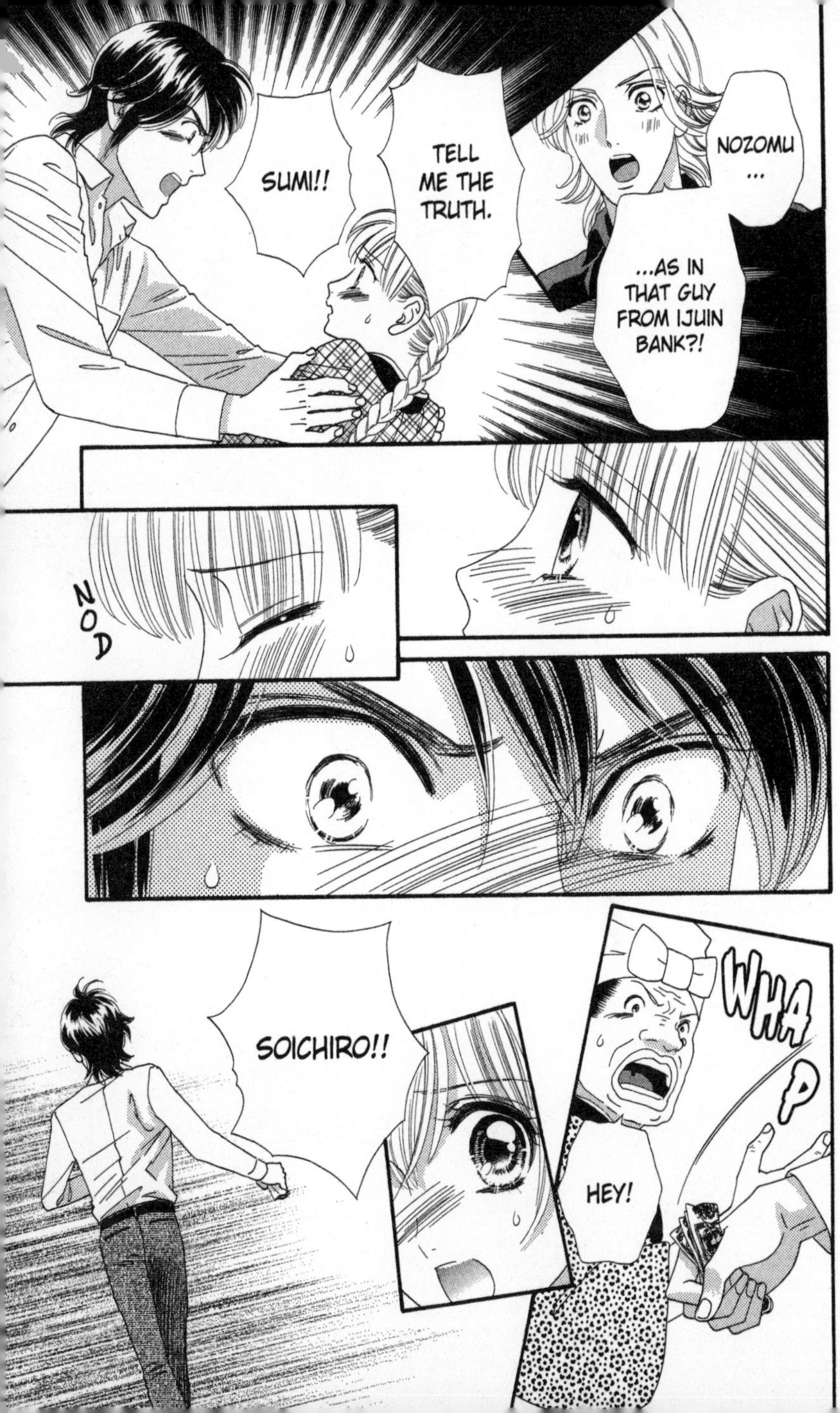
NOZOMU ...
...AS IN THAT GUY FROM IJUIN BANK?!
TELL ME THE TRUTH.
SUMI!!
NOD
WHAP
HEY!
SOICHIRO!!

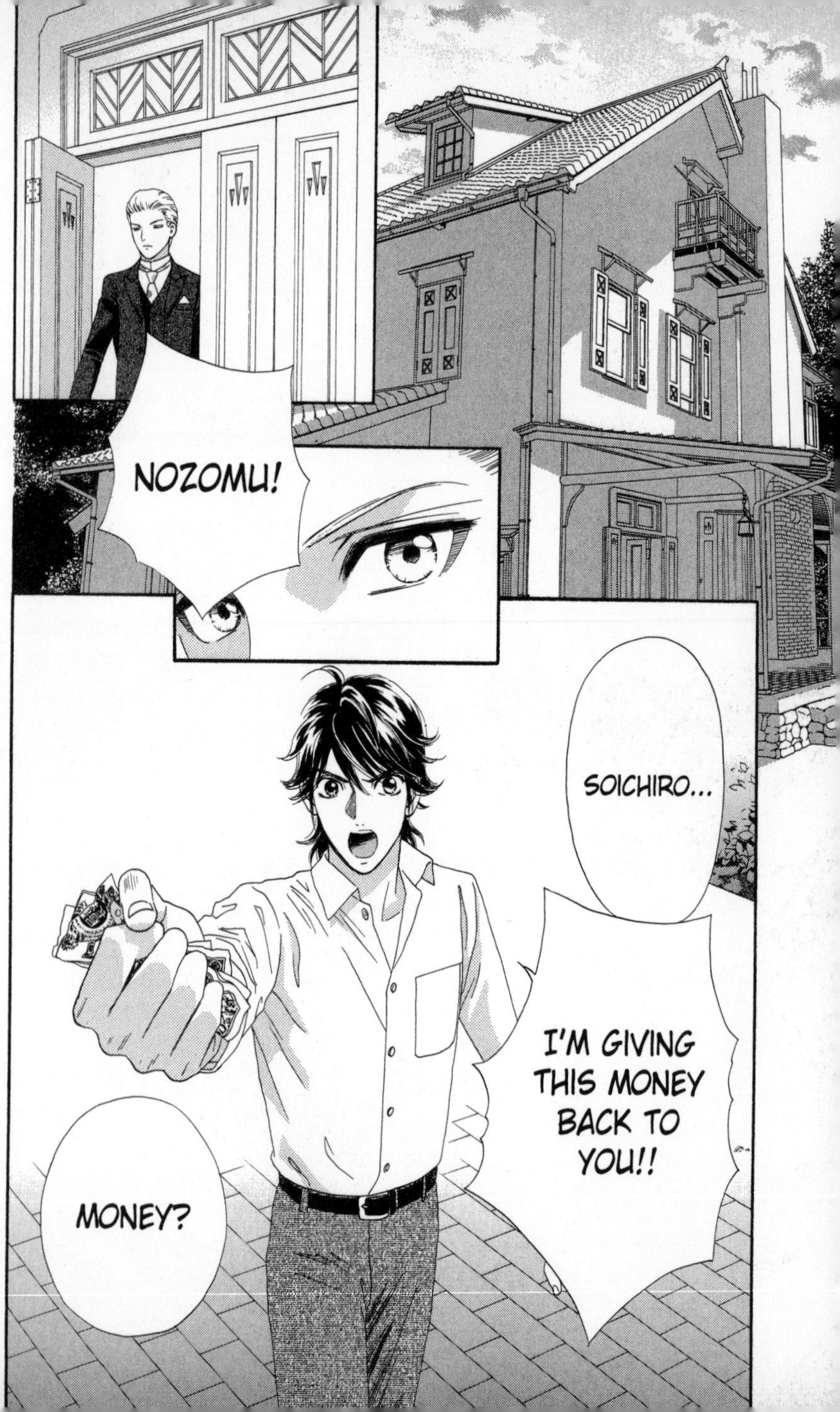
NOZOMU!
SOICHIRO...
I'M GIVING THIS MONEY BACK TO YOU!!
MONEY?

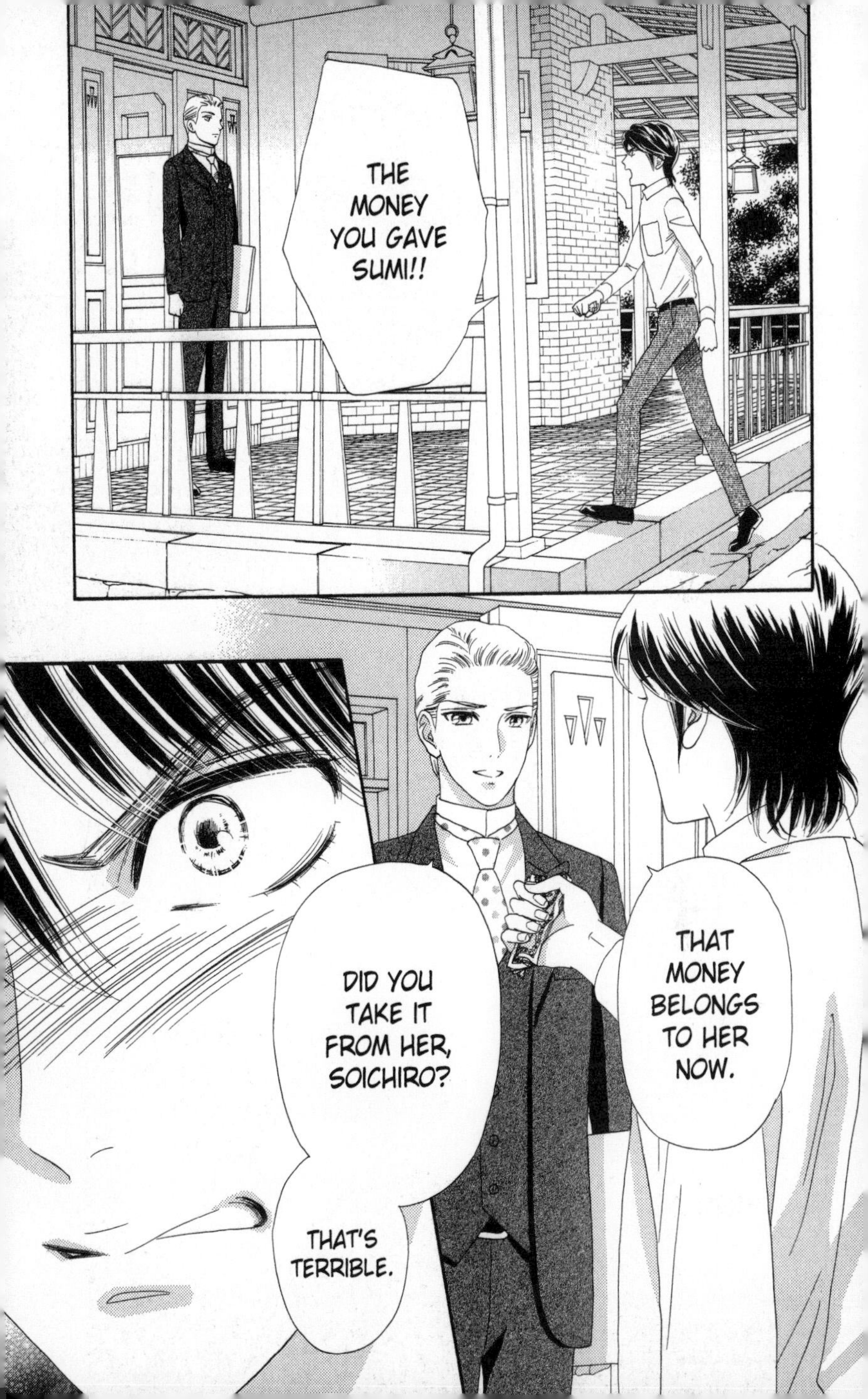
THE MONEY YOU GAVE SUMI!!
THAT MONEY BELONGS TO HER NOW.
DID YOU TAKE IT FROM HER, SOICHIRO?
THAT'S TERRIBLE.

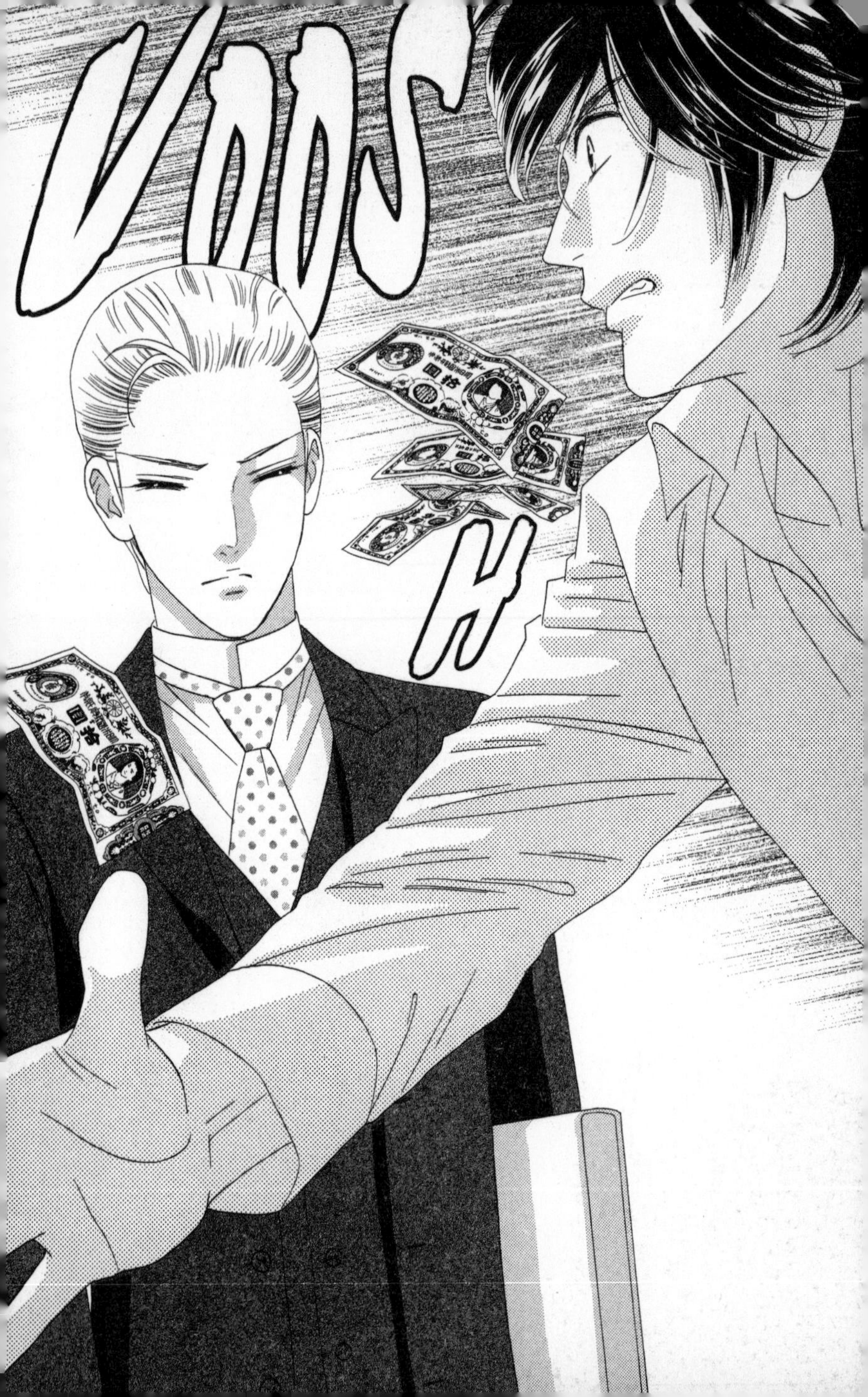
VOOSH

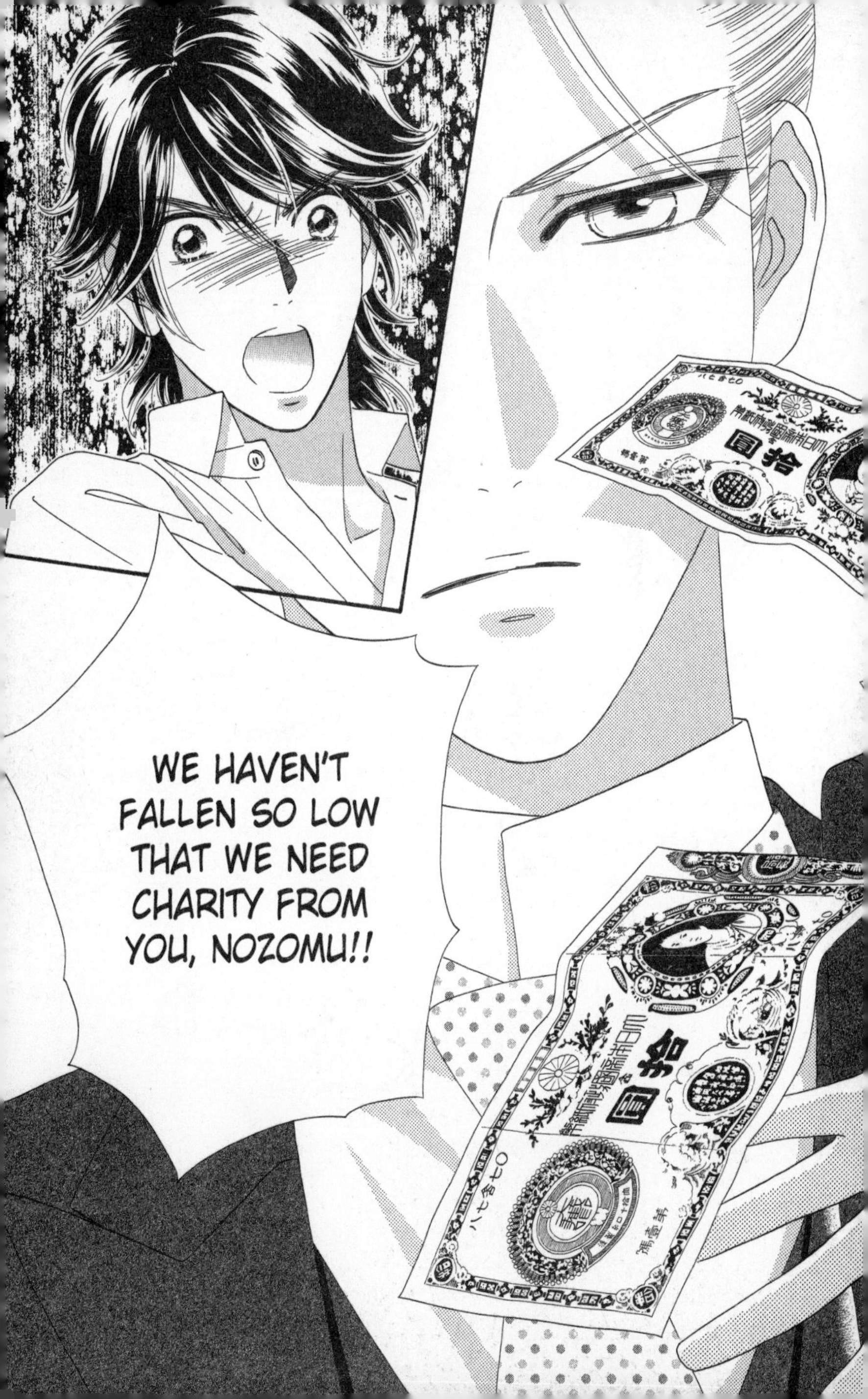
WE HAVEN'T FALLEN SO LOW THAT WE NEED CHARITY FROM YOU, NOZOMU!!

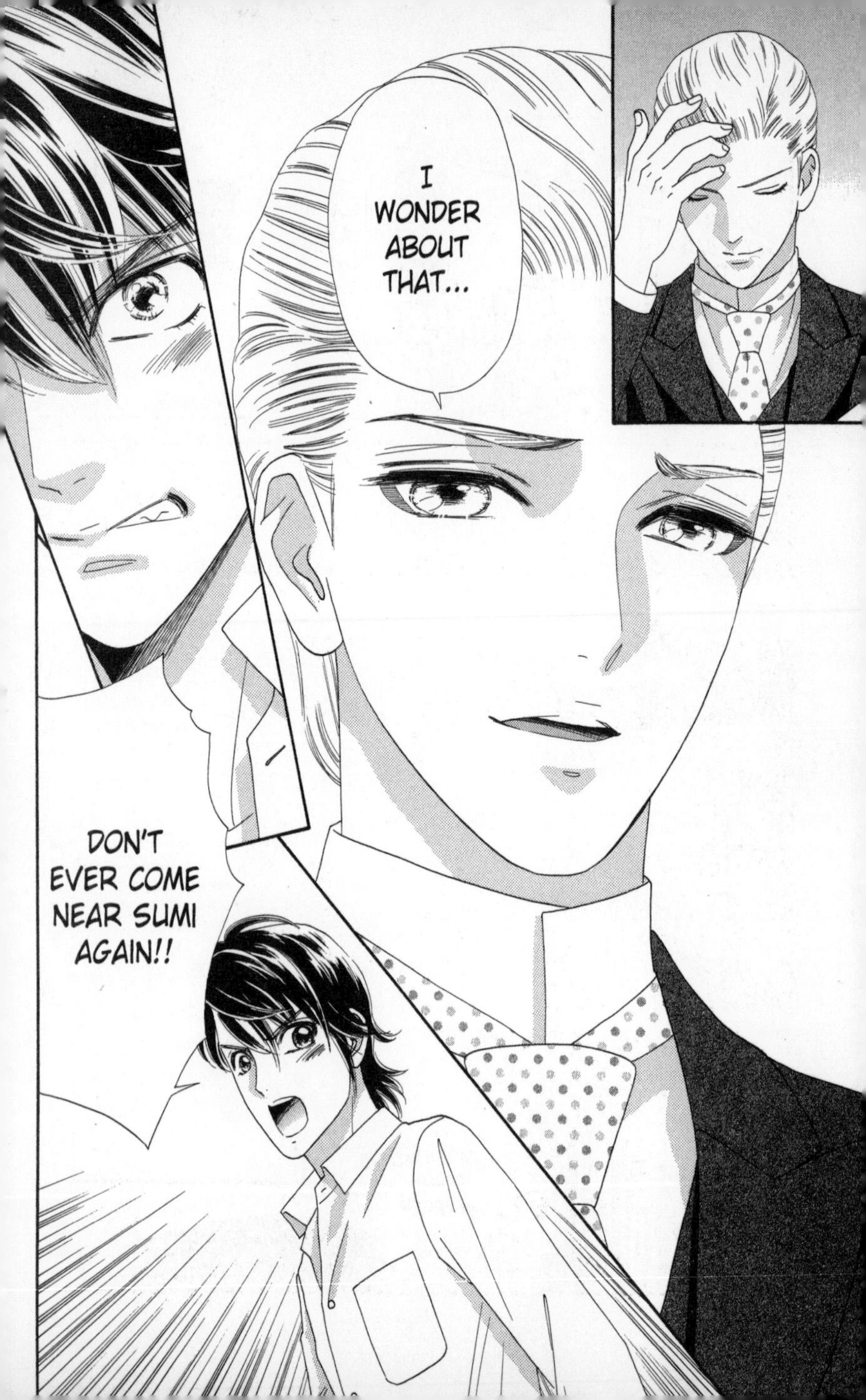
I WONDER ABOUT THAT...
DON'T EVER COME NEAR SUMI AGAIN!!

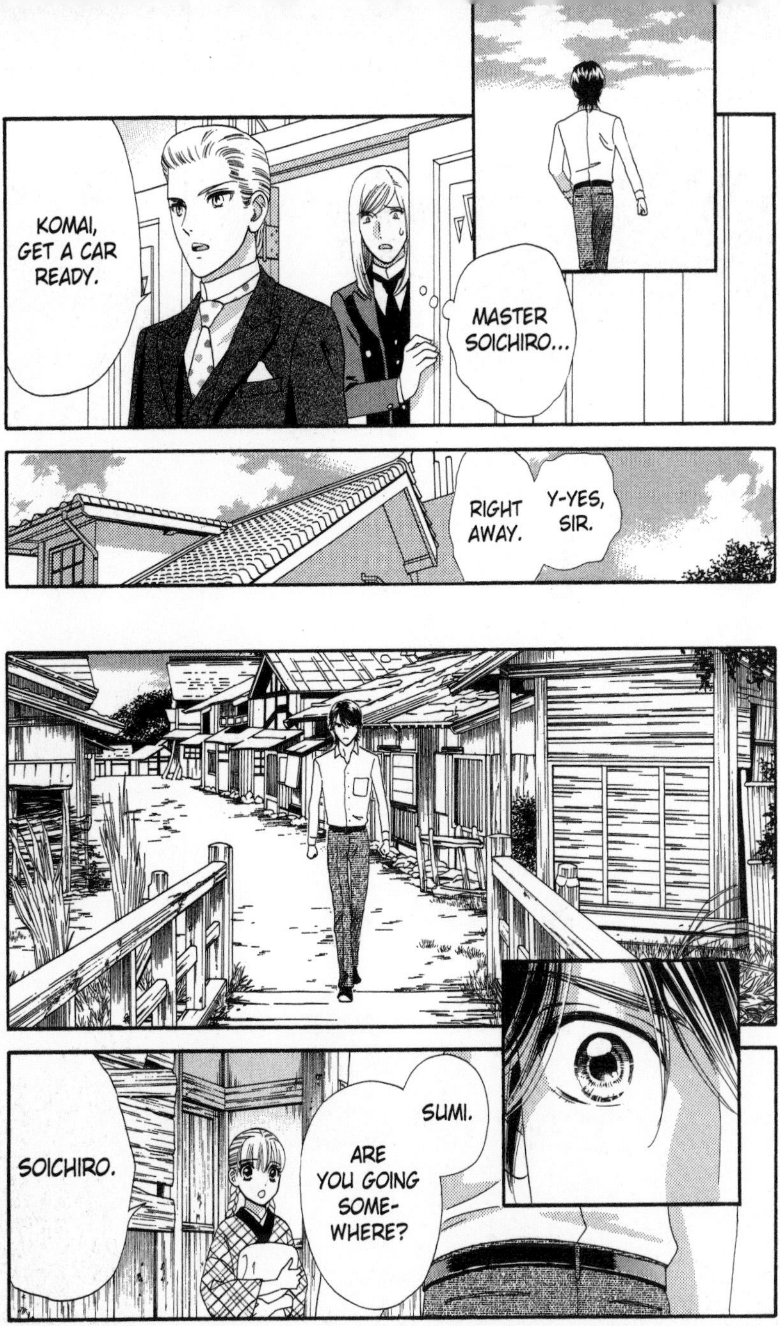
MASTER SOICHIRO...
KOMAI, GET A CAR READY.
Y-YES, SIR.
RIGHT AWAY.
SUMI.
ARE YOU GOING SOME-WHERE?
SOICHIRO.

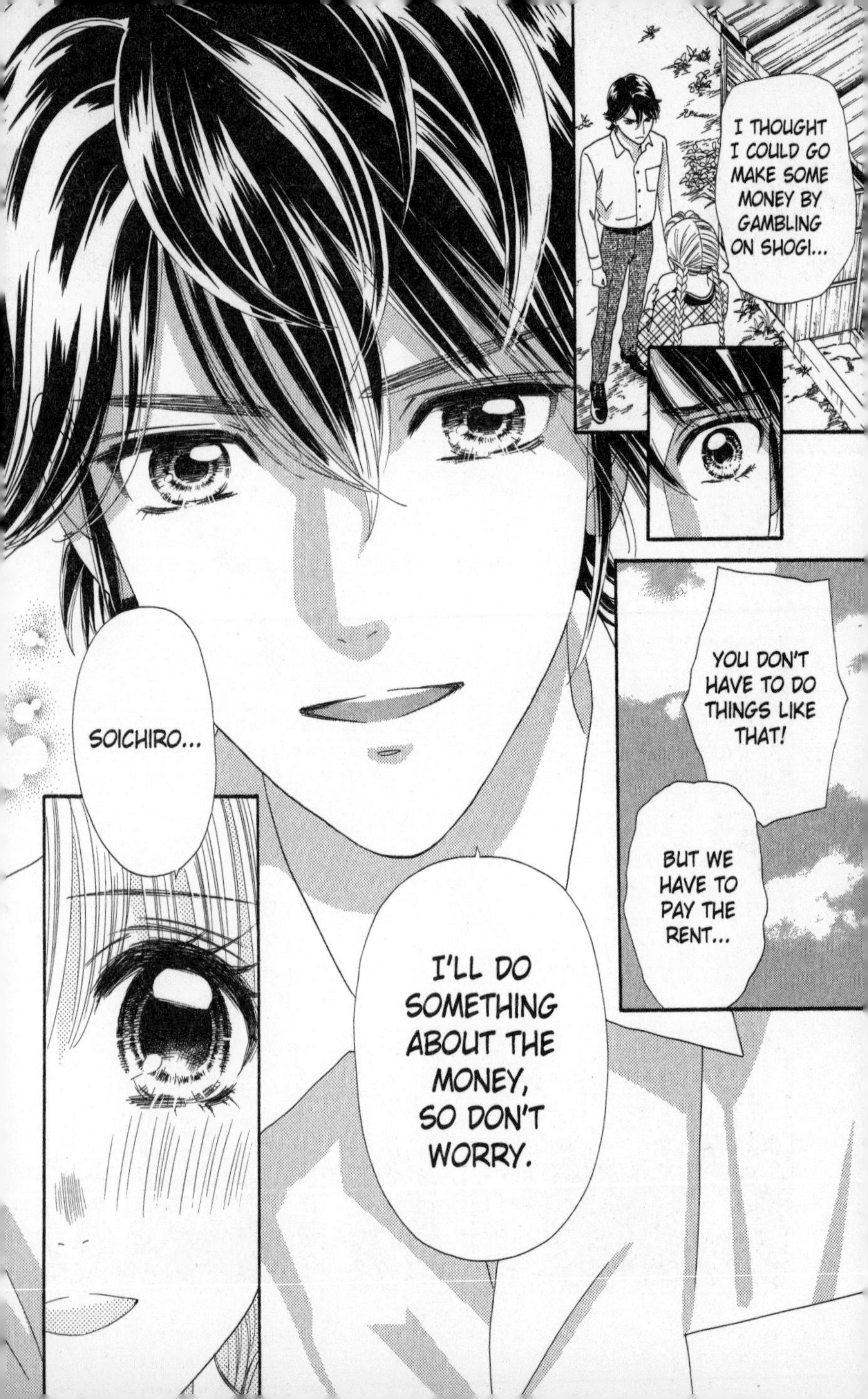
I THOUGHT I COULD GO MAKE SOME MONEY BY GAMBLING ON SHOGI...
YOU DON'T HAVE TO DO THINGS LIKE THAT!
BUT WE HAVE TO PAY THE RENT...
I'LL DO SOMETHING ABOUT THE MONEY, SO DON'T WORRY.
SOICHIRO...

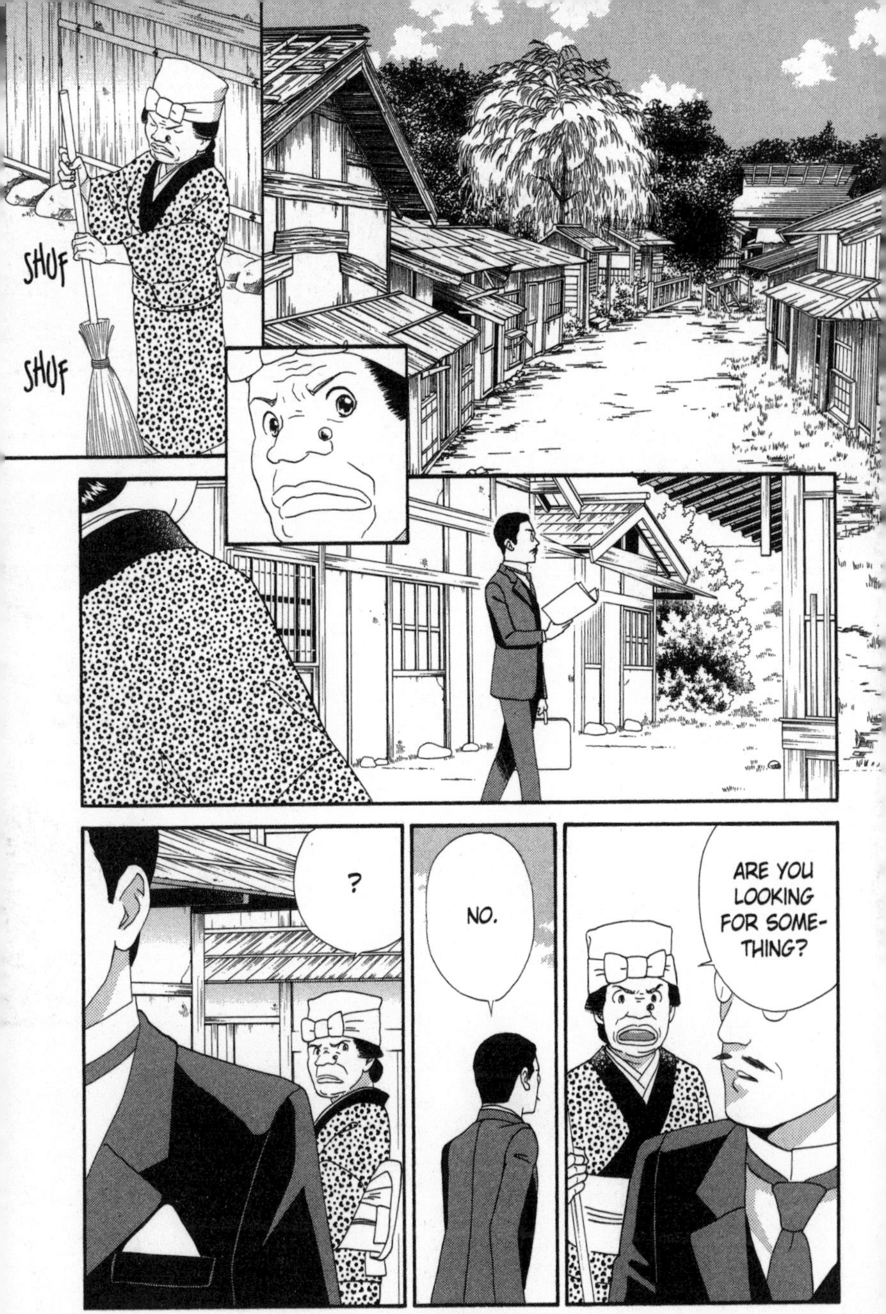
SHUF
SHUF
ARE YOU LOOKING FOR SOME-THING?
NO.
?

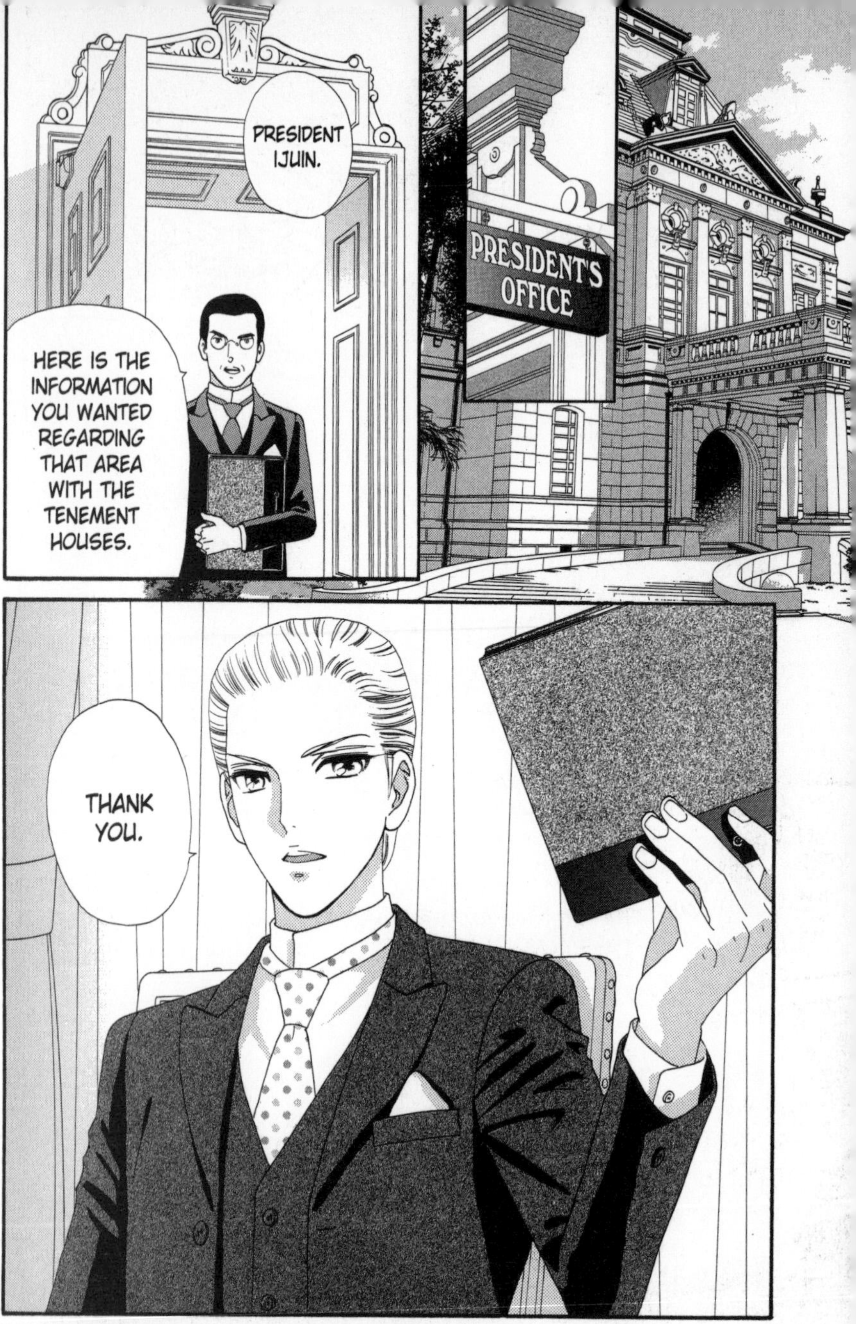
PRESIDENT'S OFFICE
PRESIDENT IJUIN.
HERE IS THE INFORMATION YOU WANTED REGARDING THAT AREA WITH THE TENEMENT HOUSES.
THANK YOU.

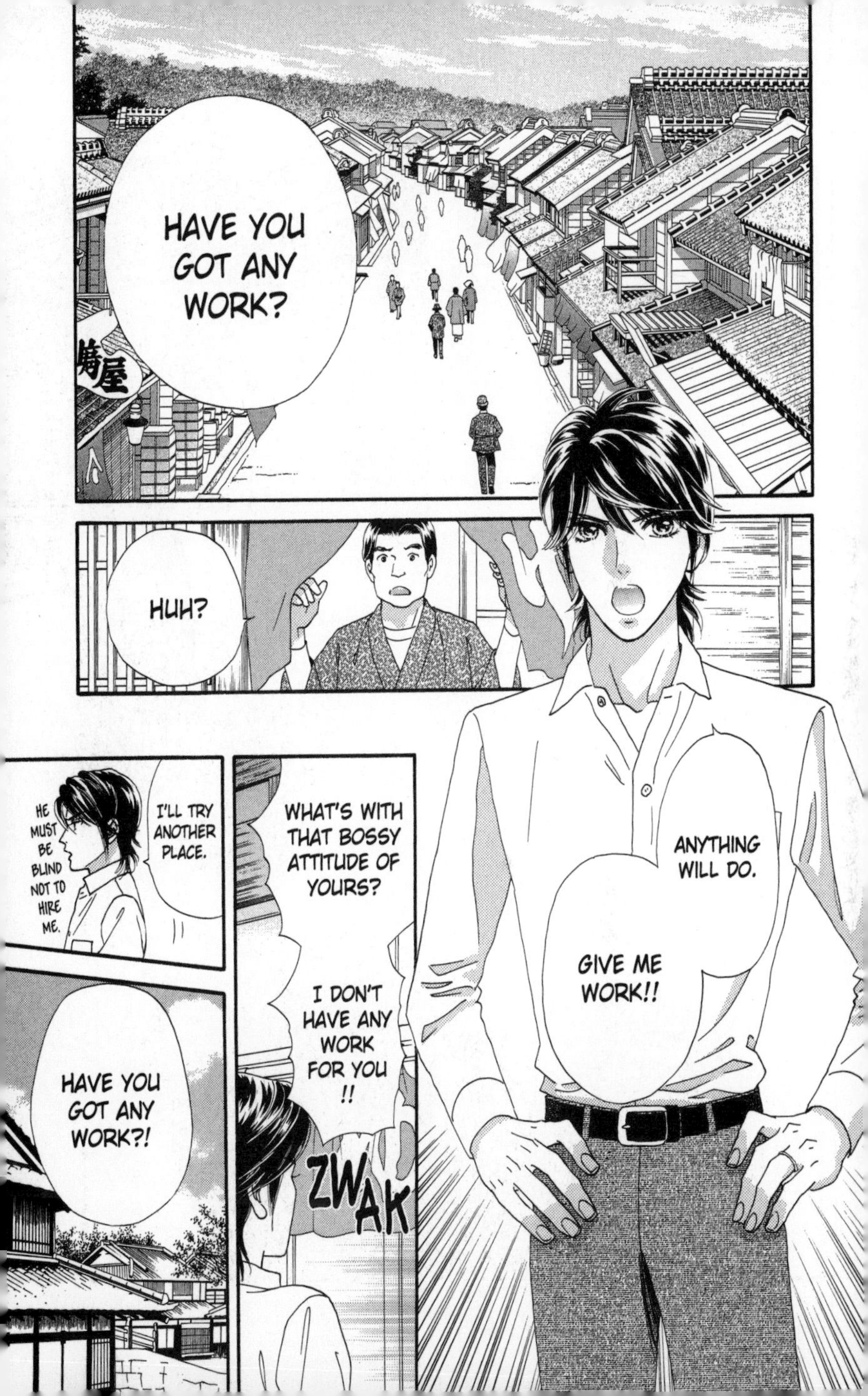
HAVE YOU GOT ANY WORK?
HUH?
ANYTHING WILL DO.
GIVE ME WORK!!
WHAT'S WITH THAT BOSSY ATTITUDE OF YOURS?
I DON'T HAVE ANY WORK FOR YOU!!
ZWAK
I'LL TRY ANOTHER PLACE.
HE MUST BE BLIND NOT TO HIRE ME.
HAVE YOU GOT ANY WORK?!

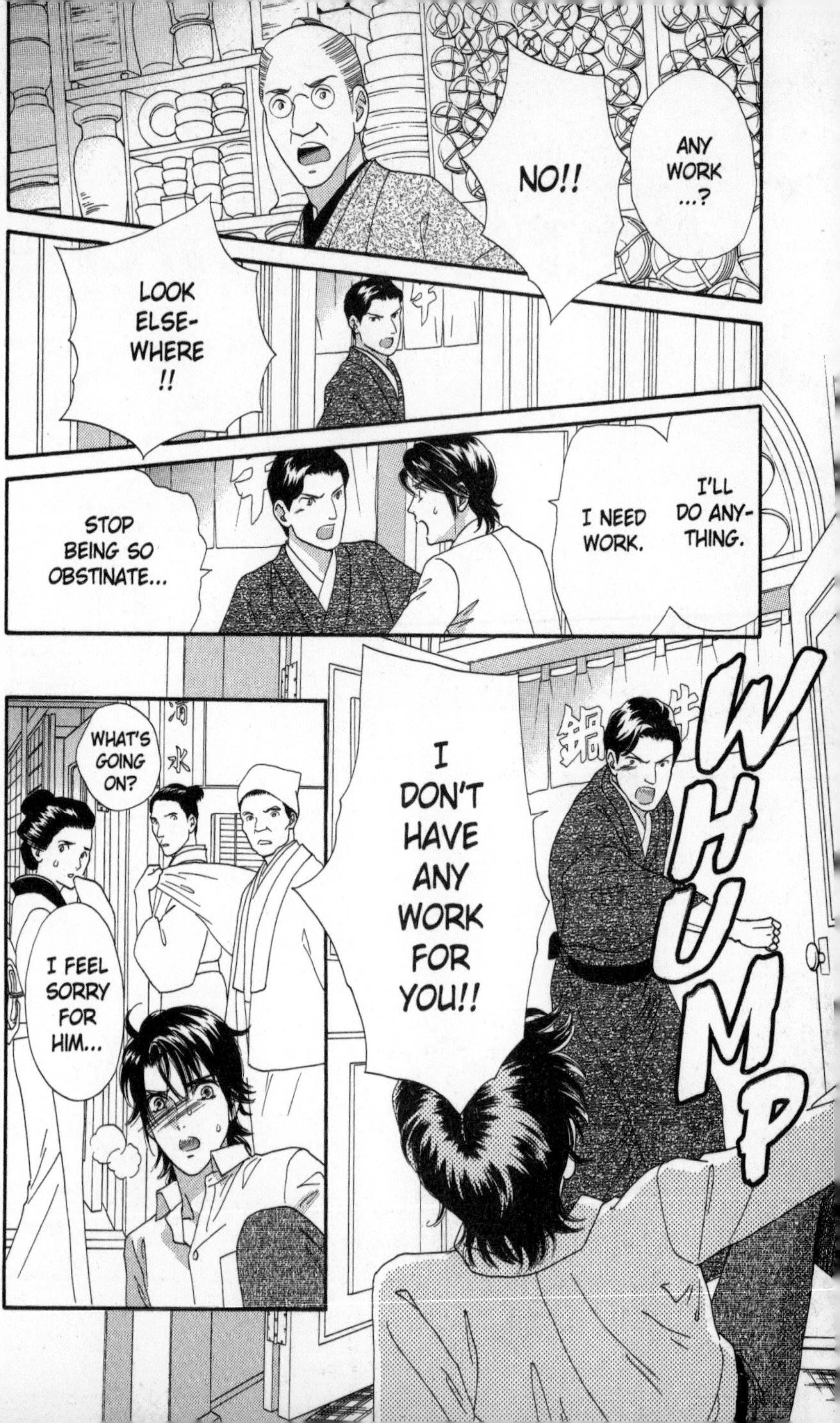
ANY WORK ...?
NO!!
LOOK ELSE-WHERE !!
I'LL DO ANY-THING.
I NEED WORK.
STOP BEING SO OBSTINATE...
WHUMP
I DON'T HAVE ANY WORK FOR YOU!!
WHAT'S GOING ON?
I FEEL SORRY FOR HIM...

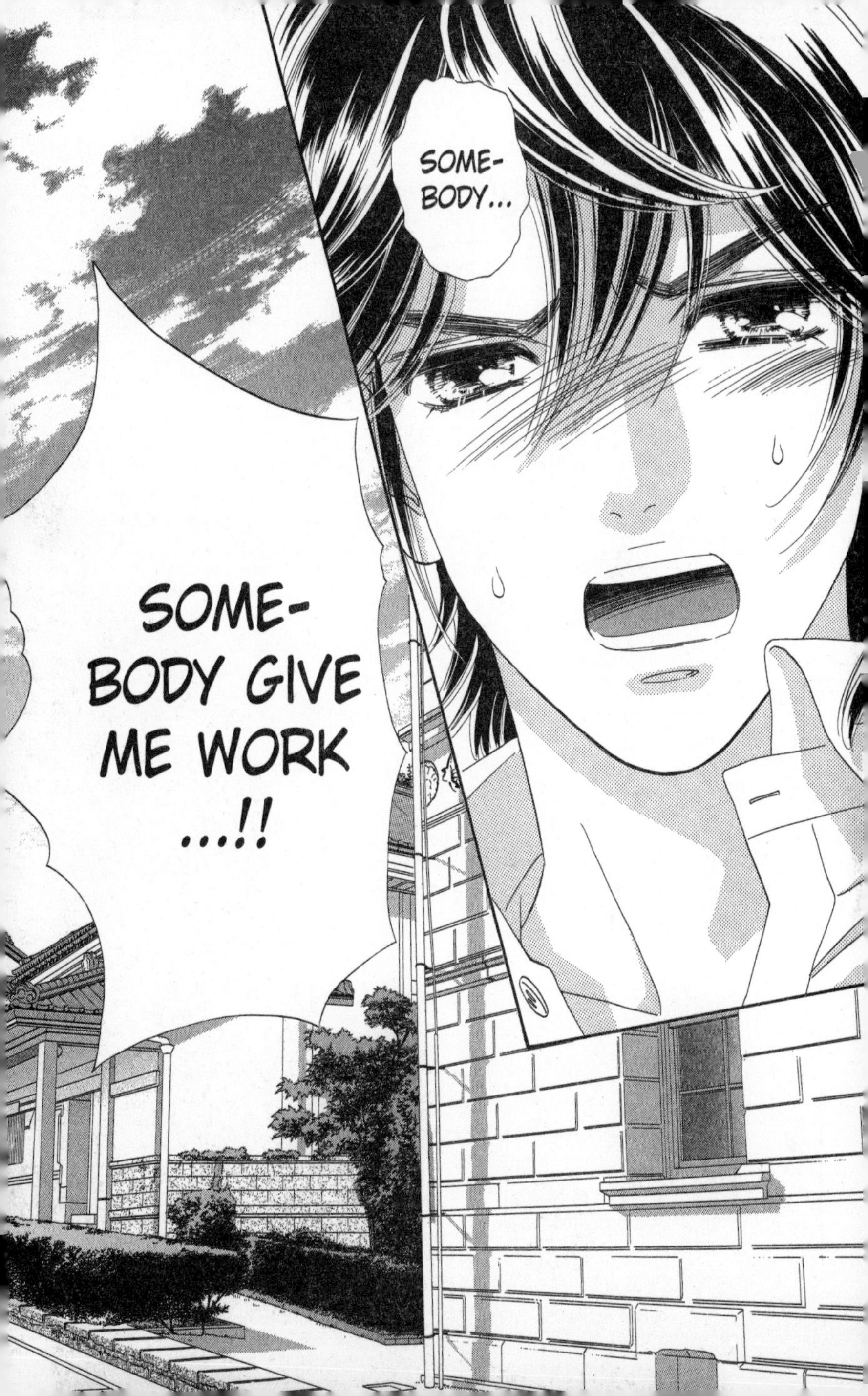
SOME-BODY...
SOME-BODY GIVE ME WORK ...!!

ATARI'S ELEMENTARY SCHOOL → MEIJI MURA

(MIE PREFECTURAL NORMAL SCHOOL, KURAMOCHI ELEMENTARY SCHOOL)

This was the main building of Mie Prefecture's Normal School in 1888. It was renovated in 1928 and then used as Kuramochi Elementary School in the city of Nabari.

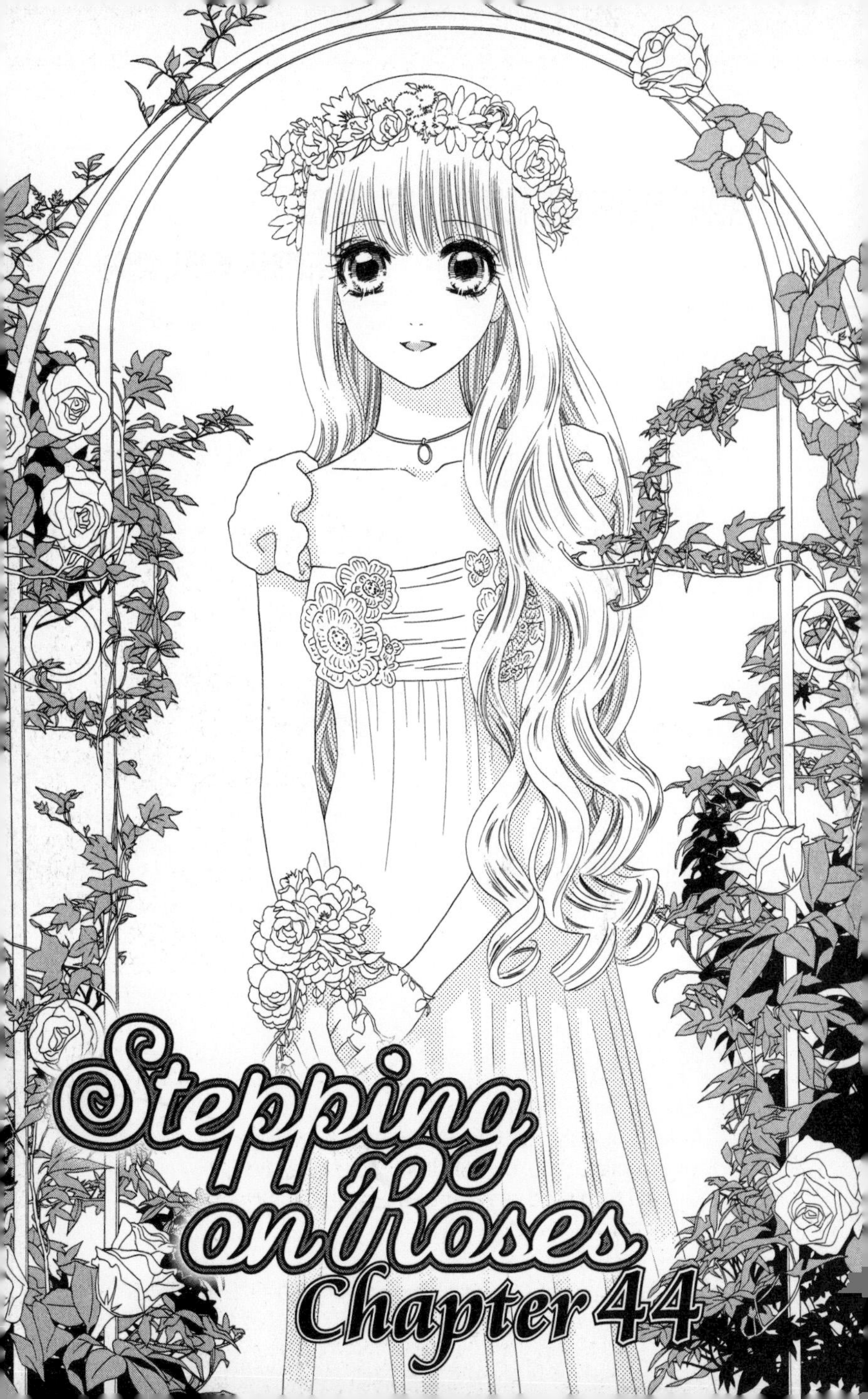
Stepping on Roses
Chapter 44

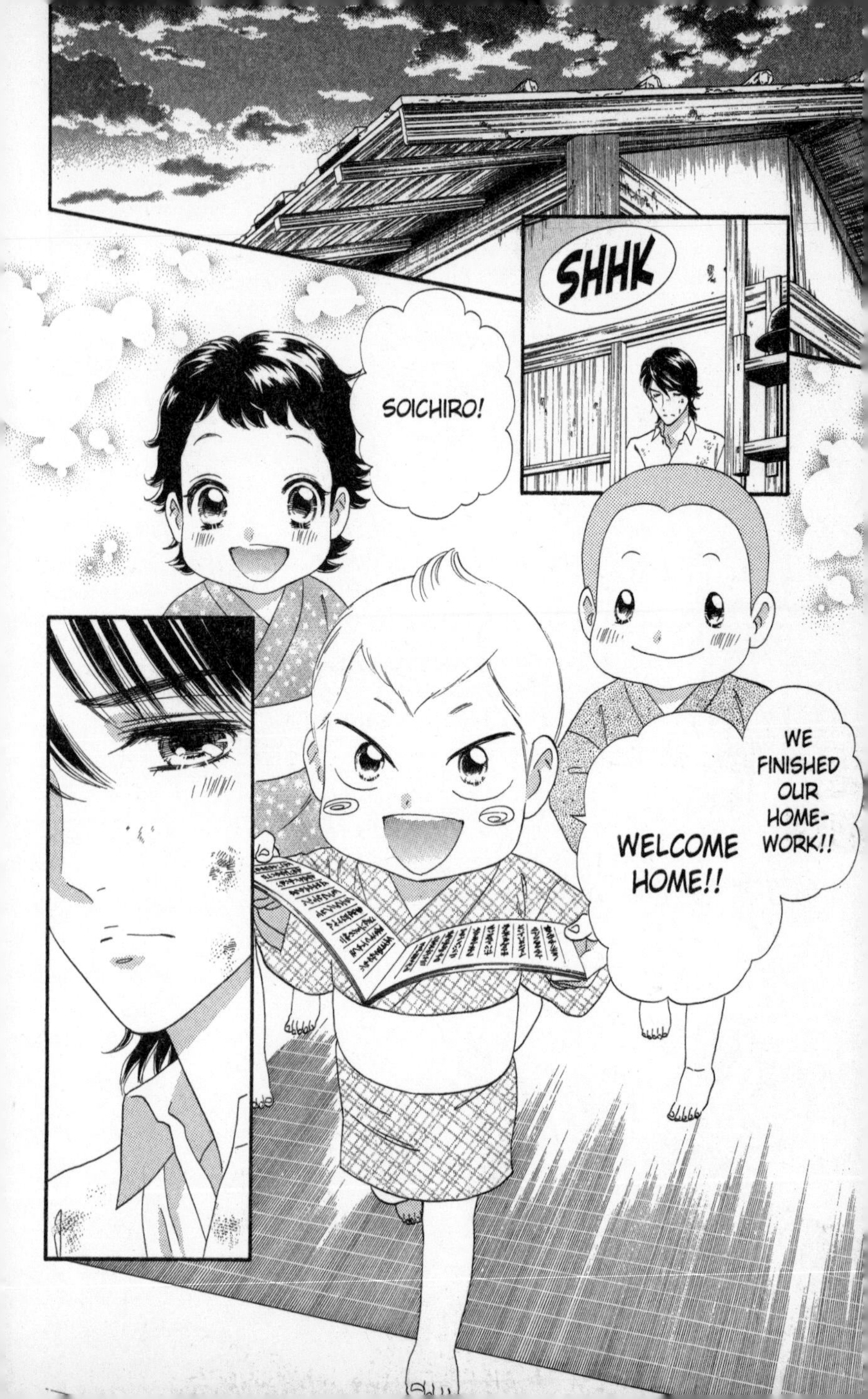
SHHK
SOICHIRO!
WE FINISHED OUR HOME-WORK!!
WELCOME HOME!!

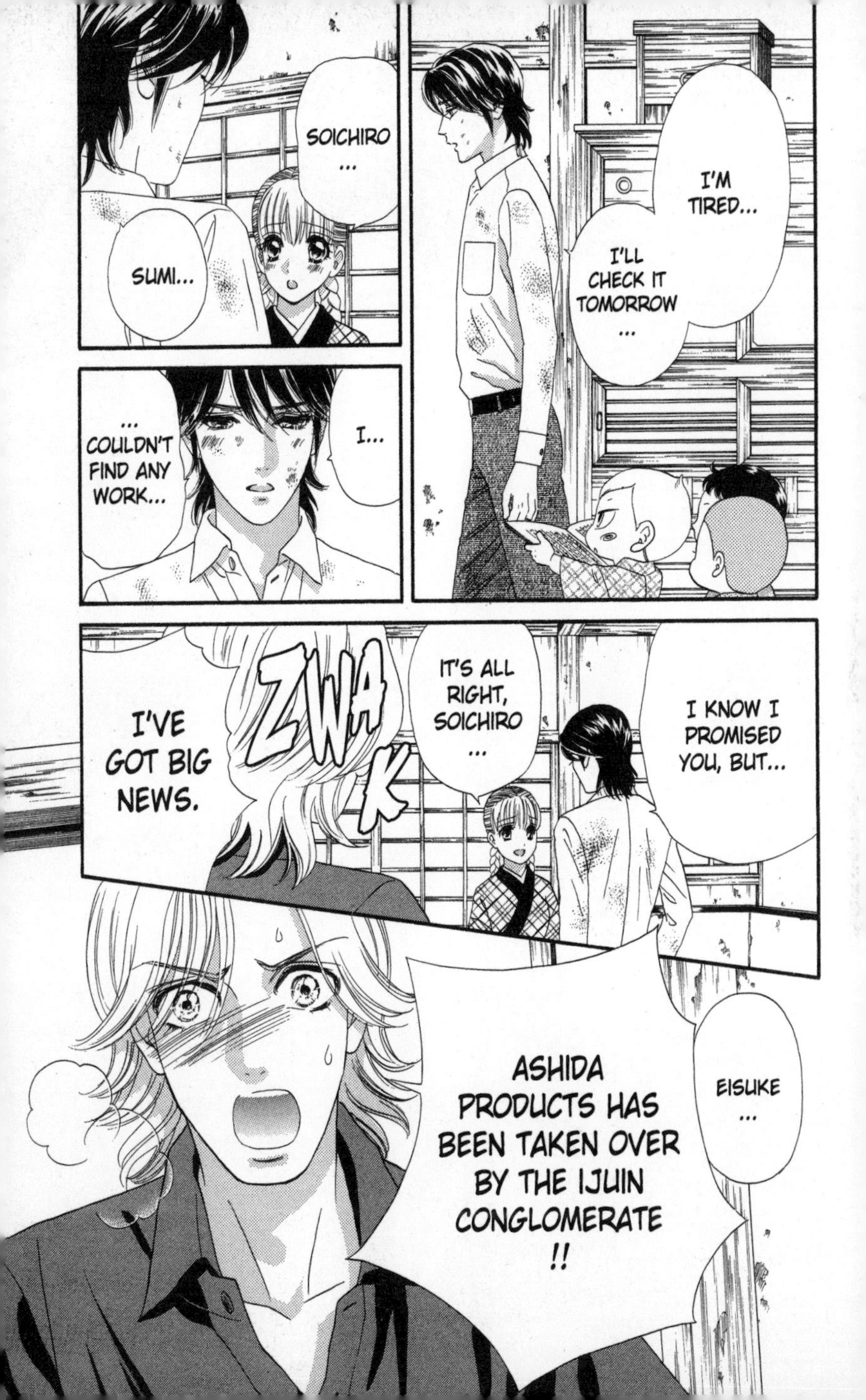
I'M TIRED...
I'LL CHECK IT TOMORROW ...
SOICHIRO ...
SUMI...
I...
... COULDN'T FIND ANY WORK...
I KNOW I PROMISED YOU, BUT...
IT'S ALL RIGHT, SOICHIRO ...
ZWAK
I'VE GOT BIG NEWS.
EISUKE ...
ASHIDA PRODUCTS HAS BEEN TAKEN OVER BY THE IJUIN CONGLOMERATE !!

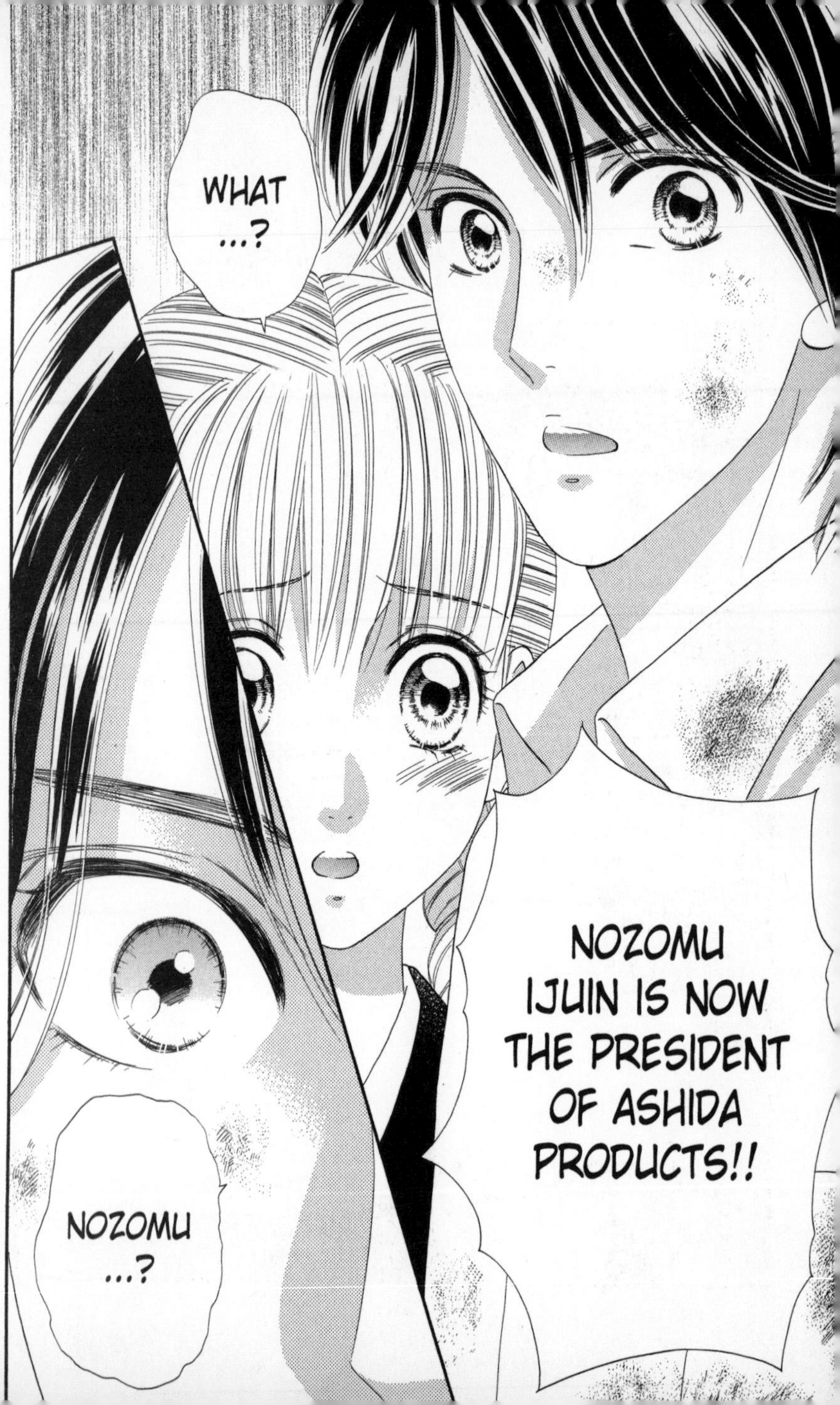
WHAT ...?
NOZOMU IJUIN IS NOW THE PRESIDENT OF ASHIDA PRODUCTS!!
NOZOMU ...?

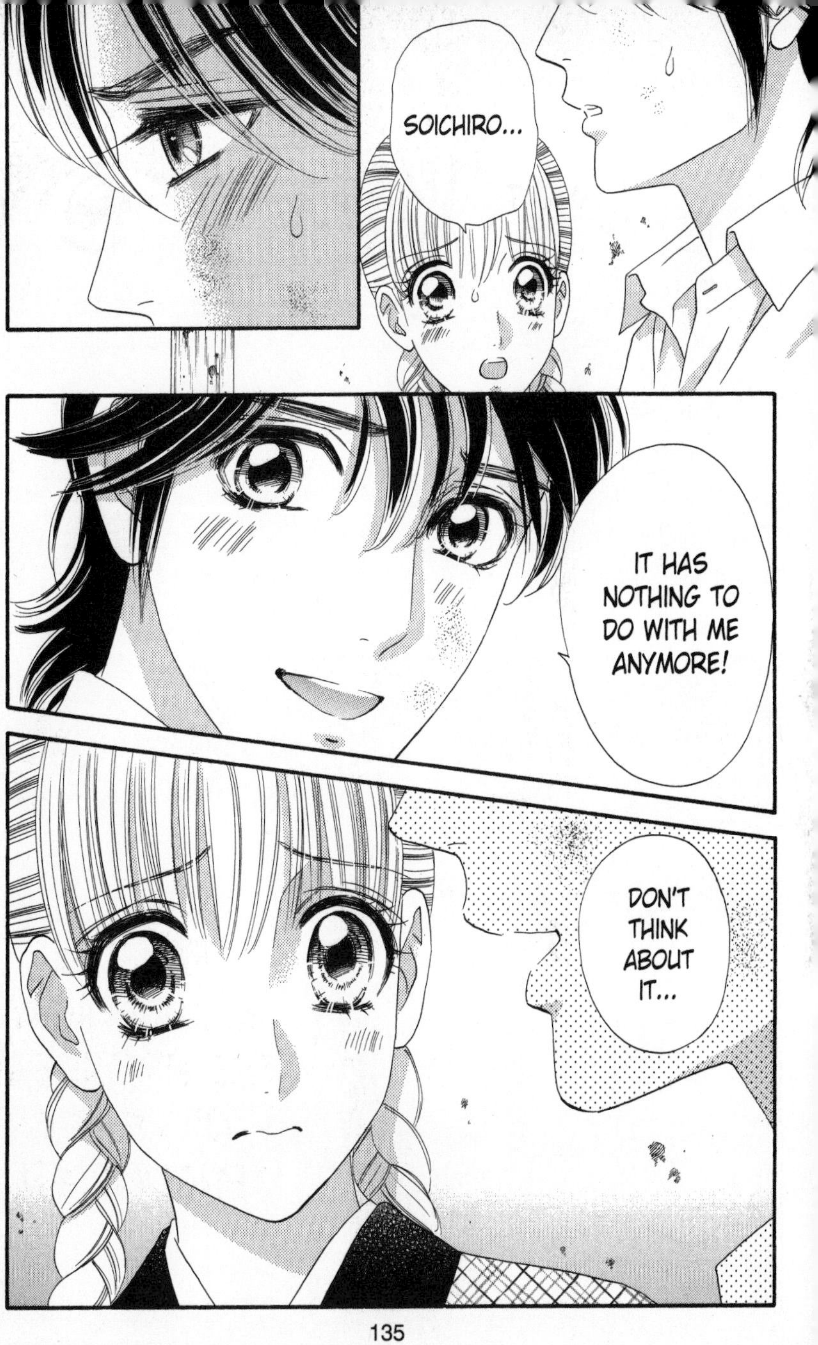
SOICHIRO...
IT HAS NOTHING TO DO WITH ME ANYMORE!
DON'T THINK ABOUT IT...

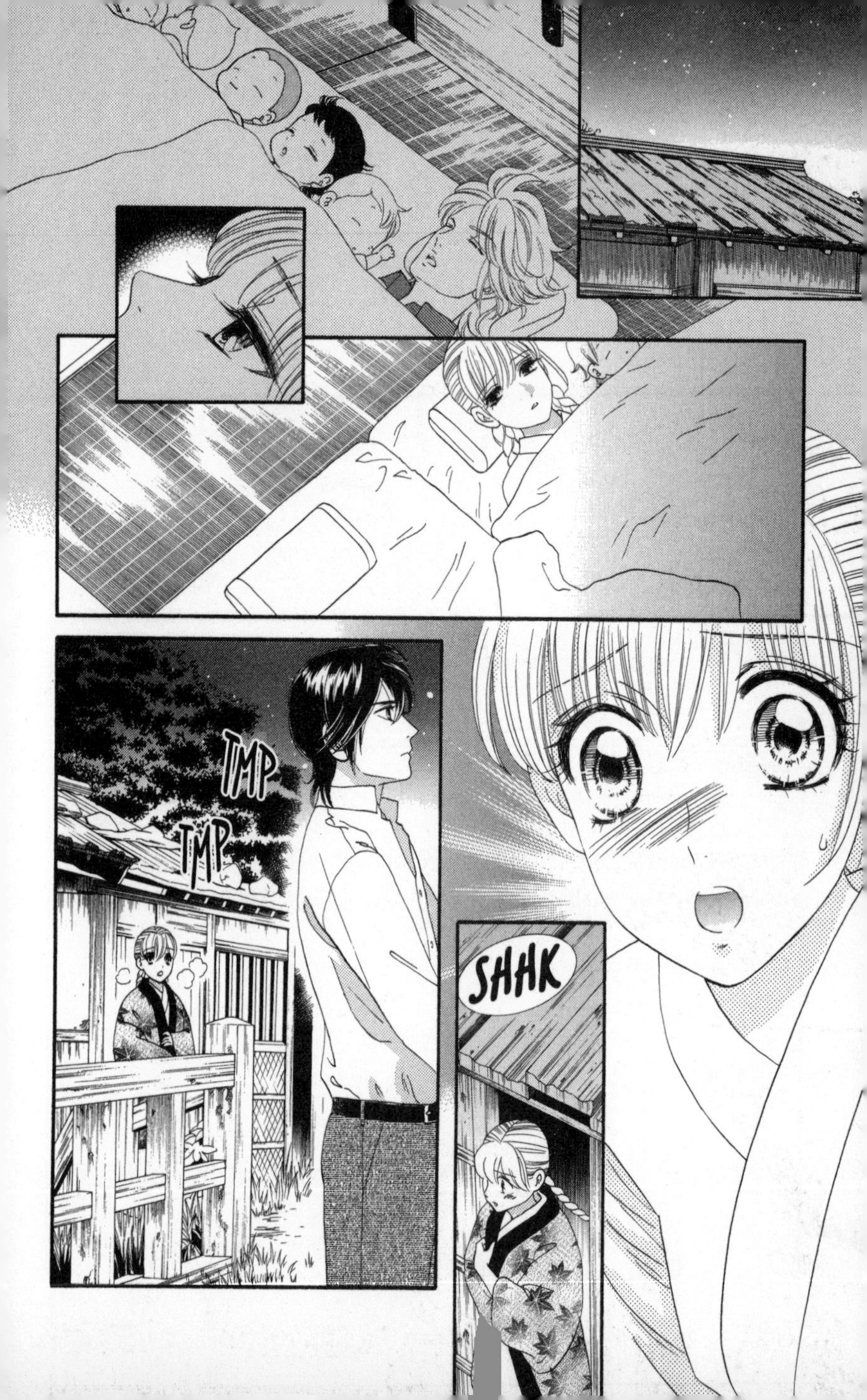
SHAK
TMP
TMP

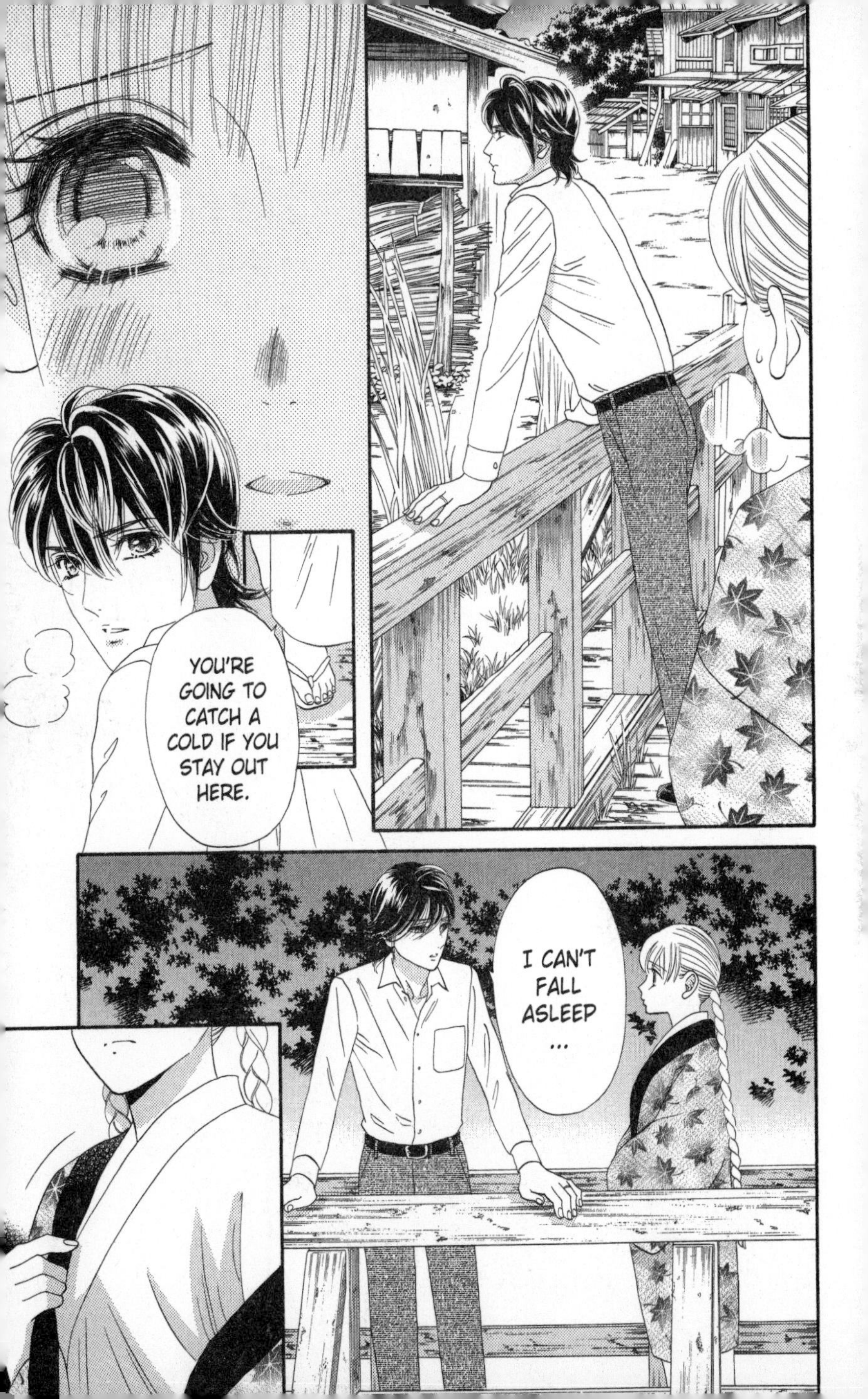
YOU'RE GOING TO CATCH A COLD IF YOU STAY OUT HERE.
I CAN'T FALL ASLEEP ...

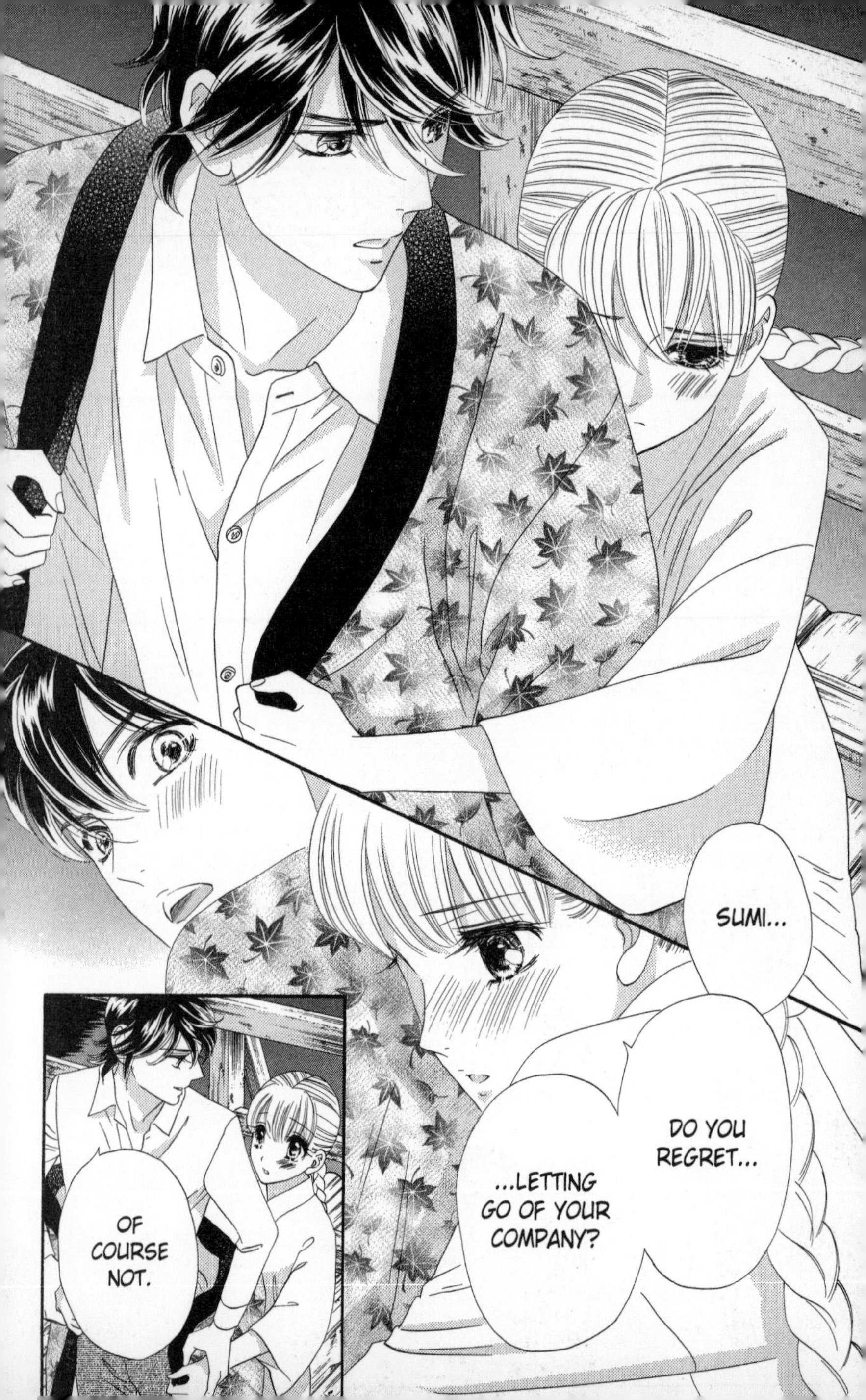
SUMI...
DO YOU REGRET...
...LETTING GO OF YOUR COMPANY?
OF COURSE NOT.

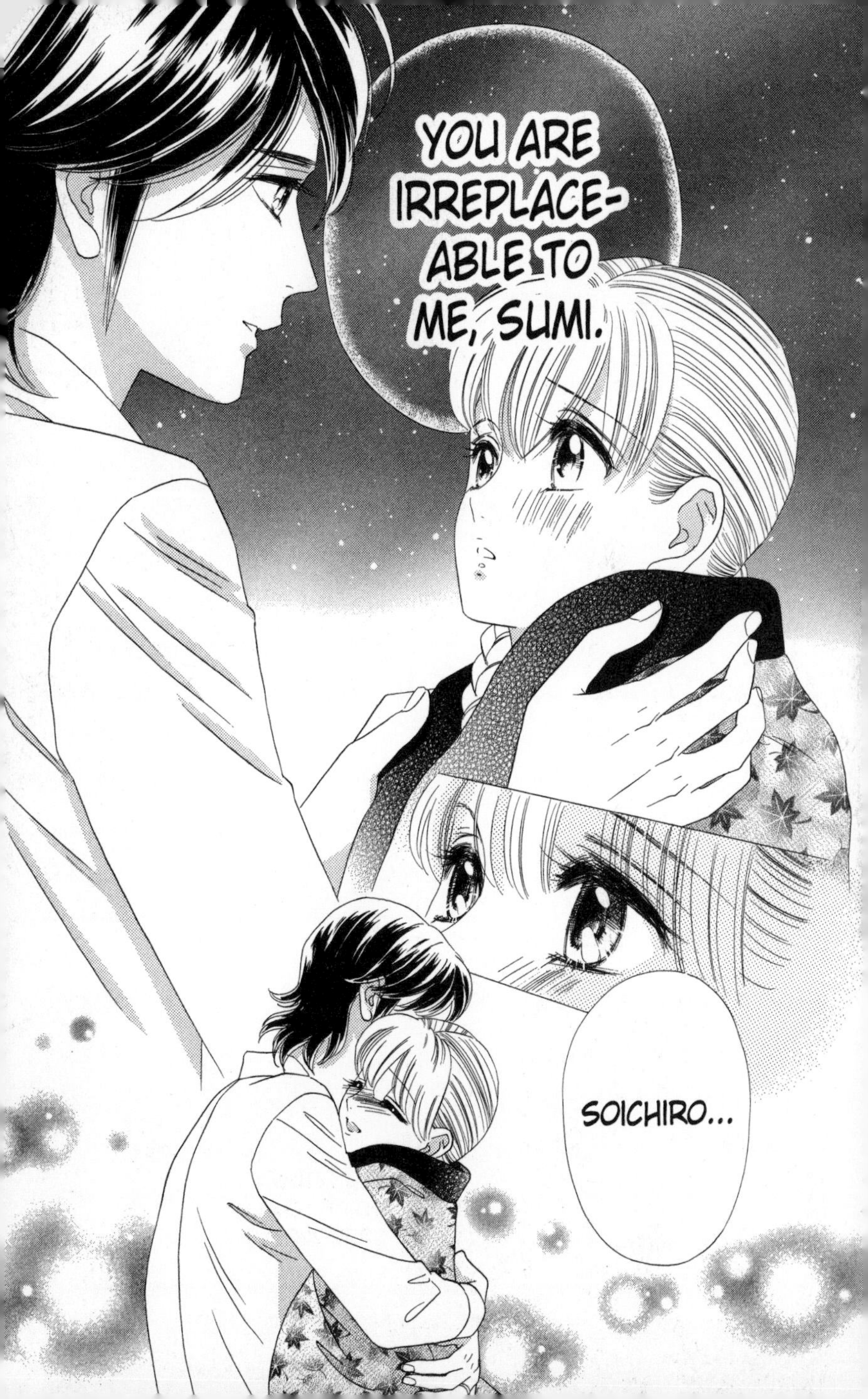
YOU ARE IRREPLACE-ABLE TO ME, SUMI.
SOICHIRO...

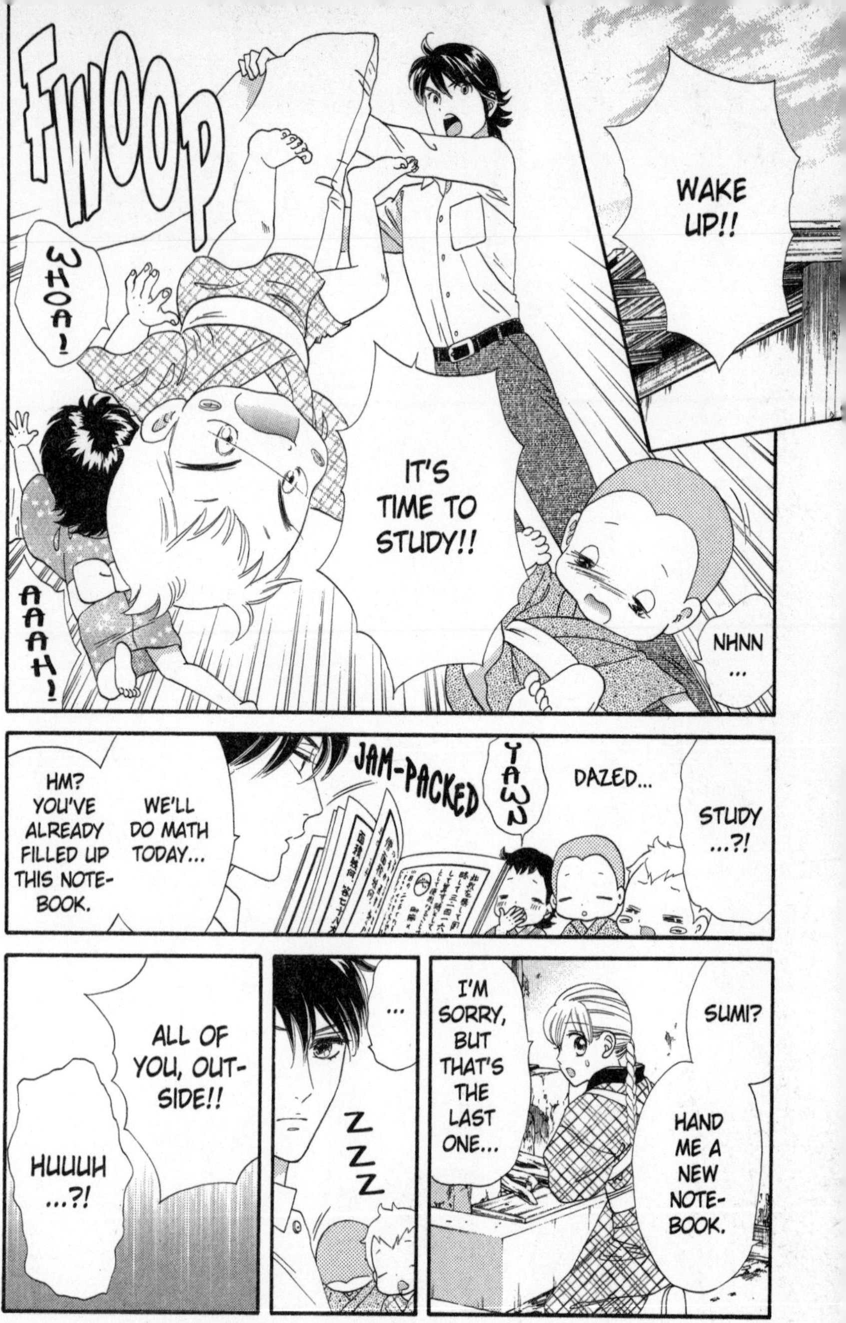
WAKE UP!!
FWOOP
IT'S TIME TO STUDY!!
NHNN...
WHOA!
AAAAH!
STUDY...?!
DAZED...
YAWN
JAM-PACKED
WE'LL DO MATH TODAY...
HM? YOU'VE ALREADY FILLED UP THIS NOTEBOOK.
SUMI?
HAND ME A NEW NOTEBOOK.
I'M SORRY, BUT THAT'S THE LAST ONE...
...
ZZZ
ALL OF YOU, OUTSIDE!!
HUUUH...?!

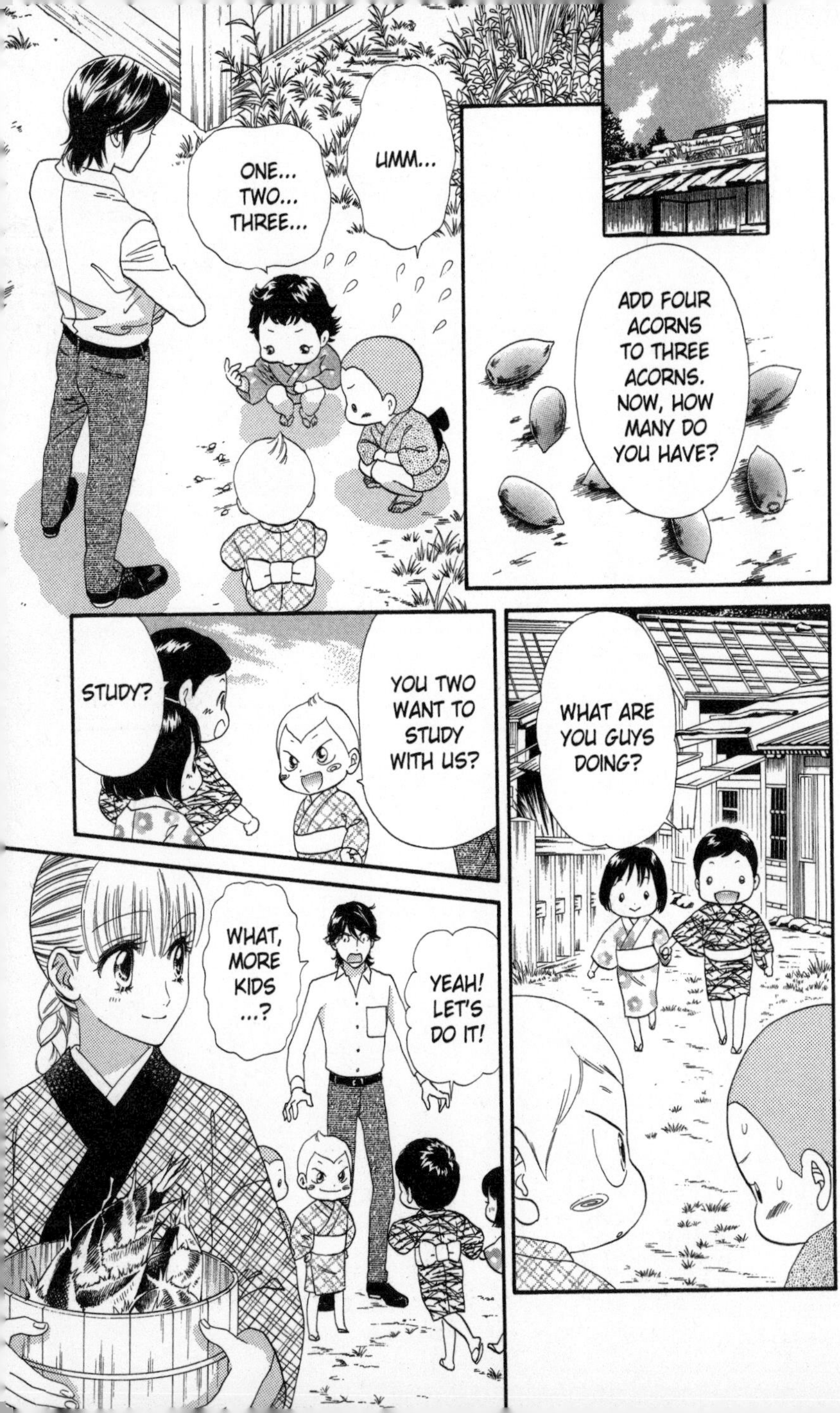
ADD FOUR ACORNS TO THREE ACORNS. NOW, HOW MANY DO YOU HAVE?
UMM...
ONE... TWO... THREE...
WHAT ARE YOU GUYS DOING?
YOU TWO WANT TO STUDY WITH US?
STUDY?
YEAH! LET'S DO IT!
WHAT, MORE KIDS ...?

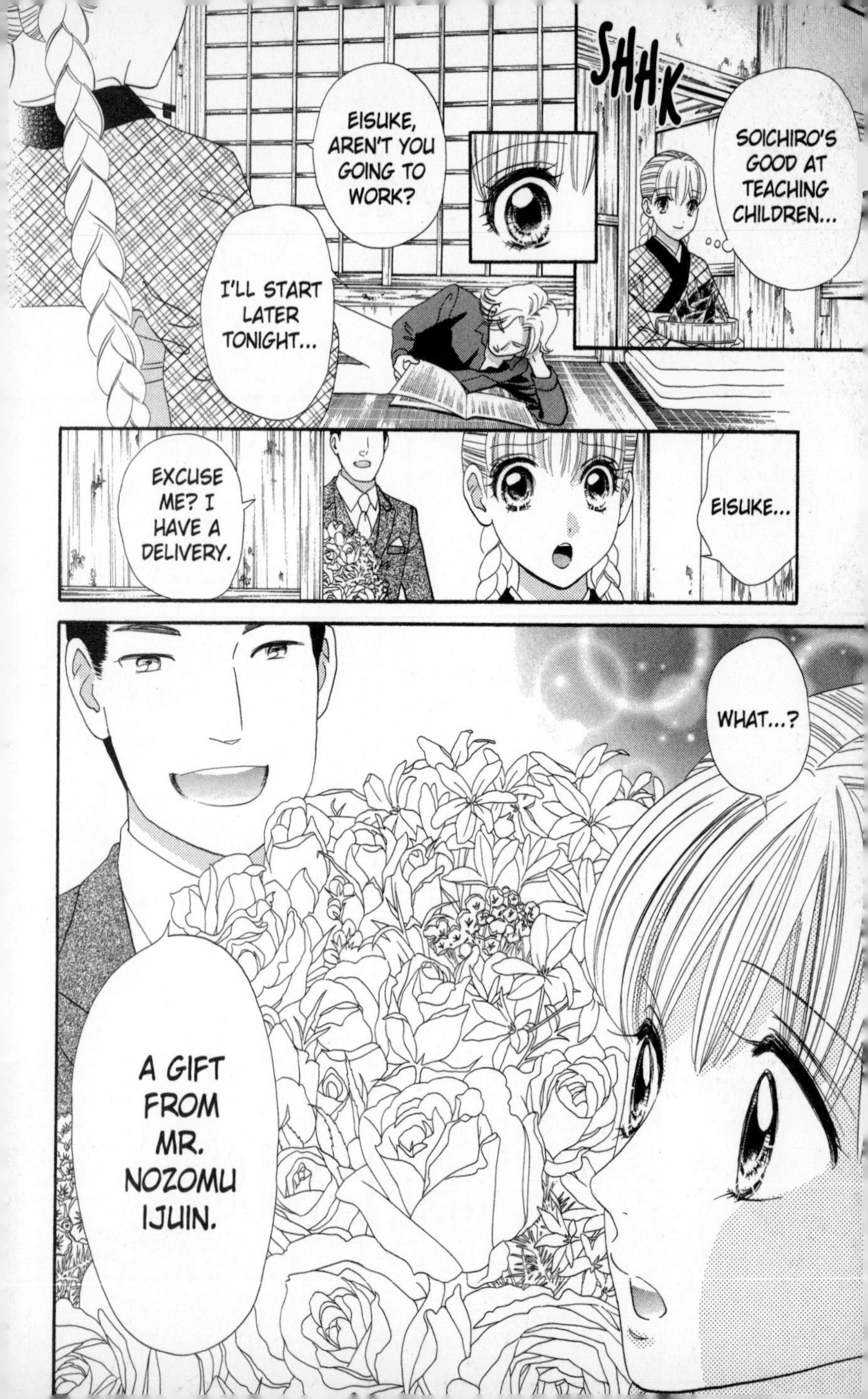
SHHK
SOICHIRO'S GOOD AT TEACHING CHILDREN...
EISUKE, AREN'T YOU GOING TO WORK?
I'LL START LATER TONIGHT...
EISUKE...
EXCUSE ME? I HAVE A DELIVERY.
WHAT...?
A GIFT FROM MR. NOZOMU IJUIN.

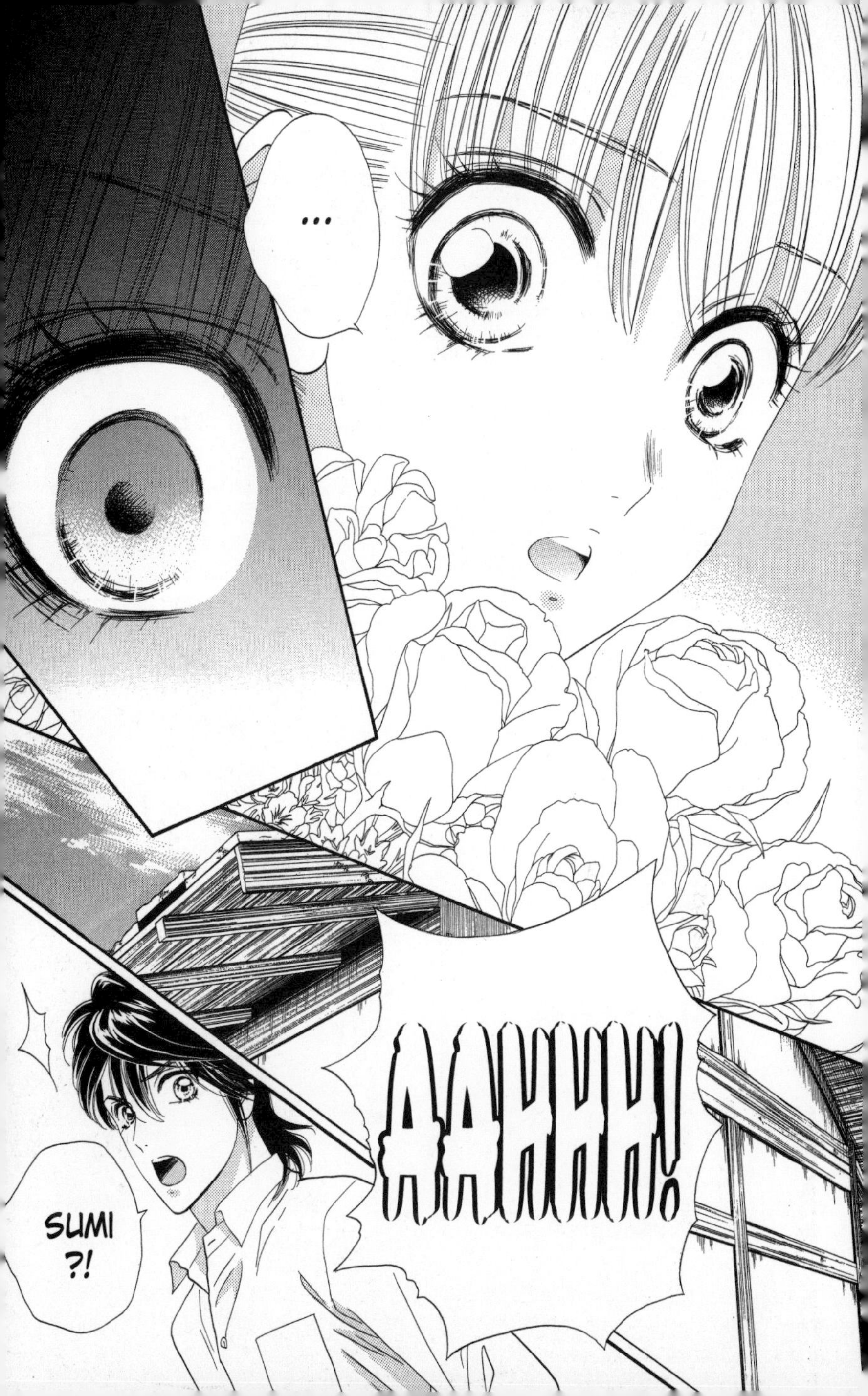
...
AAHHH!
SUMI ?!

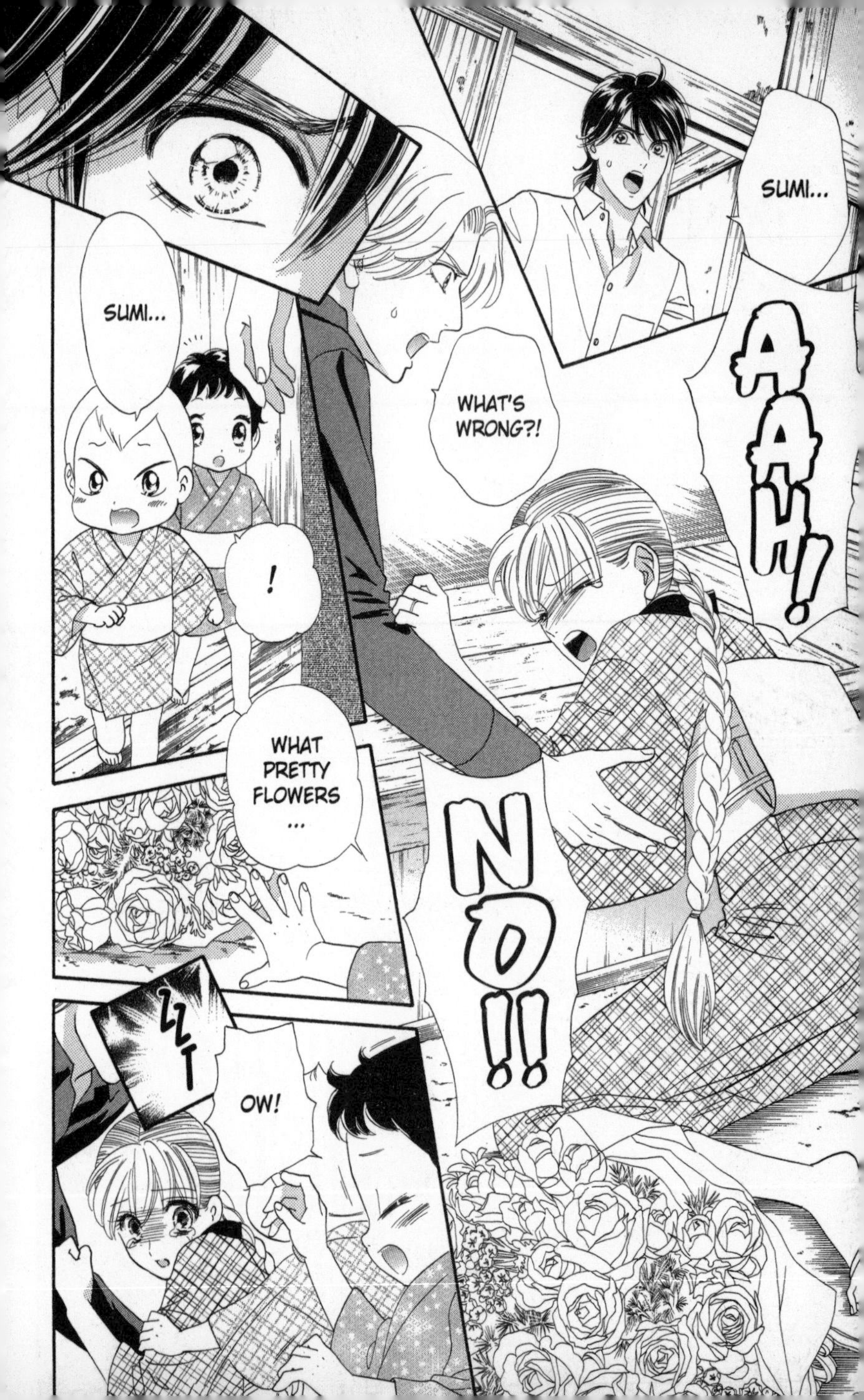
SUMI...
AAAH!
WHAT'S WRONG?!
NO!!
SUMI...
!
WHAT PRETTY FLOWERS ...
ZZT
OW!

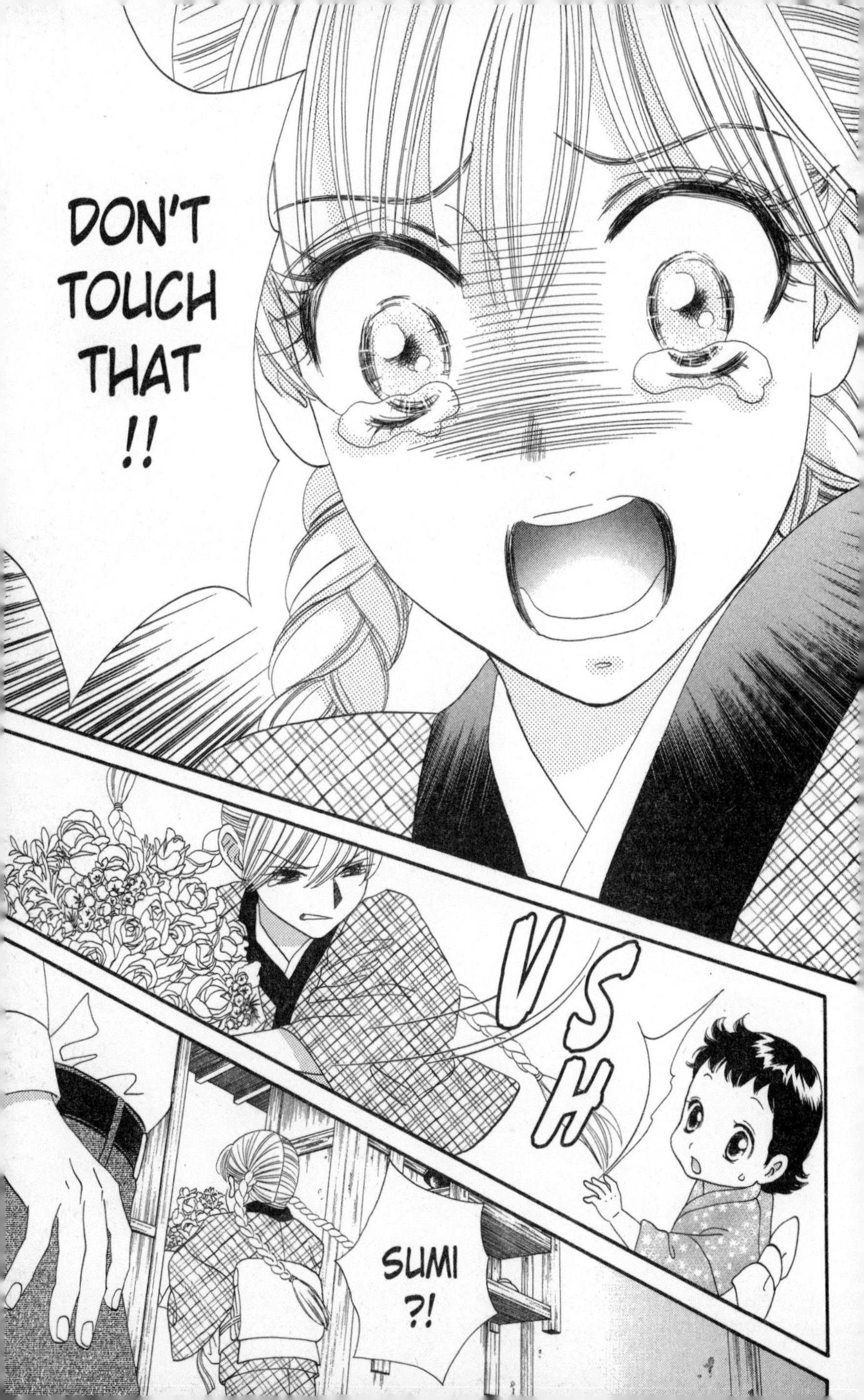
DON'T TOUCH THAT!!
VSH
SUMI?!

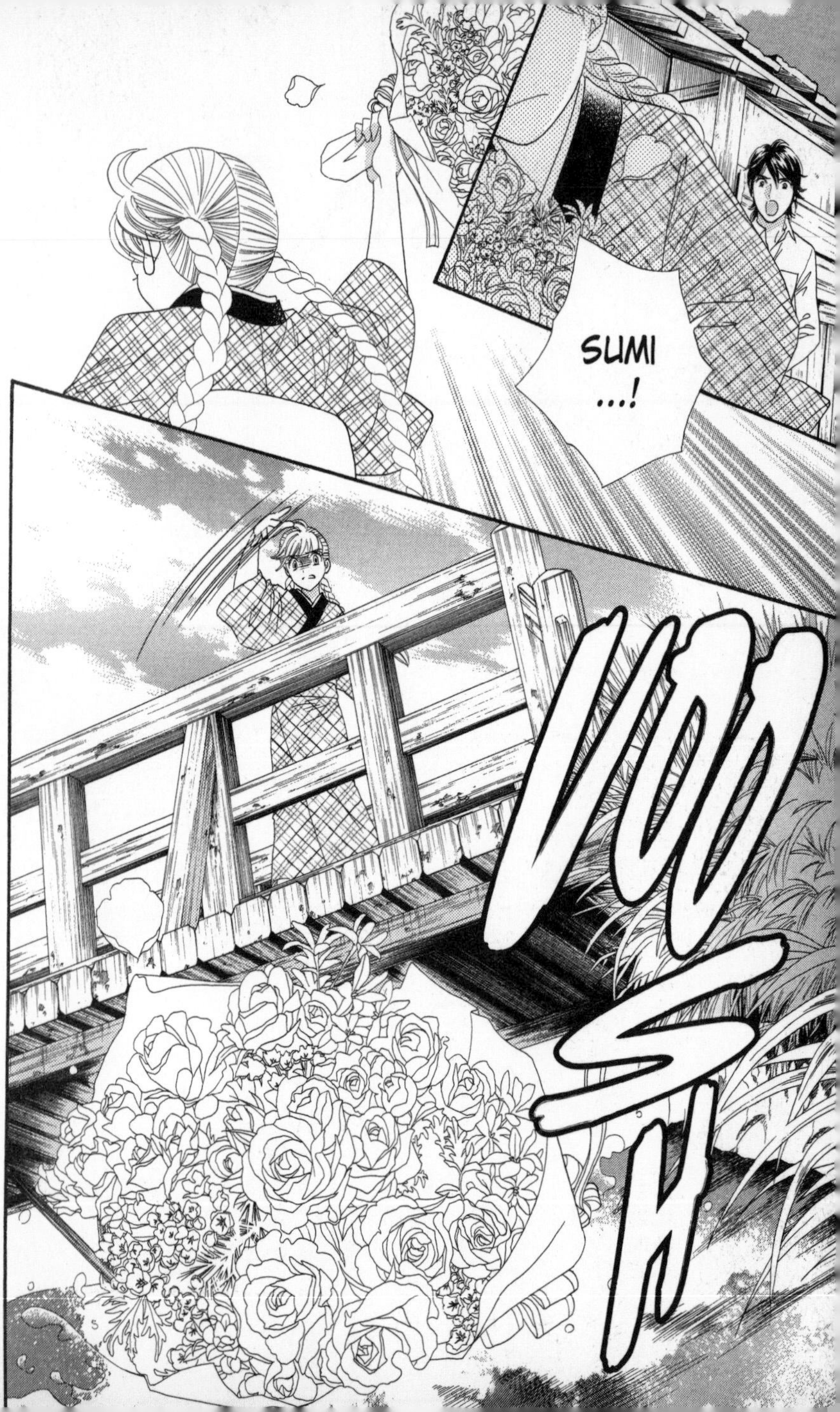
SUMI ...!
VOOSH

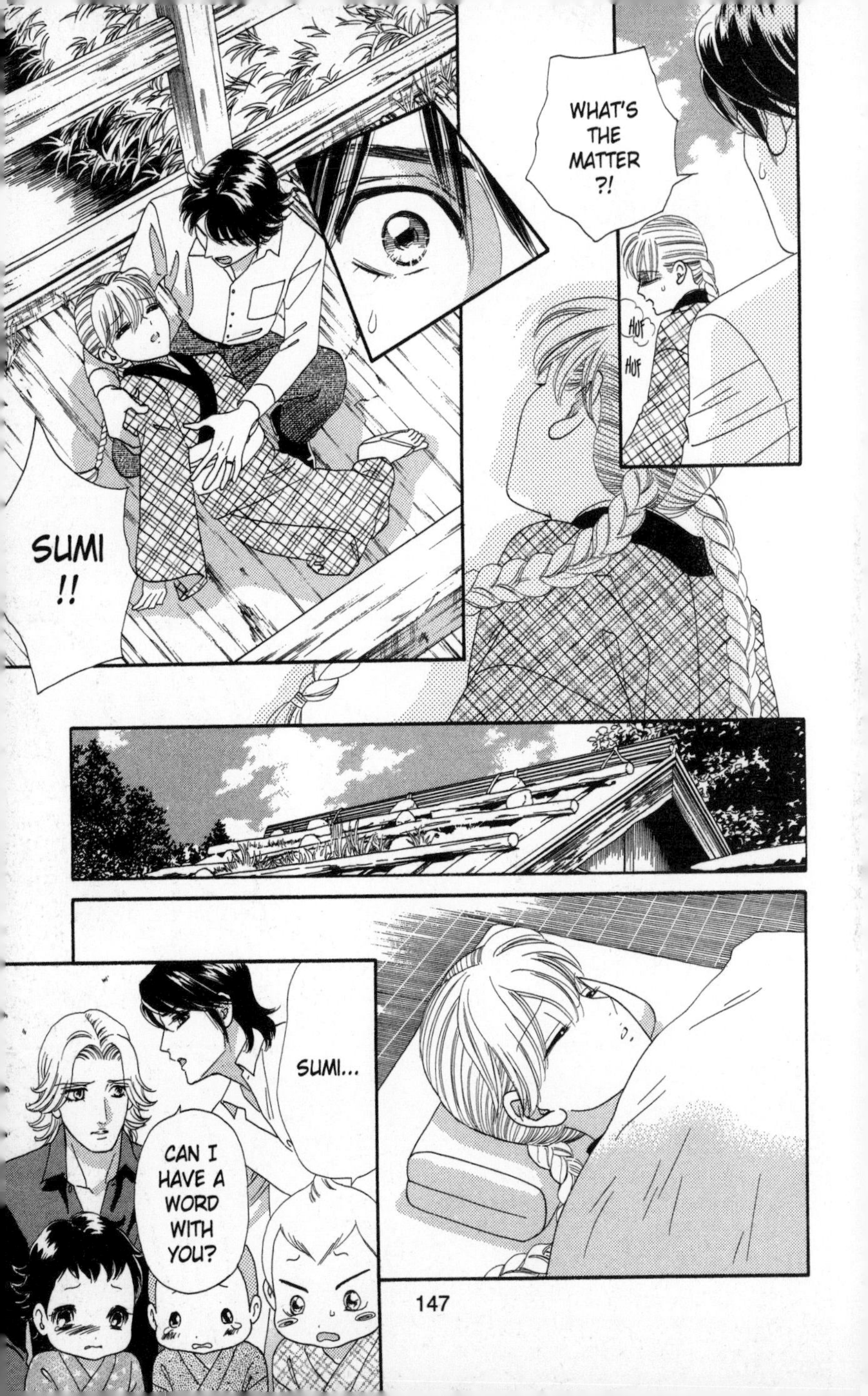
WHAT'S THE MATTER ?!
HUF HUF
SUMI !!
SUMI...
CAN I HAVE A WORD WITH YOU?

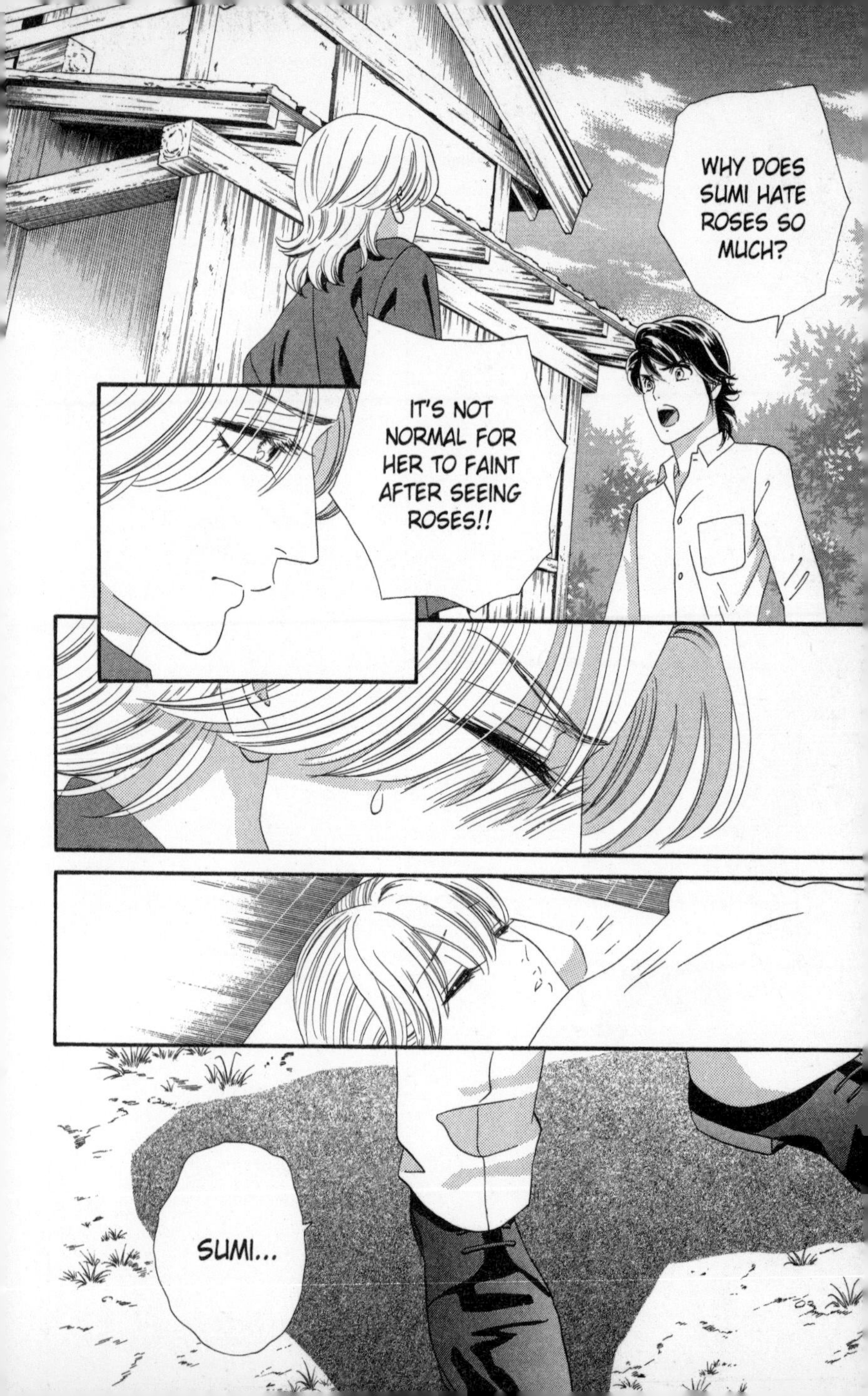
WHY DOES SUMI HATE ROSES SO MUCH?
IT'S NOT NORMAL FOR HER TO FAINT AFTER SEEING ROSES!!
SUMI...

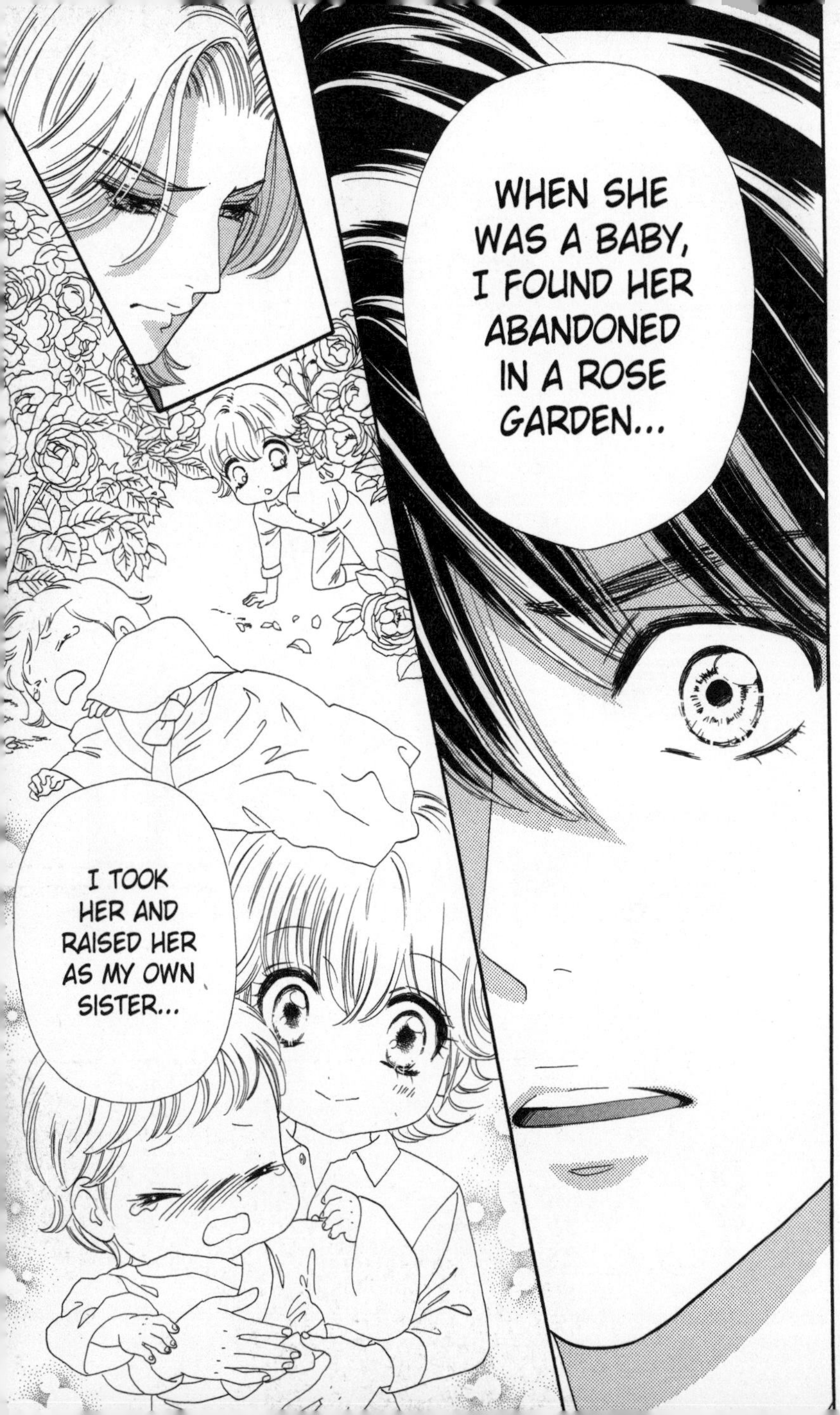
WHEN SHE WAS A BABY, I FOUND HER ABANDONED IN A ROSE GARDEN...
I TOOK HER AND RAISED HER AS MY OWN SISTER...

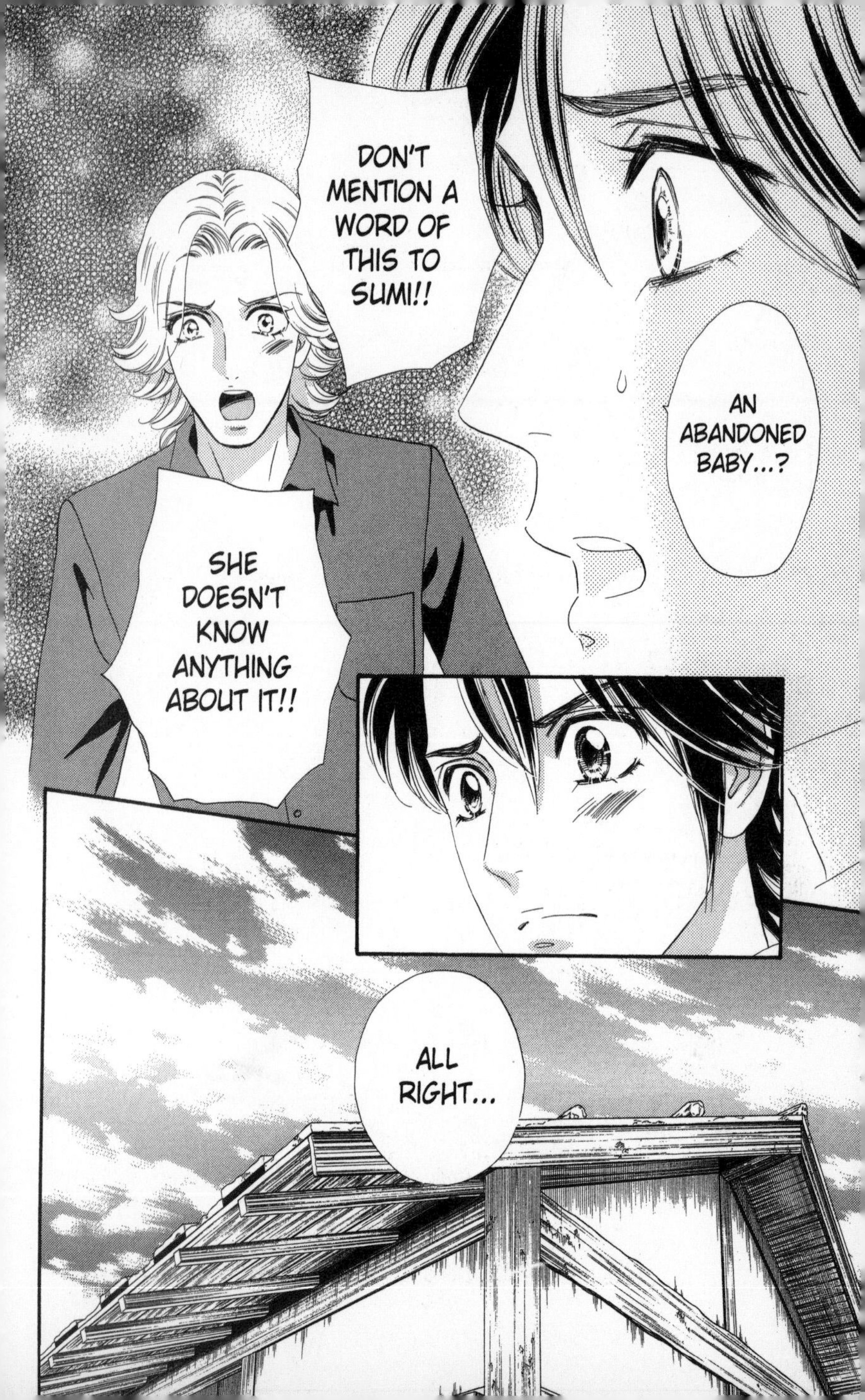
AN ABANDONED BABY...?
DON'T MENTION A WORD OF THIS TO SUMI!!
SHE DOESN'T KNOW ANYTHING ABOUT IT!!
ALL RIGHT...

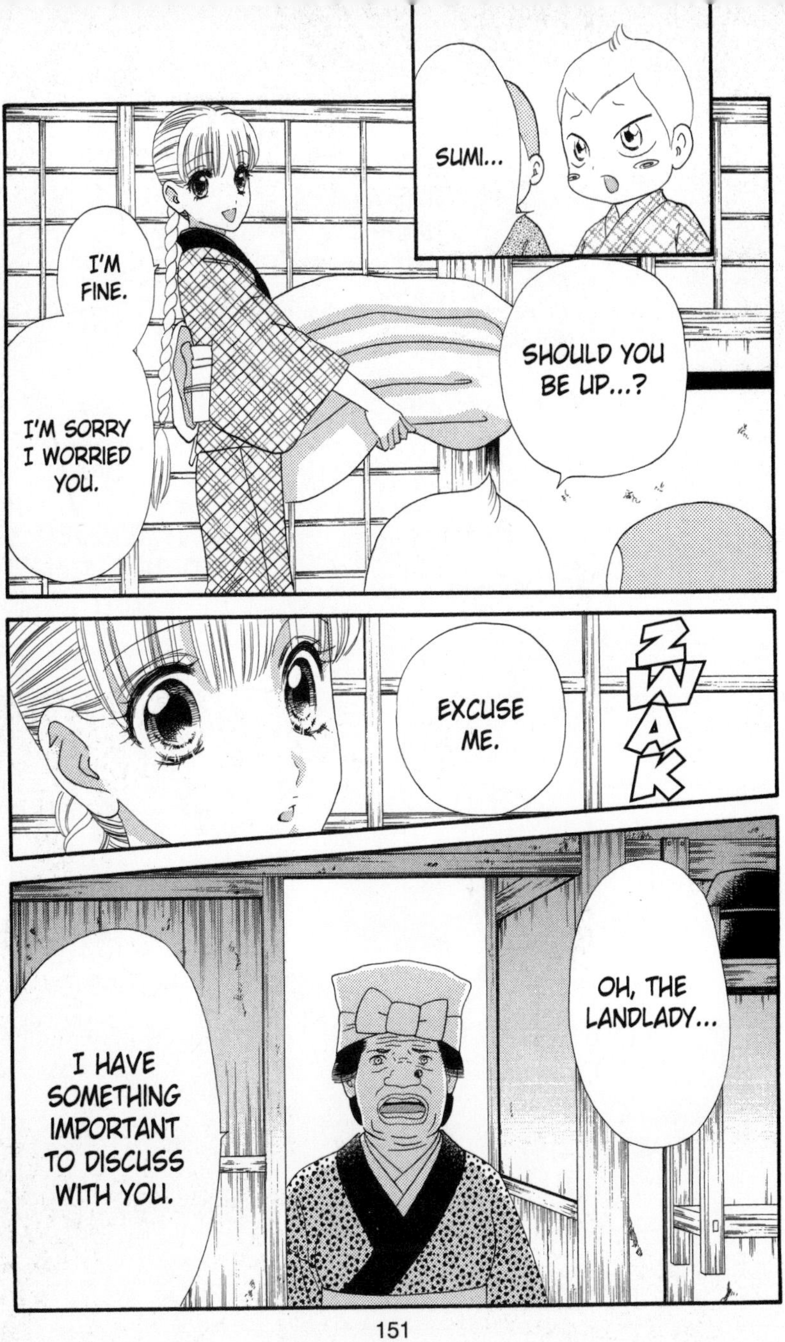
SUMI...
SHOULD YOU BE UP...?
I'M FINE.
I'M SORRY I WORRIED YOU.
ZWAK
EXCUSE ME.
OH, THE LANDLADY...
I HAVE SOMETHING IMPORTANT TO DISCUSS WITH YOU.

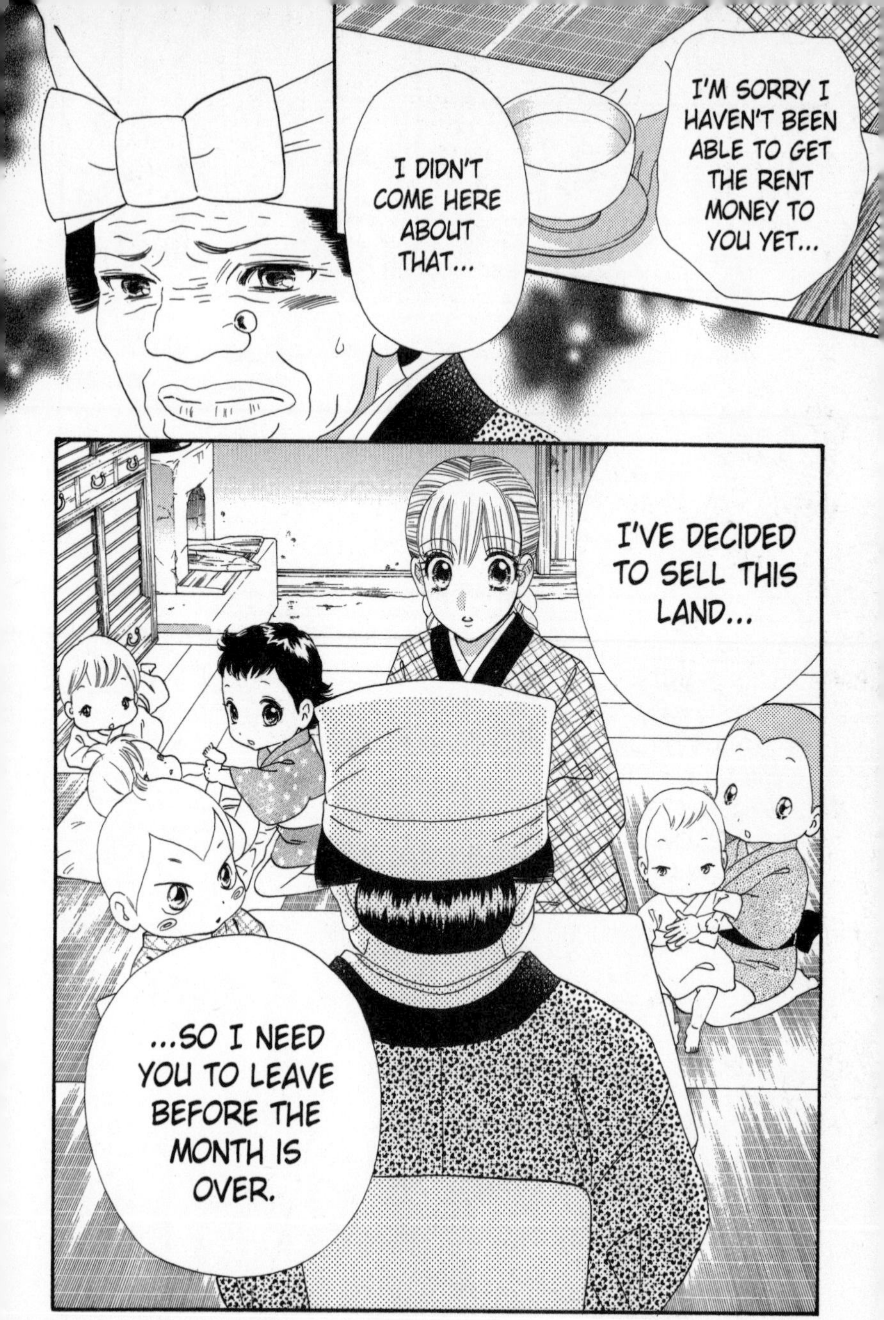
I'M SORRY I HAVEN'T BEEN ABLE TO GET THE RENT MONEY TO YOU YET...
I DIDN'T COME HERE ABOUT THAT...
I'VE DECIDED TO SELL THIS LAND...
...SO I NEED YOU TO LEAVE BEFORE THE MONTH IS OVER.

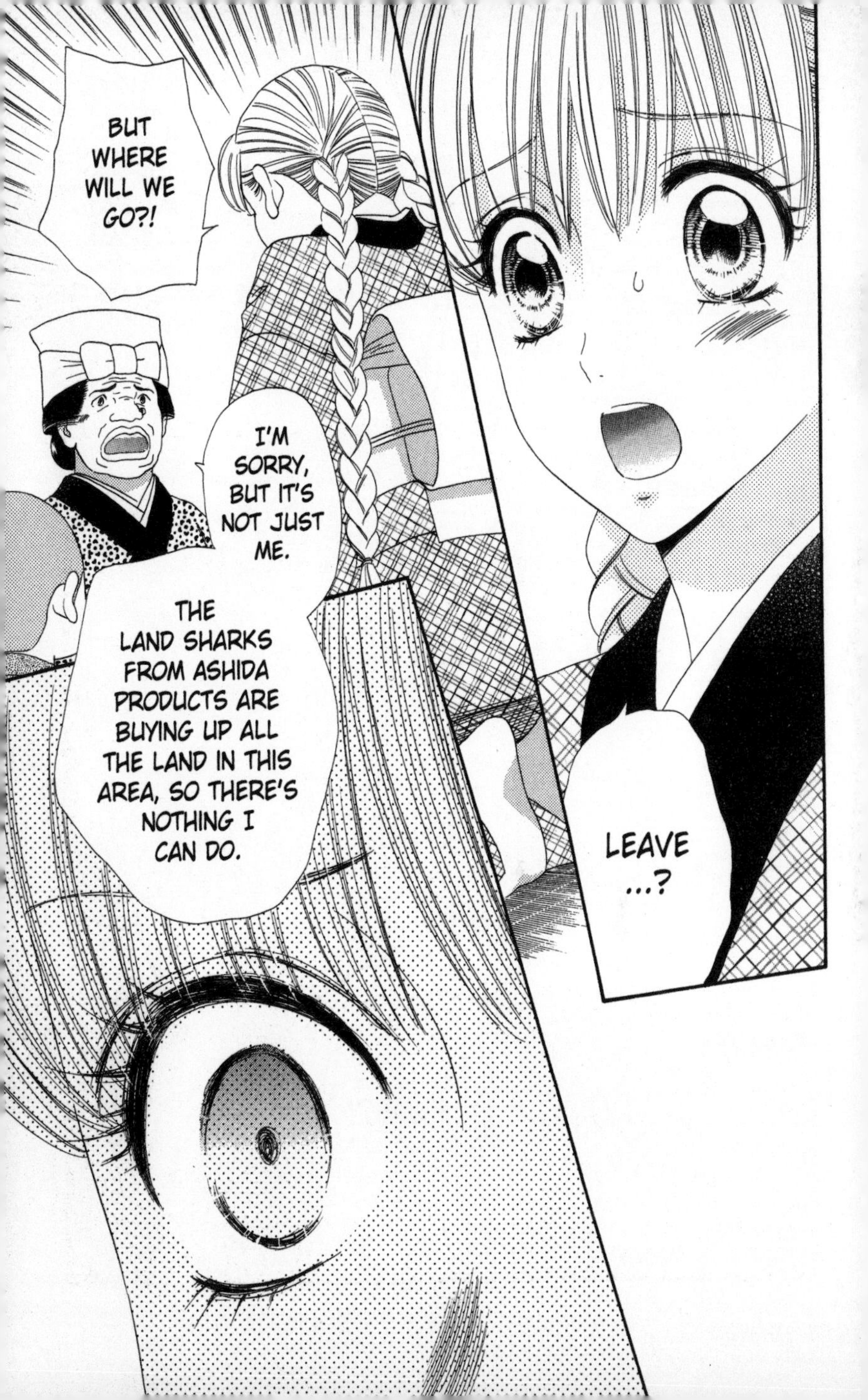
LEAVE ...?
BUT WHERE WILL WE GO?!
I'M SORRY, BUT IT'S NOT JUST ME.
THE LAND SHARKS FROM ASHIDA PRODUCTS ARE BUYING UP ALL THE LAND IN THIS AREA, SO THERE'S NOTHING I CAN DO.

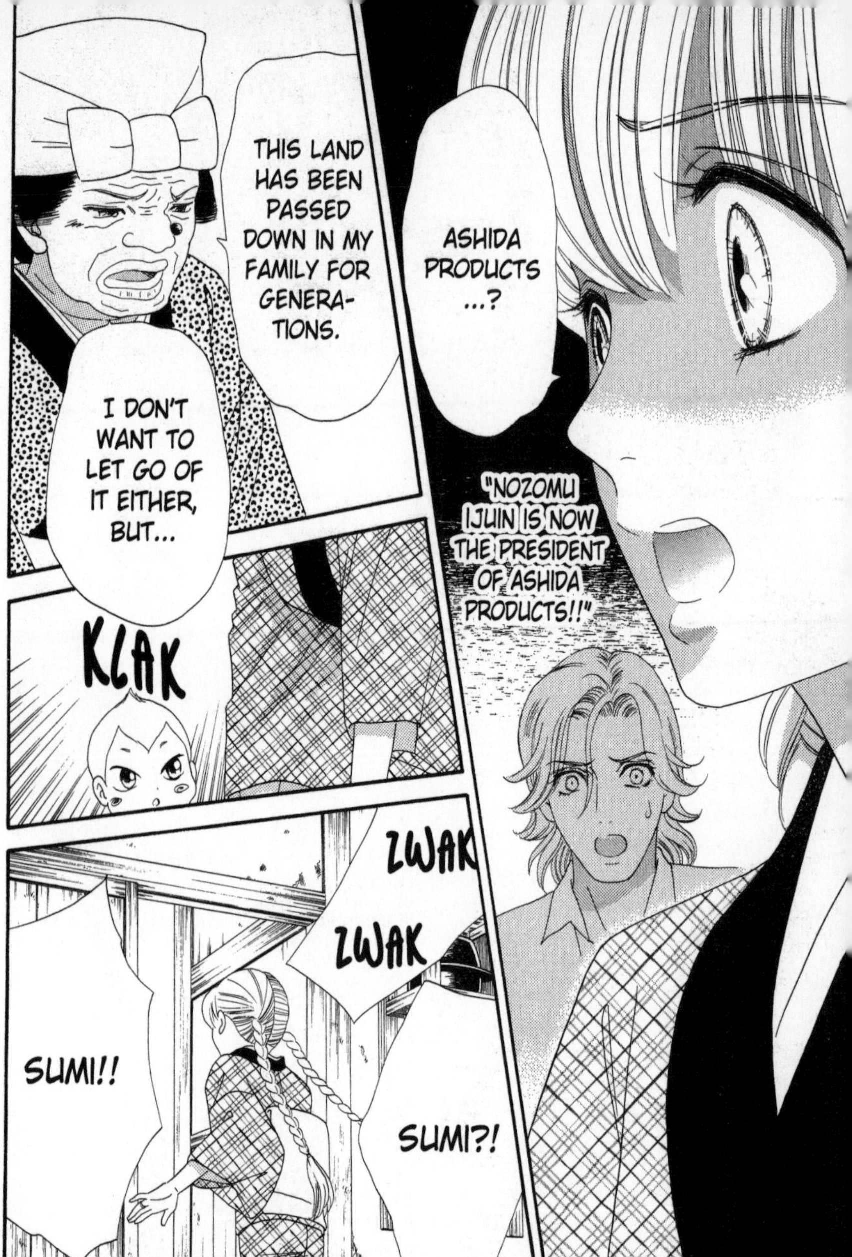
ASHIDA PRODUCTS ...?
"NOZOMU IJUIN IS NOW THE PRESIDENT OF ASHIDA PRODUCTS!!"
THIS LAND HAS BEEN PASSED DOWN IN MY FAMILY FOR GENERA-TIONS.
I DON'T WANT TO LET GO OF IT EITHER, BUT...
KLAK
ZWAK
ZWAK
SUMI?!
SUMI!!

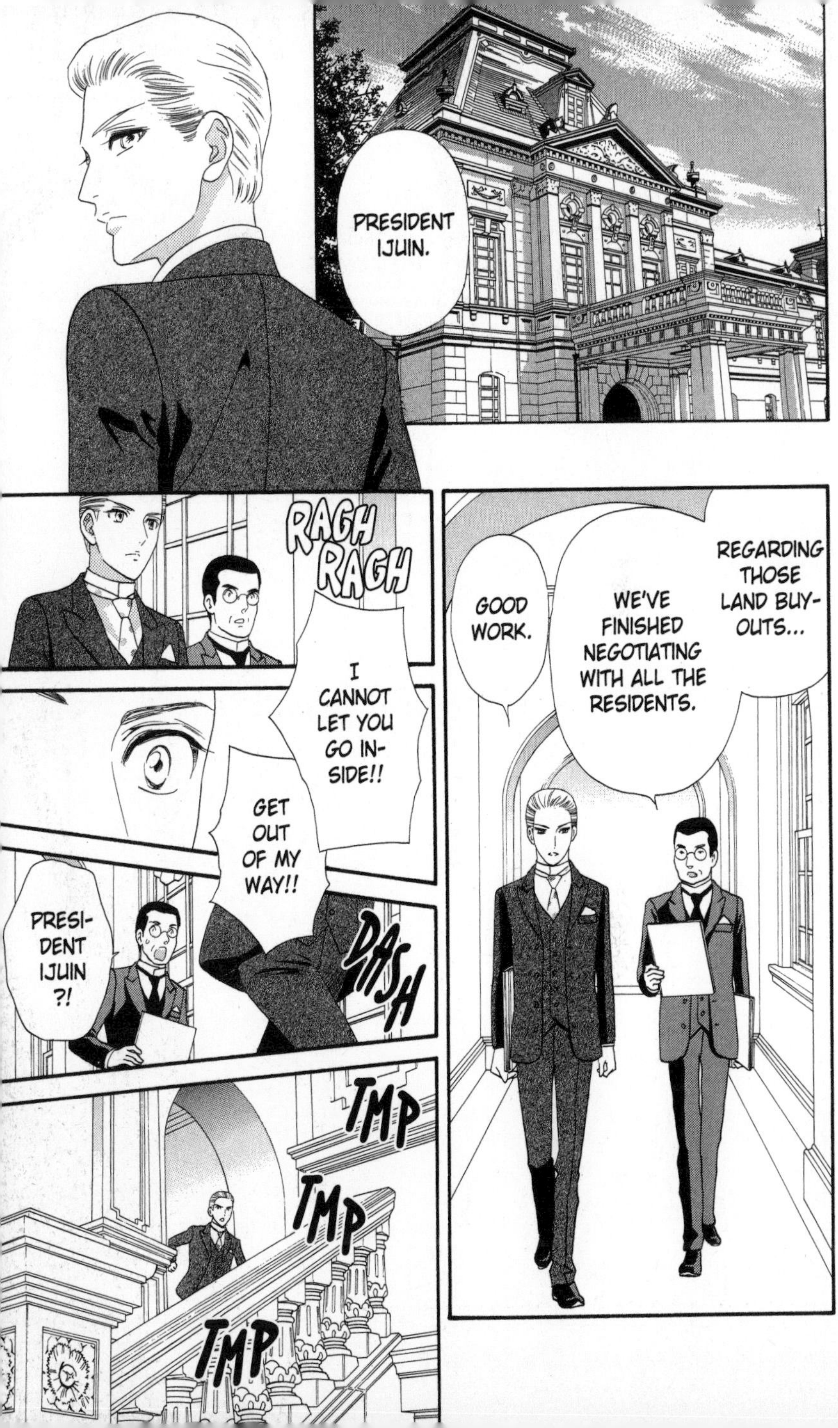
PRESIDENT IJUIN.
REGARDING THOSE LAND BUY-OUTS...
WE'VE FINISHED NEGOTIATING WITH ALL THE RESIDENTS.
GOOD WORK.
RAGH RAGH
I CANNOT LET YOU GO INSIDE!!
GET OUT OF MY WAY!!
DASH
PRESIDENT IJUIN ?!
TMP
TMP
TMP

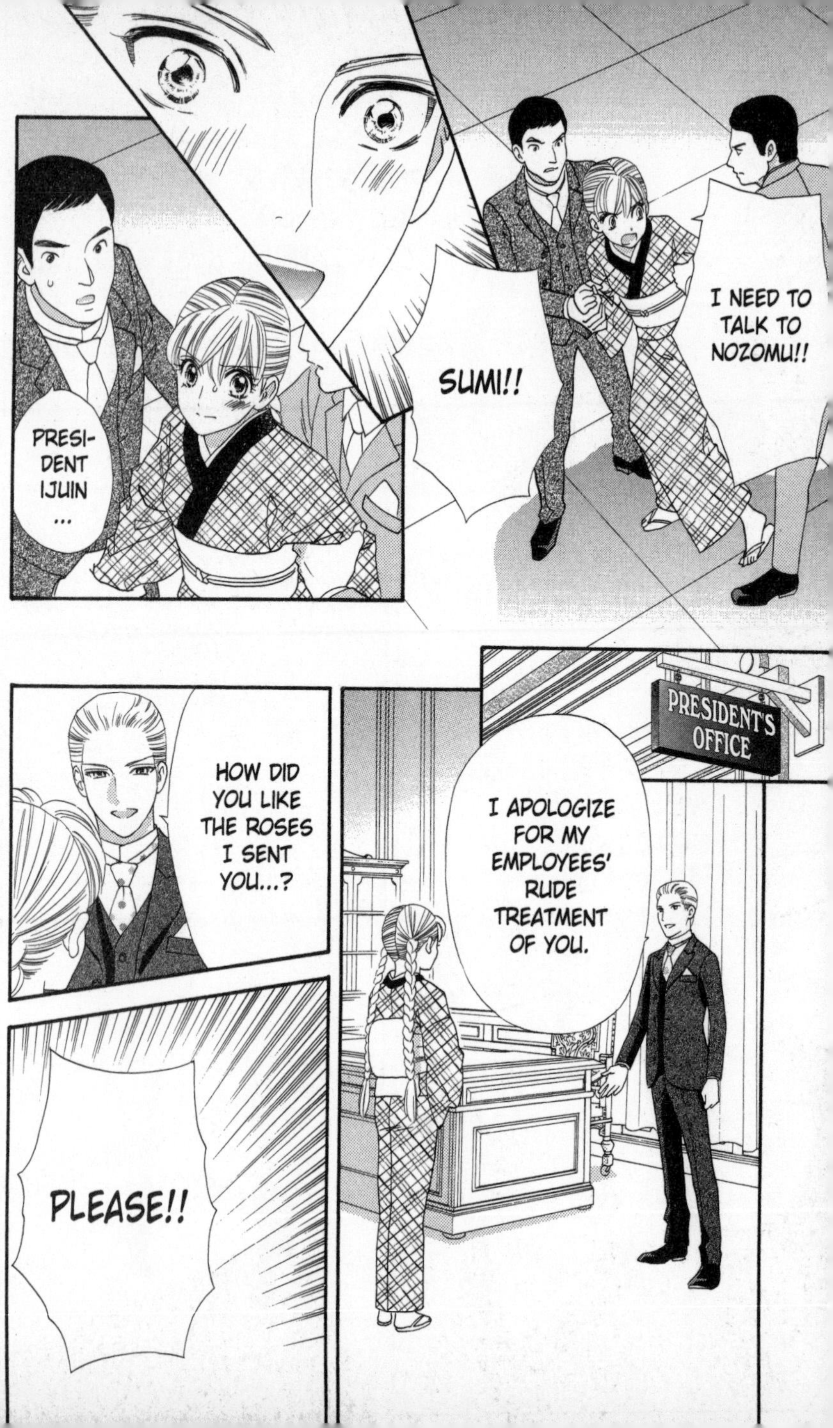
I NEED TO TALK TO NOZOMU!!
SUMI!!
PRESI-DENT IJUIN ...
PRESIDENT'S OFFICE
I APOLOGIZE FOR MY EMPLOYEES' RUDE TREATMENT OF YOU.
HOW DID YOU LIKE THE ROSES I SENT YOU...?
PLEASE!!

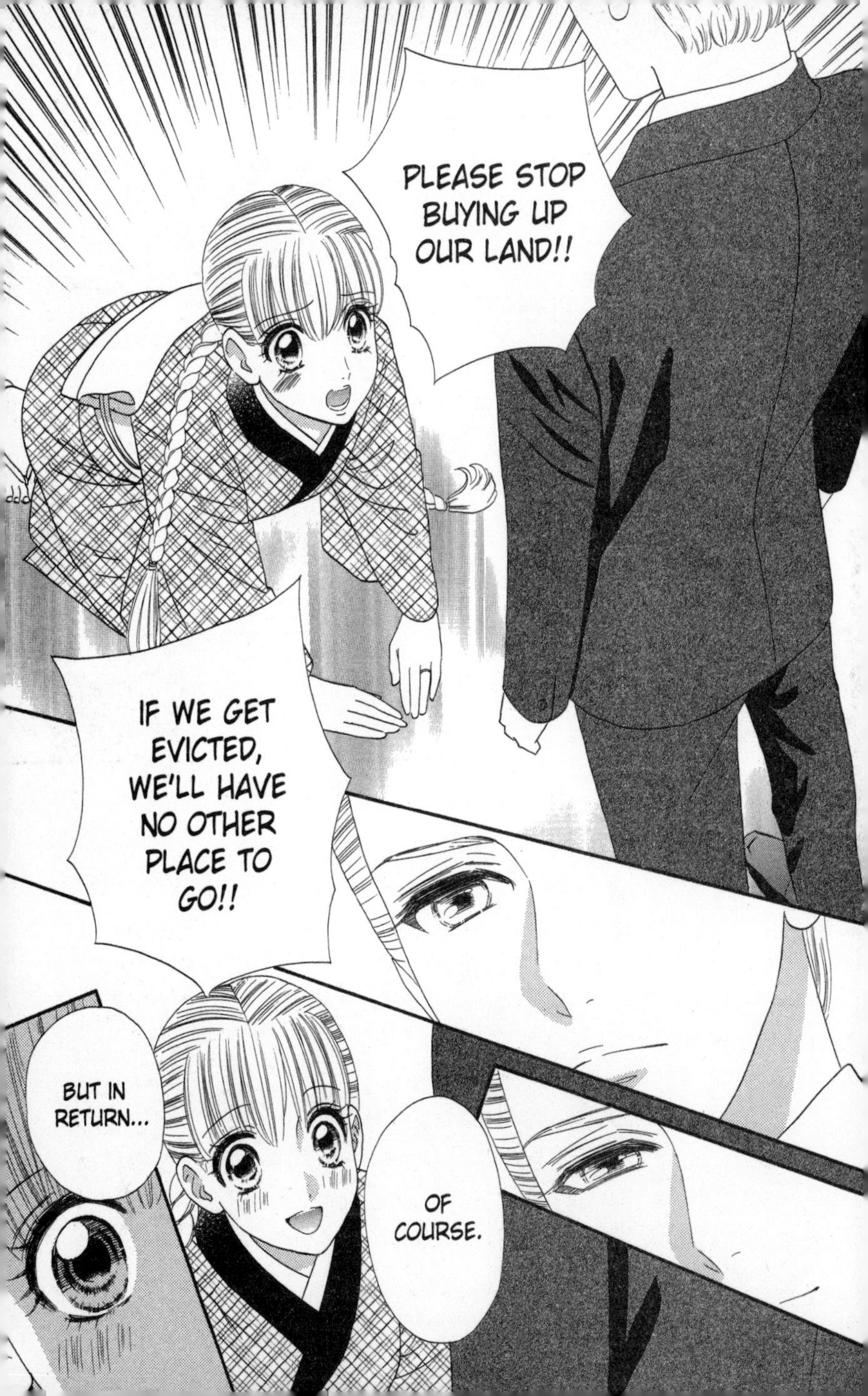
PLEASE STOP BUYING UP OUR LAND!!
IF WE GET EVICTED, WE'LL HAVE NO OTHER PLACE TO GO!!
OF COURSE.
BUT IN RETURN...

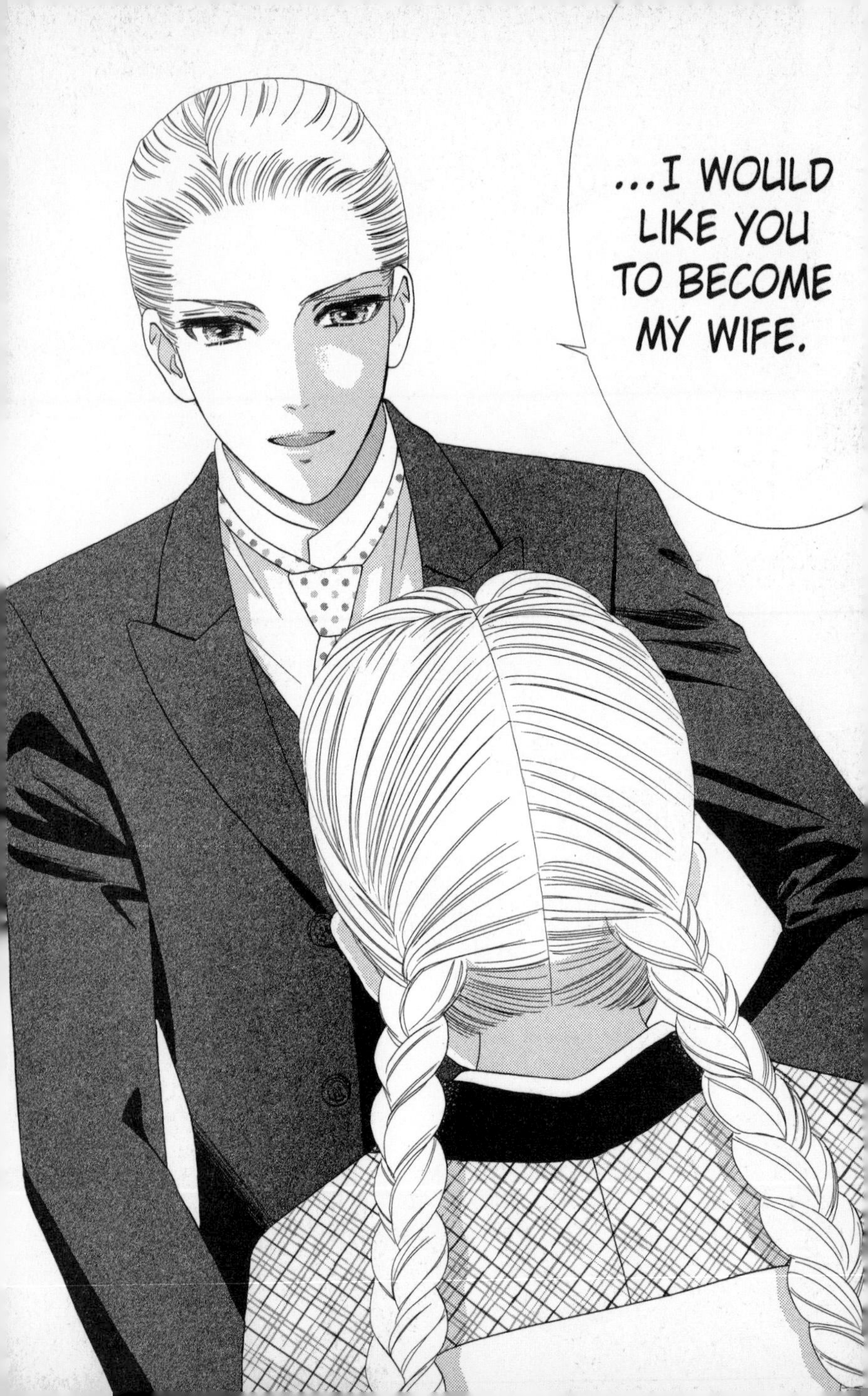
...I WOULD LIKE YOU TO BECOME MY WIFE.

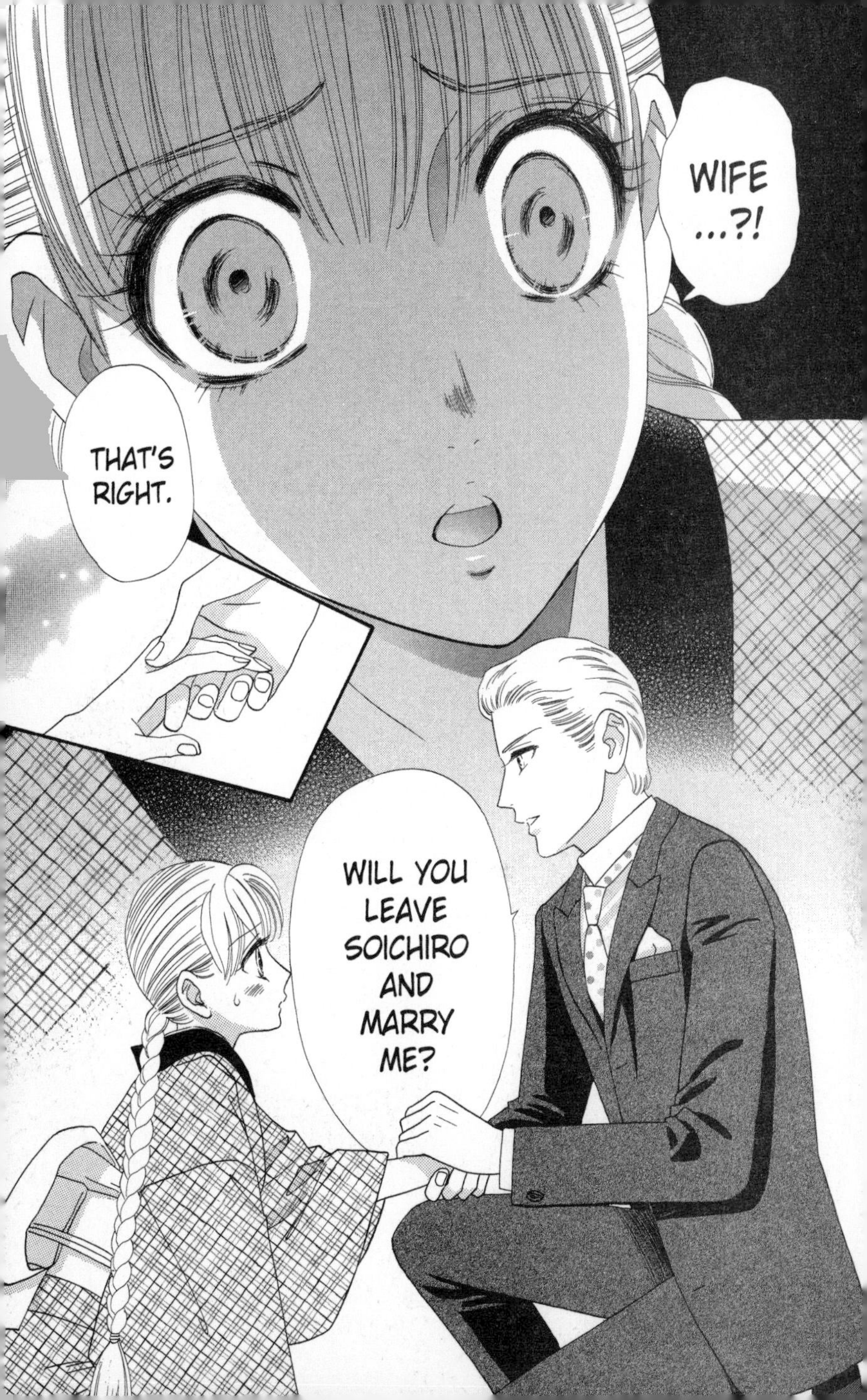
WIFE ...?!
THAT'S RIGHT.
WILL YOU LEAVE SOICHIRO AND MARRY ME?

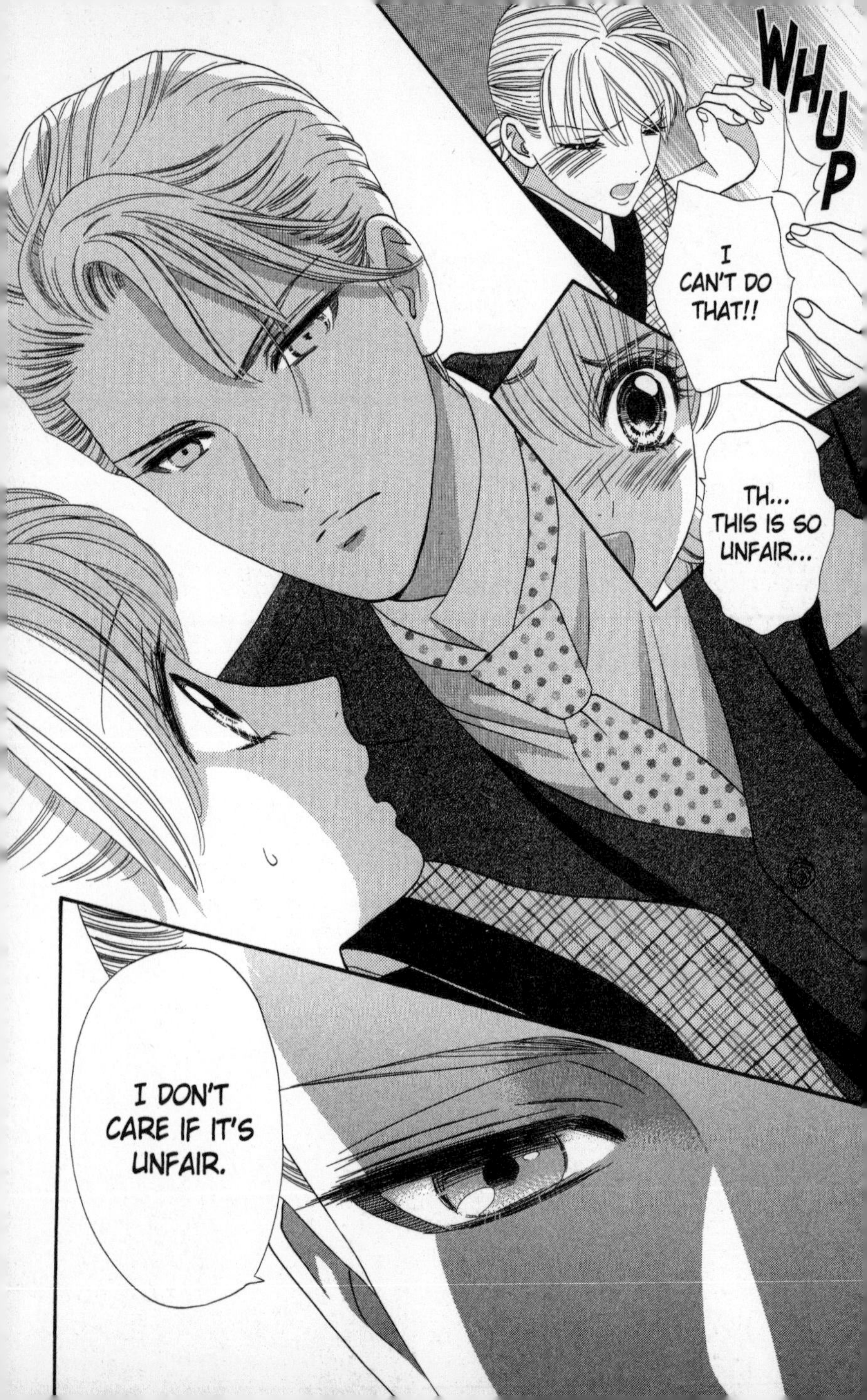
WHUP
I CAN'T DO THAT!!
TH... THIS IS SO UNFAIR...
I DON'T CARE IF IT'S UNFAIR.

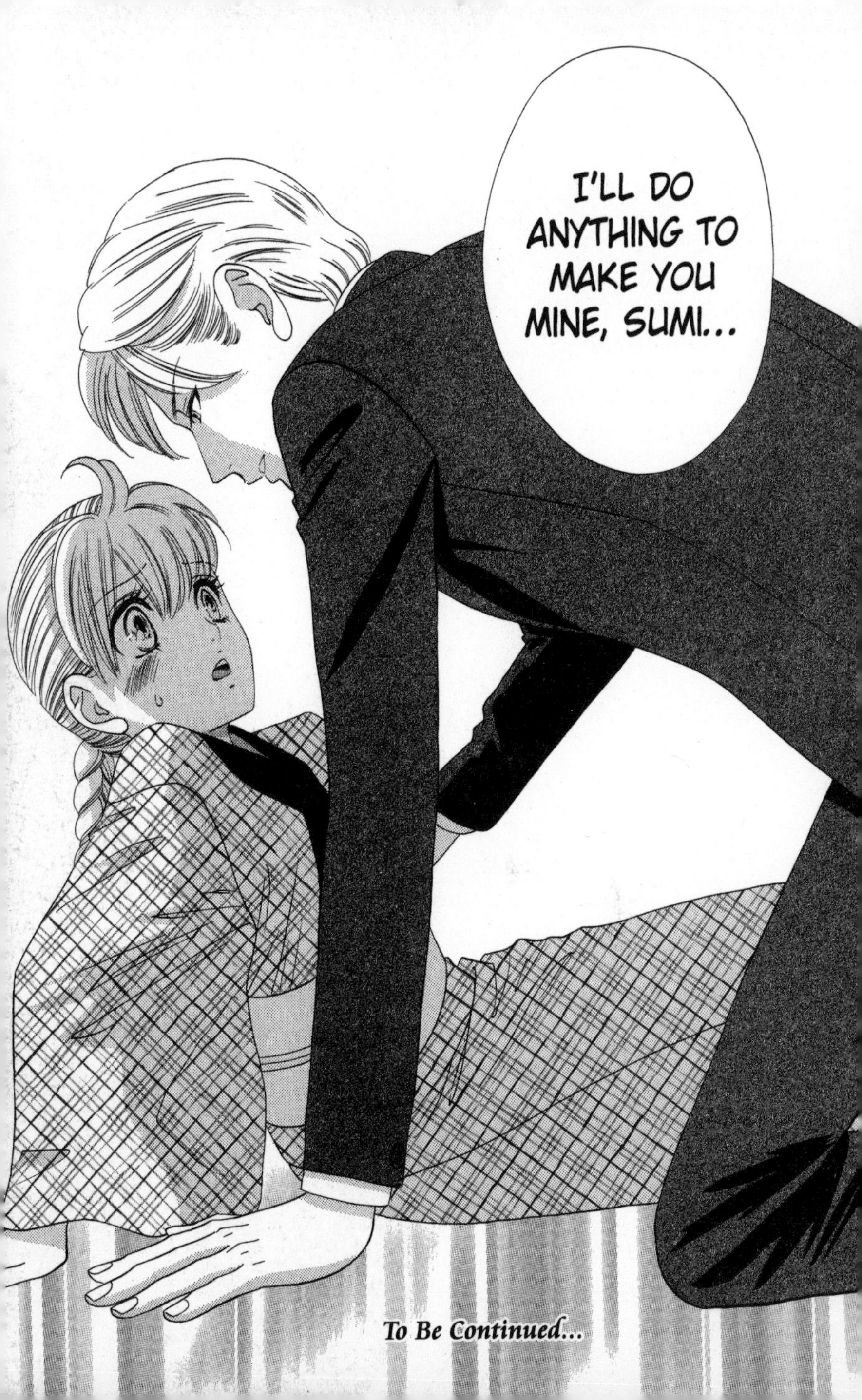
I'LL DO ANYTHING TO MAKE YOU MINE, SUMI...
To Be Continued...

Stepping on Roses

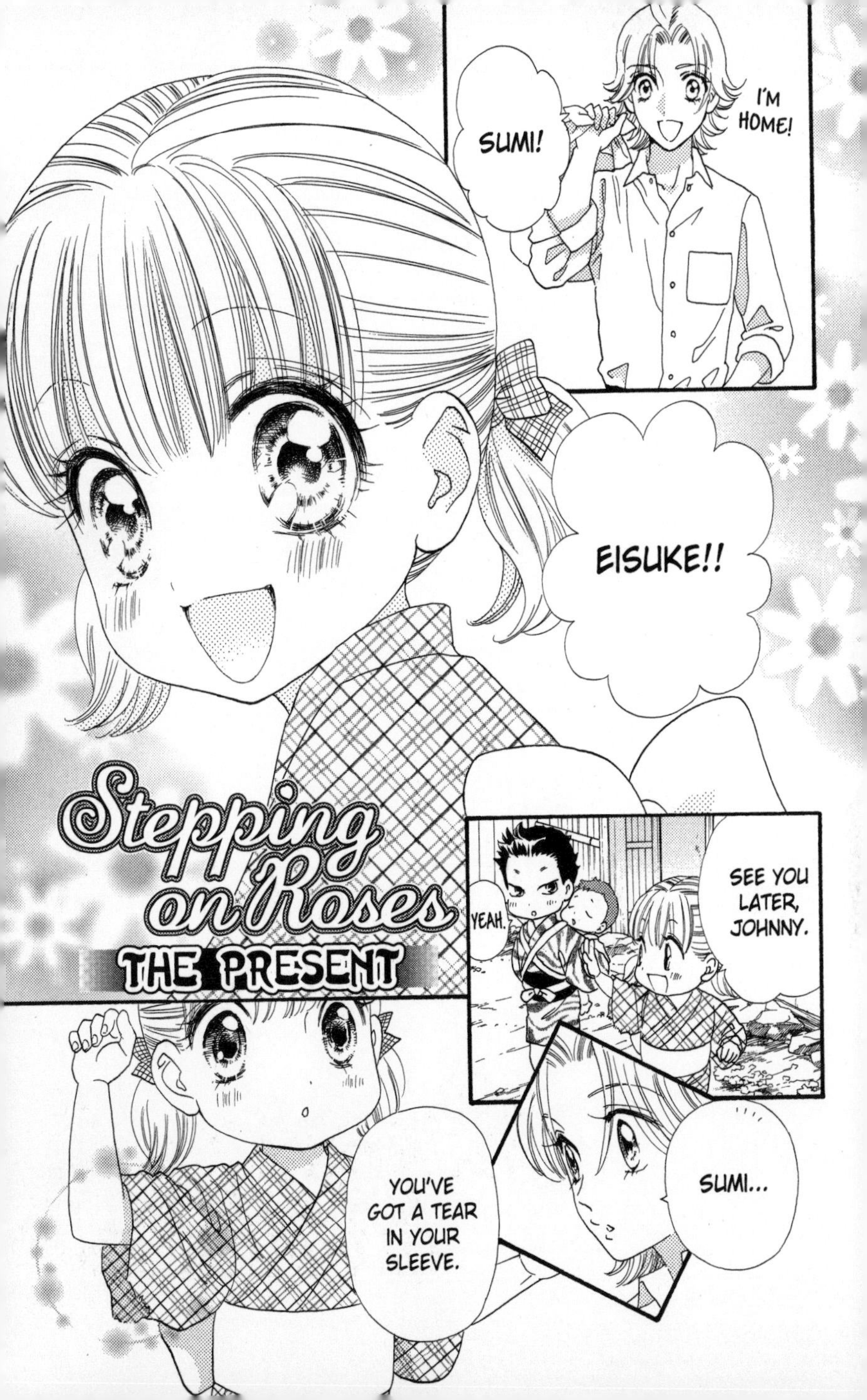
I'M HOME!
SUMI!
EISUKE!!
Stepping on Roses
THE PRESENT
SEE YOU LATER, JOHNNY.
YEAH.
SUMI...
YOU'VE GOT A TEAR IN YOUR SLEEVE.

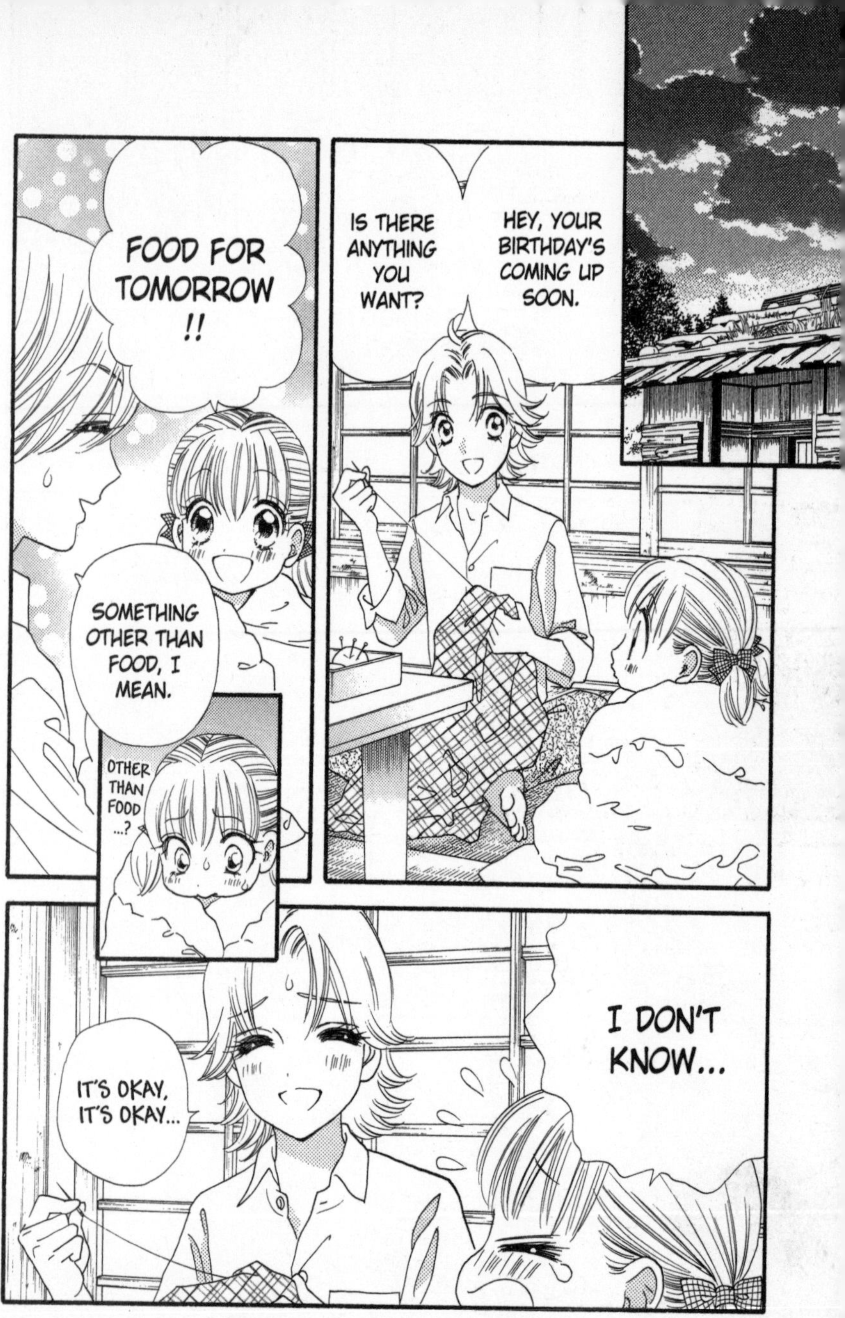
HEY, YOUR BIRTHDAY'S COMING UP SOON.
IS THERE ANYTHING YOU WANT?
FOOD FOR TOMORROW !!
SOMETHING OTHER THAN FOOD, I MEAN.
OTHER THAN FOOD ...?
I DON'T KNOW...
IT'S OKAY, IT'S OKAY...

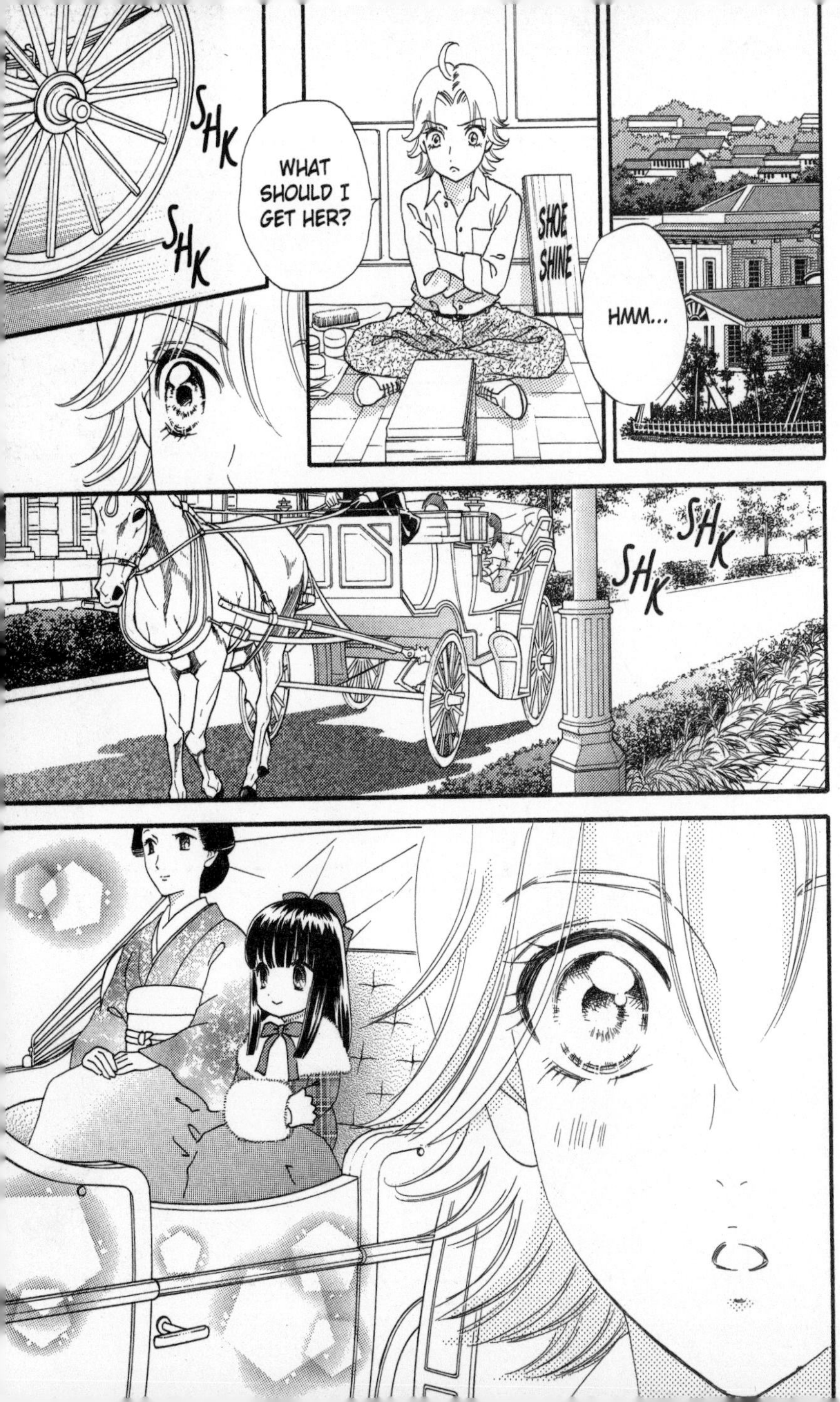
HMM...
WHAT SHOULD I GET HER?
SHOE SHINE
SHK
SHK
SHK
SHK

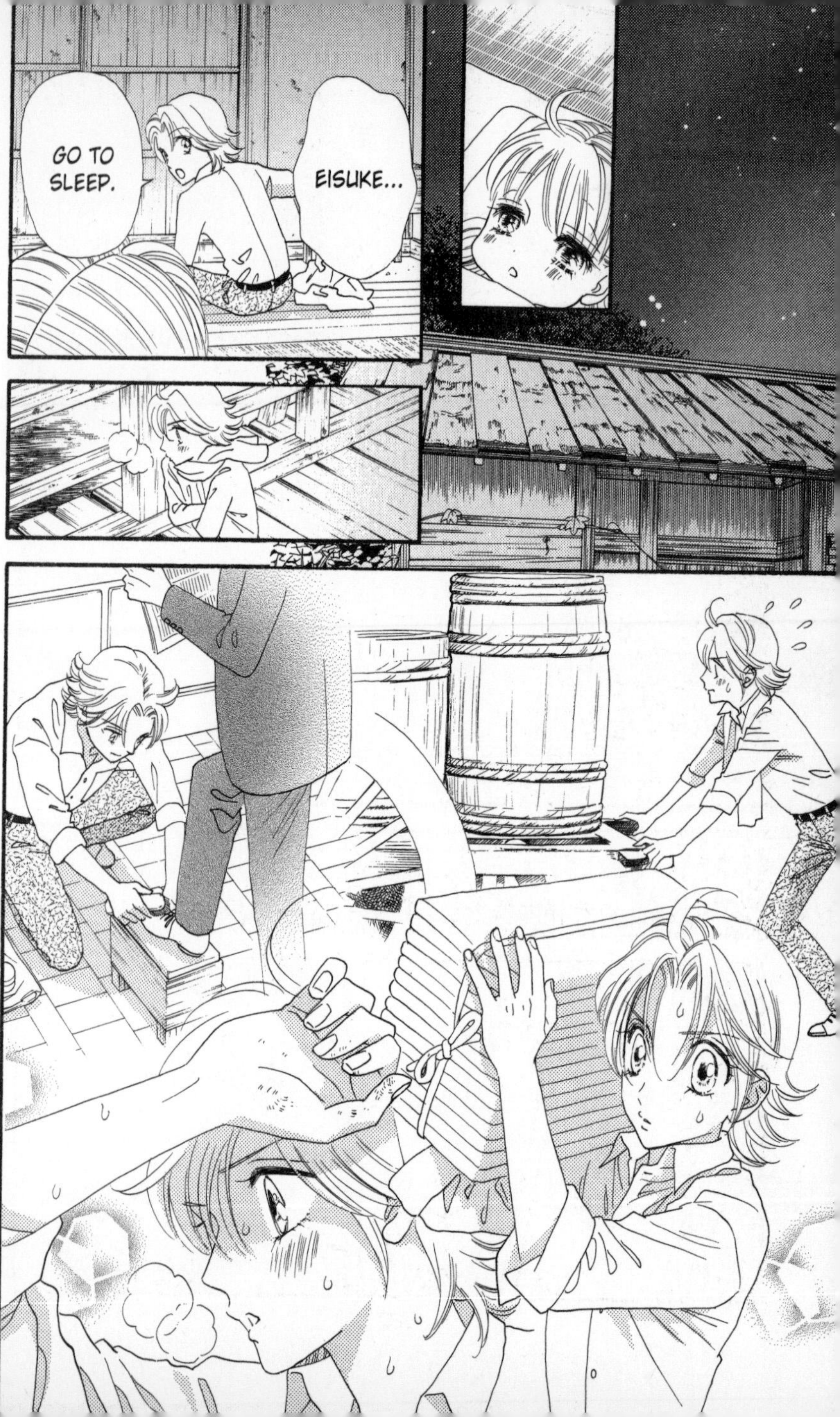
EISUKE...
GO TO SLEEP.

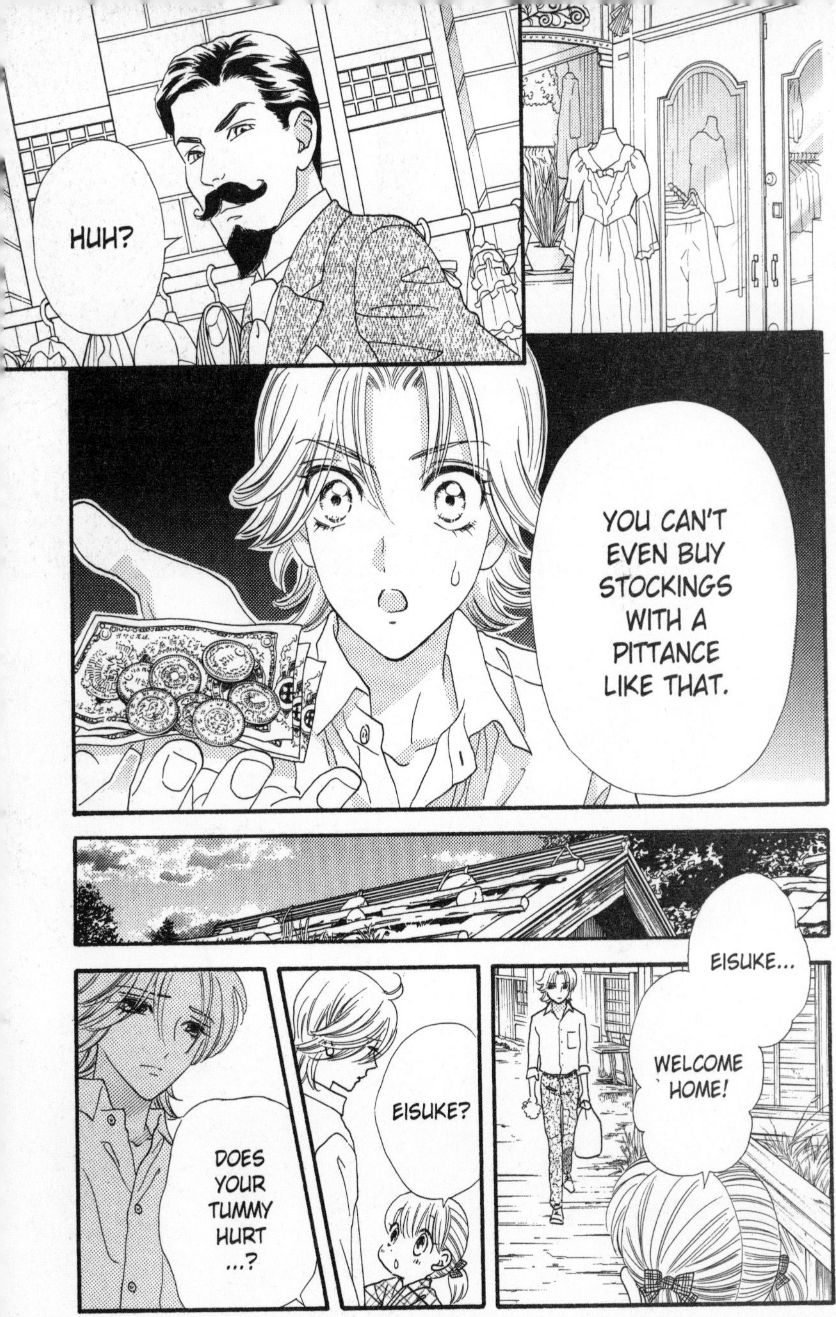
HUH?
YOU CAN'T EVEN BUY STOCKINGS WITH A PITTANCE LIKE THAT.
EISUKE...
WELCOME HOME!
EISUKE?
DOES YOUR TUMMY HURT ...?

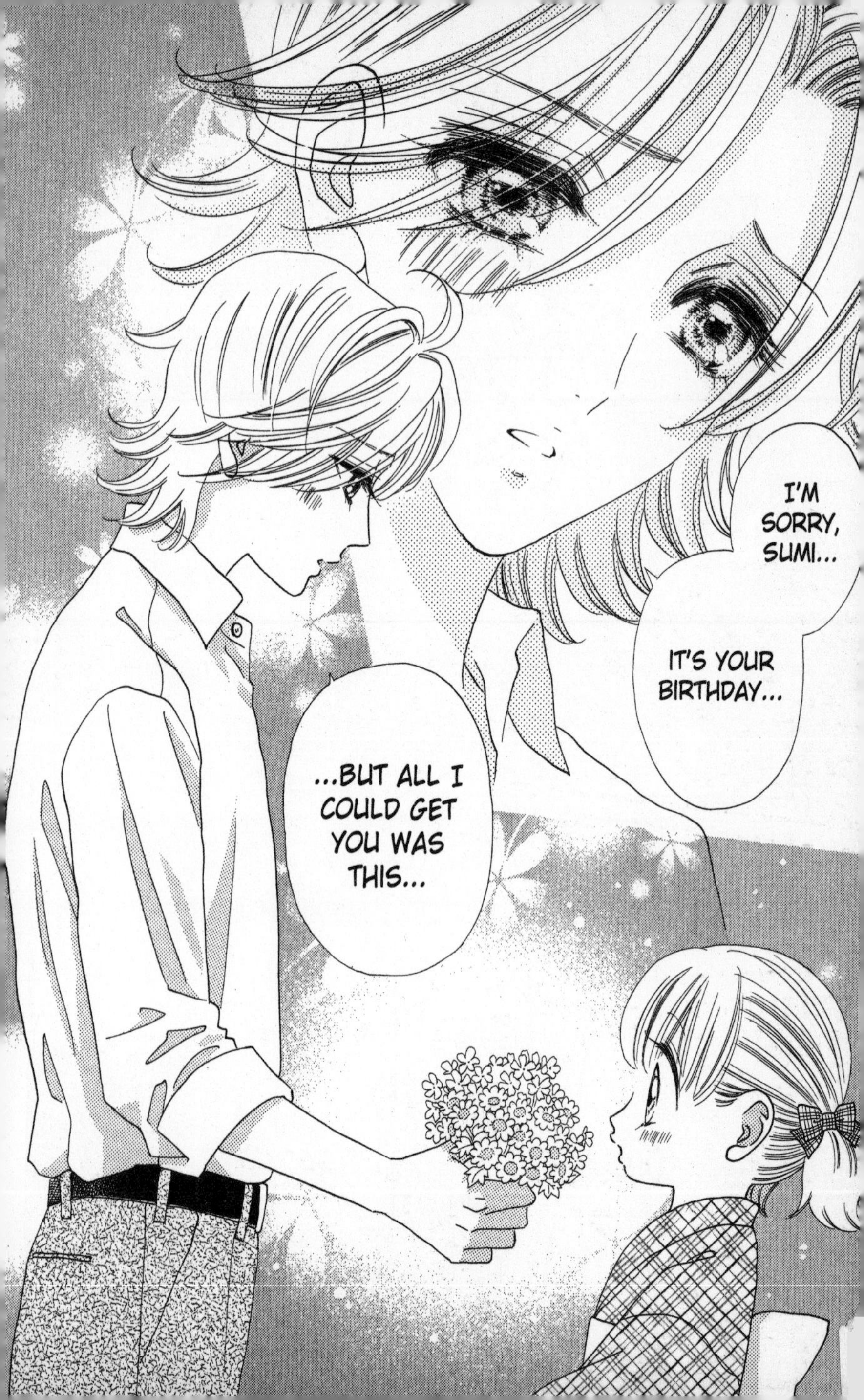
I'M SORRY, SUMI...
IT'S YOUR BIRTHDAY...
...BUT ALL I COULD GET YOU WAS THIS...

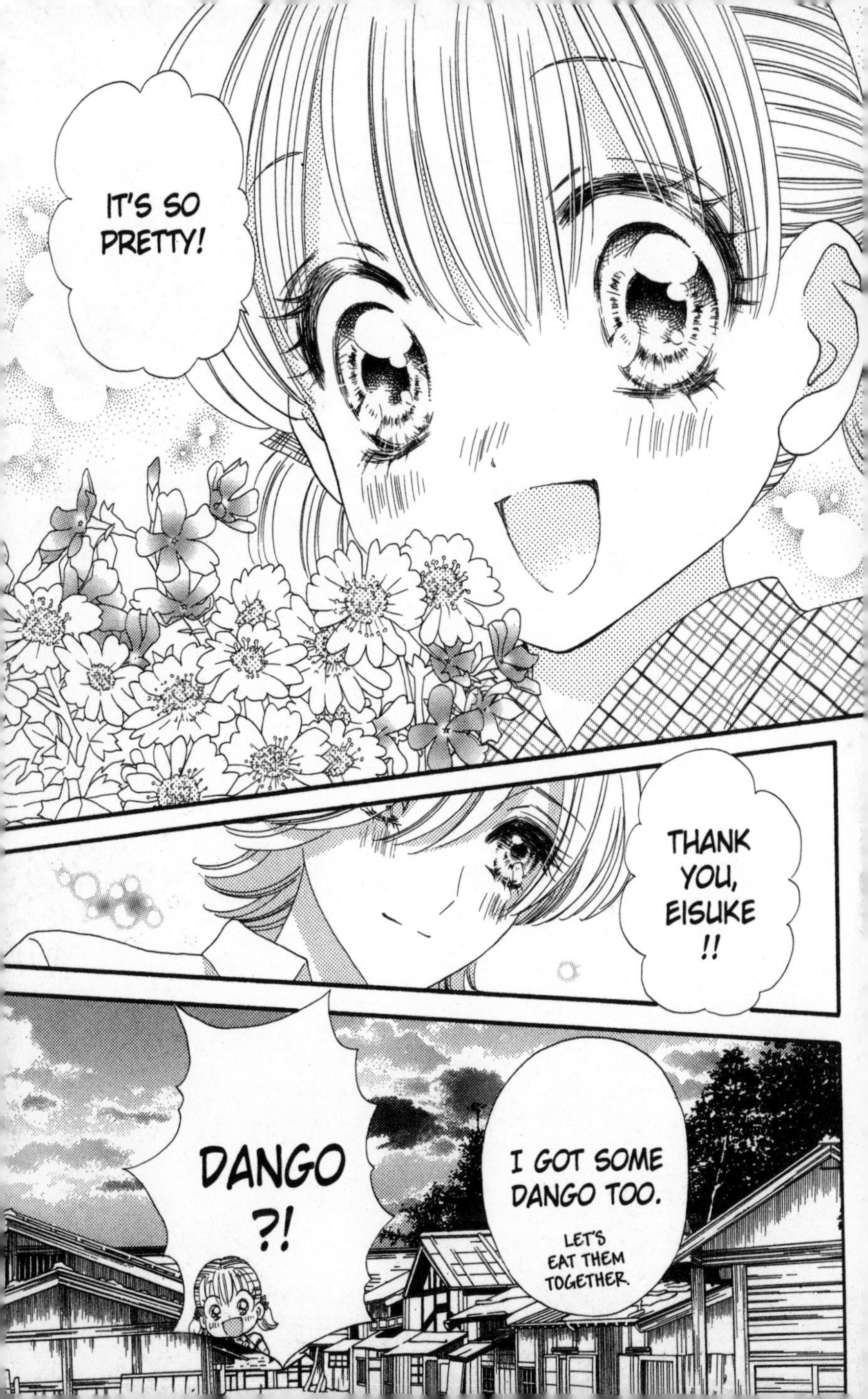
IT'S SO PRETTY!
THANK YOU, EISUKE !!
I GOT SOME DANGO TOO.
LET'S EAT THEM TOGETHER.
DANGO ?!

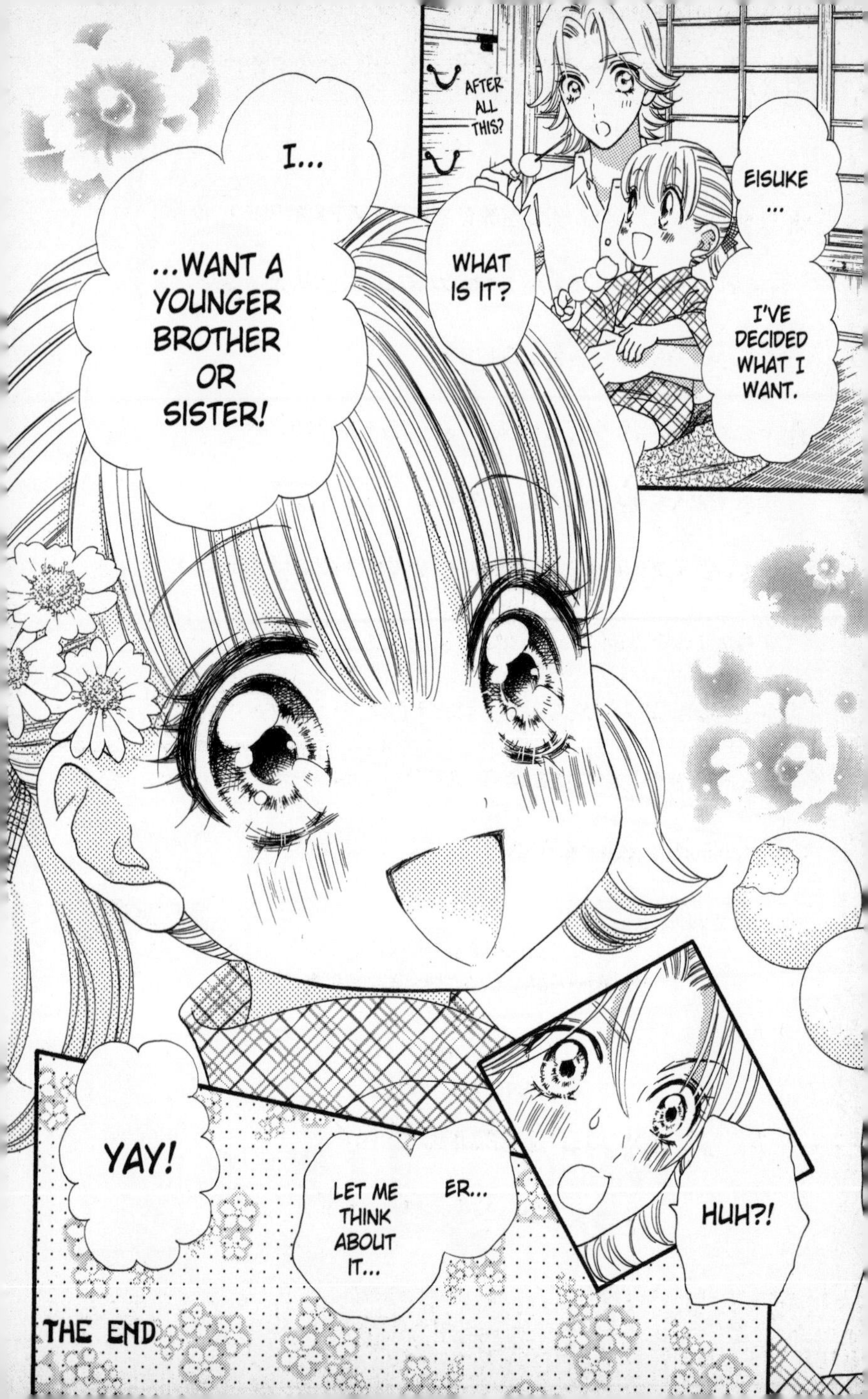
EISUKE ...
I'VE DECIDED WHAT I WANT.
WHAT IS IT?
AFTER ALL THIS?
I...
...WANT A YOUNGER BROTHER OR SISTER!
HUH?!
ER...
LET ME THINK ABOUT IT...
YAY!
THE END

✿ HOW DID YOU LIKE THE SIDE STORY? THIS IS THE FIRST TIME I DID A SHORT SIDE STORY. I REALLY ENJOYED DRAWING SUMI AS A SMALL GIRL AND EISUKE AS A YOUNG BOY. ☆

✿ THE PIECE AFTER THIS IS A CHILD-RAISING ESSAY MANGA I DID FOR A MAGAZINE CALLED *YOU*. IT'S REFRESHING FOR ME TO READ IT SINCE I DREW THIS WHILE MY DAUGHTER WAS STILL A BABY...

✿ THE MAIN STORY HAS TAKEN A SHARP TURN IN THIS VOLUME. I HOPE YOU'LL CONTINUE TO FOLLOW SUMI AND SOICHIRO'S LIVES, WHICH ARE FILLED WITH MANY UPS AND DOWNS. OH, AND NOZOMU TOO...

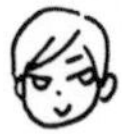
HEH HEH...

SEND YOUR THOUGHTS TO:
RINKO UEDA C/O STEPPING ON ROSES EDITOR
VIZ MEDIA
P.O. BOX 77010
SAN FRANCISCO, CA 94107

✿ SEE YOU ALL IN VOLUME 8! ~ ♡

Rinko Ueda

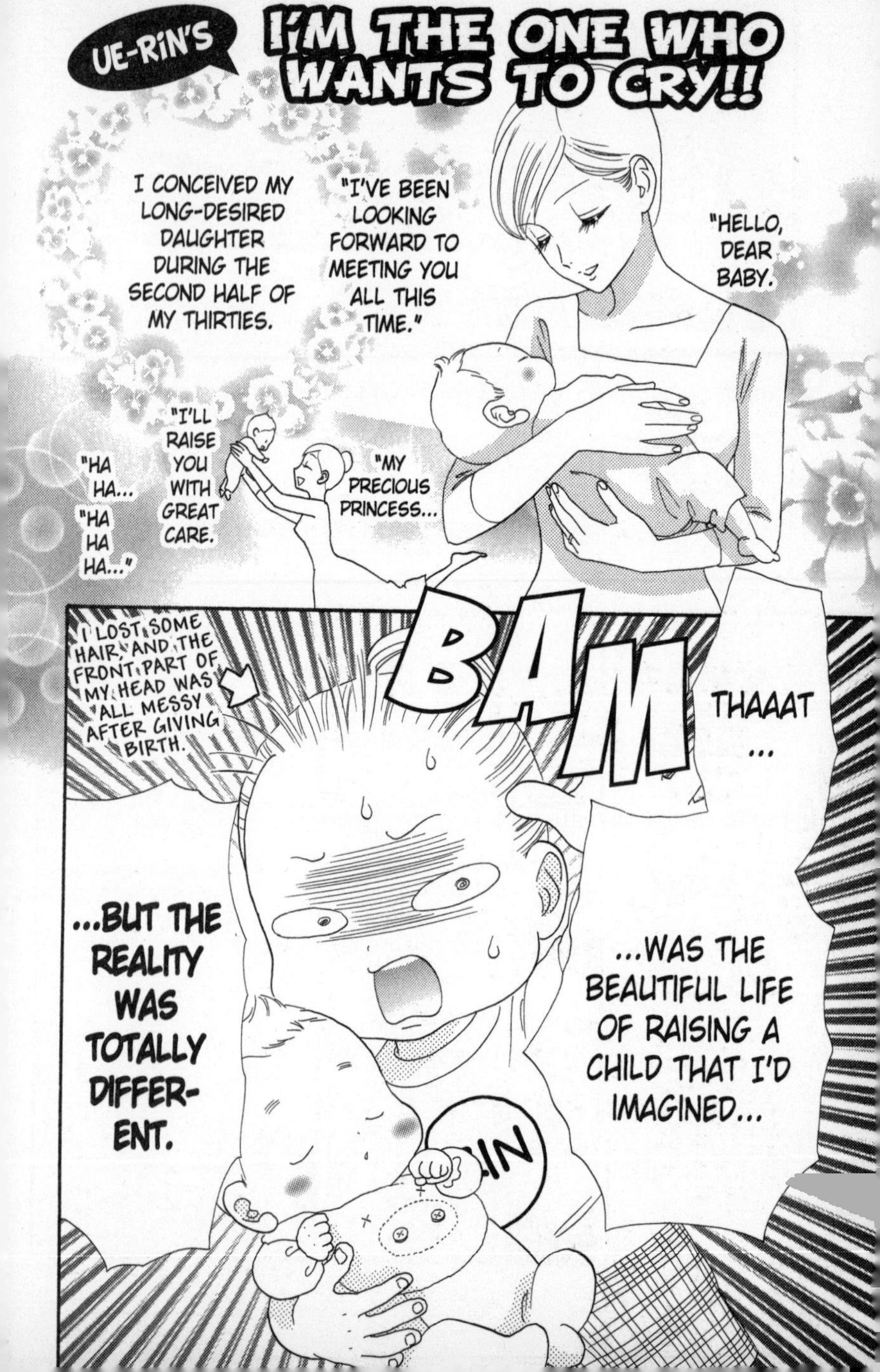
UE-RIN'S
I'M THE ONE WHO WANTS TO CRY!!
"HELLO, DEAR BABY.
"I'VE BEEN LOOKING FORWARD TO MEETING YOU ALL THIS TIME."
I CONCEIVED MY LONG-DESIRED DAUGHTER DURING THE SECOND HALF OF MY THIRTIES.
"MY PRECIOUS PRINCESS...
"I'LL RAISE YOU WITH GREAT CARE.
"HA HA...
"HA HA HA..."
BAM
THAAAT...
...WAS THE BEAUTIFUL LIFE OF RAISING A CHILD THAT I'D IMAGINED...
I LOST SOME HAIR, AND THE FRONT PART OF MY HEAD WAS ALL MESSY AFTER GIVING BIRTH.
...BUT THE REALITY WAS TOTALLY DIFFER-ENT.
RIN

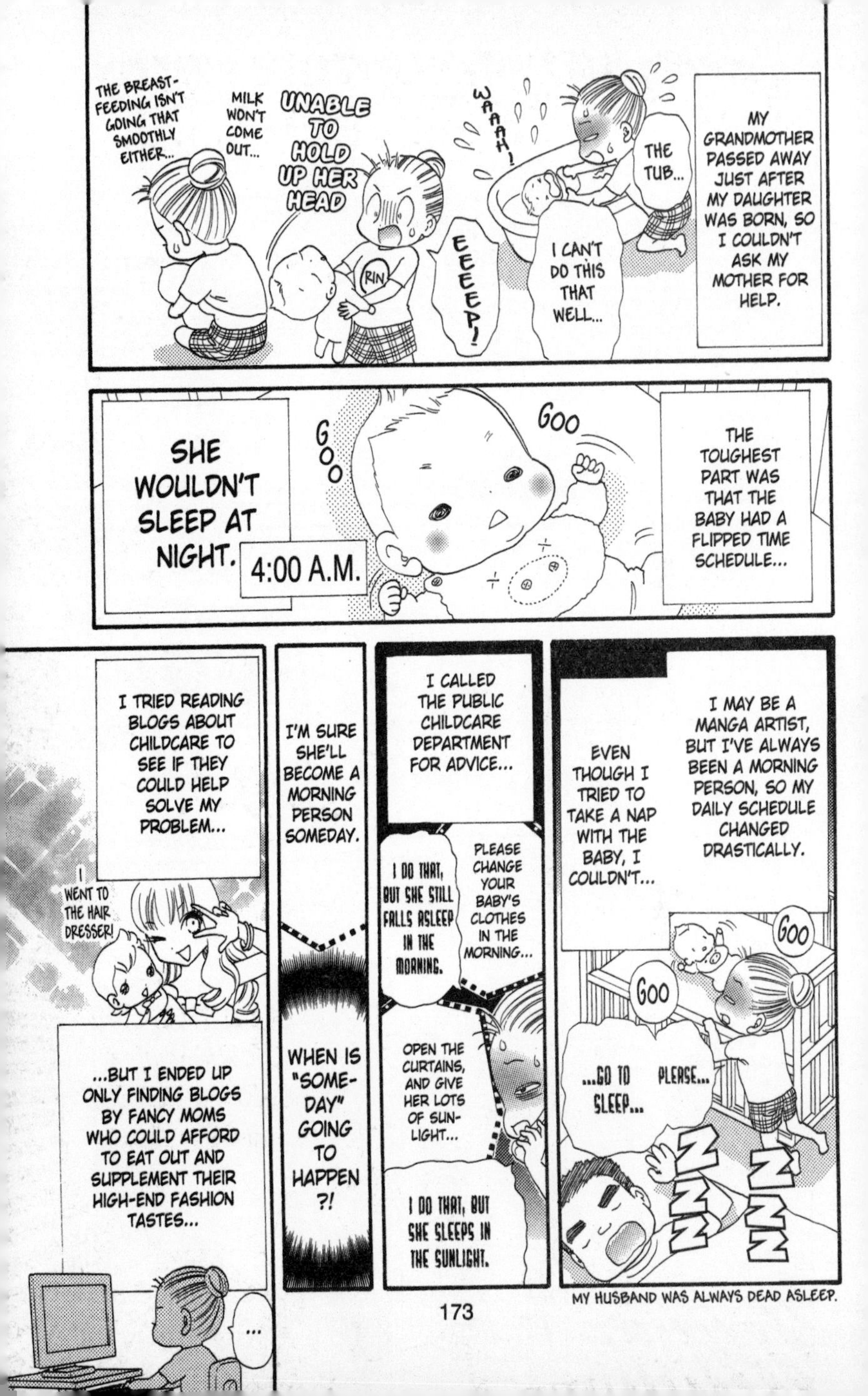

MY GRANDMOTHER PASSED AWAY JUST AFTER MY DAUGHTER WAS BORN, SO I COULDN'T ASK MY MOTHER FOR HELP.
THE TUB...
WAAAH!
I CAN'T DO THIS THAT WELL...
EEEEEP!
UNABLE TO HOLD UP HER HEAD
RIN
MILK WON'T COME OUT...
THE BREAST-FEEDING ISN'T GOING THAT SMOOTHLY EITHER...
THE TOUGHEST PART WAS THAT THE BABY HAD A FLIPPED TIME SCHEDULE...
GOO
GOO
SHE WOULDN'T SLEEP AT NIGHT.
4:00 A.M.
I MAY BE A MANGA ARTIST, BUT I'VE ALWAYS BEEN A MORNING PERSON, SO MY DAILY SCHEDULE CHANGED DRASTICALLY.
EVEN THOUGH I TRIED TO TAKE A NAP WITH THE BABY, I COULDN'T...
GOO
GOO
PLEASE...
...GO TO SLEEP...
ZZZ
ZZZ
MY HUSBAND WAS ALWAYS DEAD ASLEEP.
I CALLED THE PUBLIC CHILDCARE DEPARTMENT FOR ADVICE...
PLEASE CHANGE YOUR BABY'S CLOTHES IN THE MORNING...
I DO THAT, BUT SHE STILL FALLS ASLEEP IN THE MORNING.
OPEN THE CURTAINS, AND GIVE HER LOTS OF SUNLIGHT...
I DO THAT, BUT SHE SLEEPS IN THE SUNLIGHT.
I'M SURE SHE'LL BECOME A MORNING PERSON SOMEDAY.
WHEN IS "SOMEDAY" GOING TO HAPPEN?!
I TRIED READING BLOGS ABOUT CHILDCARE TO SEE IF THEY COULD HELP SOLVE MY PROBLEM...
I WENT TO THE HAIR DRESSER!
...BUT I ENDED UP ONLY FINDING BLOGS BY FANCY MOMS WHO COULD AFFORD TO EAT OUT AND SUPPLEMENT THEIR HIGH-END FASHION TASTES...
...

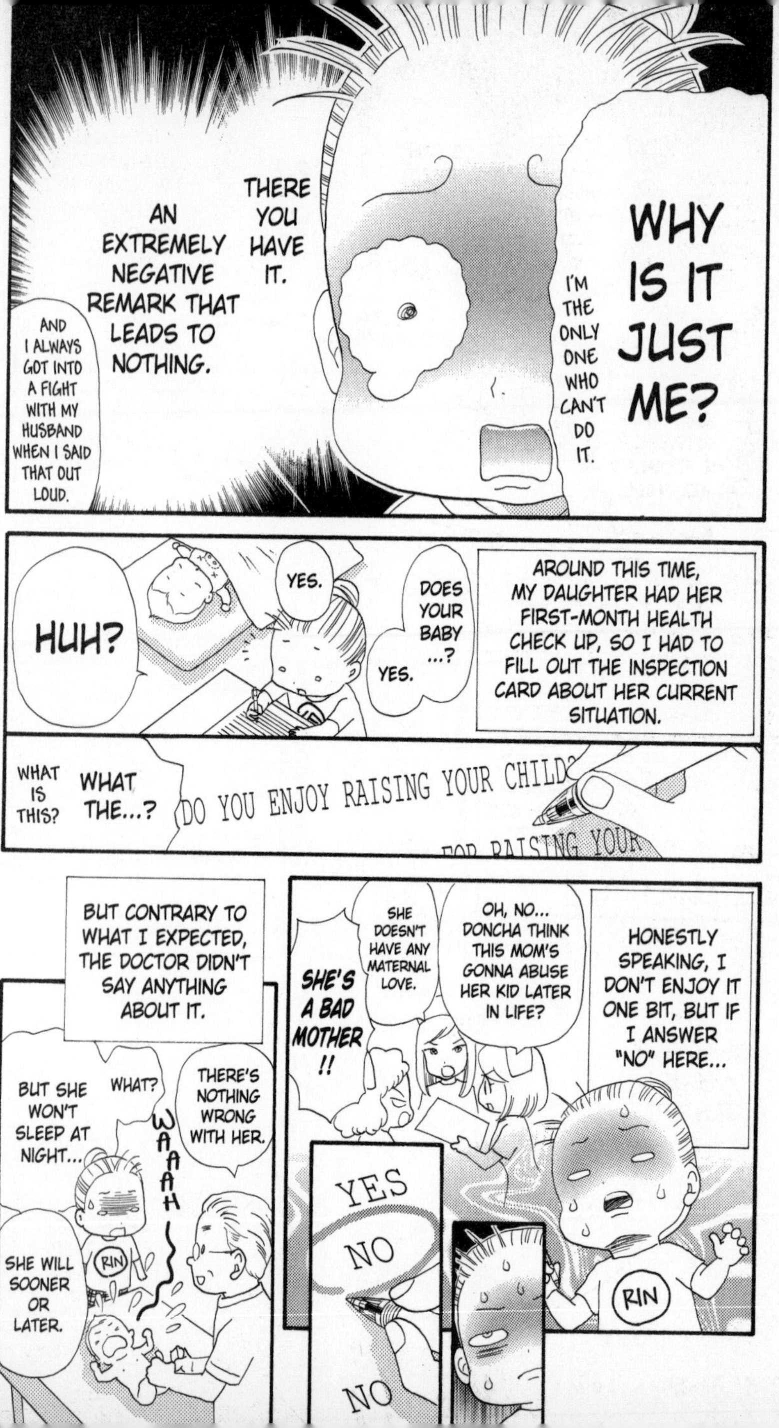
WHY IS IT JUST ME?
I'M THE ONLY ONE WHO CAN'T DO IT.
THERE YOU HAVE IT.
AN EXTREMELY NEGATIVE REMARK THAT LEADS TO NOTHING.
AND I ALWAYS GOT INTO A FIGHT WITH MY HUSBAND WHEN I SAID THAT OUT LOUD.
AROUND THIS TIME, MY DAUGHTER HAD HER FIRST-MONTH HEALTH CHECK UP, SO I HAD TO FILL OUT THE INSPECTION CARD ABOUT HER CURRENT SITUATION.
DOES YOUR BABY ...?
YES.
YES.
HUH?
DO YOU ENJOY RAISING YOUR CHILD?
FOR RAISING YOUR
WHAT THE...?
WHAT IS THIS?
HONESTLY SPEAKING, I DON'T ENJOY IT ONE BIT, BUT IF I ANSWER "NO" HERE...
OH, NO... DONCHA THINK THIS MOM'S GONNA ABUSE HER KID LATER IN LIFE?
SHE DOESN'T HAVE ANY MATERNAL LOVE.
SHE'S A BAD MOTHER!!
RIN
YES
NO
NO
BUT CONTRARY TO WHAT I EXPECTED, THE DOCTOR DIDN'T SAY ANYTHING ABOUT IT.
THERE'S NOTHING WRONG WITH HER.
WHAT?
BUT SHE WON'T SLEEP AT NIGHT...
WAAAH
RIN
SHE WILL SOONER OR LATER.

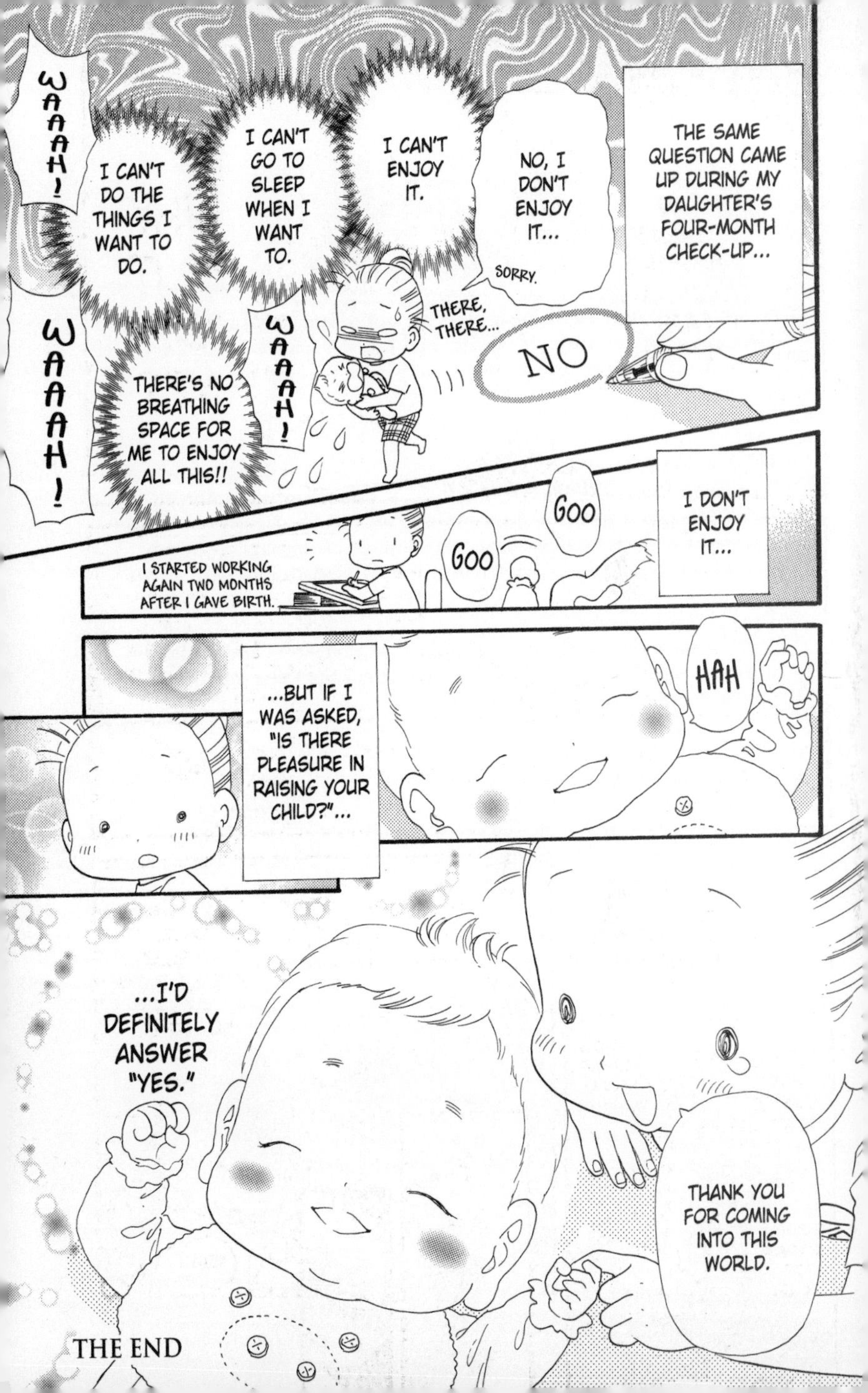
THE SAME QUESTION CAME UP DURING MY DAUGHTER'S FOUR-MONTH CHECK-UP...
NO
NO, I DON'T ENJOY IT...
SORRY.
I CAN'T ENJOY IT.
I CAN'T GO TO SLEEP WHEN I WANT TO.
I CAN'T DO THE THINGS I WANT TO DO.
WAAAH!
THERE, THERE...
WAAAH!
THERE'S NO BREATHING SPACE FOR ME TO ENJOY ALL THIS!!
WAAAH!
I DON'T ENJOY IT...
GOO
GOO
I STARTED WORKING AGAIN TWO MONTHS AFTER I GAVE BIRTH.
HAH
...BUT IF I WAS ASKED, "IS THERE PLEASURE IN RAISING YOUR CHILD?"...
THANK YOU FOR COMING INTO THIS WORLD.
...I'D DEFINITELY ANSWER "YES."
THE END

Glossary

The setting of *Stepping on Roses* plays an important part in the story, as it showcases a unique time of change and transformation in Japan. Check out the notes below to help enrich your reading experience.

Page 2: Meiji Era
The Meiji Era (1868–1912) was a time of reform in Japan during which Western models and technology were studied, borrowed and adapted for the sake of modernization. One of the slogans of this period was *bunmei kaika*, or "civilization and enlightenment."

Page 62: Yokohama
Yokohama is the capital city of Kanagawa Prefecture and a major port city located south of Tokyo. Yokohama's port was one of the first to be opened to foreign trade.

Page 69, panel 2: Shogi
Shogi is a Japanese board game similar to chess in which the object of the game is to capture the opponent's king. It's played on a board, and each player has 20 pieces. Sumi is a master at shogi, a skill she revealed in volume 3. She heads up the shogi club at Soichiro's company.

Page 169, panel 3: Dango
Round dumpling made from rice flour. They are usually served on a skewer.

Soichiro has finally given up his status and honor to live a life of poverty with Sumi.

Every time I have a meeting with my editor, I'm told, "I don't like how Soichiro continues to tuck his shirt into his trousers even though he lives in the poorhouse now," so please look forward to the moment Soichiro's shirt gets untucked. ☆

-Rinko Ueda

Rinko Ueda is from Nara Prefecture. She enjoys listening to the radio, drama CDs and Rakugo comedy performances. Her works include *Ryo*, a series based on the legend of Gojo Bridge; *Home*, a story about love crossing national boundaries; and *Tail of the Moon* (*Tsuki no Shippo*), a romantic ninja comedy.

STEPPING ON ROSES
Vol. 7
Shojo Beat Edition

STORY AND ART BY
RINKO UEDA

Translation & Adaptation/Tetsuichiro Miyaki
Touch-up Art & Lettering/Mark McMurray
Design/Yukiko Whitley
Editor/Amy Yu

Printed in the U.S.A.

Published by VIZ Media, LLC
P.O. Box 77010
San Francisco, CA 94107

10 9 8 7 6 5 4 3 2 1
First printing, March 2012

www.viz.com
www.shojobeat.com

RATED T+ FOR OLDER TEEN

PARENTAL ADVISORY
STEPPING ON ROSES is rated T+ for Older Teen and is recommended for ages 16 and up. This volume contains brief nudity and sexual themes.
ratings.viz.com

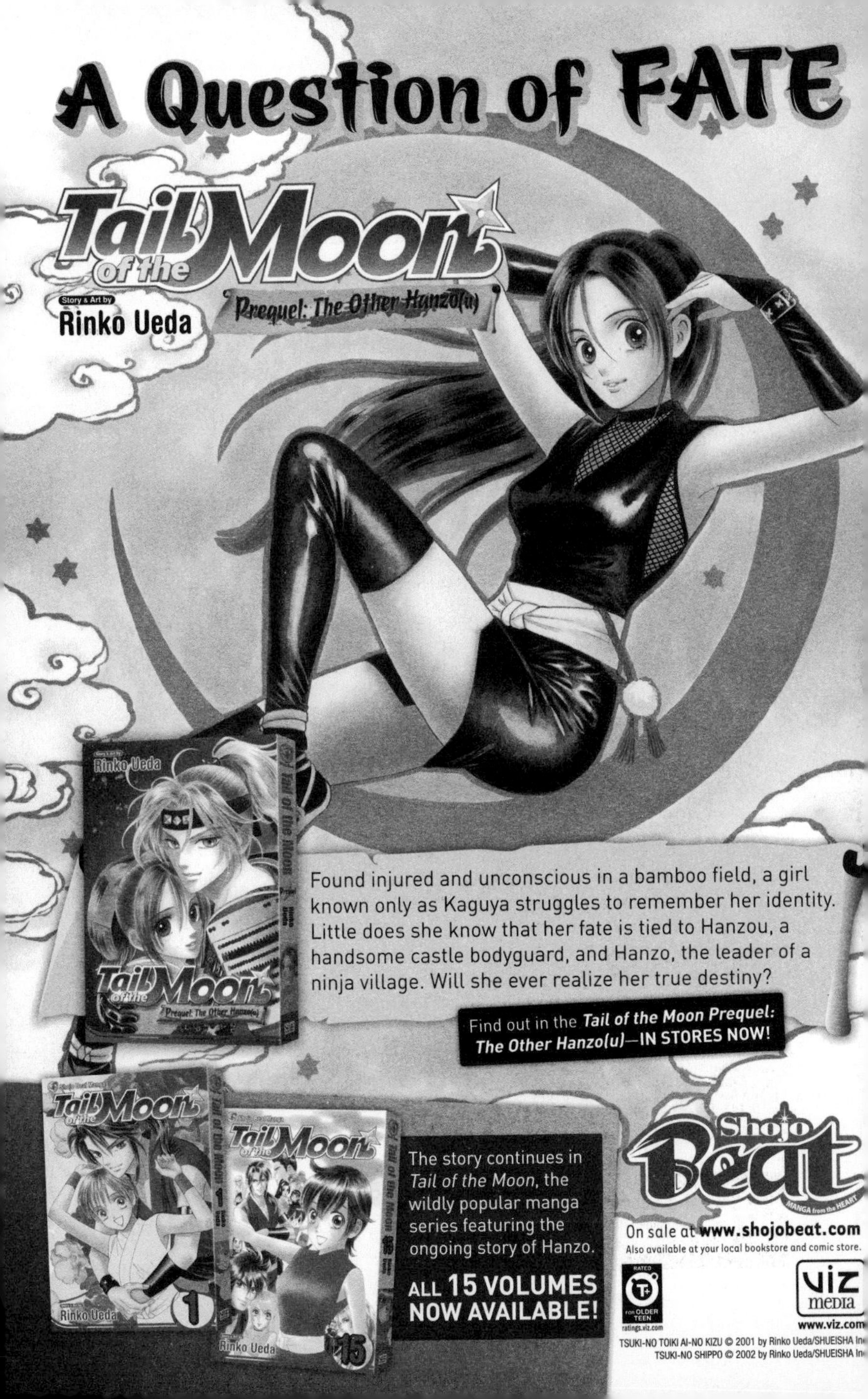

A Question of FATE
Tail of the Moon
Story & Art by
Rinko Ueda
Prequel: The Other Hanzo(u)
Found injured and unconscious in a bamboo field, a girl known only as Kaguya struggles to remember her identity. Little does she know that her fate is tied to Hanzou, a handsome castle bodyguard, and Hanzo, the leader of a ninja village. Will she ever realize her true destiny?
Find out in the Tail of the Moon Prequel: The Other Hanzo(u)—IN STORES NOW!
The story continues in Tail of the Moon, the wildly popular manga series featuring the ongoing story of Hanzo.
ALL 15 VOLUMES NOW AVAILABLE!
Shojo Beat
MANGA from the HEART
On sale at www.shojobeat.com
Also available at your local bookstore and comic store.
RATED T+ FOR OLDER TEEN
ratings.viz.com
VIZ media
www.viz.com
TSUKI-NO TOIKI AI-NO KIZU © 2001 by Rinko Ueda/SHUEISHA Inc.
TSUKI-NO SHIPPO © 2002 by Rinko Ueda/SHUEISHA Inc.

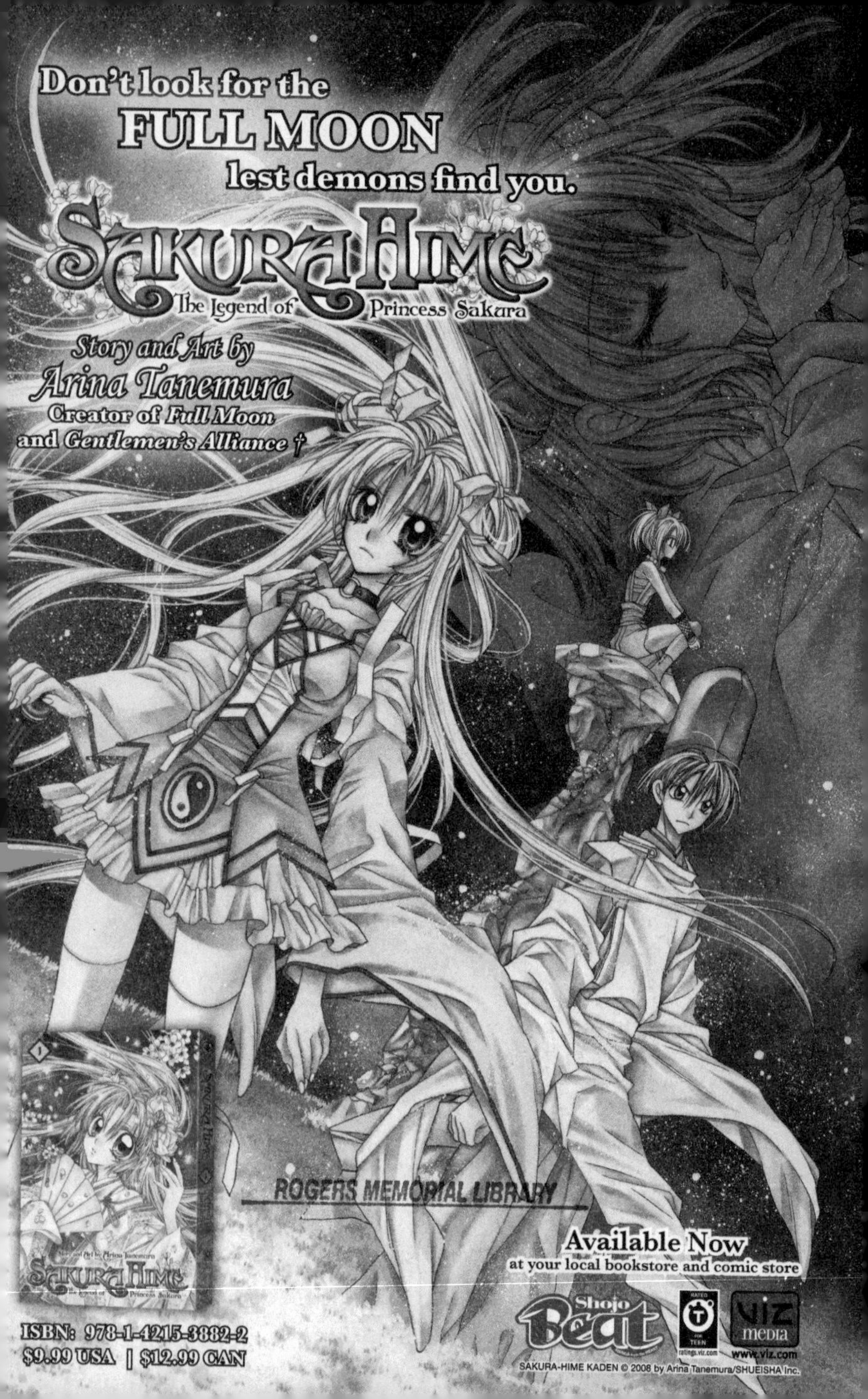
Don't look for the
FULL MOON
lest demons find you.
SAKURA HIME
The Legend of Princess Sakura
Story and Art by
Arina Tanemura
Creator of Full Moon
and Gentlemen's Alliance †
ROGERS MEMORIAL LIBRARY
Available Now
at your local bookstore and comic store
ISBN: 978-1-4215-3882-2
$9.99 USA | $12.99 CAN
Shojo Beat
RATED T FOR TEEN
ratings.viz.com
VIZ media
www.viz.com
SAKURA-HIME KADEN © 2008 by Arina Tanemura/SHUEISHA Inc.

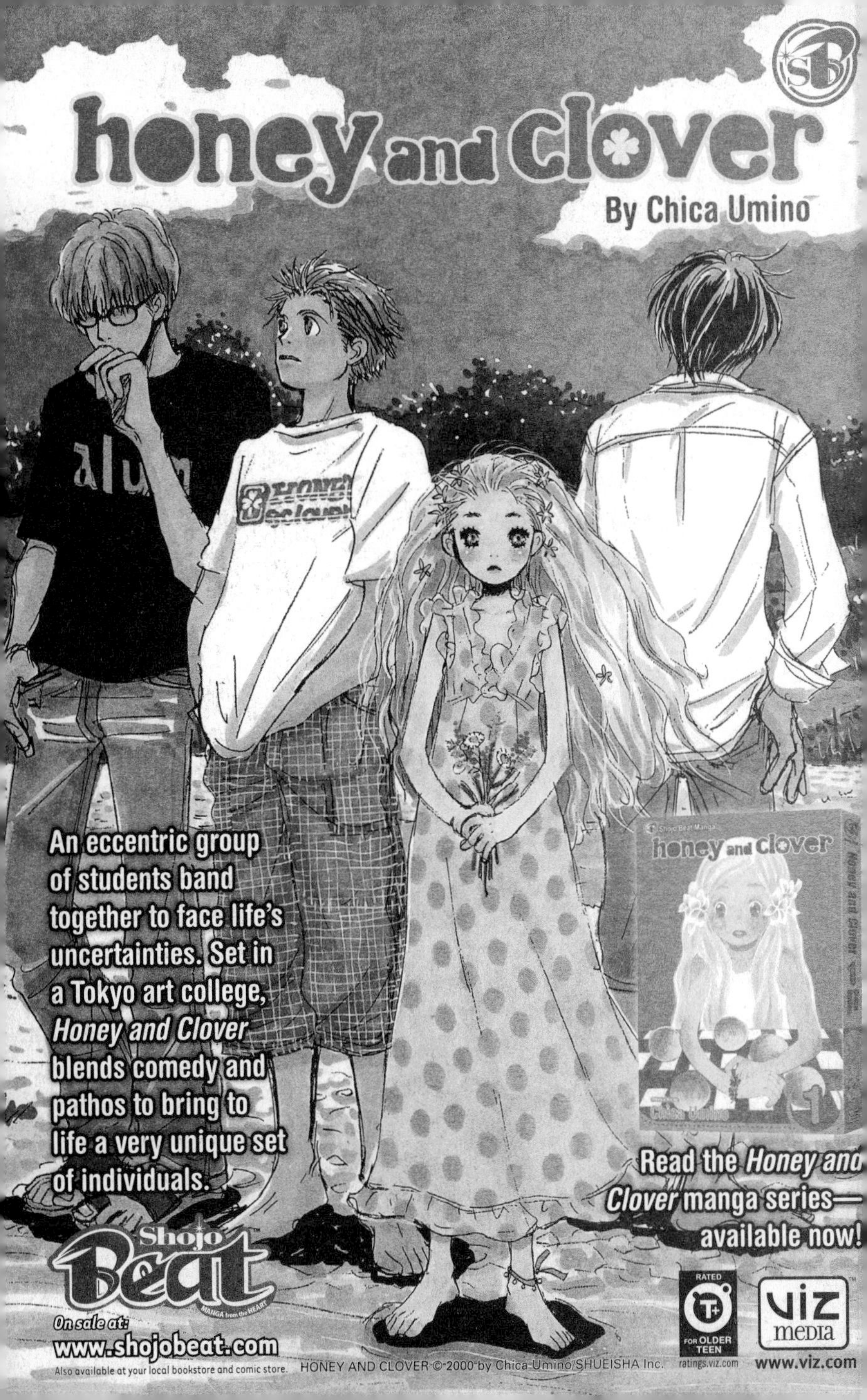

honey and clover
By Chica Umino
An eccentric group of students band together to face life's uncertainties. Set in a Tokyo art college, *Honey and Clover* blends comedy and pathos to bring to life a very unique set of individuals.
Shojo Beat Manga
honey and clover
1
Read the *Honey and Clover* manga series—available now!
Shojo Beat
MANGA from the HEART
On sale at:
www.shojobeat.com
Also available at your local bookstore and comic store.
HONEY AND CLOVER © 2000 by Chica Umino/SHUEISHA Inc.
RATED
T+
FOR OLDER TEEN
ratings.viz.com
VIZ media
www.viz.com

Kisaki is called out to California—
to fight aliens!

Mistress Fortune

Story and Art by Arina Tanemura
Creator of *Gentlemen's Alliance †* **and** *Full Moon*

Fourteen-year-old Kisaki Tachibana has psychic powers. She works for PSI, a secret government agency that fights aliens. She's in love with her partner Giniro, but PSI won't allow operatives to get involved. Just when Kisaki thinks she may be getting closer to Giniro, she finds out she's going to be transferred to California!

Bonus Color Poster Inside

Available Now
at your local bookstore or comic store

ISBN: 978-1-4215-3881-5
$9.99 USA | $12.99 CAN

www.viz.com